The Democratic Classroom
Theory to Inform Practice

UNDERSTANDING EDUCATION AND POLICY
William T. Pink and George W. Noblit
Series editors

Discourse and Power in Educational Organizations
David Corson (ed.)

Flirting on the Margins (An Educational Novel)
Robert B. Everhart

The Social Construction of Urban Schooling: Situating the Crisis
Louis F. Mirón

Continuity and Contradiction: The Futures of the Sociology of
Education
William T. Pink and George W. Noblit (eds.)

Good Schools: The Policy Environment Perspective
Charles A. Tesconi

Talking About a Revolution: The Politics and Practice of Feminist
Teaching
Cheryl L. Sattler

Assessment and Control at Parkview School: A Qualitative Case
Study of Accommodating Assessment Change in a Secondary School
Hilary A. Radnor

Working Together?: Grounded Perspectives on Interagency
Collaboration
*Amee Adkins, Catherine Awsumb, George W. Noblit, and
Penny Richards*

A General Theory for a Democratic School
Art Pearl and Tony Knight

Values-Spoken and Values-Lived
The Cultural Consequences of a School Closing
Maike Philipsen

forthcoming

Making Meaning of Community in an American High School
Kathleen Knight Abowitz

Urban School Survival
Mary Anne Pitman and Debbie Zorn

From Disabling to Enabling Schools
Roger Slee, Mel Ainscow, and Michael Hardman

From Nihilism to Possibility:
Democratic Transformations for Inner City Education
Fred Yeo and Barry Kanpol (eds.)

The Democratic Classroom
Theory to Inform Practice

Art Pearl
University of California, Santa Cruz
Tony Knight
LaTrobe University

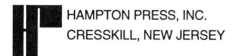
HAMPTON PRESS, INC.
CRESSKILL, NEW JERSEY

Printed in the United States of America

Library of Congress Cataloging-in-Publication Data

Pearl, Arthur.
  The democratic classroom : theory to inform practice /Art Pearl,
  Tony Knight
      p.   cm. -- (Understanding education and policy)
  Includes bibliographical references and index.
  ISBN 1-57273-218-0. -- ISBN 1-57273-219-9
  1. Education--Philosophy. 2. Education--Aims and objectives.
  3. Education--Social aspects. 4. Democracy--Study and teaching.
  5. Citizenship--Study and teaching. 6. Student participation in
  administration. 7. Curriculum planning. 8. Educational change.
  I. Knight, Tony. II. Title. III. Series.
  LB14.7.P42   1999
  370'.1--dc21   98-51060
                                                           CIP

Hampton Press, Inc.
23 Broadway
Cresskill, NJ 07626

Contents

Series Preface

Books in this series, *Understanding Education and Policy*, will present a variety of perspectives to better understand the aims, practices, content and contexts of schooling, and the meaning of these analyses for educational policy. Our primary intent is to redirect the language used, the voices included in the conversation, and the range of issues addressed in the current debate concerning schools and policy. In doing this, books in the series will explore the differential conceptions and experiences that surface when analysis includes racial, class, gender, ethnic, and other key differences. Such a perspective will span the social sciences (anthropology, history, philosophy, psychology, sociology, etc.), and research paradigms.

Books in the series will be grounded in the contextualized lives of the major actors in school (students, teachers, administrators, parents, policy makers, etc.) and address major theoretical issues. The challenge to authors is to fully explore life-in-schools, through the multiple lenses of various actors and within the contexts in which these actors and schools are situated. It is anticipated that such a range of empirically sound and theoretically challenging work will contribute to a fundamental and needed rethinking of the content, process and context for school reform.

In this book, Art Pearl and Tony Knight engage us on an ambitious project. In simple terms they set out to resurrect theory in education. In doing so, they unpack the complexities involved in developing theory that unites the core elements of

education, that is, curriculum, instruction, discipline, administration and management, research and evaluation, political control, and so on. The power of this book lies in their critique of
contemporary thinking about and practice in schools, and the
development of a theory concerning democratic schools that is
grounded in data drawn from a wide range of innovative interventions in schools on two continents. We are happy to include this
book in the series Understanding Education and Policy: our expectation is that although the message will be controversial, it will
also serve as a catalyst for a much needed conversation about the
future of schools in a democratic society.

Chapter 1

Introducing the Argument and Summarizing the Debate: Democracy and a General Theory of Education

THE INTENT OF THE BOOK

This volume asks the reader to take a fundamentally different look at education. We share with many, the criticisms of existing practice and policy. We part company with most "reformers" by concluding that proposed reforms will make a bad situation worse. Schools are in trouble because they do too well what they should not do at all—they avoid what should be addressing. The major problem with schools is that from the first grade through graduation, with an advanced degree, the intelligence of students is devalued.

The gist of our argument follows. The world is faced with difficult problems that cannot be solved without a democratic process and that become worse the more the education of the public

1

is "dumbed down" (insulting the intelligence of students). Essential to democratic resolution of those problems is a reconstructed school that prepares all students to become effective problem solvers. The goal of such a school is to prepare every person with 12 years of schooling to be an informed and responsible democratic citizen. Such a school needs to be informed by a comprehensive general theory; the theory we recommend is a democratic one.

A democratic education theory applies to every facet of education and has four requirements;:

1. Knowledge should be universally provided to enable all students to solve generally recognized social and personal problems.
2. Students should participate in decisions that affect their lives.
3. Clearly specified rights should be made universally available.
4. Equal encouragement should be given for success in all of society's legal endeavors.

Throughout this book are detailed description and analysis of each of the four requirements, while we, at the same time, maintain that democracy is a living entity that needs to be constantly rediscovered. Recommending and suggesting is not contradictory with democracy as a constantly changing living entity. The suggestions provide teachers, parents, students, and policymakers with ideas of where to begin and logic for reforming action. What we offer is the culmination of more than 30 years of experimenting with democratic education. What follows is not gospel. It is intended to stimulate vitally needed thought.

We begin our discussion with some thoughts about democracy.

THE MISSING INGREDIENT IN THE DEBATE: DEMOCRACY

What is missing in educational themes throughout the world is an encompassing educational theory that informs schooling policy and practice. What is needed is a coherent and persuasive vision to inspire all to take responsibility for their lives. Empty slogans such as "children are our most precious resources" and "children are our future" must be transformed into meaningful educational practice and policy. The lamentable condition of education, the erosion of support for "democratic" government, and the many growing crises that go unresolved can be partially laid at the door of the existing nature of education. An education that does not examine the range of plausible explanations for and solutions to important problems can only exacerbate those problems. It is our contention that only with a democratic education will it be possible for a society to develop the necessary foundation for the satisfactory resolution of difficult problems.

We present a proposed general theory at a time when the intellectual state of the academic community is in shambles and vision is almost nonexistent. In the stampede to dismiss "great narratives" (Lyotard, 1986) or to define "policy as ultimate modernist conceit," democracy has never been given a fair hearing. The university has never made a pretense of being democratic. And by insufficiently reflecting on their past thinking, a great many scholars have rushed to the conclusion that democracy, like all other "grand narratives," is an impossible project. It is our contention that large problems lack solutions not because they are insoluble or that democracy is an impossible project, but because we have not been democratic enough in our efforts. We believe that through a rediscovery and an extension of democracy as the cornerstone for a general education theory, things can turn around.

It is not just that democracy has fallen on hard times, it appears that everyone wants to embrace it and yet no one seems to want to be associated with it. In a sense, it was always thus, democracy was something people talked about but rarely did.

> The distrust of democracy is in fact as old as political thought itself. Philosophers have always approached popular rule with suspicion, preferring to link justice to reason and harmony in the abstract. The Greeks paid democracy no compliment when they associated it with the disorder of the rabble (ochlocracy). Plato, Aristotle, Polybius, and later Cicero and Machiavelli all admitted the demos into government as at best one element in a mixed constitution and at worst as a source of fraction and anarchy to be controlled and repressed at all costs. (Barber, 1984, p. 94)

Most "great systems" or worldviews,[1] did give a courtesy genuflection in the direction of democracy. But these were empty gestures. The term *democracy* was so elastic that any antidemocra-

---

[1]There were notable exceptions. Monarchism had its day, replaced currently by an analogous religious fundamentalism, and in the 20th century, fascism regarded democracy as its natural enemy. In addi-

tic practice or notion could be fitted into it. The distrust of democracy took two very distinct forms. Democracy was dramatically altered at the level of philosophy. The most celebrated and influential political thinkers-leaders of "great systems of thought"— either defined democracy in a peculiar way or limited its function.

Followers of Adam Smith believed in free enterprise and saw themselves as democrats. They went so far as to claim to be the inventors of democracy, which to them was a byproduct of capitalism. But their democracy was "thin" (Barber, 1984). Mainly defined in negative terms, it heavily emphasized "rights" that were designed to protect people from government. The major thrust of such a definition was to limit government and to make it secondary to the "invisible hand." This sense of democracy limited the citizen to a bystander role; a consumer who expressed political power by voting with his or her pocketbook. The reliance was on economic self-correction that was perceived to come about through unregulated competition. In this definition of democracy, not only was wealth and power limited to fewer and fewer people, but that was how it should be because any effort to redistribute wealth through government or other collective action would constitute a conspiracy against the marketplace and thus weaken the economy and undermine the base on which a functioning "democracy" must rest. That entrenched wealth and power could lead to subversion of elections and a decreasing number of people participating in politics were not matters of much concern. Far more serious from this perspective was interference with the invisible hand through taxation or regulation. Taxation, the mortal enemy of a so-defined democracy, was conceptualized as legalized theft. In the free enterprise definition of democracy, the poor would also benefit from an ever increasing accumulation of wealth. Adherents of this view fervently believed and still do believe that "a rising tide lifts all boats," meaning a healthy economy benefits all, albeit not equally. If it should happen that societal infrastructures crumble or the environment deteriorates, fear not, these are but temporary occurrences, and if left alone, the invisible hand will correct everything that can be corrected. Except for very limited taxation that government would use to protect private property,

---

tion, a great many respected philosophers aligned themselves in the antidemocratic camp. Dahl (1989) posed guardianship and anarchy as democracy's historical enemies. These, however, represented a very small minority "theoretical" opposition to what had been, until very recently, not only a very popular proposition, but one on a seemingly inevitable rise. In practice, as distinct from theory, the opposition to democracy has been much more prevalent.

all else should fall to an unregulated market. Such a view of the world, although dominant, did not produce universal gratification and by the middle of the 19th century, well-articulated anticapitalist responses gained credence (Marx being the most celebrated but hardly the only anticapitalist), and that thinking led to a Keynesian synthesis in the middle of the 20th century. We now find ourselves in a resurgence of capitalism ("late capitalism" according to Jameson, 1984) that, aided by sophisticated media and underwritten by handsomely funded think-tanks and political action committees (PACs) has swept even the modest tinkering advocated by Keynesians off the stage. The democracy of a global capitalistic economy is one that appears to be very comfortable with simultaneous rapid increases in wealth and poverty.

Marx (1959) also believed in a form of democracy, a communist or "cooperative society, as it emerges from capitalist society" (p. 117). His democracy would arrive once capitalism had run its course (as prescribed by his reading of "historical scientific materialism") and was overthrown by an intervening stage of socialism that in time would run its course and give way to the millennium-communism. During the socialist stage, the interest of democracy was to be served by a "dictatorship of the proletariat." The dictatorship of the proletariat was a misnomer. The proletariat, according to Marxist thought, were too numerous and too unprepared to actually exercise leadership. Therefore, a small group of leaders, a "vanguard," possessing the necessary expertise, knowledge, courage, and vision to take on the responsibility of leadership had to act in the name and serve in its interests (Marx, 1971). It was assumed that this dictatorship would have but a brief tenure before it would "wither way" with the advent of communism. Under communism, there would be no need for an active democracy because in the absence of conflict, politics would no longer be necessary. With communism, it was argued, no state function would be required because goods and services would be so abundant that "each would be able to receive according to need" (p. 119). Nowhere in the process from capitalism to communism is there projected to be a greater need for participatory democracy than was postulated in the unregulated capitalist system. Marx never hid his contempt for the possibility of significantly improving the lot of the proletariat under capitalism through democratic action. To Marx, such attempts were a waste of time, and worse, cruel deceptions. Marxists throughout the years have endorsed some version of this view. And although Marxists, particularly academic Marxists (which over the years is what people who called themselves Marxists tended to be), were distanced from the working class they chose to champion, they nonetheless found validation for their self-designated leadership by claiming legitimation through "science," and it is from science they believed that they had earned the right to be called *democratic*.

> Although orthodox Marxist writers had their own version of history and political development, it was actually quite similar to the liberal one. Democratic rights and freedoms were deemed to be merely "bourgeois" and, following Lenin's dictum that the working classes on their own are only capable of "trade unionism," it was assumed that the pursuit of socialism depended on the leadership of "the party" and the ideas of radicalized middle-class theorists and intellectuals. Neo-Marxist and New Left social theorists a la Herbert Marcuse and the Frankfurt School also wrote off working people, perceiving them to be "co- opted" by the technologies and consumerism of a booming postwar industrial-capitalism. (Kaye, 1994, p. 227)

Not all Marxists believed in vanguards, and not all socialists were Marxists. The excesses and brutalities of the Soviet Union disabused many of the belief that the dictatorship of the proletariat would be any more benign that any other dictatorship or that it would "wither away." However, even those "untotalitarian" socialists who called themselves democratic, defined a democracy that was also elitist, excluding all but a selected few from participation in policy decisions. Furthermore, discussion was organized in such a fashion that only the initiated had access and could understand the language.

> Where party life is concerned, the socialists for the most part reject . . . practical applications of democracy, using against them conservative arguments such as we are otherwise accustomed to hear only from the opponents of socialism. In articles written by socialist leaders it is ironically asked whether it would be a good thing to hand over leadership of the party to the ignorant masses simply for love of an abstract democratic principle. (Michels, 1911/1959, p. 336)

Philosophy was a level of disparagement of democracy where growing cynicism discarded democracy as a discredited "great narrative." Of at least equal importance in the decline of democracy was the disrespect it received in daily life, particularly in the practices of politics.

THE EVOLVING DEFINITION OF DEMOCRACY: THE SHORT UNHAPPY LIFE OF MANAGED DEMOCRACY

Elitism was not by any means restricted to the left or the right. The center was just as anxious to dispense with anything that remotely resembled government "of the people, by the people and for the people."

How could a mass democracy work if all the people were deeply involved in politics. (Berelson, Lazarsfeld, & McPhee, 1954, p. 318)

The notion of democracy as a working principle guiding civic life began tenuously. Only a very small minority was favored with suffrage. This was true for the Greeks, but also for the democracies that rose with the advent of the enlightenment. There was little trust in people as a result of either the Great Revolution of 1688 in England or the American Revolution in 1776. As property, racial, and gender restrictions to vote were removed (not without great struggle), and the vote became near universally available to adults, new concerns about the practicality of democracy were raised.

Particularly important for our thesis is that although the vote was being made universally available, no parallel activity was being made to ensure that voters were receiving the knowledge and experiences needed to enable them to perform as competent citizens. Citizenship preparation in schools, the logical place for such preparation, was minimal and mostly directed to cementing an allegiance to the state and the existing economic system (we deal with social reproduction theories later). Thus, it is not surprising that as politics emerges as a scientific discipline, empirical studies reveal that the average citizen is generally uninformed and disinterested in political life.

Three very different approaches were constructed in the 20th century to manage democracy,[2] and thus protect it from a general public that was assumed to be uninformed, irresponsible, untrustworthy, and impossible to enlighten. As one aspect of democracy was expanded with the increase in the right to vote, mechanisms and influences were created to buffer the swings that

---

[2]Managed democracy is our term, others define the changes we talk about as modern democracy and contrast it with the more participatory in theory, classical democratic theorists (see Pateman, 1970).

an unmanaged populist democracy was likely to produce. Thus, it was that interest groups, political parties, and leaders were promoted as a means by which democracy could be managed and thereby protected from the people.

Interest Groups. Bentley (1908) is generally recognized as the founding father of group theory. He viewed politics as a struggle among groups, each acting in their own interests. It was not until the 1950s (Gross 1953; Truman, 1951), that competition between interest groups was elevated to be a guiding principal of government. Bentley believed democracy would be judged by balance of power in groups. Truman and Gross found democracy in the pluralistic struggle among diversified groups. Groups thus compensated for individual failure. Dahl (1956) defined democracy as the free interaction of diverse minorities. That no one group would dominate was a sufficient guarantee of democracy for group theorists (Dahl, 1958, 1959; Polsby, 1963). They presumed that, unlike individuals, groups would have an equal opportunity for participation and could therefore prevent domination by a single group. Interest group theorists, like all the elitist managers of democracy, looked askance at too much citizen participation (Margolis, 1979). They believed that interest groups were democratic because they espoused democratic values and that dissenters of any policy always would have sufficient resources to assure a continuation of democratic values (thus becoming an interest group). Interest group theory had a great influence in both Great Britain (Beer, 1956, 1958, 1969) and in the United States.

Party Democracy. Wallas (1962) reached the public the same year as Bentley, but he brought to politics a very different focus. His interest was on the individual and the consequences individuals had on democracy. To him, political behavior was largely irrational, based on instinct and emotion, not reason. He sought to develop a scientific theory of democracy that he could empirically substantiate. His emphasis on science had a great influence on political science, more in the United States than in Great Britain. His ideas captivated Lippman, who in turn popularized them in the United States. According to Wallas, the political party was the most effective modern adjustment of political institutions to human nature. Parties did not rely on intellect of citizens, but built images through easily recognized symbols and slogans, that is, by advertising. "Elite and responsible" party leadership is a quite familiar concept to 20th-century Britons. The Conservative Party has long presented itself as a party of and for, but not by the people. Schattschneider (1942, 1960) argued that a responsible party system that offered voters meaningful choice was the sine qua non of democracy.

Leadership and Socialization. Schumpter, in his celebrated work, *Capitalism, Socialism and Democracy* (1942), found classical democratic theory to be unrealistic because it assumed a recognizable common good and a common will of the people to achieve that good. He found no evidence for either assumption. Like Wallas, he saw people responding to appeals to emotion not reason, and what was rational for one individual was not necessarily rational for the state or a subdivision of the state. Like Mosca (see Meisel, 1962), Schumpter believed that political regimes changed only when one elite replaced another. He turned classical democratic theory upside down, insisting that although the people may choose the leader, it is the leader who has the freedom of choice in governing. Therefore, it follows that the success of democracy solely depends on the quality of leadership. The average citizen needs only to recognize his or her unfitness to govern and turn over that responsibility to the leaders for democracy to work. Schumpter believed it would not be necessary to guard the guardians because only competent individuals with strong morals would aspire to leadership. Political scientists provided evidence that leaders, far more than the average citizen, espoused the values of democracy (Key, 1961; McClosky, 1964). Schumpter supported an educational system that stressed leadership training in elite schools, whereas the schooling for all others would be aimed toward developing the willingness to accept less than a leadership role in the system. The schooling Schumpter recommended corresponds quite closely to the system currently in operation.

Berelson et al. (1954), on the basis of empirical findings, concluded energetic participation was harmful to democratic government because the average citizen was neither conscientious nor knowledgeable. Moreover, they argued that even if those conditions were remedied, high levels of participation would produce a political deadlock at best, and a social breakdown at worst. They believed that the United States was a democracy, and whatever faults it had lay with the status of democratic theory, not in the readiness for citizens to behave responsibly.

Elitist conceptualizations of democracy was widely accepted by empirically oriented political scientists (Kornhauser,
1959; Lipset, 1960) and found its way into political science
textbooks, but not into high school government textbooks, which
continued to extol the virtues of a universal participatory democratic theory that was neither supported by experts nor informed
by political practice.

Liberal managed democracies prospered throughout most
of the 20th century. Few found much to criticize in a democracy
managed by elites. The economy grew, the standard of living rose,
government was accepted as credible by most people even if their
involvement in it was minimal. However, a managed democracy
began to fall apart in the mid-1960s. Parties, leadership, and
interest groups lost credibility. Disillusionment with the U.S.
government grew with the Vietnam war, widespread African-
American uprisings in American cities, unprecedented simultaneous high unemployment and high inflation, misdeeds by President
Richard Nixon, and a growing concern about the environment. In
Great Britain, adding to a sense of disgruntlement, was the
reflaring of violence in North Ireland, a rapid rise in racial violence, and high unemployment coupled with rapidly rising prices.
Australians also felt the frustrations of an economy out of control
and the divisiveness of Vietnam, and were jolted by the unprecedented sacking of Prime Minister Whitlam by Governor General
Kerr in 1975. Add to political happenings the cultural change that
was powerfully reflected in the growing popularity of the Beatles
that gave voice to rapidly rising antiestablishment attitudes.
Whatever the combinations or concatenations, the "Humpty
Dumpty" that was managed democracy had a great fall and no
interest group, leader, or party has been able to put it back
together again. Leadership no longer inspired confidence, interest
groups no longer maintained equilibrium, and loyalty to political
party diminished to near nonexistence. The vacuum that was created by the demise of managed democracy has been filled with
unfocused anger. There has been little desire to reconsider democracy. How could there be when so little discussion or analysis of
democracy filtered down to the average citizen? Democracy was
wrapped in rhetoric that students were being prepared to defend,
even die for, but were never encouraged to understand.

DEALING WITH THE NOW: APPEALING TO THE LOWEST COMMON DENOMINATOR OF UNDERSTANDING

At its best, democratic politics is about . . . "the search for remedy" (Arthur Schlesinger, Jr.). The purpose of democratic politics is to solve problems and resolve disputes. But since the 1960s, the key to winning elections has been to reopen the same divisive issues over and over again. The issues themselves are not reargued. No new light is shed. Rather, old resentments and angers are stirred up in an effort to get voters to cast yet one more ballot of angry protest. Political consultants have been truly ingenious in figuring out endless creative ways of tapping into popular anger about crime. Yet their spots do not solve the problem. Endless arguments about whether the death penalty is a good idea do not put more cops on the street, streamline the criminal justice system, or resolve some of the underlying causes of violence.

The decline of a "politics of remedy" creates a vicious cycle. Campaigns have become negative in large part because of a sharp decline in popular faith in government. To appeal to an increasingly alienated electorate, candidates and their political consultants have adopted a cynical stance that, they believe with good reason, plays into popular cynicism about politics and thus wins them votes. But cynical campaigns do not resolve issues. They do not lead to "remedies." Therefore, problems get worse, the electorate becomes more cynical—and so does the advertising. At the end of it all, the governing process, which is supposed to be about real things, becomes little more than a war over symbols. (Dionne, 1991, pp. 16-17)

As the old systems of mediating power became obsolete, they were replaced by direct seductive public appeals tailored to mesh with an emerging technology. The politics that has emerged consists of consultants packaging political figures and people voting their ignorance. Commentator after commentator has provided different spins to what has become a generally recognized condition (Greider, 1992; Hutton; 1995; Jamieson, 1992; Kelly, 1992; Saul, 1997). More than ever before, the political life of any society is at the mercy of public opinion that is increasingly fragmented and removed from a factual base. The intellectual elite have gone off in one direction, the vast majority of people in another. Although power has most certainly been concentrated in fewer and fewer hands, the power has become in many ways illusory and the ability to govern has not been facilitated by such concentration. To the contrary, problems remain unsolved, and possible solutions remain untried. An ignorant public mobilized by naked appeals to blind emotions cannot govern, but such a public can cause enormous amount of mischief. Such a public is able to frustrate and sabotage attempts by entrenched elites to govern. Hutton (1995), in his analysis of the present state of democracy in the United Kingdom made the following points:

> What is needed is the development of a new conception of citizenship. If a well functioning market economy requires skilled workforces, strong social institutions like schools and training centres, and a vigorous public infrastructure, these cannot be achieved if the governing class cannot understand the values implicit in such bodies. (p. 25)

During the "whoop-de-do" days of an elitist-managed democracy there seemed to be little need and perhaps even less desire to educate citizens to citizenship responsibility. Indeed, an active, informed, and participatory ordinary citizen had been discouraged. Thus, it should come as no surprise that in a 1990 survey conducted by the Times-Mirror Center it was revealed that, "Today's young Americans, aged 18 to 30, know less and care less about news and public affairs than any other generation of Americans in the past 50 years" (Cohn, 1992; Harwood, 1992). When managed democracy came apart, campaigns bypassed the traditional mechanism of parties and finessed the give-and-take of interest group politics and made direct appeals to loosely connected individuals. The campaigns were negative and were reduced to short "soundbites" and anger-inspiring visual images. A winning campaign was one that could most effectively use modern technology—computers and television—to take maximum advantage of a disinterested and uninformed electorate. What we reap is what we have sowed. Americans hate politics (Dionne, 1991) because they never were prepared for responsible political involvement.

Although discussion and debate has gone off in every possible direction, there has been a near unanimous conclusion that recent elections in the United States, Great Britain, Australia, or anywhere else, fail to meet minimal democratic requirements. Blame has been attached to the "media," the "family," multinational corporations, political parties, and the character of those who have aspired to leadership. None of these are attributed to be as good as they once were. Schools have not been spared in this spate of wholesale condemnation. The most spirited attack on schools centers on their failure to achieve the conservative mission of minimally skilled, passive, and docile workers and submissive political followers. What has not been brought to public recognition is the possibility that we are in trouble precisely because the schools have accomplished far too well their antidemocratic mission. They have done exactly what the elites who have managed democracy wanted them to do. These elites, who point fingers of blame at everyone but themselves for the deterioration of public life, refuse to accept any responsibility for influencing public schools to discourage students from an active and informed participation in political life. These discouragements took the form of deliberate antidemocratic classroom activities and instruction on the one hand, and opposition to necessary curriculum and instruction that would prepare students for active informed citizenship on the other.[3]

With very few exceptions, schools have worked at cross purposes to democracy. If ordinary people were to learn to become competent citizens, they would not be able to learn it at school. What students do learn in public-supported schools is to distrust government. And this they learn well.

An antidemocratic thrust to schooling had less disastrous consequences in the past because problems to be solved were far less complex than they are now; managed democracy worked reasonably well; and other agencies and institutions provided some form of political education that varied considerably in devotion to democracy, but when added to the mix provided a more informed citizen than is currently the case.

Unions, fraternal organizations, and a less monopolized media brought a range of thought to the public. Not too long ago, political campaigns had educative value because candidates were forced to discuss issues. With the decline of out-of-school political education, we urge schools to take up the slack and assume a major responsibility for preparation of competent citizens. We provide more specifics on the current pervasiveness of antidemocratic education and contrast it with the specifics of a democratic school throughout the text.

---

[3]There has been a reawakened concern in preparation for civic responsibility that we discuss at depth in later chapters. We do not believe that a rediscovery of civics or a revitalization of history is a sufficient move toward democratic education.

THE NEED FOR A GENERAL THEORY

Merely attaching the term *democracy* to education will not significantly alter current practice. Education needs a general theory.
And because theory, like democracy, has become suspect, it is
important that we are very clear about our meaning of a general
theory. Theory in education must not only inform educational
practice and policy, it must also be capable of specifying and
defending educational goals. With respect to goals, theory establishes the case for desirability and feasibility. But theory must
also inform process. By combining goals with clearly defined
processes, the necessary elements of good theory—explanation and
testability—are established. Without powerful arguments for
desirability and feasibility on one hand, and explanation and
testability on the other, theory degenerates to what it has become
in the postmodern age—whatever anyone wants it to be. Sutherland
(1988), in stating her case for the importance of theory of education, made the following point: "Our theory is not simply a
statement about what is: theory of education is a statement of what
should happen and which actions are most likely to bring about
this effect" (p. 4).

The Importance of a General Theory. An education theory
meets the criteria of general only when it is applicable to every
aspect of the educational process. The same theory applies to
development, curriculum, instruction, "discipline," evaluation,
research, and administration. At the present time, education is
plagued by theory that does not meet criteria of desirability, feasibility, explanability, or testability, and is also unable to bring
coherence to curriculum, discipline, pedagogy, evaluation, development, and administration. In fact, theory when viewed across
different aspects of education is, as Dunne (1954) remarked
about the Democratic party in the United States in 1901, not on
"speaking terms with itself" (p. 165).

**A Possible Paradox: Is Not the Specification for Democratic
Education Incompatible With the Call for Open-endedness
and the Insistence that Democracy is Constantly Being
Reinvented?**

Having just lambasted educational theory for inconsistency, are
we not guilty of exactly the same offense? Throughout this book,

we insist that democracy is an ever developing concept and that it needs to be continuously reinvented and yet we also provide very precise almost prescriptive recommendations and suggestions. Furthermore, we take the position that democracy cannot be mass delivered to classrooms but must emerge at the classroom level and grow from classroom to classroom. How can something invented as a unique experience in each classroom grow exponentially? That is not as contradictory as it might first appear. Democratic classrooms will be unique (as are authoritarian classrooms trying to meet top-down-mandated identical curriculum). Each classroom will differ in important attributes, but a democratic education will also share some critically important values, principles, and culture. For democracy to be invented, it must start with some grasp of the thinking that spawned it. What continues to be constant are certain principles and these can only be altered and refined after put to rigorous test. We present as fundamentally distinguishing qualities of a democratic classroom the following:

- persuasion and negotiation in place of coercion or laissez faire "choice";
- inclusivity rather than exclusivity;
- a problem-solving curriculum that includes personal and social problems and is made equally available to all students;
- equal participation in decisions that affect student lives, a very limited number of rights that are inalienable for all students; and
- equal encouragement to classroom success for all students.

Our long-term goal for the democratic classroom is that all students, upon completion of high school are capable of fulfilling the requirements of an informed, active, and responsible democratic citizen.

Each of these principles and the goal can be made sufficiently precise to meet the criterion of testability. Each is sufficiently robust to be tested for desirability. Each has sufficient history for credibility.

To begin a discussion of democratic education without such principles, and without a record of accomplishment based on the application of such principles, is far worse than mere irresponsibility; it amounts to abandoning education to democracy's enemies—guardianship and anarchy (Dahl, 1989). The paradox would be to ask people to invent democracy and not provide them with suggestions, recommendations, and proposed goals. Democratic education advances when adults (teachers, etc.) propose and defend and invite students to come up with counterdefensible proposals. Democratic education is unlikely to occur when adult leadership is abandoned. To the contrary, democratic education will not develop without strong democratic leadership. In this volume we indicate what democratic leadership looks like.

Democratic education is the logical extension of long history that provides the basis for its future development. We would be remiss in this chapter if we did not single out for special attention John Dewey because he is justifiably recognized as the champion of democratic education and his successes and failures are necessarily instructive to anyone trying to resurrect democratic education.

THE CONTRIBUTIONS OF JOHN DEWEY

Dewey made his presence known at about the time scientific management was gaining control over education. Dewy represented both a part of that movement and opposition to it. He emerged as an early American left-leaning. As such, he begged for comparison with Marx. Their differences are marked. The dialectic for Marx was conflict between classes; for Dewey it was competing ideas. Marx put his faith in the dictatorship of a vanguard; whereas Dewey was committed to his version of democracy. While at the University of Chicago with Jane Addams and other associates, he tested his ideas in the crucible provided by Addam's Hull House and the laboratory school he established in 1896 as "a cooperative society on a small scale." In the laboratory school, he applied his developing theory of "learning by doing" (*The School and Society*, 1900). He left the University of Chicago in 1904 for Columbia University, where he remained for more than three decades producing his most important works. It was his intent to reach a general public and alert them to social problems and critical issues that were confronting American industrial democracy. His writing style and his distance from mainstream politics to a large extent undermined his intentions. Dewey had range and diversity. His influence on-century philosophy, aesthetics, education, legal and political theory, and the social sciences rank him among the most important thinkers of the century. Dewey was no ivory tower academic.

Dewey played a leadership role in most of the social causes of his time, however, for all of his political and social cause involvement's it is difficult to establish Dewey as a political activist. Despite his professed pragmatism, his politics were far more expressions of moral conviction than concerted and organized efforts at a "search for remedy."

Critical to an understanding of Dewey was his aversion to modern urban life. He believed that urbanization led to a loss of sense of community and purpose that was to be found in small towns and farm communities. In the absence of community, the scale of the city, its diversity, and its disconnection with tradition overwhelmed the individual. Dewey believed that restoration of community would promote both individual and societal growth. He designated the school to be the agency to restore community (Dewey, 1916). Here we find one of many significant differences between our understanding of the role of the school in helping build a democratic society and Dewey's. We do not believe the school can restore community, although certain aspects of desirable community life can be modeled there. We believe that the primary goal of the school should be to prepare a responsible, informed, and active citizen. That is both more challenging and more modest than what Dewey proposed.

As an educational theorist, Dewey argued that schooling should connect with home and social life. To Dewey, schools are places where students learn to live by living, and learn morality by engaging in moral behavior. Dewey was vehemently opposed to passive learning—the belief that knowledge can be handed down from teacher to student. He believed that knowledge was an active process that required constructive effort on the part of the knower. To Dewey, knowledge was power to cope with the environment and ultimately dominate it, but power was also mastery of processes that could be applied to life-long experimentation and readjustment. Although Dewey believed knowledge can have future utility, his emphasis was on the child's immediate interests and aptitudes and not on future needs or aspirations. By cultivating the interests of the child, school changes from subjects to topics. He wanted to show students the social value of education and its interdependence with society. His laboratory school gave students real-life problems to solve. He tried to connect the school to the community and engage in social life, arguing that school should be the center of community life. He was convinced that his laboratory school would foster the type of efficient learning and good social habits to enable students to effectively cope with a chaotic city.

His educational program was developmental; younger students concentrated on household activities (similar to Montessori and her work with the Italian poor), older students were faced with more challenging problems. In Dewey's school, the younger children in play and work, learned to weave, garden, and construct things from wood and metal. As they grew older they learned how science emerged from these kinds of activities and in this way Dewey believed the artificiality of science as a subject was reduced. The teacher in the Dewey classroom acted as a guide and supervisor who was knowledgeable about process and rich in experiences, ready to answer questions but unwilling to deliver answers to students.

For all of his fame and notoriety, Dewey never had much influence on U.S. schooling. Although student-centered, his curriculum is not unlike an "unpragmatic" school. He is less absolute, but his working hypotheses are not that much different than absolute truths. The progressive movement is far more William Heard Kilpatrick than Dewey and it is Kilpatrick who set the stage for the modern open school—allowing a child to decide what it is he or she wants to learn (Kilpatrick, 1936, 1983). Dewey (1938), in his last major work on education, criticized progressive educators for homage to the same abstract principle of freedom for the child that he had earlier espoused.

Dewey never did fit well into his times. He was too right for the left, which at the time was strongly Marxist, but he also was far too left for the right or even the mainstream. He was too academic for the average citizen, but also too involved in the world for most academics. His laboratory school was just that, a laboratory; it did not have to deal with the real world of public education with its growing top-down intransigent bureaucracy, unruly students, and a teaching staff widely differing in competence and philosophical orientation. Although his school was an unchallengeable success, it operated under conditions very different from the typical urban school. The laboratory school began with 16 students and 2 teachers. Before it closed its doors it had 140 students served by a staff of 23. That pupil-teacher ratio would make any public school teacher drool with envy. The laboratory school demonstrated possibilities that could only become realities if applied to existing bureaucratic systems. Dewey made little inroads in those systems. It was difficult for him to make those inroads because he was far removed from them. He did not write in a style that a general public or even the typical teacher could understand. His writing was dense and his arguments difficult to follow. And although it is undeniable that Dewey has much to contribute to the development of a democratic classroom, and all interested in such a project would profit much by revisiting him, there is much in him that is problematic for democratic education. It is difficult to conceive of a democratic process without also envisioning clear democratic goals. We believe that educational process should have predictable impacts on societal structures. At the very least, the attributes of a successful graduate should be defined with sufficient precision that there can be assessment of accomplishment. Without clear goals it is almost impossible to meaningfully evaluate the value of the education. Evaluation of a classroom without long-term objectives reduces one to insist that one is doing good because one feels good about what one is doing. The democratic classroom as is presented here is derived from work in public schools with all of public school difficulties. Democratic education to us is democratic means toward democratic ends, in existing school systems. Our democratic classroom is designed to grapple with society as it is and try to move it in a democratic direction. Dewey organized his classroom into projects that met student interests. We believe that student interest is a necessary, but insufficient element in a democratic education. The primary goal of our democratic education is an informed, competent, and involved citizen, which requires a balance between personal and social interests and a far more active teacher-leader than the ones who functioned in Dewey's laboratory school.

Mostly, however, Dewey is deadly serious. Our democratic classroom is sustained by humor. Humor is the primary attribute of the democratic teacher. On the board in every democratic classroom should be printed in bold letters: "If we are not having fun we are not doing it right." The importance of humor is not to be found in Dewey.

As we try to place Dewey in a historical context, we find that it is not he but his followers that confound us. Dewey reversed the problem that Clarence Darrow attributed to himself when he said, "I suffer much from being misunderstood, but I would suffer more if I was understood." Dewey suffered from being misunderstood by followers who reduced him to relatively simple processes, group projects, or activities dictated by student; and thus they removed from him his essence—his deep-seated interest in society.

DEMOCRATIC EDUCATION, NOW MORE THAN EVER

This argument for a general education theory with democratic education as its base is presented at a time of deepening crises. We are living in a paralyzed world seemingly unable to address even its most simple problems and overwhelmed by an increasing sense of powerlessness in the face of growing poverty, crime, environmental degradation, violence, intolerances, inadequate health care, and so on. Part of the powerlessness stems from an inability to think deeply about anything, part from an inability to conceptualize the inter-connectedness of problems, and part from the lack of visions of a world capable of solving problems. Part of the difficulty is organizational—implementing actions that are contagious (i.e., encouraging active and meaningful mass citizen participation in the achievement of a desired goal). The needed conceptualization, appropriate organization, and contagious action are addressed in a democratic education. In fact, democratic education is designed to treat all the issues that current education fails to address or worsens.

You can have equality; you can have culture; but you cannot have both. (T. S. Eliot, said to G. H. Bantock; Bantock, 1970, p. 78)

Moreover, with democratic education, it is possible to do what Eliot held to be impossible. Some would characterize our belief in the potentiality of democratic education as overly ambitious. Perhaps. But a major argument we have with education past as well as present was that it was insufficiently ambitious, and we have suffered greatly as a consequence.

The General Characteristics of a General Theory of Democratic Education. At one level, democratic education provides a philosophical underpinning to education. It elevates it from the routines and rituals that have falsely been defined as "basics" (essentialism). It also provides a philosophical alternative to the elitist (and exclusionary) demand for perpetuation of the classics (perennialism). Democratic education defines the moral boundaries within which all elements in a pluralistic and diverse society can engage in meaningful discourse. The invitation to the center not only unfreezes debate; it is an invitation to examine ideas now discussed, if at all, only by isolated groups. Education itself, its purposes and practices, becomes an exciting topic in a democratic classroom.

One of the grounding assumptions of democratic education is the recognition that humans by nature are an environmentally altering species. Each generation substantially and permanently changes the world for the next generation. Each generation thus is condemned to invent the future. In an active democracy, there is an implied mandate for everyone to participate in the creation of that future.

With the realization that the world 20 years from now will be markedly different than today, a democratic classroom challenges and encourages students to envision the active role they will play in designing change, and to accept the responsibility for what they will help produce. Democratic education provides all students with the same opportunity to gain the knowledge and specific citizenship skills to be important conscious participants in the creation of posterity. Recognizing the world will change in no way requires the teacher to be an advocate for a particular direction of change. No two teachers need to support the same future. Nor do teachers need to believe in democracy to function effectively in a democratic classroom. They merely need to present their ideas and support them openly with logic and evidence. The restriction on a teacher opposed to democracy is identical with the restriction imposed on the teacher who supports democracy; both persuade and negotiate, neither coerce. Could a democratic classroom allow a teacher to express sentiments in favor of Nazism, anti-semitism, racism, suppression of gays and lesbians, or patriarchy? A satisfactory discussion detailing freedom of expression of teachers and students is more than can be accomplished in an introductory chapter. We elaborate extensively on this issue later in the book. However, as general rule, in a democratic classroom students sample a wide variety of proposed futures, ways of thinking, and benefit from rich discussion of them. The democratic classroom is also fundamentally different from a "social reconstruction" that is characterized by partisan advocacy of a particular strategy or a narrow range of possibilities.

DEMOCRATIC EDUCATION, NECESSARY FOR THE SUCCESS OF MODERNITY: A RESPONSE TO THE CHALLENGES OF POSTMODERNISM

Modernity is the transient, the fleeting, the contingent; it is the one half of art, the other being the eternal and the immutable. (Baudelaire, quoted in Harvey, 1989, p. 10)

It is difficult for formalized education to orient itself to postmodernism because it never came to grips with modernity. Modernity has had trouble coming to grips with itself. Modernity has had many different interpreters. It was seen by Baudelaire as the joining of the ephemeral with the eternal. Modern has meant transformation and the breaking of boundaries, but it has also meant disintegration. Modernity is filled with contradictions. Modern writers have stressed insecurity, chaos, and disrespect for the past. Other philosophers, critics, and analysts (Cassirer, 1951) trace modernity to the Enlightenment and the replacement of religion with science and through science a solution to all problems leading ultimately to "the perfectibility of man" (Passmore, 1970). Inherent in the Enlightenment ideal were the gains that would result from education. It is through rational analysis that contradictions could be resolved and complex problems solved. And yet the requisite education that could make the Enlightenment more than another failed project was very rarely permitted into schools, and when attempted were almost always crushed by strong counterforces. The Enlightenment required serious treatment of serious issues. In schools, everything is sugar-coated, and the contradictions that could be energizing forces are swept under the rug. Schools have never been able to shake loose from a premodernist hold. The school is an anachronism rooted in the distant past and disconnected from a functioning world.

We once described the university as an institution made obsolete with the invention of the printing press. It made a lot of sense to go to where the book was when there was only one book. To this day, the university stubbornly maintains a hierarchical organizational structure faithfully modeled after the Catholic Church of the Middle Ages. Professors control who among the lower ranks will be permitted to join them, and so on down the order. Ornate edifices are built for the university president that would be the envy of most Cardinals, and if that was not enough, faculty swelter in Cardinal-like robes while students in robes signifying inferior status, march to "pomp and circumstance" in commencement or graduation exercises.

There have been some concessions to modernity; the university is more beholden to money interests than was true in the renaissance. Veblen (1918), a victim of the university failure to deal with one of modernity's characteristics—diversity—looked at this feature of the university in the early part of the 20th century. Today we know that Veblen understated the case. The hold that large corporations have over the university strengthens as public support of education declines. And although the university takes on a tinge of modernity and perhaps postmodernity by including women and people of color in positions of authority, these have not changed its essential structure. Moreover, these concessions, significant in some ways, and insignificant in others, have not moved the university to reexamine its mission. In fact, changes in higher education reflect the centrifugalization of intellectual life. Mission is too grand a term to be included in postmodern vocabulary and as a consequence, the university has shown decreasing interest in defining itself—except as an efficiency-driven, rational-organizational model of corporate planning.

The preuniversity school organization does not have the historical tradition of the university. It emerged as part of modernist efficiency and commitment to scientific principle. Such approaches to management are unraveling, not as belated attempts to catch up with the times, but rather from premodernist forces such as religious fundamentalism and early modernist unregulated capitalism. Both of these forces are "odd couple" allies in the effort to privatize choice in public schools. In one sense, however, the differences in management style between the university and elementary and high school education is insignificant. When it comes to admission to the academy, it is higher education that plays the tune to which kindergarten to 12th grade education dances.

Schools' inability to respond to or influence the direction of modernity is also reflected in attempts to maintain a rural character. Modernity was "very much an urban phenomenon" (Harvey, 1989, p. 25). To this day, schools maintain a holiday schedule to correspond with the harvest. In the absence of historical grounding, "cowboys" (as referenced by Ronald Reagan and John Wayne) become more real than Albert Einstein, whose caricature is reified, not by what schools do, but by what schools do not do. The failure of schools to deal with the challenges of diversity and urbanization makes fantasy real and reality fantasy.

One aspect of urban life—diversity—has traumatized the antiquated school. The modern city is distinguished from the premodern rural by the rich diversity of experiences. Education not only does not deal with diversity, it attempts to coerce all students into a bland sameness. Tepid overtures toward appreciation of diversity (e.g., recognition of its existence), is treated superficially leaving the core fundamentally unchanged.

For our purposes, Harvey's (1989) four-phase division of modernity is very useful. The first, spawned by the

Enlightenment, began as an extraordinarily optimistic centripetal movement, energized by the belief in the infinite capabilities of human once the great powers of science were unleashed. Clearly, education was to play a significant role in helping humans toward "perfectibility." It was in this period that organized education came into existence and the optimism of the Enlightenment was embodied by Horace Mann and the common school, although his influence came at the time the belief in the Enlightenment was beginning to wane.

> Education is the orphan of the enlightenment. (Barber, 1992, p.10)

Harvey's Phase 2 of modernity is an Age of Ideology that began in the middle of the 19th century, and was triggered by the shrill rhetoric of antagonistic movements. Marx and Engels, with their *Communist Manifesto* in 1848, were critical agents in the development of this phase of modernism. With an increased emphasis on differences and divergence, the center was evacuated and increasingly the Enlightenment became Gertrude Stein's Oakland. "There was no there, there." The Enlightenment was fueled by belief in a utopian future. It was to be posterity's gift to the species. But heaven on earth remains believable only when there is perceptible progress in that direction. By the mid-19th century there was little indication of movement toward such a wondrous goal. The city with its crowded poverty and squalor was anything but splendid. The Irish politician, Sir Boyle Roche, reflected the spirit of the times, "Posterity be damned. What has posterity done for us." It was a time when self, class, religious, ethnic, and race interests rose to the surface. It was also the beginning of difficult times for schools. These differences were not ones that schools were prepared to address. With the Age of Ideology, the world went off and left schools mired in the past.

In modernity's Phase 3, came the ascendancy of myth. The arts were shaken from an earlier foundation by an explosion of experimentation in the early part of the 20th century. The phase began in 1910 according to Virginia Woolf, or 1915, if D. H. Lawrence's version is accepted (Harvey, 1989). Those experimentations added significantly to literature, dance, music, and the pictorial arts. However, traditionalists decreed these explosive expressions to be immoral, or in bad taste, and did not permit them in schools. With the rising gap between the culture of the times and the culture permitted in schools it is not too surprising that students became increasingly estranged from both what teachers taught and the new cultural experiments. It thus follows that students, basically left on their own, would gravitate to television that pandered to them (e.g., MTV) and other postmodern diversions.

Phase 4 of modernism reflected "the machine age" and World War II. In this phase, modernity becomes unhinged. The rush of technological advance coupled with the rise of Hitler and the later fall of Communism produced widespread alienation. The Enlightenment dream was reduced to either a colossal hoax or an example of silly pretentiousness of human beings. In either instance, with the fall of modernity comes postmodernity. And how does schooling cope with this new way of making sense of the world, or more accurately, deal with a world where making sense is considered to be a hopeless endeavor?

NOW TO POSTMODERNISM

The first business of educational reformers in schools and universities—multiculturalists, feminists, progressives—ought to be to sever their alliance with esoteric postmodernism; with literary metatheory (theory about theory); with fun-loving, self-annihilating hyperskepticism. As pedagogy these intellectual practices court catastrophe. They proffer to desperate travelers trying to find their way between Scylla and Charybdis a clever little volume on Zeno's paradoxes. They give to people whose very lives depend on the right choices a lesson in the impossibility of judgment. They tell emerging citizens looking to legitimize their preferences for democracy that there is no intellectually respectable way to ground political legitimacy. (Barber, 1992, p. 125)

Postmodernism is generally applied to cultural forms that emerged in the 1960s and claim "reflexivity, irony, playfulness and the mingling of popular and high art forms." From the outset, one of our problems with postmodernism is its treatment of language. Language is a critical component in postmodernism (and poststructuralism), perhaps the most critical component. Postmodernists have come to view action with deep suspicion. They are far less concerned with what a person does than with what a person says. Preoccupation is with "text" and "voice." Sameness is viewed as acquiescence to coercion. Eschewing sameness has led to near reverence for difference and multiple interpretations. Thus, a new Orwellianism has come into existence. Words can mean whatever anyone wants them to mean. Postmodernists are fascinated with power. This is especially true of two of postmodernist's most acclaimed leaders, Foucault (1984) and Lyotard (1986). But in the process of discussing power, the word is transmogrified to be indistinguishable from powerlessness. *Irony* is another defining feature of postmodernism, but what does irony mean? And how does it become distinguishable from opportunism or cynicism.

Postmodernists call themselves "playful," but it is a humorless playfulness. These attributes of postmodernism (power or powerlessness, irony or cynicism, grim humorlessness or playfulness) connect with or influence education in many largely unrecognized ways.

Postmodernism ascended as a diatribe against humanism and the Enlightenment legacy (Bernstein 1985; Spanos, 1993). It rejected abstract reason and any project that consciously seeks to improve the human condition. Postmodernism must, therefore, reject as ludicrous or meaningless anything resembling an all-encompassing general theory of education with democracy as its core. Considering our investment in democratic education, one would not expect from us a favorable stance toward postmodernism. We side with Barber in our analysis, but we come to our conclusion somewhat differently. Barber was most concerned with the activities in higher education where postmodernist influence has been most significant and visibly contested. Our attention is directed at children and adolescents in school where they have become the battleground on whom postmodernist, modernist, and even premodernist conceptualizations are contested.

Our concern, and hopefully the concern of anyone hoping to stave off the catastrophe that postmodernism is hurtling us toward, is reflected in the question of how humanism and reason have reached such a disrespected state. What implication does this have on an attempt to generate any general theory? Did democracy become a lost cause because human progress was doomed from the beginning as a project beyond human capability? Or, did humans try to go forward without the necessary accompanying intellectual equipment (education for democratic citizenship) for general human progress? Was it possible to achieve a democratic end in the absence of democratic means? Was it reason that failed humans, or was failure inevitable once access to the development of reason and the opportunity to have reason recognized was limited to elites? We argue that postmodernism is the logical consequence of hostility toward not only all grand narratives but to democracy, specifically.

> There is, perhaps, a degree of consensus that the typical postmodernist artifact is playful, self-ironizing and even schizoid; and that it reacts to the austere autonomy of high modernism by impudently embracing the language of commerce and the commodity. Its stance towards cultural tradition is one of irreverent pastiche and its contrived depthlessness undermines all metaphysical solemnities, sometimes by a brutal aesthetics of squalor and shock. (Eagleton, 1987, p. 192)

Although the term *postmodernism* emerged in architecture (Jencks, 1977), it has been applied to almost every human activity. It began, according to Jencks (1977), at precisely 3:32 p.m. on July 15, 1972, when the prize-winning St. Louis Pruitt-Igoe housing development was demolished because it was deemed "unfit for human inhabitants."

With postmodernism came a change in the scope of planning. The grandiose associated with late modernism was replaced with small-scale organic integration into the surrounding environment. Modernist planners had tried to master the metropolis; postmodern planners believe the urban process cannot be controlled. The fatalism about the urban environment and its pernicious influence on youth has resulted in generally lowered expectations, which has been felt most directly and savagely in the urban ghettos (Kozol, 1991). The general disrespect for planning has undermined efforts to bring a quality education, no matter how defined, to the inner city (and from our perspective everywhere else). A chilling signal of what postmodernists have in mind for education is their willingness to replace "unfit for human" habitation public supported housing with homelessness (see Table 1.1) (Harvey, 1989). The dismissal of the grand has led to a fascination with the minimal.

Postmodernists accept the ephemeral, the fragmentation, the discontinuity, and the chaotic; they make no effort to transcend or alter any of these conditions. Some even claim that there is progressive potentiality in these conditions.

Lyotard defined postmodernism as the "death of the grand narratives" that had been used to make sense of the world. What

Table 1.1. Modernity or Postmodernity.

Fordist Modernity	Flexible Postmodernity
Economies of scale/master code/hierarchy	Economies of scope/idiolect/anarchy
Homogeneity/detail division of labor	Diversity/social division of labor
Paranoia/alienation/symptom	Schizophrenia/decentering/desire
Public housing/monopoly capital	Homelessness/entrepreneurialism
Purpose/design/mastery/determinacy	Play/chance/exhaustion/indeterminacy
Production capital/universalism	Fictitious capital/localism
State power/trade unions	Financial power/individualism
State welfarism/metropolis	Neoconservatism/counterurbanization
Production/originality/authority	Reproduction/pastiche/eclecticism
Blue collar/avant-gardism	White collar/commercialism
Interest group politics/semantics	Charismatic politics/rhetoric
Centralization/totalization	Decentralization/deconstruction
Synthesis/collective bargaining	Antithesis/local contracts

Note: From Harvey (1989).

does all of this mean for education? Obviously, education becomes yet another postmodern problematic.

Democracy is one of the prize conceptions of the Enlightenment. It had the potential to be one of the great accomplishments of modernity. But democracy was too great a leap to be attempted, and efforts were made to work around it. Our argument is that education was never organized for democracy and, as a consequence, democracy, never given a try, could well be the most serious casualty of postmodernism.

We are aware that as we advance our proposal for democratic education all aspects of modernity are being jettisoned by postmodernists. We believe that democracy will survive postmodernism, but if such is to be the case, a powerfully persuasive case has to be made for it.

What We Bring to the Table

To establish credibility of our cognitive democratic paradigm, we draw heavily on our extensive experiences as program developers and participants in democratic initiatives in education. In our nearly three decades of collaboration, we consistently rejected simple single-variable explanations of school culture and have approached every situation as one that has the potential for change. Where that potentiality lies and how constituents can be mobilized to take advantage of it are vital considerations in the process by which democratic change can be introduced to produce a democratic result.

A characteristic of our work has been the application of democratic principles to action research. Our "subjects" have been involved in designing programs and evaluating results. The distinction between subject and researcher, teacher and student has been consciously blurred.

Our work features three main characteristics. First, we challenged the deficit theories that postulate intellectual inadequacy in underclass populations. We introduced programs to show that students who have been tested and found intellectually inferior or have been "diagnosed" as suffering from irreversible learning deficiencies, can perform on every established school achievement measure fully as well as students who have been designated as superior or "gifted." Thus, we produced results that are contrary to a social reproduction thesis. We engaged in such investigations in a variety of social settings where the usual structural arrangements were consciously altered and the cognitive and behavioral changes noted. From this work, we established as part of our democratic theory, equal encouragement, sufficiently precise to be tested systematically. Equal encouragement adds a different dimension to equal opportunity, which has been a crucial and particularly difficult project for schools in recent years.

Second, each of our programs was designed to test our then understanding of democratic education. The synthesis of all that work has us to describe ourselves as cognitive-democratic-social reconstructionists. The precise meaning of these words become clear in the body of this work.

Finally, we viewed and tested a dialectical cognitive hypothesis that the individual and the culture were in a mutually influencing relationship. In a democratic classroom, cognitive growth is maximized by consciously planned opportunities to reflect on organized efforts to change the social and physical environment. In the democratic classroom, students are not only active learners, they are prepared to be agents of change. Our view of education is diametrically opposed to a static system organized for linear acquisition of "knowledge" with little attempt at helping students understand the dynamics of the processes that are involved in learning. We also oppose an education that renders the student powerless to impact culture and social structure. We have been drawn to the work of Vygotsky (1937, 1978), who is now enjoying a revival, although we believe we go beyond Vygotsky in our definition of education and the identification of its democratic components. We are equally opposed to authoritarianism (guardianship) and to an laissez faire education (anarchy) where students are left to determine what it is they will or will not learn.

Defending Democratic Education in the Absence of Independent Ground

Postmodernism came into existence when the credibility of all established authority crumbled. Neither natural nor scientific law can provide an adequate defense for school policy or practices. In the absence of the independent ground of God, tradition, or science, how can democratic education be defended?

> Strong democracy [formally defined] as politics in the participatory mode where conflict is resolved in the absence of an independent ground through a participatory process of ongoing, proximate self-legislation and the creation of a political community capable of transforming dependent, private individuals into free citizens and partial and private interests into public goods. (Barber, 1984, p. 132)

It is Precisely Because There is no Independent Ground That Democratic Education Becomes Necessary. Independent ground was the primary justification for schooling. Pre-enlightenment education drew its inspiration from God; much of that school was devoted to mastery of the Bible (Koran, Talmud, etc). Post-Enlightenment education had science as the ultimate authority. Without unchallengeable authority, educational decisions can only be justified by persuasive argument. The test of the quality of a decision shifts from the leader to the led and in blurring the distinction between the two. It is precisely because of the lack of credibility of established authority that schools have lost both a sense of purpose and the loss of control. Teachers no longer can demand obedience and few possess the theory or skills to be persuasive.

Not everyone acknowledges the loss of credibility of independent ground. What has been termed *right wing fundamentalism* has made its presence known in schools. The more the authority of God is challenged in the classroom, the more aggressively fundamentalists insist educational decisions must be based on "God's" word. Fundamentalist efforts to influence runs the gamut from curriculum to school organization. The call for reestablishing the authority of God in school decisions has produced shrill interchanges and has had chilling effects on curriculum. These efforts, Although occasionally successful, are always divisive and represent a serious challenge for public schools.

"Science," as independent ground, has not lost its adherents. Science continues to be called on to justify curriculum, instruction, student potential for learning, discipline, and so on. The resurgence of the religious influence in schools runs counter to movements toward democratic education, but so too do efforts to establish science as an arbitrary basis for educational decisions. We contend that education based on either an unchallengeable God or an unchallengeable science cannot deal effectively with the developing crises in or out of school.

How We Differ. The preponderance of school analysis has come from scholars who see themselves as objective "umpires" resolutely positioned "outside the system." Theirs is an indispensable role in the development of a solid body of knowledge on which sound educational policies and practices can be grounded. There is undeniable strength in such efforts. But there are also weaknesses in the form of biases and gaps. Too much of contemporary educational research is wrapped in an exclusive academic stratosphere and fixed in a language that is designed to be not understood by classroom teachers, parents, and others interested in schools. This book attempts to provide a balance. We eschew objectivity in favor of active participation in the educational process. The umpires can tell you what has and has not worked. They have difficulty explaining successes and failures. They cannot go beyond their data with any degree of certainty (and their findings suffer the distortion that comes from distance). In our work, we have attempted to test the limits and our interpretations push the possibilities (with the distortion that comes from proximity). Our analysis has been vastly underrepresented in the discourse and its inclusion adds missing ingredients to the discussion and in the process can elevate the contribution of the "umpires."

Although the vantage point from which we approach schooling differs markedly from the university-based one, we are, nonetheless, intrigued by contemporary critical analysis. We agree with much of it. However, we also find it inadequate for informing social policy or practice. Critical theorist analysts are particularly helpful in their analysis of social reproduction, but inadequate in proposing approaches to replace social reproduction with viable forms of social reconstruction.

We can be classified as posthumanist, however, we do not limit ourselves to criticism of an outmoded, palpably undemocratic humanism. We propose a democratic reconstruction. Criticism without defensible proposed remedies is likely to be counterproductive. In the absence of crisp, clear, and coherent proposals, the logical consequence is a paralysis that will give way to a brutal authoritarianism confronting increasingly violent anarchistic fractions and enclaves (Kaplan, 1994). Because postmodernist critics were unable to stay with the procession, they find themselves hopelessly out of step with the changing times. They respond by lashing out at a world they have stopped trying to comprehend, insisting it is incomprehensible.

We face daunting and complex problems. Little in the way of serious solutions to these problems have been proposed. The emphasis in the intellectual world has been on esoteric analysis that includes denunciation or dismissal of anyone daring to devise a solution to any problem. If the problems are difficult, it follows that the need is for better thinking and/or more research. More academics must be willing to leave the musty enclaves that have become for them intellectual traps and interact respectfully with broad segments of diverse populations. We believe that only when all elements of a society are involved in the search can effective solutions to complex problems be found. We further believe that places need to be found or created where courses of action can be proposed and subjected to the widest possible range of critiques and assessments. One such place should be a school. A democratic analysis establishes the foundation on which a plan of action can be carefully constructed with the reasonable assurance that there will be popular support for and ownership of the plan. It is that simple and that difficult.

Democratic education enables individuals to get out of the personal and become political. Probably nothing distinguishes our notion of democratic education more than our disagreement with the proposition that "the personal is political." If politics is a means by which problems held in common are solved in common, then it follows that politics can only occur where is movement from private to that which is shared with others. We agree with Dionne (1991, p. 16) in his citing Schlesinger's notion of politics as "search for remedy" (i.e., the means by which a decision is reached to resolve a conflict).

It is premature to announce the end of great narratives (Lyotard, 1986). There has been an abdication of all but one great narrative, capitalism or more apt, economic rationalism, as represented by the seemingly omnipresent and all victorious marketplace. The monopolization of social thought by the "market" is not a vindication of postmodernist thought. It is an indictment of it.

> For postmodernists, it is simply too late to oppose the momentum of industrial society. They merely resolve to stay alert and cool, in its midst. Consciously complying and yet far from docile, they chronicle, amplify, augment it. They judge it as little as it judges itself, Determined to all or nothing they are passionately impassive. (Kareil, 1989, p. ix)

The Marketplace and Education. There presently exists a similarity of broad educational themes across western and eastern European countries. With the fall of communism and a general disintegration of socialist intellectual thought into shrill and increasingly arcane criticisms of "grand narratives," a deregulated market dominates all discussion of social policy. As previously mentioned, a self-management and market-driven concept has been translated into calls for parental "choice" with parents defined as consumers of a market-generated commodity. Choice is a central feature in a patently undemocratic market approach to education, just as choice is a central feature in the democratic school. The market choice differs greatly from choice in our version of a democratic school. In the marketplace version, choice is used to obtain a competitive advantage over other students. Choice is incorporated in a system designed to separate winners from losers. In actuality, in the market approach to choice, it is the elite schools that do the choosing, with unchosen students forced to opt for openings in schools with decreasing power, until those students with the least going for them find that their choice is restricted to schools that also have the least going for them. In that definition of choice, it is not what the school can do for the child, but what the child can do for the school. It is also a system guaranteed to reinforce social reproduction (Ball 1994a; Gewirtz, Ball, & Bowe, 1995).

In a democratic education, choice meets both the goal of the right to movement and the guarantee of equal encouragement. The market choice contributes to the centrifugalization and decentering of society, whereas democratic choice is linked to centripetal-ization and the reestablishing of a center. How these two approaches to choice differ in practice and policy is explained in the following chapters.

The challenge in the 1990s and into the 21st century is to create a public education system that prepares all students to deal effectively with inescapable challenges. Such a school encourages all students to empower themselves with knowledge and citizenship arts that can be used to help solve important problems (important because students believe the problems are important). Although in this book we call for considerable change and a paradigm shift away from the present market alternatives in education, we also recognize that we cannot move back to a humanist tradition that attempted to impose a unitary culture on students and inadequately and often brutally dealt with diversity. We cannot stay with either a hopelessly inadequate and rigid premodernist conservatism or with the muddling deconstructive nihilistic postmodernism, both of which are fragmenting and centrifugalizing. The inability of postmodernist critics in education to devise a coherent plan of action for the future of education on the basis of their research is a serious weakness in their thinking and an abdication of responsibility to the community that sustains them. We do, however, applaud their role in the wider social protest against the destructiveness of certain features of modernism, particularly the destruction of local culture. They have made a powerful contribution in their careful dissection of government policy and its impact on micropolitical levels of schooling. Although we are put off by the difficult language by which postmodernist critiques are presented, we are acutely aware that the publicly impenetrable discourse is not an affectation. It is designed to decenter debate. Our goal is to recenter debate and bring everyone into it in a universally understandable language.

The Magnitude of the Challenge

Schools amble along as if the world is the old world yet. From everywhere come signs and signals of the dangers that lie ahead. We are hurtling toward a precipice. It is not too late to change directions. We have been forewarned from every possible direction.

Sampson (1992), Chancellor (1990), and Kennedy (1993) are not "gloom and doomers." They tend to be careful, balanced, and, if anything, overly optimistic. But they are among a growing consensus that call for a totally new approach to education. None propose specifics; none qualify as a democratic educator. But a democratic education does address everything Kennedy and almost every other analyst of the world condition brings to our attention.

The gap between government and governed looms wider than ever, and Britain is run by one of the most centralized and least accountable systems in the industrial world. The complaint is familiar: a century ago Disraeli warned that "centralization is the death-blow of public freedom". . . the British in the last decade have seen concentrations of power which the Victorians never dreamed of. The central control has tightened, and the countervailing powers outside Whitehall have been weakened. The Church, the Law, the universities and the monarchy have all lost influence. The middle ground of high-minded or non-political people, "the great and the good", has been eroded. Town halls and provincial cities have been by-passed. Individual schools and hospitals may gain financial autonomy; but they are becoming accountable less to their locality, and more to Whitehall.

Parliament, while proclaiming its sovereignty, allows still more decisions to be taken by the party-machines, the executive, the cabinet and the Council and Commission in Brussels. (p. 154)

Businessmen were the first to become supranational, followed reluctantly by politicians and diplomats. It is this time-lag which has caused the "democratic deficit"—the bleak phrase which itself suggests that everything can be measured in money. (p. 156)

Modern society is so complex that decisions always seem to be taken somewhere else. But no democracy can be effective unless the public is allowed to know how, and where decisions are taken, and given some sense of participation. (Sampson, 1992, p.162)

The strength is there, but it is being sapped by a combination of weaknesses—a thousand wounds we find difficult to heal. We have weakened ourselves in the way we practice our politics, manage our businesses, teach our children, succor our poor, care for our elders, save our money, protect our environment, and run our government. (Chancellor, on the future of the United States, 1990, p. 23)

If my analysis is correct, the forces for change facing the world could be so far reaching, complex, and interactive that they call for nothing less than the reeducation of humankind. (Kennedy, 1993, p. 339)

As we move toward the 21st century, there are a number of challenges that teachers and students simply can no longer avoid. These become key elements of the curriculum of the democratic school. At the close of the 20th century, we encounter fundamental and cataclysmic changes in human history. The political, economic, social, environmental, cultural, and technical changes are unparalleled. Chaos, as defined by "themeless juxtapositions" (Kaplan, 1994), more than planning, characterizes much of this change.

If the future is to be understood and brought under human control, students must be prepared to be an integral part of the challenge. Democratic education is not an exercise in predicting futures. It presents students with problems, allows them to marshal evidence (do research) and helps them find solutions to those problems. The primary challenge is to help students overcome a pervasive sense of helplessness that is the logical consequence of having been denied comprehension of the workings of the complex system of which they are a part.

CHALLENGE AS CURRICULUM: TOWARD A PROBLEM-SOLVING CURRICULUM THAT ADDRESSES REAL AND IMPORTANT PROBLEMS

A central feature of a democratic school is the preparation of students for solving important and pressing social and personal problems. In a democratic classroom there is balance between curriculum designed to help individuals solve personal problems and curriculum organized to help citizens solve problems that they share as community members. It is recognized that if the emphasis is too much on the social, students will rightfully resist. If the emphasis is too much on the personal, students' attention will not be alerted to the impossibility of solving personal problems in an unraveling world. Some of the pressing social issues that become the curriculum of a democratic school are cited here:

1. An ecologically sustainable society. Curriculum must be developed that enables students to propose desirable and feasible ways to achieve environmental stability by preventing the depletion of nonreplenishable resources; the increase in pollution that poisons land, sea, and air; and the massive changes in populations—overpopulation of some species coupled with the extinction of others. Such

curriculum would require students to examine the appropriateness of such concepts as *gross national product; consumption;* and consider the viability of an ecological theory of value (Pearl, 1971). Students would be asked to evaluate the ecological impact of various models of global economies on the livability of the environment.

2. An economy that meets human needs while achieving a full, fair, and gratifying employment society. Students will be given the opportunity to evaluate various approaches to a free market economy, as well as a variety of alternatives to the free market in an effort to determine which approach is most likely to generate a full, fair, and healthy work environment without endangering the environment. The consideration of a future economy would include discussion of conversion from a war to a peace economy and the redirecting of facilities and resources to first define and then to meet human needs. Such challenges would include careful considerations of planned apprenticeships in the human services to take the place of current credentialling procedures (Knight, 1993; Pearl & Riessman, 1965). It would also open up discussions involving redefinitions of work and the possible creation of a variety of new forms of work.

3. Nonviolent approaches to conflict resolution. The end of "the evil empire" has not produced peace. If anything, war is breaking out all over and is not subject to traditional resolutions (Kaplan, 1994). Students need to be able to analyze the changing face of war and to devise schemes that replace international and within-nations disorder and bloody confrontations with working systems through which disputes are settled without violence.

4. Just and humane societies. A just society is an equal encouragement society. It is one in which different understandings of justice are considered and issues of putative injustice (e.g., racism, classism, sexism, ageism, etc.) are carefully considered and proposed approaches to rectification are debated, tested, and evaluated. Students are encouraged to consider moving from hierarchical and confrontational arrangements of race, ethnicity, and gender to relationships based on equitable treatment of women, minorities, and the entrenched poor.

5. Crime-free and caring societies. A humane society comes to grips with increasing social instability marked by

unacceptably high levels of crime and violence by conscious efforts to construct a workable civil society that can reduce violence and criminal behavior while also scrupulously respecting rights and meeting other democratic requirements.

6. Elimination of world poverty. The challenge starts with at least 2 billion people presently living below the poverty line. Poverty is not exclusively a third-world problem. Nor does it distinguish the capitalist economically developed countries from the former Eastern Bloc. Within "wealthy" developed nations there are increasingly larger proportions of citizens mired in abject poverty.

7. Moving from the monocultural nondemocratic cultures to the multicultural democratic cultures. Tribalism, ethnic conflicts, and religious differences present to the 21st century many of its most difficult challenges, including recognition of the rights and values of the "fourth world," the indigenous populations existing within modern societies. "Mabo" land rights in Australia can be treated as a case study, as can the somewhat similar claims of Native-Americans, and "Black" immigrants in the United Kingdom. At issue is how diversity can be incorporated into a coherent integrated whole that allows for both common understanding and the appreciation of difference.

8. Planning cities of hope. The challenge is to be able to merge economic development, urban planning, and community services in the recreation of local communities. The modern international style with its emphasis on centralization, economic rationalization, and a global economy destroys local culture and decenters communities. Students in democratic classrooms learn how to create a viable community and defend its feasibility and desirability.

9. Marshaling technology for socially useful purposes. Technology has intended and unintended consequences. Most current presentations of a high technology future are dystopic. Students need to examine how technology can be organized to better serve humanity. Students need to distinguish myth from reality in the highly promoted "information society." They need to be given the opportunity to perform research that will enable them to dis-

tinguish information from disinformation. Students need to be able to weigh the difficult ethical issues related to the use of technology.

Each of these problem areas are difficult, but because they are interrelated, the solutions are even more difficult because all these problems must be solved simultaneously. Given the enormity of the problem, it is not difficult to understand why people feel powerless and why intellectuals limit themselves to criticism rather than proposed interventions. In the chapters that follow we discuss how a transition from a fragmented "subject"-based curriculum to a problem-solving one can be conceptualized, and how such a curriculum can be organized developmentally. It is through the solving of real problems that students learn to develop a social consciousness, develop arguments designed to persuade others by logic and evidence, and listen to the logic and evidence of other proposals. Democratic education is most effective when classmates, teachers, and community leaders consciously try to influence each other.

As difficult as responsible intellectual debate leading to shared support of social intervention is, it is only half of the curriculum of the democratic classroom. The other half involves the development of healthy, independent, and personally responsible individuals. Although issues of employment, poverty, and the environment can only be resolved through collective understanding and collective action, there are aspects of life where privacy and individual choice must be respected if a civil society is to be preserved. A democratic education is directed at assisting students to make responsible choices in job or career selection; social connections; culture-carrying activities; constructive use of leisure; sexual practices; the use of psychoactive substances; and the nature of relationships with friends, mates, and children. Many of these matters currently are thrown willy-nilly into the curriculum with little or no informing theory, and with little or no impact on thinking or behavior. A democratic education is as much concerned with the growth of individuals as it is with the advance of society. How a balance between the social and the personal can be obtained is treated throughout this book

We Have No Unique Claim on Democracy. Well before Dewey, there were calls for democratic education. Many today recognize the severe limitation, inequity, insensitivity, and, at times, outright brutality of current classroom practices. In the pages ahead we examine many of the attempts to either retrieve a democratic education or to establish one where none has existed before. The more democracy becomes a topic for conversation, the better it will be for schooling. But there are also pitfalls and booby traps. It is important that the discussion lead to clarity of vision and to crisp analyses. Making school a happier place does not necessarily make it democratic. Sensitizing students to the realities of the world does not necessarily make the classroom democratic, cooperative learning is not necessarily democratic, nor is a multicultural, antiracism curriculum. The test of a democratic education is the difference it makes in the lives of students and to the community to which they belong.

CONCLUSION

A society that is divided, disillusioned and bewildered, that has lost confidence in its own character and its purpose, cannot expect to achieve unity through schools. (Commager, 1980, p. 47)

Commager is a wonderful historian. Few approach him in his ability to read and apply history, However, in this quote, we believe he has it wrong. A society cannot expect to achieve unity solely through schools. But, it is also true that a society cannot be brought back from disillusionment, disunity, and bewilderment without a revitalized democratic education. The trivialization of schooling contributed significantly to our present condition. We go forward to present the case for a school that could contribute to revitalizing society.

The fate of the country . . . does not depend on what kind of paper you drop into the ballot-box once a year, but on what kind of man you drop from your chamber into the street every morning. (Thoreau, 1981/1854, p. 674)

We believe that a general theory of education that will guide a democratic school can exert influence on other agencies and institutions in subtle and complex ways. Among its most important influences will be to a competent citizen who will "drop on the street" prepared to positively influence "the fate of the country"—and the world.

Chapter 2

The Role of the Schools and the Importance of a General Theory of Education

The intent of this chapter is make the following points:

1. A general theory is vitally needed to deal with educational issues.
2. A general theory based on clear and specific democratic principles is preferable to existing and proposed theories.
3. Privatization, although presented as the epitome of democracy is inadequate as a general theory, and grossly undemocratic.
4. Educational theory needs to be developed and tested from the ground up.
5. The classroom, not remote governmental centers or research institutes is where important educational change occurs.

6. The more ordinary and undistinguished by special features the classroom is the more the useful it will be in testing theory and initiating wide sweeping change.
7. Teachers, parents, and students have vital roles to play in the development of educational theory.
8. The more university scholars work as equal status partners and collaborators with teachers, parents and students, and the less they define themselves as outside experts, the more useful they will be in helping to develop and test theory.
9. The classroom, as distinct from "all" classrooms or a large array of randomly selected subjects whose performance is contrasted with comparable controls, is where theory is tested; partly because a general theory brings local community into its development, partly because only when students play an active role can there be meaning attached to evaluation, partly because the classroom is a logical place for the restoration of community to begin, and partly because only in a classroom can there be the balance and integration between frameworks and other centralized initiatives and the inclusion of ideas and interests of local communities. Each new classroom test is not only replication but also provides opportunity for refinement and establishing the limits of applicability.

Advancing a general theory is fraught with philosophical and practical difficulties and must be done cautiously. The theory will work to the extent that it draws on a solid body of evidence and is so logically constructed as to be readily and universally understood. Which means if a such grand theory is to gain general acceptance, the beginning test of it must be small.

Ultimately, a theory works to the extent it can be applied successfully first in one class-room, and then with refinements that emerge from reflections on small-scale tests, can be extended to all classrooms. This approach is necessary because we have learned to our chagrin that grand schemes created by our very best minds working in rarefied air, crash when put to test in the classroom. Teachers resist, deflect, or ignore such theories because they are denied ownership. Centrally determined policy also bewilders students and infuriates parents. Here we make the case that the average, ordinary, regular classroom is the only place where sound educational theory can be developed and then only when teachers, students, and parents play important roles in its development.

When the classroom is at the center of educational discussion, talk about democracy and its four requirements becomes possible.

Only when all having vital interests in education (stakeholder is the fashionable expression as we write) are brought into discussions and given the opportunity to express themselves fully will theoretical understanding about curriculum be attainable.

That discussion will be most fruitful to the extent to which all students are encouraged to participate equally in decisions that affect their lives.

That discussion will be most fruitful to the extent all students enjoy equally specifically defined rights, among which are: freedom of expression, privacy, a system of due process and rights of movement.

That discussion will be most fruitful to the extent to which all students are equally encouraged to succeed in all of the classroom's activities.

Theory development and evaluation go hand in hand. Only when all students carefully examine the classroom experiences and participate in the generation of data and otherwise assess classroom performances will it be possible to accurately evaluate a general theory. University-based scholars and high-level bureaucrats will better understand educational theory, and assess its applicability, when they enter into a classroom and engage in mutually respectful extensive and unrestricted interchanges with students and their parents.

THE NEED FOR A GENERAL EDUCATION THEORY

Given the state of world affairs and the trend evident in world educational systems to elevate market-driven choice to the status of theory, development of a comprehensive general theory that can provide precise definition of educational goals and the means to accomplish them has never been more important. It is precisely at this time that retreat to the margins would have the most tragic results. Our general theory—democratic education—is organized to encompass the widest range of educational activities including the following: knowledge as organized into curriculum, instruction, learning and cognition, classroom management, governance, budgeting, and administration.

There is nothing more practical than a good theory (attributed to Kurt Lewin)

The Deliberate Construction of Theory

Schooling has always been guided by some semblance of theory.
Rationales have been concocted to explain the actions taken in
classrooms. Education theory, for the most part, has been ad hoc,
vague, low level, and more directed to description than to precise
explanation. The guiding raison d'être for most schools throughout
history was to teach only those things that were necessary for the
perpetuation of the dominant culture. Instruction was conducted
within the family or in a close-knit homogeneous communal unit.
Even these simple systems were not free from controversy.
Because the species by nature permanently alters the environment every generation, all cultures have experienced the tension
created by efforts to hold on to the past and movements to some
meagerly defined future. Until very recently the pace of environmental alteration has been slow and an education with heavy
emphasis on transmitting to the next generation a particular version of the past met with little organized resistance. Only rarely
did preoccupation with past knowledges, values, arts, skills, and
belief systems pose a threat to the survival of the culture, and
never was such an education perceived to be a threat to the continuation of the species. There were occasional tensions.
Pythagoras found the Greeks relentlessly unreceptive to the
square root of 2. And the fate of Socrates was sealed when he was
found guilty of corrupting Athenian youth through his teachings.
His crime, like Galileo's many centuries later, was extending
teaching beyond education's acceptable mission (i.e., the perpetuation of existing dominant culture).

In recent years, feminists have stripped the mask of liberal democracy to reveal its patriarchy and to some extent the
curriculum and instruction has been modified to accommodate this
change in understanding (Yates, 1993). There have been similar
modifications in curriculum to treat racial bias in the most
palatable and superficial ways. Not so with class. In the United
States and Australia, the myth of a classless society is not challenged in the formal curriculum. The environment has become a
recognized subject in schools and students engage in ceremonial
acts and anti-litter campaigns to demonstrate their commitment
to a iivable world.

It is our contention that intermittent jabs at difficult topics will have little or no effect. We argue further: Only when curriculum is incorporated within a general theory can it significantly influence a student to become an active and informed citizen.

The call for significant changes in education has only recently surfaced. In relatively stable societies with tightly bound codes and entrenched systems of authority little discussion about the nature of education took place and outright opposition to established authority was not tolerated.

The schooling the young received through the centuries was patently unfair. It was designed for social reproduction. Those at the top of the social ladder were provided the education to keep them there and those at the bottom received the paltry portion necessary for community survival. But, even though unfair, what existed, as meager as it was, was a workable, if not a very important, system. There was a close correspondence between the education provided and citizenship responsibilities as limited as these were. The education met employer requirements, although *employer* is a quaint term for most of human history where the dominant economic activity was labor-extensive agriculture.

Education changed dramatically with the advent of primary and secondary means of production. The evolution of shipping, mining, and manufacturing changed the landscape of employment and the organization of society. The rapid and widesweeping changes that accompanied the industrial revolution led to the creation of a system of mass formal education (i.e., the public or government funded school). That public school, created in the first half of the 19th century and rearranged in the first half of the 20th century, is what current reformers are trying to patch together, although the pace of change in the world today far outstrips the magnitude of change that led to the creation of the public school. It is the rate of change that overwhelms educational theorists, reformers, and practitioners, And yet it is the rate and direction of change that a general theory of education must address.

In the 20th century, new modes of production have come into existence, and disappeared. The locus of power moved from the local community to the nation-state and then to multinational corporations operating in a global economy—all within the span of a single century.

In the 20th century, a credential society was created! Nothing more characterizes the change in the importance of education than the authority given to it to grant credentials. In a credential society, the school issues visas to different areas of the work world and to places where power is brokered. The school, rather rapidly and somewhat imperceptibly, was transformed from a relatively unimportant institution into the primary instrument of status flow. When schools gain such power they draw interest and concern. In the not too distant past what happened in the classrooms was a matter for each local community to decide. But with change in status ineluctably came concern over "standards," norm-referent testing, teacher licensing, and other formalized regulations. The rise in school importance had implications for both individuals and for the society. Business leaders wanted assurance that schools were preparing the type of worker they needed. Pillars of the community, shocked by the decline in morality, wanted schools to do something about teaching values. Parents could not understand how the adorable 6-year-old they had entrusted to the school had been transformed into a 15-year-old monster. Teachers could not understand how parents could be so negligent and irresponsible to send a 15-year-old monster to school. Parents wanted schools to be safe places. Teachers wanted schools to be safe places. Students wanted school to be safe places, but they also wanted someone or something to shake up the place and bring some excitement to an otherwise dreadfully boring enterprise. But maybe, most important of all, the changing role of the school in a credential society with insufficient good jobs to go around stimulated "concerned" parents to enroll their children in the best school and otherwise do whatever it might take to gain a competitive edge. And so, parents search for the "right" school, the "right" teacher, the "right" computer, the "right" subject choice, the "right" phonics program and so on, hoping that by doing so they have stolen a march on other parents. The extent to which desire for a competitive edge impinges on equity and equal opportunity is a matter a general theory must address.

The desire for competitive edge is a major impetus for choice initiatives that are discussed later in this chapter. Competitive edge also presents a challenge for middle-class civil libertarians, who in theory desire an equal playing field for all children while at the same time do everything they can to help their children get ahead in an increasingly cut-throat competitive world.

The impetus for a competitive edge in a shrinking opportunity structure has had a chilling impact on the debate over purposes and processes of schooling. Insufficient emphasis has been given to the destructiveness of "getting ahead at the expense of others" mentality in the education debates. Insistence on a competitive edge is to a large extent the response to the perception of the opportunity structure. If there is widespread belief in the inevitability of shrinking economic opportunity and an ever widening gap between the rich and poor, it is not at all surprising that parents would do what they could to improve the likelihood that their children be rich rather than poor. And there is a widespread belief in the inevitability of shrinking economic opportunity. In fact, that is about the only area of agreement among Whites, Blacks, Hispanics, and Asian Americans in the United States.

> Pessimism united the races. A majority said they feel the American Dream is fading for them and for their children. Good jobs, they said, are harder to find. So is decent housing. Schools are getting worse, not better. Those in America's growing black middle class said they felt particularly vulnerable, expressing fears that tough times and discrimination could wash away their gains. (from responses to a survey of 1,970 randomly selected Americans, including 802 whites, 474 Blacks, 352 English-speaking Asians, and 252 Spanish and English-speaking Hispanics. (Morin, 1995, p. 6)

That particular actions taken to support competitive edge can lead to an increasingly unstable and unsafe society is not given much consideration in what passes for public debate on education. To the contrary, getting ahead is often coupled with support for get-tough crime measures, opposition to tax increases, school cuts and mergers, decline in support for school desegregation, and withdrawal of support for "social" programs. The logical consequences of these trends has not been matters for serious discussion. What should be thought-provoking essays (e.g., Kaplan, 1994) are not incorporated into educational theory or practice. Nor for that matter are the more vivid dystopic futuristic motion pictures (*Blade Runner, Escape from New York*, and the *Mad Max* series) that probably inform the future visions of students far more than anything that takes place in the classrooms.

A general educational theory has something pertinent to say about pessimistic themes found in the lyrics embedded in the music that teenagers listen to, or the "reality" films such as *The Trainspotters*. No adequate educational theory can avoid dealing with the condition of the economy, the appropriate function of government, "power" as it is and as it can and should be. It is through enriched conversation about all that is real in a student's life that educational theory develops. Part of the application of democratic educational theory in schools would have students actively participate in discussions about "government," the economy and their role in it. In these conversations, students should be encouraged to imagine the world as they would like it to be, and what it would take to make such an ideal real. We have in the past criticized educational theory and practice as exercises in dream killing. The dream killing takes the form of limiting discussion, placing a ceiling on aspirations, or by the most painful of all deaths for youth, consciously planned boredom. A significant characteristic of a general democratic educational theory is the encouragement that it gives students to dream.

The organization of work and the condition of the economy are only some of the many very difficult issues that need to be addressed in a general educational theory. Given the magnitude of emerging problems outlined in chapter 1, it is extremely doubtful whether a stable society can be achieved with an education whose major purpose is cultural transmission, the elders passing on to youth the accumulated richness of the past through "myriad cultural activities."

Education that began as an informal process and evolved into a large, cumbersome, bureaucratically managed institution, needs to be recast as the primary agency devoted to preparing all of society for its future challenges. It falls to the school to take on a large measure of this considerable responsibility. Schools cannot be expected to solve the world's problems, but schools must play a pivotal educational role in the equal preparation of all students for active and informed citizenship, if those problems are to be solved.

Because the task of educating for an uncertain, difficult, and foreboding future must be fundamentally different than the education of the past, it follows that the theory that guides and informs such an education must also be different than the theories that guided the education of the past.

Sorting out Educational Theory

Educational theory comes in all sizes and shapes. There are theories of knowledge, theories of development, theories of learning and cognition, theories of instruction, theories of classroom management, and theories of organization. What passes for theory in most classrooms is bits and pieces taken from all, or some of those just mentioned. This is most evident in preservice courses for aspiring teachers.

Lecture series, electives, and course requirements are too frequently assembled without a sense of theoretical coherence. There is often little correspondence between the theory of knowledge and the theory of instruction or discipline, or for that matter between any formal theory and classroom activity. The more education has been subjected to attack the more it has abandoned coherent theory. It is our contention that only with clarity and thoroughness in the development of theory, and seriously applying it to classroom policies and practices, will it be possible to encourage debate on what it will take to stabilize society and address problems.

Theories of Knowledge

Nondemocratic theories of school-delivered knowledge can be classified into three categories: essentialism, perennialism, and existentialism (or romantic humanism). Each of these are informed by a philosophy, and it is often difficult to distinguish the knowledge component from other aspects of the philosophy.

The "Basics" as Important Knowledge. The term given to an education limited to basic information is *essentialism*. Essentialism emerged in the 1930s as a reaction to progressivism (Bagley, 1938), regained momentum in the 1950s and 1960s (Bestor, 1953, 1955), was reestablished as "back to basics" during the 1970s, and later further reinforced with emphasis on "competency-based" curriculum and skills measurement (Goodson, 1992). It is a no-frills, practical approach to education. The focus is on abstract problem solving, minus social-personal context. It operates from a principle of disinterested inquiry, meaning that students approach learning as passive consumers. Whether this kind of logic allows the development of social and moral identities in students is questionable. It is conservative and authoritarian in its approach to knowledge. Important knowledge is that which essentialists insist every child must know to be able to function adequately in society. Essentialists organize knowledge by subjects. Essentialism informs the report published by the commission appointed by U.S. President Ronald Reagan (National Commission, 1983), and Schools of the Future legislation in Victorian schools (Australia; DES, 1993) The basic subjects that essentialism calls for are reading, writing, and mathematics in the elementary schools and English, mathematics, history, geography, government, science, foreign languages, physical education, and the arts in the secondary schools (Down, 1977). Other subjects (strands and key learning areas) are added to the 1990s version (DES, 1993). Each strand contains major subject content and processes connected to each key learning area. This is basically a framework model of curriculum design. It draws from three streams of curriculum theory: (a) behavioral objectives or in recent terminology, *out-comes-based* education (OBE), in which teachers are expected to place students at particular developmental levels in relation to eight "key" learning areas and learning assessment profiles (LAP); (b) the essentialist tradition with an emphasis on subject-based content areas, skill instruction, and assessment procedures; and (c) what has been described by Hargreaves (1989) as the cultural restoration model defined as the new progressivism," which may include the values of flexibility, team work, and communication). [The core emphasis of new curriculum forms is on learning process rather than knowledge and content.] The language of this education emphasizes performance, accountability, and inputs and outcomes. Essentialists require students to master certain facts and skills; they are not much interested in ideas. Essentialism is as much defined by what does not happen in schools as by what does happen. Essentialists insist that there is a limit to what schools can be expected to accomplish and attempting more than schools can realistically be expected to do only leads to a decline in standards and student performance. Thus, essentialists insist that broader social issues should not be addressed in schools, nor should schools try to influence the conditions and situations in which many students find themselves. Essentialists believe that other agencies have the responsibility to treat living conditions, sexual practices, and psychological growth and that schools should be limited to only teaching the basics. Teachers should teach only what they are authorized to teach, and students should demonstrate that they have learned what their teachers have taught by regurgitation and by performance on tests that meet rigidly defined standards. Essentialism makes little effort to meet any of the four requirements of a democratic education. The knowledge is not organized to prepare the student to solve any important problem, and thus for us, essentialism is far too basic to meet either student interest or societal need.

    We believe essentialism fails because it insults the intelligence of the student. And that, more than anything else, provokes resistance. With essentialism the major emphasis is on literacy, but there is no effort to convince students of the importance of literacy, nor is there an attempt to enliven the educational process. What many if not most students find intrinsically interesting in the primary grades becomes for most excruciatingly boring the longer they remain in school.

Essentialists make no effort to involve students in any decision that would affect their lives (in fact, it is such education that essentialists denounce). The importance of students' rights are minimized and there has been no serious examination of the possible inequity of such a system. Equal education from an essentialist perspective is teaching everyone the same subject in precisely the same way (*exposition* is the dominant teaching model used) and using the identical standard to evaluate the performance of every student. Although essentialists do not meet our requirements of democracy, they nonetheless stake a claim on democracy, insisting that mastery of the basics is the sole defensible prerequisite for democratic citizenship. Requiring more, according to essentialists, constitutes either indoctrination or intrusion into areas where education does not belong. Curiously, essentialism is frequently criticized for its attempt at indoctrination. Indoctrination could conceivably be a serious criticism if students were the least bit interested in what was going on in the classroom. A more accurate charge is that essentialists unprepare students. Students emerge from schools knowing very little that can be applied to real-life problems.

From an essentialist view the deterioration of school standards coupled with a lack of emphasis on basic skills has produced functional illiterates and thus has threatened democracy. From our view, because so much of what goes on in classrooms is a concentrated effort to implement essentialism, it is essentialism that has to accept the responsibility for the functional illiteracy that endangers democracy.

The "Great Works" as Important Knowledge. The term given to an education limited to great works is *perennialism.* Perennialism, like essentialism, is conservative and authoritarian in its approach to knowledge. To perennialists, the goal of education is to help students know "truth." Perennialists believe that all important truth is contained in the great works of culture that have withstood the test of time. Truth to perennialists is unchanging and that is what makes it "perennial." Students are encouraged to delve deeply into the great works, to savor them, and discuss and reflect on them. Perennialist schooling involves ideas more than the accumulation of skills or facts. The appeal is to cognition. To perennialists, lack of student interest or complaints about subject relevance is itself irrelevant and schools should not pamper whiners or dilute subjects to appease complainers. The student is encouraged to be an active learner of a curriculum that is rigidly structured and unamendable

> Conservatives do not deny the existence of undiscovered truths, but they make a critical assumption, which is that those truths that have already been apprehended are more important to cultivate than those undisclosed ones. . . . Conservatism is the tacit acknowledgment that all that is finally important in human experience is behind us; that the crucial explorations have been undertaken, and that it is given to man to know what are the great truths that emerged from them. Whatever is to come cannot outweigh the importance to man of what has gone before. (Buckley, 1968, p. 182)

Perennialists do not try to meet our requirements of democratic education. They make no effort to organize knowledge for problem solving. Students are not included in the decision making, students are not granted rights, nor is there much interest in equality. Inequality, after all, is one of the truths that has stood the test of time and is rarely challenged in this model. In fact, what is common to this model is the reverential nature of its teaching style. Nonetheless, important leaders among the perennialists insist that perennialism is consistent with democracy (Adler, 1982a, 1982b; Hutchins, 1936). They argue that every student receiving a perennialist education is exposed to the great truths out of which democracy emerged and it is in these great works that the solutions to all of our present problems can be found (although Pateman, 1985, among others has revealed how the great works have been used to oppress women).

In practice, perennialism has been the education for the elite, whereas essentialism has been restricted to those deemed to be intellectually unworthy. This allocation is one of the means by which social reproduction has been maintained.

> Education implies teaching. Teaching implies knowledge. Knowledge is truth. The truth is everywhere the same. Hence, education should be everywhere the same. (Hutchins, 1936, p. 27)

Self-Awareness as Important Knowledge. There are many terms given to an education that limits important knowledge to awareness of self, *existentialism, romantic humanism,* and *open education* are among the most often used. Existentialism or romantic humanism is child-centered education. The knowledge of this approach to education is that which facilitates individual growth. In essence, each student chooses what it is he or she wants to learn. The primary knowledge is self-discovery. The most noted proponents of such education have been Maslow (1958, 1971), Neill (1961), and Rogers (1969).

Child-centered education claims to be democratic. The primary justification of that claim is the authoritarian nature of essentialism and perennialism that it opposes. The democracy supported by such an approach is one that features *negative freedom,* the removal of restriction on the individual. It is what Barber (1983) called "thin" democracy and fails to meet critical elements in our definition of democratic education. There is no effort to develop a body of knowledge that equips every student to solve critical social problems. And although students do make decisions that affect their lives, these are individual decisions. Community is a significant feature of an "open school" but the community is restricted to those who share the philosophy. Rogers' T-groups supposedly develop sensitivity to other individuals, but that is as far as it goes (or because this philosophy currently is in free fall, as far as it went). The establishment of a larger than individual entity created by a community of diverse individuals struggling to discover or invent a common ground, and to which there is general allegiance, is not something emphasized in an education that turns its attention inward and whose mission is self-discovery. Rights are emphasized in existential education, but there is no balancing of rights with responsibilities. It is assumed that a self-actualized person will be responsible, but the nature of that responsibility is not specified. And the issue of equality is never seriously joined. It is believed that a self-actualized person by definition is a good person, and good people are not racists, sexists, or otherwise prejudiced. And if everyone was educated to full self-development, everyone would be good, there would be no prejudice, and we would all live happily ever after in a society dedicated to equality (as well as peace, justice, etc.). Such a definition of equality is too broad to be useful in a world where institutional practices are organized to perpetuate inequities, and organized efforts are required for significant change. In essence, the growth of self-centered education coincided with the emergence of an ego-centered society and has contributed significantly to the rise in inordinate selfishness that a democratic education attempts to address. It is the attitude of the "me" generation, far more than organized conservative thought, that has led to the political paralysis a democratic education seeks to remedy.

> To begin, [existential education] . . . rules out three conventional notions, that education is primarily an agency of society, set up to perpetuate a cultural heritage; that it is a pipeline of perennial truths; and that it is a means for adjusting the young to life in a democratic community. In place of these, let education exist for the individual. Let it teach him to live as his own nature bids him, spontaneously and authentically. (Kneller, 1961, p. 428)

Learning How to Create a Better World as Important Knowledge. The term given to an education designed to create a better society is *social reconstruction.* The goal of social reconstruction is to give students the knowledge necessary to change society. Its most celebrated proponent, Counts, gave it expression during the great depression of the 1930s. Prompted by a society sinking in seemingly insoluble economic difficulty and enmeshed in rapidly growing social problems resistant to traditional treatment, Counts exhorted professional educators to serve as agents of social change. In his most famous work, *Dare the Schools Build a New Social Order?* (1932), he encouraged teachers to ally with labor, women, farmers, and minority groups in a campaign to form a new society. Counts criticized Dewey and other "progressive" educators for failing to generate a theory of social welfare. He maintained that the child-centered approach was inadequate to ensure the necessary skills and knowledge that an education must provide in the 20th century.

In recent years, Marxists and critical theorists have made similar appeals for social reconstruction (Apple, 1979; Aronowitz & Giroux, 1985). Social reconstruction theorists, by not specifying curriculum, rights, how, where, and when students will participate in important decision making and developing a means by which equality can be attained, do not meet our definition of democratic education. Nor do they emphasize to the extent to which we do, the importance of balanced treatment of controversial issues.

Redefining Leadership

In our understanding of democratic education, neither teachers nor students are directed to the type of future society to be created. A democratic school does not choose sides and thus bias knowledge. It is not premised on the belief that it will be led by feminists or any other critics of existing society. It is not a school that sexists, racists, or homophobes enter at their peril. Its goal is not to dare to change society. Its goal is to prepare students to provide leadership for inevitable change by organizing the curriculum so that students can participate in the debate about change. In a democratic classroom, students become aware of conflicting arguments and the logic and evidence that support different proposals. It is the responsibility of democratic teachers to ensure balance by bringing to the classroom the widest range of different positions on a particular topic. Students should be as much encouraged to be conservative as they are to be liberal or radical. The quality of a democratic education is not determined by the direction the debate takes, it is determined by the quality of the debate—the extent to which students learn to marshal evidence and build coherent cases for different positions and proposals. The role of the teacher is to challenge all positions. (How overtly racist and sexist arguments are treated in the debate is discussed in chapter 7, which deals with rights, particularly the right of expression and the limitations to such a right.)

The Advantages of Democratic Educational Theory

One of the arguments for democratic educational theory is recognition of the weaknesses in nondemocratic education. Democratic education needs to be considered because both conservative and humanist theories have failed dismally.

Some reasons why conservatives fail follow:

1. They are unwilling to allow for true debate on critical issues, including important knowledge.
2. They assert an independent ground for resolution of differences (God, tradition, science, or some other established authority) that many students do not find credible.
3. By their closed mindedness they refuse to recognize changed conditions.
4. They are unable to specify particular problems that schools should help students address.

In fact, conservatives prominently position themselves as opponents of problem solving education. Conservatives are not opposed to indoctrination. To the contrary they like indoctrination. They simply want to do the indoctrinating.

> Education is largely a matter of indoctrination any way you look at it, and . . . there is no reason to presume unintelligence or shallowness in an "indoctrinator." Socrates was neither unintelligent nor shallow, nor, for that matter, was Adam Smith or Lenin. But they did not approach a classroom as a vast hippodrome, where all ideas "start even in the race," where the teacher must interfere with none, because the right idea will automatically come romping home ahead of others. Their method lay rather in exposing the latent disabilities in all but the winning contestant. "The Socratic manner," Max Beerbohm reminded us, "is not a game at which two people can play." (Buckley, 1968, pp. 82-83)

In the last decade, conservatives elevated the troubles of schools into a worldwide political issue. Presidents and prime ministers, having failed to solve any other important problem are promoting themselves as saviors of the schools. What they are selling is snake oil. A decade of highly publicized "reforms" have only made schools worse. The reforms failed because they went in a direction opposite from what was needed. An already rigid and authoritarian system was made more authoritarian and rigid under the guise of liberal (thin democracy) reforms.

A powerful argument against conservative education is its authoritarianism. It makes little sense to claim to prepare students for democratic citizenship while denying them any opportunity to practice democracy.

Failure, and logical inconsistency, are less powerful criticisms of authoritarian education than is student resistance to it. At an earlier time, it might have been possible to coerce students to education, although this was always marginally successful and only worked for a small proportion of students. Authoritarianism is no longer possible. Authoritarianism not only drives students from school, but in that process undermines the credibility of the authority and this contributes significantly to high incidence of drug use, high rates of teenage pregnancy and sexually transmitted diseases, violence, hours wasted transfixed before the television, and the development of a culture that not only does not connect with schools but is actively antagonistic to it (Knight, 1997; Willis, 1990). The resistance to education is not only a problem for education, it is a greater problem for society. Students who resist education are not prepared to solve the problems they will necessarily face and they also resist accepting any responsibility for those problems.

> Many politicians of our time are in the habit of laying it down as a self-evident proposition, that no people ought to be free till they are fit to use their freedom. The maxim is worthy of the fool in the old story, who resolved not to go into the water till he had learnt to swim. If men are to wait for liberty till they become wise and good in slavery, they may indeed wait forever. (Macaulay, 1924, p. 35)

Liberal approaches to education as reflected in individually centered humanism (existentialism) also fail to prepare students for emerging societal and personal problems, although the reason for failure is just the opposite to the problems posed by authoritarian education. Child-centered education fails because it does not generate strong or appropriate adult leadership. Such education is not resisted by students, but the education they receive does not provide then with the knowledge necessary to adequately confront either personal or social challenges. Because "liberal" teachers do not attempt to persuade, there is no more acceptance of responsibility for societal problems in students subjected to that kind of teaching than there is in students who have been exposed to an authoritarian education. The disinterest in politics is if anything more encouraged in liberal classrooms than in conservative classrooms. Furthermore, liberal education provides no moral position to guide students in drug use, sexual relationships, violence, and so on Although the goal of liberal education is personal development, there is little evidence to show that the permissiveness of a child-centered education has led to a more healthy development (e.g., the ability to resist substance abuse or to establish mutual respect in interpersonal relationships). The argument that Counts made against progressivism more than half a century ago applies to current student-centered education. In fact, a child-centered approach is even more inadequate now in providing necessary skills and knowledge to meet the challenges of the 21st century than it was when it failed to meet the much less difficult challenges of the 20th century.

Postmodernism as an Inadequate Response to Educational Challenge. Postmodernist critiques can be seen as a response to the static and exaggerated features of existing education. As such, postmodernism could be seen as our ally in treating existing education. However, considering postmodernist thought as our ally would be not be fair to postmodernists nor to us.

The theory that undergirds democratic education makes logical sense. It is consistent with future expectations. Students do not resist it and from it they develop the knowledge to solve complex problems. A major responsibility of tomorrow's education will be to "reconnect or even restructure the future with the past" and thereby help young people create the future. For students to reach mutually accepted social as well as personal goals, learning-rich environments must be created and students must be organized to interact in nonauthoritarian patterns with educators, peers, and various community leaders who serve as resource persons, and with other learning resources inside and outside the school . Such an education will require new and fundamentally different alliances at both institutional and personal levels and new kinds of noncoercive learning contracts between the learner and authoritative, as distinct from authoritarian, leadership in social institutions (Dalin & Rust, 1996). Once it is recognized that current conservative and liberal approaches to education do not work, and as a result youth problems grow and societal problems remain unsolved, democratic education, at least in theory, deserves careful consideration.

PRIVATIZATION

Although presented as the epitome of democracy, privatization is an inadequate presentation of democratic education or general theory, and fails to meet democratic requirements. Our version of democratic education is broad and comprehensive. As such, it varies significantly from the more limited management theory that has dominated most public school discourse and informs the free market approach to education. Broad comprehensive theory brings both specificity and wholeness to the classroom. A general theory connects every facet of educational practice. Management theories are limited to the management side of education and are silent on curriculum, "discipline," cognitive development, and so on.

The collapse of the Soviet Union and its satellites gave great impetus to privatization. The market was elevated into the grand theory status applicable to everything. It has become in many minds synonymous with democracy. Thus, it came to be that the Soviet collapse has been accompanied by privatization moves throughout a world that advertises itself as democratic. Privatization has resulted in wholesale selling off of public enterprises, and withdrawal of resources from long-established government activities, the boundaries between public and private have been deliberately obliterated. Government has been presented and to a large extent has been perceived as antithetical to freedom and thus by implication to democracy (Soros, 1997). The deconstruction of government has been incorporated into postmodern rhetoric and posturing. Thus, privatization is presented as a desirable alternative to public monopolized education.

Chubb and Moe (1990) are among the most acclaimed proponents of privatization. They couch their arguments in attributes normally associated with democracy—choice, empowerment, equality, and so on—and enumerate the benefits that will accrue to both the individual and society once the state-school monopoly has been broken with the subsidization of private schools. Privatization is presented as protection against the "excesses of democracy," in which "democratic" control is a game of "winners" and "losers" with "winners" having their way with the "losers" and the "losers" having to pay for it. Even so skimpy an allusion reveals great differences in Chubb and Moe's understanding of democracy and in ours. In fact, Chubb and Moe's democracy and our notion of democracy have virtually nothing in common. When Chubb and Moe indict "democratic" state schools, they more than strongly suggest that a significant shift away from winners and losers will occur when the state monopoly is broken. Winning and losing applies to any system with more appetites than there are means to satisfy them. Some aspects of winning and losing are defensible; others are impossible to eliminate. Winning and losing in education is extraordinarily complex and deserves a much more thorough discussion than Chubb and Moe are either willing or able to give to it. This book in its entirety is about winning and losing and bringing attention to ways reward systems can be reconstructed and thereby the definitions of winning and losing changed. This book is also about fairness in ways people are declared to be winners and losers.

Ball (1994) provided a crisp and clear summary for privatization's case against the public school "monopoly": Funding support (taxation) is not linked to client satisfaction; the absence of profit undermines motivation resulting in "conservative, self-serving, minimalist and survivalist strategies," and, mission is

distorted and more interest is directed to teacher working conditions than to student learning. Privatization is presented as the
logical alternative to Ball's summary because: private school pro-
prietors have strong incentives to please the client; resources will
be diverted to schools that are responsive to client concerns and
away from those that are not; and natural selection will occur, the
nonresponsive school will either improve or go out of business.

We do not attempt here to weigh the relative merits of a
proposed free market approach and state schools as currently
constituted. Our interest is in educational reform and the organization of schools that has the greatest potential of generating both
a citizen and a society that can solve its problems. Thus, we give
short shrift to most of the current debate on privatization.

Privatization as Efficiency. Depending on definition, it is
entirely possible that private schools will be more efficient than
any configuration of public schools. Mussolini made the trains run
on time, a powerful argument for fascist efficiency, an awful
argument for justifiable society. Efficiency is an elusive concept.
It is meaningless unless attached to clearly articulated and powerfully defended goals. It makes no sense to determine whether
private schools or public schools can more efficiently do what
should not be done at all. It is in the elevation of efficiency as a
standard that the inadequacy of privatization as a general theory is
revealed. It is silent where it should be eloquent. Given private
sector propensity for advertising, patrons of private schools
might be attracted to something very different from what has been
offered and confused enough to not recognize the difference. It is
not at all clear that by any definition private schools will be more
efficient than public schools (Ball, 1994; Gewirtz et al., 1995).

Choice. Choice is an important characteristic of democracy. In democracies, citizens exercise choice. The primal unreflec-
tive popular support for the vague concept of democracy that most
people support reduces to the "perceived" availability of choices.
Choice in democracy is broad and interconnected. In democracies
that are more illusion than real, citizens are led to believe that
they choose their leaders, places, and types of residence, modes of
transportation, access to public facilities, what they watch on
television, and a wide range of goods and services. In weak democracies, citizens can choose religion and sexual preference (perhaps?). Whether citizens can choose to have abortions in a
democracy has not been settled. There are other problematic areas

as well. But if it could be established that privatization improved the ranges of choice over what is (or could be) available in state schools it would be making a strong case for its democratic qualities. Our general theory calls for markedly increasing choice in public schools. What that means and how it can be accomplished comes later.

Choice in privatized education is an illusion. When compared with state schools, the privatized experiments provide even fewer choices. Former U.S. President George Bush used his office as "bully pulpit" to whip up support for privatized choice in education. All he wanted, he said, was for every poor child to have the same choice in schooling that his parents made available to him. The savage cruelty of that remark and the unrealizable expectations it encouraged cannot be overstated. The elite private schools he attended—Phillips Academy in Andover, Massachusetts, and Yale University, where he majored in economics, was captain of the baseball team, and graduated with Phi Beta Kappa honors in 1948—are schools with existing long waiting lists and therefore could not accept voucher students even if they were so inclined. But they are not so inclined. What gives the schools that George Bush went to their exalted reputations is their exclusiveness. They are elite because they choose the students they want and drastically limit admissions to just those students. Students are not given the opportunity to choose them. If such schools were made available to everyone they almost assuredly would be similar to the public school they have worked so hard not to be. That George Bush was disingenuous in his desire to open Phillips to everyone is not our major unhappiness with his statement. The elite private school is private enterprise by invitation only. These schools are not established to give competitive advantage to their students. The students who attend these schools are loaded with advantages years before they get there. These schools are places where a certain tradition is inculcated and sustained. A style of leadership is ingrained. Whether these schools better prepare students for democratic citizenship, the skills and knowledge to solve the important problems of a society is discussed later. For the moment, it is only important to realize they have nothing to do with choice.

No one would take seriously the idea that Phillips and Yale or Melbourne Grammar and Melbourne University or Eton and Oxford University will become egalitarian. A few untraditional students, a very, very, few untraditional students, may be allowed to enter, but that would be for show and far too few to make significant changes in those schools' customs and culture. The recruiting of a few people from lower classes to elite institutions does not mean that the insights gained will be used to help the communities, the neighborhoods, the "cultures" from which these students came. To the contrary, these recruits will be asked to serve the class to which they are being drawn and will have great difficulty sustaining contact with a home base. Some argue that draining poor communities of this potential leadership makes community efforts at self-help that much more difficult.

The power of the argument for choice through privatization is at the next rung down, in the school with a strong academic traditions, powerful instruction, high standards—the schools for members only. These could be the more real alternative to the state school. Many such schools exist in the United States, England, and Australia, some religious some secular. But these schools are not unique to the private sector. Such schools not only currently exist as state schools, they thrive. There are public schools, like the well-reputed private counterparts, that pride themselves on their selectivity. A Boston Latin, a Bronx School of Science, a Lowell High School in San Francisco, a Melbourne High School, are state schools that maintain exceedingly high standards, rich traditions and well-regarded teachers. Remarkably, the state-run elite school is able to maintain all of its wonderful attributes while encumbered by bureaucracy and intransigent teacher unions (two targets of privatization proponents). And even more remarkably, they operate at a fraction of the cost of the comparable private institution. At this level, public enterprise is far more efficient, if efficiency is measured as output by unit cost, than is private enterprise. The high-standard state school is far from democratic, but then no one has seriously argued that it was intended to be. In both the high-standard public and private school instances, choice is limited. The highly selective elite state school, nonetheless, is more elastic and more accessible than the comparable private school. Both of these schools serve the identical purpose. Both exist to provide the highly restricted number of specialized professionals and highly skilled technicians the society needs. Both provide a competitive advantage to students. Thus, such schools are not likely to grow in number or size. From a broad-based social policy perspective, it makes little sense to generate more highly educated professionals, and so on, than a society can absorb (some insist we have already gone too far). At the level of upwardly mobile individuals, increasing the number of such schools, public or private, adulterates and dilutes the advantage. Add to all of this, high-status schools take time to develop and they are expensive. Thus, privatized choice as a measure to improve the quality of education cannot be defended either by logic or evidence.

The argument in favor of privatized choice becomes a cruel joke when its allusions and illusions are directed to accessing super elite private schools (or some mythical newly created equivalents). It loses its allure when stood in comparison to existing high-status state schools. Privatization is unmitigated savagery when projected as a lifeline to students buried in urban ghettos and similar concentrations of poverty. Nothing could be more cruel or dishonest than to hold up privatization as hope for students stuck in the misery that slum schools have been allowed to become. It is this targeted population that will receive the "benefits" when Californians vote on a revised Voucher Initiative in 1998. The needs of these students are real, the response is pure hypocrisy. It is impossible to defend any existing education inflicted on poor children anywhere in the world. The "great equalizer" common school has become a transparent hoax (Kozol, 1991). Sapped of resources, surrounded by squalor and crime, and guided by theory riddled with class- and race-biased deficit theses that establish limits on what children can learn, the urban school is an unmitigated disaster. Given the severity of the situation, privatization could, at superficial glance, be seen as a fresh approach, a new start, an extrication from hopelessness. But not so. None of the real problems of urban education are addressed by privatization. There is no plan to infuse the ghetto or the slum with resources, or to improve the quality of instruction, or to guide it with general theory that rigorously meets a criteria of equal encouragement. To the contrary, what is proposed is less of the same. Privatization will limit choice because an already underresourced state system will lose funding. Privatization will encourage fly-by-night operations—"Kentucky Fried" schools and "Safeway " merchandising (Kenway, 1995). If held to arbitrary standards, the rate of failure of private schools will be very high, forcing continual relocation of students. About half of all private ventures fail within 2 years, so why would there be reason to believe the situation would be different for private schools? If an effort is made to keep private schools economically alive by eliminating regulations and standards, the abuse of students will be enormous. What assuredly will happen is that a few inner-city private schools serving a handful of students will produce spectacular results that in all likelihood will be transient.

These will be celebrated in the media. When we began to write this chapter we surmised that many voucher schools would be inadequate and would fail midstream. Before we had completed our writing our hunches were substantiated. The following story reveals how insubstantial privatization is. The story we cite is from schools in Milwaukee, hailed by Chubb and Moe (1990) as the vanguard of the voucher movement.

Milwaukee Voucher Schools Close

Two Milwaukee voucher schools have unexpectedly closed and two more are struggling to survive, leaving hundreds of children stranded at mid-year. The closings have fueled public concern over the voucher schools' lack of accountability, and voucher supporters are increasingly split over how much to allow state regulation of the private schools.

Critics of the voucher program have long argued that lack of accountability is a significant problem. Many voucher schools, however, have resisted regulatory oversight. The problem exploded in January when two voucher schools closed amid charges of financial irregularity and possible criminal activity.

Exito Education Center closed at the end of January and its director faces criminal charges of issuing $47,000 in worthless checks. The school reportedly received an overpayment of about $90,000 from the state for students that were not enrolled at the school. Exito had reported in September that 174 voucher students and 90 non-voucher students were attending the school. An audit in January found that the school had 124 voucher students and no non-voucher students. By the time the school closed, it had only 61 voucher students. (By state law, only 65% of the students at the private schools may receive vouchers.)

Milwaukee Preparatory School closed in February, likewise plagued by questions about its enrollment and finances. An audit could not be completed, however, because of missing financial records. The school had received $315,362 from the state in payments for voucher students allegedly attending the school, but may be obligated to return up to $300,000 due to exaggerated enrollments, according to the state Department of Public Instruction. In September, the school said it had 175 voucher students out of a total of 200 students. By the time it closed in February, there were about 80 students at the school and 9 of the 12 teachers had left because they had not been paid. The founder, meanwhile, abruptly left town in December.

Two other voucher schools are facing possible closure due to financial difficulties. Administrators at Medgar Evers Academy said the school's staff had not been paid regularly, while at Woodson Academy, the school' s teachers have been forced to take pay cuts. (Miner, 1996, p. 19)

If nothing new is done, public schools will continue to limp along serving the vast majority of impoverished students, and continued failure with these students will be the subject of periodic sensationalist media exposés. The successful inner-city private schools will be highly selective, not necessarily in admissions, but with those students allowed to remain in the school. Because the number of openings in the successful private schools will be pathetically few, parents desperately trying to liberate their children from intolerable conditions will be literally climbing over the bodies of neighbors and friends to gain admittance, thus contributing to the destruction of what little is left of community. Privatization in the ghetto is one lifeboat for a sinking Titanic. Choice, in that situation, is selecting who to save. Privatization is an expensive, brutal, divisive, and unnecessary means to "save" a handful of students. Privatization is unnecessary because successful state school alternatives exist in ghettos and slums, as Deborah Meier (director of Central Park East in New York City from 1974 to 1994) among others has demonstrated (Meier, 1995). These public alternatives serve more students, are more readily accessible, and are positioned to exert more influence on theory, policy, and classroom practice than private schools have ever been able to do. Because the move to privatization has been silent on theory, or more accurately presents privatization as the grand narrative, the treatment of students in ghetto private alternatives will be informed, as the most celebrated private alternatives have been informed, by the most retrograde approaches to theory, witness Marva Collins[1] and her classics emphasis in her Chicago private

---

[1] Few have gotten as much publicity and done more for the privatization cause than African American Marva Collins and her Westside preparatory School. Born into a wealthy family in Monroeville, Alabama, Collins came with her mother to Chicago after her parents were divorced. She attributed to her father her respect for self-pride, nonconformity, strong values, uncompromising beliefs and strength. She graduated from Clark College Atlanta, in a secretarial course. Unable to get a job as a secretary she turned to teaching. Back in Chicago she married Clarence Collins, a draftsman, and mothered Eric, Patrick, and Cynthia. She secured a teaching position without completing any methodology courses. This lack of "preparation" did not hamper her

school that, although highly acclaimed, has never been adequately evaluated, especially on admission criteria, retention of students, and post-schooling careers.

Privatization not only offers little in the way of real choice, in many ways it threatens existing choices in state schools. Every penny that the state will provide to a private school comes from the state school budget, which means that as private schools proliferate, public school budgets are reduced accordingly. Public schools, even the most underfunded, offer ranges of programs from the traditional academic to vocational tracks (as corrupted as these choices are by emphasis on social reproduction). Students in those schools are introduced to music, theater, dance, chorus, specialized science, design, sport, and so on. With each reduction, generalized school offerings are negatively affected and choices are eliminated. The choices lost will not be reclaimed by private alternatives available to only a tiny minority of students and even these students will find their choices often transitory.

---

advancement as a teacher. Her "innovative" methods, however, got her into trouble with the "system." She was not popular with her colleagues. In 1957, with help from neighbors and advice from the Alternative Schools Network, she opened her own school in the basement of Daniel Hale Williams University, a Chicago community college. Her approach strongly emphasized phonics and the classics (which was hardly innovative). With increased enrollment, the school moved to the top floor of her home. Her teaching method emphasized the instillation of confidence, pride, and self-esteem. She tells her students she loves them, sets for them high standards, demanding that they meet them. She teaches self-respect, self reliance, and moral character. Two years after opening her school, the media found her—the centerpiece being the CBS TV special The Marva Collins Story. With a $50,000 grant from the W. Clement Stone Foundation, Collins moved to a new facility and a spot on a 1979 60 Minutes with Morley Safer. She soon had 200 students and 15 teachers. With fame came job offers—positions as Secretary of Education for the Reagan administration, and Los Angeles County Superintendent. Saying she wished to remain with "her children" she declined. Some detractors accused her of accepting federal money (which she claimed she would never do), and inflating test scores. Detractors have not hampered her growth. She extended her influence with a branch school in Cincinnati with sponsorship from the rock star formerly known as Prince. The connection to the rock star is interesting because the performer's mother was one of the paraprofessionals brought into one of the model democratic programs featured in this book, New Careers. From her beginning involvement in the Minneapolis program, she was able to establish herself as an influential educator and earn two master's degrees.

Privatization, evaluated on its own terms, is no panacea and may even be worse than the inadequate system it is trying to replace. It most certainly will not lead to more equity or a "more perfect union." We agree with Ball's (1994) conclusion that "the market works as a class strategy by creating a mechanism which can be exploited by the middle classes as a strategy of reproduction in their search for relative advantage, social advancement and mobility" (p. 126). We go further; privatization also helps the dominant classes by effectively dividing the dominated and under-mines attempts at resurrection of community. This brings us to an analysis of privatization in the context of our general theory.

Choice in school only fits within a general theory of educa-tion when the choices made in school enhance life choices. It is only when a school choice translates into real power that choice is significant. When school choices lead to significant choice and thus power in the political arena, to wide ranges of choice in employ-ment, to choices in community and cultural life, and to choices in meeting interpersonal challenges can it be said that value is attached to choice in schooling. A general theory consistent with democracy would direct students to increased life chances in the community. A general theory of education organizes students to create plus sum games where there are more winners than losers. Such a general theory raises to consciousness community devel-opment, ways to increase employment opportunities, ways to appraise governmental priorities, the development of communi-ty-based culture, and the organization by the community of appropriate services (which would include education). In that light, privatization should be described as an antichoice alterna-tive to government-funded schools, already hobbled with too few activities designed to enhance life choices.

When we examine privatization in the light of our four requirements of a democratic education—important knowledge, participation, rights, and equal encouragement—what seems weak and inadequate becomes totally unacceptable.

Privatization and Important Knowledge. Advocates of pri-vatization have been rather silent or very conservative when addressing curriculum. Silence about curriculum is not the major problem with privatization. The major problem is the fractional-ization it promotes under the guise of choice. The splintering into enclaves will prohibit the broad exchange necessary for reaching some generally understood conception of important knowledge. Such centrifugalization makes possible the creation of a few "democratic" private schools. In these schools, students would apply themselves to the solution of critical problems. At times, this proposition seems so attractive that we consider establishing such a school. We would have little trouble attracting 50 to 100 students disaffected with the schooling they receive. We could certainly lure a few of our former students to help us teach. We could locate a site and we would be in business. And if the past is any predictor of the future, we would be very successful, maybe so successful that television movies would again be made of our efforts. And we would have replicated Dewey's mistake, a laboratory school with no prospect of generalization. We would have constructed "a circle of truth" (a term attributed to Freire). Our students could speak only to each other. Meanwhile, there would be schools of every possible ideological description, each generating its own circle of truth. It is not that each school would not have a solution to the race problem, the economy, the environment, gender relationships, the role of government, a guiding system of values. Each likely would. What would be missing is what is missing today—debate. A general theory reintroduces *debate.* That debate is meaningful only with diversity. State schools have and will continue to have far more diversity than private schools, particularly if diversity is understood to include differences in worldviews. Diversity is the greatest asset the state school has. Because the school operates with an inadequate general theory, its greatest asset has become its greatest liability.

Complicating the problem is the generally held view that students are consumers of education. From a democratic education perspective, students and parents cannot be reduced to educational consumers. They must be producers of knowledge. If the student (and/or parent) as consumer is rejected, the argument for a market approach to education disintegrates.

Privatization and Participation. If it was possible to restore a managed democracy and if meritocracy was all that Bell (1973) said it was, then the impact that privatization would have on informed participation would be unimportant. If a managed democracy headed by elites in a hierarchical system could be made to work, then privatization of education could make a good deal of sense. It must be understood that a managed democracy would be cruel and unjust. Little attention would be given to reducing poverty. It would be a society with an ever-widening gap between the rich and the poor. Prisons would overcrowd as soon as they were built and building prisons would become a major growth industry. It would be a society of drugs and violence. But it would exist. Events over the past two decades conclusively demonstrate the impossibility of a managed democracy. What has emerged is a society where the uninformed vote their biases and paralyze society. Governance functions at two levels that are almost disconnected from each other. Elites control the macroeconomy with policies that concentrate wealth in ever fewer hands. At the level of interpersonal interaction, elites no longer rule; in fact, they never have been less powerful. They maintain the illusion of power by recreating themselves into whatever an uninformed populace wants at the moment. Privatization of schools cannot remedy that situation at either level. It can only make matters worse. Schools will largely be organized around biases. Participation and leadership in such situations will not only be situation-specific, but extremely limited in scope.

Rights and Privatization. By opting for the limited right of privatized choice, students in effect surrender all other rights. Each school is free to define rights in its own way. There may be some formal and ritualistic allegiance to the principle of rights but only with a general theory that privatization by definition militates against can there be the kind of instruction and curriculum that would lead to a full understanding and appreciation of rights. Private schools, by definition, are distinguished by their individuality. Each is distinctive by what it does and who it admits. Some private schools will be adamant in their opposition to the notion of rights. Others will restrict the number of rights and limit them to only the most "responsible" (e.g., docile). Others will emphasize rights. It is exactly that kind of confusion that a general theory attempts to eliminate, not by imposing a rights dictum, but by inviting into a discussion everyone whose goal is the realization of a common understanding of rights.

Equal Encouragement and Privatization. Equal encouragement is an impossibility in any privatized scheme, no matter how it is conceived or constituted. Equality under any market-defined education is defined as equality for *consumers.* Even that limited definition cannot be met under existing notions of private enterprise. Privatization strives to provide competitive advantage not equalized opportunity. That is why parents choose to put their children in them. The rub is that equal encouragement is also exceedingly difficult in state schools. Pressures toward hierarchy not only run deep but are constantly recurring. When we strive to identify entrenched opposition to our general theory, we can expect teachers and administrators to be most adamant in opposition to student rights; parents, particularly upwardly mobile parents, to equal encouragement. How such opposition is met is discussed in considerable depth later in the book.

Educational Theory Needs to be Developed and Tested From the Ground Up

Grand narratives have not plagued education; top-down-initiated moves to reform education has. First, the experts who designed them were conceptually confused. Education to them is a jumble of concepts. And this is as much true for the liberal or radical proposed reforms as it is for the more recent conservative ones. Second, the top-down initiatives will be necessarily resisted and sabotaged (not always consciously) by those who work in the classroom.

No better example of the meaninglessness of a theory-less top-down-exalted exercise can be found than that provided by the Carnegie Foundation for the Advancement of Teaching (1995) report of U.S. elementary schools. This report, one of the largest studies ever undertaken and 3 years in the making, concluded that too many elementary schools use class time poorly, are isolated from their communities, and do not adequately teach language skills or promote civic virtues. To bring schools back on track, a simple alternative to the "reform(s)-of-the-month" that have "created a lot of confusion"—the basic school—is recommended. A basic school creates strong ties to parents and neighborhood leaders; enlarges the responsibility of teachers; emphasizes reading and language skills; brings more flexibility to the class to promote creative learning; integrates subjects; and promotes honesty, compassion, and respect for others. To make sure that this new educational smorgasbord is complete, it rounds up the usual group of palliatives: schools (no more than 500 students per elementary school); reduced class sizes (no more than 20 students per class); bilingualism (more stress on Spanish); technological upscaling (one computer per five students and a television and videotape player in every classroom).

The salient submerged message in the report is that because we have no idea where you are going, it is best to slow down. That would make a modicum of sense, if the world was willing to do the same. Not recognized by the authors of this report or by Ernest Boyer, the former commissioner of education and then president of the Carnegie Foundation, was the futility of trying to reform education without a guiding theory. The problem with elementary schools was not that they were trying to move too fast with a "reform-of-the-month." The problem was rudderlessness. As Boyer allowed and we agree, lack of direction causes less "perceptible" harm in elementary schools than it does in middle schools and high school. Insufficiently recognized is that the lack of comprehensive and coherent theory in elementary school paves the way for the calamitous events noted in later grades.

None of the Carnegie recommendations are wrong, or harmful. Parental and neighborhood involvement; greater opportunity for teachers to exercise leadership; sustained student investment in reading and other uses of language; more classroom flexibility and the promotion of creative learning; integrating subjects; and developing a shared values system that includes honesty, compassion, and respect for others will be found in a democratic classroom, as will increased use of technology and smaller classroom sizes. But not as unconnected bits and pieces, nor as mantras or slogans. Each element of the democratic classroom derives logically from a theory of education that has clear purposes and principles and is an analyzed response to the problems that have been encountered in the classroom. It makes no sense to intensify reading instruction in the elementary school without attending to the resistance encountered to reading in high school. Developing a shared values system that includes honesty, compassion, and respect for others cannot happen by fiat, nor will such values materialize as a result of exhortation. Those values develop as part of a general theory dedicated to resurrection of a particular type of community.

It is sad that Carnegie pays no attention to Carnegie. In 1990, the same foundation issued a report on higher education campus life in the United States and Boyer provided the preface for that report (Carnegie Foundation, 1990). In 1990, Carnegie found increased tension on university campuses generated by deeply rooted prejudices (these tensions have increased markedly since then). Moreover, the report noted "the breakdown of civility on campus" (p. 2). The proposal for redress was the creation of an open, just, and fair, disciplined, caring, and celebrative community. Celebrative meant rituals "affirming both tradition and change (that are) are widely shared" (p. 55). The earlier Carnegie report addresses reality to a far greater extent than does the later. It brings to surface what should be generalized recognized problems, although in both reports, solutions are weak and platitudinous. The diagnosis of a university in the first report is equally applicable to the secondary school. In both, the notion of community may be vitiated when "fragmentation of knowledge, narrow departmentalism, and an intense vocationalism . . . are the strongest characteristics of (the) education" (p. 63). A problem for all levels of education is the loss a sense of community when people are increasingly imprisoned in a private realm. None of this negates the necessity of a common infrastructure. A balance can be struck between individual interests and communal concerns. But that balance can only occur when there is movement in such a direction and when that movement is informed by a coherent theory. An open, just and fair, caring, and celebrative community cannot be created in the absence of a conscious effort to make that an educational goal. And that goal cannot be attained unless it is reflected in the curriculum, the decision-making process, the security to participate that can only be provided by specified guaranteed rights and when the community is organized to provide equal encouragement to all its residents. In other words, for there to be a common infrastructure there must be a theory that is consistent with such a goal.

Ball (1993) dissected the destruction to education by right-wing top-down edicts that have dictated education reform in Great Britain to an extent beyond anything attempted in this century. He described the effect on three curricular areas: music, geography, and history. In each, "cultural restorationists—the hard-line old humanists of the New Right"—have exerted exceedingly powerful influence, although the takeover has not been smooth or necessarily decisive. We share with Ball his indictment of a music curriculum that has no place for performance and limits instruction to the appreciation of classics in which Duke Ellington is somehow included; a backward turn to simplified and fragmented geography; and a history that glorifies British accomplishments. What Ball also needed to consider is why these efforts are doomed to fail. They will be overcome by student resistance. The classics can be force-fed to students but that does not mean they will be digested. Simplified geography will not be learned. A glorified British history can have transient success and help make a Falklands campaign popular enough to elect conservative politicians. But such education will not sustain popular following in something prolonged and indecisive as the Vietnam War. Nor will it develop the characteristics needed to be informed citizens. Where Ball became unpersuasive was when the only alternatives to the hardline right-wing takeover he could find were top-down

liberal alternatives: music that includes an emphasis on performance, an integrative geography, and a history that reveals the
oppressiveness of British empire at least to the extent it is glorified. Students will resist the well-rounded academic's effort to
create curriculum with same ferocity they resist the hardliners.
Ball's more desirable alternatives are just as inadequate as that
which he rightfully condemns. And that is as much true for the
"reform" efforts made by the Labor Party in Victoria, Australia
and all of the foundation inspired initiates in the United States
among which Carnegie has been in the forefront

The state of California has issued a series of guidelines
called, *It's Elementary* (California Department of Education,
1992), *Caught in the Middle* (California Department of Education,
1987), and *Second to None* (California Department of Education,
1992). Each were products of task forces consisting of state
bureaucrats, school administrators, teachers, academics, and
business leaders. The guidelines are a synthesis of what is
believed to be desirable practice. The curriculum and the organization draws on research findings and everything in it seems to
make marvelous sense: active rather than passive learning, integrative and thematic curriculum, celebration of diversity,
authentic assessment, utilization of "brain" research findings; a
remarkable grabbag of seemingly worthwhile ideas uninformed by
anything resembling a theory. Although gussied up, it was still the
old world. The curriculum, although struggling for interdisciplinary connections, was nonetheless stuck in subjects. Problems
were recognized but there was no commitment to involve students
in a search for solutions.

In the four areas we singled out as critical for a democratic education that is held together by a general theory (knowledge
organized for problem solving, participation in decision making,
rights, and equal encouragement), the guidelines are largely
silent. What needs to be understood is that all of these efforts we
discussed have been top-down and the reason the California guidelines were warmly embraced for a short while was due to a fairly
close correspondence to ongoing consensus of "best" practice.
That these same guidelines were largely repudiated when a conservative government took power was not surprising because student performance had not changed significantly and little effort
had been made to win a constituency for these overblown reforms.

The Classroom, Not Remote Governmental Centers or Research Institutes is Where Important Educational Change Occurs

It is important that very specific examples of theoretically driven education be cited to empower the drive for educational change. One of the problems of a top-down approach to education is that its effects can only be presented in exceedingly abstract and general terms.

Education has meaning when it addresses significant events in identified real individual lives located in real communities confronting real problems and when real positive change in life circumstances can be clearly attributed to education. And only when those changes can be fitted into a general theory is it possible to generalize accomplishments.

At an earlier time, before massive funding and computerization, it was commonly understood that theory in the social sciences was developed by working close to the roots. Brunswik (1956) introduced the concept of *ecological validity* to psychology and Barker (1964) attempted to implement it. Independently of the movement in psychology, universities developed laboratory schools to simulate the real school life. However, the "lab" school did not attract a representative sample of students and teachers worked in nonrepresentative situations. Universities abandoned laboratory schools and ecological validity is no longer a priority concern of social scientists. Rather than moving closer to the subject being studied, academics increased the distance between themselves and what they research. The change is a logical consequence of changes in technology, structure, and means by which status and security are attained in the academy. In recent years, huge research institutions replaced the solitary worker or small team approach and the relevance of the research suffered accordingly. Computers transformed research. When it became possible to assimilate, store, manipulate, and deliver vast amounts of data, researchers tended to be measured by the size of the project and the ability to bewilder an audience with massive statistical findings on a large number of subjects. All of this has not advanced theory, it has camouflaged the dearth of theory and the emptiness of the social sciences.

An education organized by a general theory cannot be developed from a distance. It cannot be developed from statistics obtained on a small number of attributes that are connected by a statistical process and where small differences can be hailed as significant. The place to develop and test a general encompassing theory is in a single classroom. Such a test exposed nonsense masquerading as theory and builds the understanding necessary to overcome resistance and sabotage to a developing theory. The theory gains power and credibility when tests are replicated in more and more classrooms. Each test provides opportunity for refinement. The beginning must be small and growth depends on its ability to adequately explain the totality of education. This is very different from the widesweeping short-lived fads that have characterized education this past half century.

Using School-Based Initiatives

The individual school site is the place to initiate school reform, not to meet some anarchistic decentering value. Nor is it an illusion that disguises and facilitates authoritarian centralized control, but is an opportunity to initiate a process that can lead to democratic recentering. Reform has to begin somewhere. The schools we now have cannot in some wholesale manner be magically and instantly transformed into something fundamentally different. There has to be a strategy for change that requires the establishing and nurturing of beachheads.

Where does one start a democratic classroom? Wherever there is interest in one. That is why current talk of decentralization and site-based planning has potential for democratic reform. We are aware that much of decentralization in the United States has been little more than a mirage (Bimber, 1995).

> Decentralization, which includes innovations like site-based management and school-based decision making, is based on the assumption that reducing bureaucratic controls will prompt teachers and principals to exert greater initiative and to tailor instruction to the needs of students. It has failed, the study says, not because the premise is flawed but because the true locus of power remains where it has always been—with school boards, central office staffs, and state authorities. (Bimber, 1995, p. 1)

And although in the four high schools that Bimber studied, breakthroughs were limited and the locus of power remained where it had been, there were nonetheless considerable differences in the way these schools operated. And if he had explored more deeply, he would have found very large differences within each school. Not all teachers taught the same, the same subject was presented differently to different classes of students, not all parents were the same. It is fascinating to note how much critical theorists, poststructuralists, and the like, persevere over difference and never use existing differences to initiate educational reform. The differences within a school are as interesting as the similarities between schools, but are rarely noted in educational research. Bimber concluded that the main reason for lack of change brought on by moves toward decentralization was organizational or institutional intransigence, the control of resources continued to be a central responsibility. Having been involved with efforts to decentralize and bring more management to the site, we recognize the difficulty, but our conclusions are far different than Bimber's. Decentralization cannot produce significant changes unless the attempted changes are theory-driven, and that policy formation and implementation are owned by those communities to which change is directed. Currently they are not. Trying to relocate the locus of power is meaningless in the absence of theory. Why would anyone expect that a particular site with all the differences within it, would, when trying to make a site decision be significantly different in its collective understanding of education from those who make decisions at some central location. Minority voices get drowned wherever they are voiced, particularly when the lack of serious thinking about education is ubiquitous. Furthermore, the variables that have been used to critique decentralization may be the least important. It is incontestable that budget allocations and assessment tends to be centralized, however, the critical activities of schooling—the nature of relationships between teachers and students—have always been decentralized. No central mandate can determine how teachers relate to students nor can central authority dictate how ideas will be communicated. The nature of relationship in a classroom constitutes the heart of education and that is where reform can and should begin.

In Great Britain, Ball (1994), reflecting on the move there for decentralization concluded that "the autonomy of schools is more apparent than real." He maintained that "the state" is able to "retain considerable 'steerage' of the goals and processes of the education system (while appearing not to do so)" (p. 10). This variation on the mirage argument again reflects lack of leadership and vision at the school site. Ball did allow in the complicated nexus of policy and practice that "policies are incomplete" (p. 11). Expressing himself in postmodernese, he said policy is created in the "trilectic of dominance, resistance and chaos /freedom"

(p. 11). However, he did recognize a "third space." It is in that third space that educational change can take place if informed by a coherent general theory. The third space needs more than defini- tion, it needs exploration not as problemizing, but in search for solution. In Great Britain, as in the United States and Australia, moves toward decentralization should be seen as an invitation for exciting innovation. The rhetoric of school autonomy creates spaces and provides room for debate and change. Unfortunately, too many educationalists are preoccupied with the discovering of limita- tions, flaws, and mirages.

The Preparation of a School Charter

In Victoria, Australia, decentralization requires each individual school to establish a school charter, with the following provi- sions:

> Quality self-managing schools will be characterized by: effective, leadership, effective management of staff, a sys- tematic approach to planning, effective, efficient financial and human resource management, directly responsive to program priorities and requirements, effective decision- making practices that, where appropriate, involve the whole school community, regular feedback on performance to sec- tions of the school and to individuals, active promotion of the school in the community, recognition of the principles of merit and equity, widespread opportunities for the develop- ment and leadership skills, a work environment free from sexual harassment. (DES, Victoria, Australia, 1993, p. 2)

On the face of it, these propositions are laudable, even commendable. Who could possibly oppose any of the recommenda- tions? They are in fact too marvelous for words. Australian decentralization, like decentralization in the United States and England, is a mirage, and will remain an illusion in the absence of clearly defined educational goals. It has all of the liabilities pre- viously cited. The desired student outcomes are not defined. In the absence of that definition, local management becomes an exercise in social and personal futility because the criteria against which they will be judged is centrally determined—a standardized test or some variation thereof. The school is in effect told that it can take any route it wants as long as the student ends up where central authority wants her or him to go. If the school does not want to go to the decreed station, too bad. That is where the educational train is heading. Worse, in actuality the local school is asked to prepare students for a trip, a very long and arduous one, and the destination is kept secret. And yet, for all of the obvious pitfalls, deficiencies, slippery motivations, and outright deviousness, the charter school is yet another opportunity to test theory and begin the arduous process to true school reform.

In summary, the classroom (as distinct from "all" classrooms or a large array of randomly selected subjects whose performance is measured on arbitrary and traditional criteria and is contrasted with the performance of comparable controls, is where theory is tested) is where educational reform begins. The classroom is the place to test and develop theory. A general theory requires all of the community to be part of its development, in collaboration with student, parents, and teachers, educational researchers and theoreticians could benefit from Robert Burns' Ode to a Louse' and not take umbrage at its reference.

> Oh wad some power the gifie gie us
> To see oursels as ithers see us!
> It wad frae moniea blunder free us,
> an foolish notion.

A general theory must explain the responses to educational interventions of all the students that are affected, and only in a classroom is it possible to make those observations and collect sufficient relevant data on all the students for the theory to be given an adequate test. Assessment can be demystified and purged of bias when students play an active role in helping construct assessments and help interpret meaning and that is only possible when the test is organized within a circumscribed area, like a classroom. The classroom is a logical place for the restoration of community to begin at least as a simplified model. And the classroom is the best place to evaluate frameworks and other centralized initiatives and balance that evaluation with ideas and interests of the local community. Decentralization initiatives, for all of their deficiencies, should be viewed as an opportunity for rediscovering the importance of the classroom.

The More Ordinary the Classroom and Undistinguished by Special Features, the More the Useful it Will be in Testing Theory and Initiating Widesweeping Change

The closer the beachhead is to a typical classroom the more likely it will catch hold. Too often in education, it was believed that a special place, a laboratory, had to be created for a new theory to be constructed. A laboratory reduced variables and eliminated distractions. All too often, what was eliminated was what the theory had to address. In beginning a test of a general theory, the choices may be limited, but the obligation remains to test in real-life complex situations. The theory will only have value to the extent that it applies generally. Or, it can define the conditions of its applicability. For example, if the theory is able to provide predictable results in classrooms of 20 students but not in classrooms of 30 or more, that is not an indictment of the theory, but the conditions of its use. At the present time, we can say very little about what theory works where. An adequate test of a general theory requires that it be applied across a wide spectrum of classrooms. The quicker the theory can be tested in regular, normal operating conditions, the quicker it can be determined whether it meets the requirements of a general theory.

Teachers, Parents, and Students Have Vital Roles to Play in the Development of Educational Theory

Only a few teachers have been asked to help with theory development. The few have not been representative of the profession. It is safe to say that most teachers throughout history have resisted intellectual theory. Teachers have not been interested in theory or knowledge creation, nor have they, in general, wanted to become involved with controversy. It is our contention that avoiding theory or controversy in education is no longer possible. It is the recognition of the inevitability of conflict and controversy that leads us to advocate democratic education. Democratic education does not end controversy, to the contrary, democratic education brings controversy into the center and establishes it as a central and necessary feature of the schooling process. But controversy cannot be constructive unless there is a means for resolution and that is where a general theory is crucial. The general theory not only provides ground rules for debate, it also establishes criteria to be used to resolve debate. However, there cannot be democratic education without teachers playing a leadership role in both the development of the theory and in its implementation. The exclusion of teachers from involvement with theory has had a significant downside. The relegation of teachers to technicians has caused them to become hostile to theory. ". . . educational theory and other non-classroom based explanations are excluded from discussions because teachers deem them culturally inadmissible" (Hargreaves, 1989, pp. 38-39).

Hargreaves insisted that teachers find education theory to be "culturally inadmissible." He argued that teachers reject theory in initial training and forever after (Hargreaves, 1989). What has made theory culturally admissible is the nature of the theory, the manner by which it was developed, and the language with which it has been presented. Teachers need to be drawn toward theory, not repelled by it. Teachers need to be encouraged to participate in the development, refinement, and the testing of theory, not excluded. A theory constructed by remote academics and imposed on teachers should be culturally inadmissible. In fact, Hargreaves may have it backward. Because university academics have removed themselves so far from the field of action, their analysis may be so distorted and their data so irrelevant that a coherent, adequate, comprehensible, comprehensive, and workable formal educational theory may now be culturally inadmissible to precisely those who pride themselves on their capacity to build and understand theory. The cultural inadmissibility of theory in the academy could possibly be found in Hargreaves suggestion that teachers concerned with moral development consult Kohlberg or Durkheim. We have consulted both and find both irrelevant. Durkheim, no matter how interpreted, is woefully inadequate as an informing theory for today's classrooms.[2] Kohlberg's approach to values not only lacks empirical validation but has elitist and possible sexist overtones that we find incompatible with a democratic education.

---

[2]Ohlin and Cloward (1960) tried to apply Durkheim to the treatment of juvenile delinquency in a celebrated handsomely funded demonstration, "Mobilization for Youth." It was a massive effort and although interesting in its accomplishments and important historically, Durkheim proved to be difficult to translate into modern conditions and when translated far removed from practical program initiatives. Not too much time transpired before Ohlin returned to Harvard and Coward went on to other non-Durkheimian enterprises—guaranteed annual income, welfare reform, and so on.

Theory construction, knowledge creation, and strategy of implementation go hand in hand, integrally synthesized into an ongoing dynamic process. The development of theory in which teachers have played an important role identifies teachers who are ready for theory and they, in turn are entrusted with the responsibility to reach out to more and more teachers. Ultimately, it is primarily through teachers that other necessary actors in the development of democratic educational theory are introduced to theory development. It is primarily through teachers that parents, students, and others who have been excluded from the debate and the formulation of policy can be drawn into the creation of workable educational theory. Involving teachers in the vital political process of transforming theory from an academic exercise into everyday practice demonstrates one of the requirements of a democratic education—participation in decisions that affects one's life.

Why has there been such resistance to theory? Theory is difficult. Theory requires serious debate. And perhaps, of greatest importance, the means by which people are drawn to teaching and prepared for teaching has been antithetical to theory. If teachers are to find theory culturally admissible, it is necessary that schools of education also find theory to be culturally admissible. That is not now the case.

Cultural inadmissibility is reinforced by a systematic denial of parents and students from the decision-making process. Parents and students should not be reduced to objects on which theory is to be tested. They are part of the development team. They are brought into the discussions about theory, their contributions are actively sought and taken seriously (Gill, 1975; Knight, 1995). At every stage of theory construction and in every area of implementation—curriculum, pedagogy, discipline, assessment, organization, and management—parents and teachers must be viewed as partners in the enterprise, or what passes for theory should be culturally inadmissible. Perhaps teachers, parents, and students can recognize bad theory and that is what they find culturally inadmissible.

UNIVERSITY SCHOLARS AS PARTNERS IN RESEARCH

The more university scholars work as equal status partners and collaborators with teachers, parents, and students, and the less they define themselves as outside experts the more useful they will be in helping develop and test theory. Good theory and good education practice will develop when university scholars work collaboratively in the classroom with teachers, parents, and students. That is not likely to happen quickly, nor is it desirable for all university-based educationalists to leave the hallowed halls for the hurly-burly of urban classrooms. Such a migration is not necessary (Hargreaves, 1996). For the university to play a useful role in educational theory and practice, a significant number of scholars need to situate themselves in the classroom while the others respectfully pay attention to what the field-based theoreticians and researchers are doing.

Educational Change as Exponential Function or Building a Movement for Democratic Education

Exponential function is at the heart of democratic change in any situation or in any context. Movement to more democracy in a world dominated by concentrated media beaming messages to passive populations requires the creation of means by which ordinary individuals can become a part of the idea transmission process. Without devising an effective person-to-person communication system, democracy becomes an impossible project. And democracy has been viewed as an impossible project because people refuse to consider democratic possibilities. The concept of *power* has been usurped and the usurpers have made it generally inaccessible. The Foucaults of the world have been extremely effective in articulating how power has been misused. Power in a Foucaultian analysis is remote and unaccountable. Although power is often presented as the topic of discussion, the real emphasis is on powerlessness. Current social commentators appear to be obsessed with powerlessness. Democracy is not about powerlessness, nor is it about illusory power. It is about a process of developing power and continually checking on the validity of such power.

If one was to apply a exponential function to human communication and ask a group of students, "if 10 of them were to leave this room and were able to persuade 10 others to vote 'the green party' and these 10 in the next minute would persuade 10 others, and those 10 others in the next minute, how many minutes would it take for everyone in Melbourne or Moscow or Santa Cruz to be persuaded?" This incidentally, is a math problem we use in a problem-solving eighth-grade class. The answer, of course, is less than 7 minutes. Students immediately bring to our attention the lack of realism of this exercise, which permits us to continue the discussion by pointing out that persuading everyone in Melbourne, and so on, is not a requirement in a democracy, nor are we limited to 10 minutes. What this "math" problem is designed to reveal is the potential power that each of us possesses, and how we can broaden the range of our influence if we work in collaboration with others. The example cited brings back into focus other democratic qualities previously mentioned. The effectiveness of such communication depends on inclusiveness. One cannot communicate with people with whom there is no connection. It also speaks to the importance of citizenship skills, the capacity to communicate effectively; civility, a bearing that draws people to you rather than drives them away. And perhaps, most importantly, a body of knowledge sufficiently persuasive as to influence others. Thinking of democracy as exponential function opens up many areas for discussion, some of which we return to later.

Exponential function as a calculated strategy is the process by which a democratic education is introduced into education. A good theory is tested in a single classroom, any classroom initially, and gains credibility when it is successfully replicated in more and more classrooms. Once a theory is shown to be useful it can be generalized as well as refined through a process of contagion. This can be done in various ways as we indicate in the final chapter of this book.

SUMMARY

In this chapter, although ranging across a wide range of issues, two central points were made. First, that education needs a workable general theory, and second, theory needs to be developed and tested at a local site and to be built and refined from the ground up.

Chapter 3

Meeting the Goal of Student Participation in Decisions That Affect One's Life: Developing the Skills for Responsible Political Empowerment

The only compelling justification for a *public* school is preparation for democratic citizenship. And here public schools fail miserably. In this chapter, we discuss what the school must do in the area of curriculum if the goal of universal competent citizens is to be obtained. We analyze the current situation that continues to be an only slightly updated version of reliance on courses in history and government, augmented by exceedingly limited participation in student governments. This approach, we believe, does more harm than good and much evidence supports our conclusion. We describe what schools should be doing, the particular kinds of knowledge that are needed, the use of cooperative learning, com-

munity service, and a very much expanded role for student government. With the decline of elitist-managed democracy, a society
can be no stronger than its least prepared citizen. The argument
for equal encouragement is most obvious in citizen preparation.
People will work in different stations and the importance of their
work will vary greatly, but in a democracy everyone's vote is
equal. It falls to public schools to ensure that all students are
equally prepared to use the vote wisely. However, as important as
it is, a carefully considered vote is the least of the responsibilities of a competent citizen.

If there is one universal defining characteristic of youth
in the world, it is the widespread feeling of exclusion from the
circles where important social decisions are made. Perhaps of
greater significance is the lack of knowledge about governmental
processes. The lack of knowledge coupled with growing disrespect
for political institutions, are the logical consequences of an education that not only does not prepare for democratic citizenship,
but works in ways that discourages interest in either democracy
of participation in politics.

Politics is the means by which decisions are reached under
conditions of conflict. Democratic politics and democratic education are intimately connected. In democratic education, everyone
is equally encouraged to be equally informed on the vital issues of
the day, all are equally encouraged to participate equally in the
decision making, all are guaranteed equally specifically defined
rights, and effort is made to persuade all that democratic principles are violated when decisions reached provide economic or
social advantage for some at the expense of others. A major
emphasis of democratic education is to provide all students with
citizenship skills.

Preparation for democratic citizenship is the major
defense of government-funded schooling. Only public schools have
the potential of maintaining the diversity necessary for meaningful political discussion. Only in public schools is it possible to
generate the widest range of the public debate on critical issues
and prevent the pernicious narrowing of focus and the closing of
the mind to a wide range of alternatives. Only with preparation of
competent citizens can a unifying vision be developed that is
essential for the overcoming of political paralysis. Preparation
for democratic citizenship simultaneously enables the student to
function in an existing world while participating in its change.
The goal is to prepare everyone to be active, responsible, and
informed citizens.

KNOWLEDGE IN A DEMOCRATIC CLASSROOM PREPARES ALL STUDENTS TO MAKE INDEPENDENT AND INFORMED CHOICES ON IMPORTANT SOCIAL ISSUES

Democratic education organizes curriculum so that all students are able to devise a defensible solution to a generally recognized important problem, evaluate the logic and evidence used to support different proposals for the solution of the problem, and conceptualize the political tactics and strategy that would be required for implementation of the solution.

Preparing students for citizenship responsibility has always been an explicit purpose of public education. Although the founding fathers of the United States may have had considerable reservations about the desirability and feasibility of democracy, they were of one mind that the democracy could only exist to the extent to which the population was educated for citizenship responsibility. From John Adams, an adamant opponent of democracy, through the meritocratic Thomas Jefferson, to the moderate George Washington there was an awareness that democracy required an enlightened citizenry.

> Liberty cannot be preserved without a general knowledge among people.
> —John Adams

> Every government degenerates when trusted to the rulers of the people alone. The people themselves are its only safe depositories. And to render even them safe, their minds must be improved to a certain degree. . . . An amendment of our constitution must here come in aid of the public education. The influence over government must be shared among all the people. If every individual . . . participates of the ultimate authority, thee government will be safe.
> —Thomas Jefferson, Notes on Virginia 1781-1785, Query 14.

> Promote then as an object of primary importance, institutions for the general diffusion of knowledge. In proportion as the structure of a government gives force to public opinion, it is essential that public opinion be enlightened.
> —George Washington, Farewell Address, 1796

THE STUDY OF HISTORY AND DEMOCRATIC CITIZENSHIP

History has long been generally recognized as vital for citizen preparation. In the United States, as far back as 1892, the National Education Association, in its effort to define secondary school curriculum needs for the noncollege-bound, appointed nine subcommittees; the subcommittee with the responsibility for history, civil government, and political economy chaired by Wisconsin University's President Charles Kendall Adams concluded all students in a democracy needed broad-based knowledge of the past and recommended 4 years of history as that which would be needed for an "understanding of human affairs and (for) intelligent citizenship" (Jackson & Jackson, 1989, p. 4). Over the years, history has lost its privileged position; ". . . dislodged from its lofty perch as 'queen' of the social studies by the proliferation of social sciences, electives, and other courses" (Ravitch, 1989, p. 59). The result has been less emphasis on history in the middle grades and fewer world history courses in high school, further adulterated by short-lived fads and intellectually degraded by demands for "immediate social utility and thus (history's) advocates had difficulty claiming a place in the curriculum" and as ". . . the curriculum incorporated more courses that seemed socially useful or were intended to teach social skills, the time available for history shrank" (Ravitch, 1989, p. 61). Ravitch excoriates current practice—the curriculum and its teaching. The curriculum is bland and efforts to appeal to student interest has failed. Students view social studies to be the most boring and irrelevant of all their courses, no mean accomplishment because none of the other courses are viewed as exciting or relevant. Social science textbooks are "compendious, superficial, and dull" (Ravitch, 1989, p. 64). The curriculum is repetitive and too rushed for in-depth study and taught in a perfunctory manner by unprepared teachers (Ravitch, 1989). The Bradley Commission has made a spirited effort to resuscitate the study of history, arguing that its study is essential for the two "foremost" aims of U.S. education, "personal integrity" and "preparation for public life as democratic citizens" and useful for a third, "preparation for work" (Bradley Commission, 1989, pp. 21-23). The recommendations to meet these critical goals were the following:

1.   That the knowledge and habits of mind to be gained from the study of history are indispensable to the education of

citizens in a democracy. The study of history should, therefore, be required of all students.

2. That such study must reach well beyond the acquisition of useful information. To develop judgment and perspective, historical study must often focus upon broad, significant themes and questions, rather than the short-lived memorization of facts without context. In doing so, historical study should provide context for facts and training in critical judgment based upon evidence, including original sources, and should cultivate the perspective arising from a chronological view of the past down to the present day. Therefore it follows . . .

3. That the curricular time essential to develop the genuine understanding and engagement necessary to exercising judgment must be considerably greater than that presently common in American school programs in history.

4. That the kindergarten through grade six social studies curriculum be history-centered.

5. That this Commission recommends to the states and to local school districts the implementation of a social studies curriculum requiring no fewer than four years of history among the six years spanning grades seven through twelve.

   The Commission regards such time as indispensable to convey the three kinds of historical reality all citizens need to confront: American history to tell us who we are and who we are becoming; the history of Western civilization to reveal our democratic political heritage and its vicissitudes; world history to acquaint us with the nations and people with whom we shall share a common global destiny. It follows . . .

6. That every student should have an understanding of the world that encompasses the historical experiences of the peoples of Africa, the Americas, Asia, and Europe.

7. That history can best be understood when the roles of all constituent parts of society are included; therefore the history of women, racial and ethnic minorities, and men and women of all classes and conditions should be integrated into historical instruction.

8. That the completion of a substantial program in history (preferably a major, minimally a minor) at the college or university level be required for the certification of teachers of social studies in the middle and high schools.

> *The Commission is concerned by the minimal, fre-*
> *quently insubstantial, state requirements for historical*
> *studies in the education of social studies teachers. The*
> *kind of historical instruction we believe to be indis-*
> *pensable requires prior study of the subject in depth.*

9. That college and university departments of history
   review the structure and content of major programs for
   their suitability to the needs of prospective teachers,
   with special attention to the quality and liveliness of
   those survey courses whose counterparts are most often
   taught in the schools: world history, Western civilization, and American history.

> *The Commission is concerned that the structures*
> *and requirements of the undergraduate history major*
> *are too frequently inchoate, and that insufficient atten-*
> *tion is paid to courses demonstrating useful approaches*
> *to synthesis, selection, and understanding of organizing*
> *themes. (Bradley Commission, 1989, pp. 23-25)*

The Bradley Commission embellished its recommendations
with various instructional and curricular implementing suggestions that would inculcate "history's habits of minds," the inclusion of "vital themes and narratives" (revealing a concession to
postmodernist thinking), "a listing of analytical and comparative
topics central to the teaching of American, western civilization, and
world civilization organized by levels of development and concluding
with recommendations for appropriate teaching (pp. 25-44).

In the series of essays included in the Bradley Commission
volume on historical literacy was Nash's (1989) fascinating
History for a Democratic Society: The Work of All People. Nash
clearly was interested in preparing students for democratic citizenship. His contribution dealt with the elitist bias of historians
and attempts to remedy that distortion by noting the powerful
contributions to historical change made by two very ordinary
people: Ebenezer MacIntosh in the American Revolutionary War,
and nearly 200 years later, Rosa Parks in the Birmingham bus
boycott.

We find the condemnations by the Bradley Commission of
how history is taught to be convincing. We further believe that
enlivening history and treating it in depth is an essential component in preparing students for democratic citizenship, but here
we part company. We believe that if all of the Bradley recommen-

dations were followed to the letter, which would be very difficult, if not impossible, we would be no closer than we are now to preparing students for citizen responsibility. We do not analyze point by point the specifics of the Bradley Commission's recommendation because the whole falls far short of what is needed for an adequate preparation for democratic citizenship. The Bradley Commission recommendations, when considered from a competent citizen perspective, reduce to a more rigorous and invigorating irrelevancy. Although it is undoubtedly true that, "History will never be restored as a subject of value unless it is detached from vulgar utilitarianism" (Ravitch, 1989, p. 68), it is equally true that history will not be restored as a subject of value unless students perceive it to be useful for the solving of important problems, something that neither Ravitch nor others on the Bradley Commission seem to understand. The Bradley Commission is yet another document extolling the virtues of the Enlightenment. It is a declaration of faith—the expression of the belief that once a student really knows history, she or he will use that knowledge to inform citizenship behavior. Not only is there neither logic nor evidence to support such a claim, the argument is insufficiently attractive to motivate many students to study history. For all of its insistence that knowledge of history is essential for informed citizenship, the discussion generated by the Bradley Commission is too abstract and the problems to be solved too poorly defined to be a stimulus to democratic citizenship. The commission is too preoccupied with what students do not know about history to get to the task of describing in detail how that lack of historical knowledge specifically interferes with competent citizenship. Or more to the point, the commission does not make clear what history a student needs to know to become a responsible citizen. None of the contributors to the Bradley Commission report present a decipherable case for how or what history is to be taught so that it will inform universal citizen competence.

The study of history is critical for competent citizenship. The history that students need to learn is the history of effort expended in trying to solve a particular problem. If the problem is designing a work world (see chapter 4), students need to know the history of work and the impact on the work world by social policies designed to alter work, as well as how that history produced unanticipated consequences (which is a far cry from what the Bradley Commission recommends).

The most germane history that students need to know is the history of democratic thought and its application to the political process. The social studies curriculum as currently advertised, purports to teach such a history. It falls far short. Moreover, the history that the Bradley Commission recommends also fails because it is no more organized for problem solving than that which it seeks to replace. Students are far too passive and detached in what is an insufficiently "enlivened" history curriculum to solve the specific problems required by informed citizenship. Even those students who will pay attention, and there is little reason to believe there will be any more than is currently the case, will be hard pressed to apply what they have learned as passive absorbers of this deeper and broader history to solve any problem. The Bradley Commission, like all current educational reforms, have it backward. The problem comes first, the history follows as one ingredient of an integrated solution.

It would not suffice if an ideal history was presented to students and organized for problem solving. For problem solving, students must become historians. It is vital that students engage in historical research. Although accessing original source material is necessary, probably the most exciting form of historical research is oral history. Depending on the nature of the problem to be solved, students can tape-record interviews with persons who have made history—a stevedore who had been involved in the organizing of the docks in the 1930s; a tribal elder recounting a brave's life of 60 years ago; a veteran Mexican (or Lebanese to Australia) migrant who can trace the changes in his or her lifestyle that technology and globalization has caused; a jaunty 80-year-old feminist reliving the fight for suffrage. Students would have to do what all historians struggle to do—sort truth from fiction, fact from interpretation, and significance from insignificance. That individuals differ dramatically in their assessments is a powerful history lesson. That the differences in selection and interpretation of historical data is influenced by political ideology, gender, ethnicity, and race is another important lesson. That the rules of perception apply to historians to the same extent as they do to everyone else is yet another valuable lesson. Historians see what they believe to be true. Their worldviews shape where they search, what questions they ask, and how they interpret their findings. Liberal historians see the world differently than conservatives. Traditional historians find little in common with revisionists. Once students learn this, they are ready to attack history as a discipline. They are also prepared to identify what a historian must do to establish a common understanding as a basis for arriving at a solution for a pressing problem.

Today, students are well aware that "their" (Australian, English, or American) democracy is flawed (Gunn, 1996). But they have no idea how it got that way or what it would take to connect it to their personal lives (Australian Electoral Office, 1983). Students distrust government, but they do not know why, nor can they define the characteristics of a trustworthy government. Students must be encouraged to participate in learning, discovering, and producing a history directed toward solving the general problem of a "more perfect union." The U.S. founding fathers, for example, were under no illusion. They knew they had not created the perfect society, but their doubts are rarely included in the taught histories of that society, nor is sufficient attention given to the differences that divided them.

The philosophical differences that brought tensions to the 19th century continue into the present as sources of disagreements and unresolved tensions in modern society. (The Bradley Commission is helpful here, but only to the point of elaborating the differences that existed at the time.) The inclusion of people who made unrecognized contributions to democratic movements— women, slaves, White males who owned no property—is vital to the democratic project. (This is what Nash, 1989, meant by a history for a democratic society, but we do not feel that mere inclusion of the excluded is sufficient reform to orient students toward accepting the responsibility of democratic citizenship.) Unless history is taught as unresolved conflict brought forward and expressed in ever-changing contexts and organized for solving persistent unresolved major problems, little good can come from its study. Not one of the original concerns about democracy has been removed from the list of current problems. All of Plato's concerns about democracy are alive and well. Governance has always been difficult and may be getting more so.

No historian can feel very optimistic about the human prospect. We face a very ominous future and unless the history is taught in such a manner as to equally encourage all students to be leaders in the creation of a desired future, they are likely to be very unhappy with what they inherit.

From history, students should learn why there is a deep-seated fear of democracy. To understand how difficult the project of a more perfect union is, students should be given every opportunity to appreciate why propertied classes demand special privileges, why great effort was made to morally justify slavery, and why arguments for excluding women from first-class membership in society continue to recur. Textbooks cannot teach such history, but textbooks can be the launching pads for such instruction. Once a basic foundation is established, and that foundation identifies areas of disagreement as well as agreement, students are encouraged to engage in research, assemble and present findings, and debate conclusions. The goal of that debate is not to reach a consensus or to arrive at a democratically established official history to replace ordained official histories, but rather to marshal arguments for different solutions to modern problems of governance. In this particular instance, the problem to be solved is inventing a government best able to attend to the needs of all of its citizens.

PLAYING WITH HISTORY

The study of history has to be an invitation to vision. It must stimulate imagination. History devoid of imagination is worse than useless. Playing with history and using history to unleash imagination is a crucial component in the preparation for democratic citizenship. History has become a deadly subject for many (if not most) students because of the way it has been taught. Reciting facts of the kind that Ravitch said students cannot do is what has killed interest in history (although she tried to make the case that the facts are needed to add substance to concepts). When history is understood by students as necessary research for the creation of a better union, there is relevance, intellectual growth, and the potential for excitement. When that happens, so too will pertinent "facts" be remembered. The study of history will not necessarily produce a better government, but such study can play a significant role in preparing a citizen to continue the pursuit of a more perfect union and that preparation should be the public school's primary goal.

The study of history for problem solving is not passive absorption of a bland synthesis of historical knowledge, nor is it passive reading of traditional and/or revisionist historians. The study of history consistent with the goal of preparing a democratic citizen is active and unruly. The history of racism, for example, cannot and should not be cleansed of its ugly brutality, what the conservatives in Australia call the "black arm band" view of history. Racism will be countered only when fully addressed. But the teaching of that history cannot become an excuse to exact revenge on people for whatever their forbears may have done, or even on those who sustain its practice today. History is not a search for moral superiority. It is a search for solution of a recognized problem. Finding inequality and degradation in history does not produce a solution. Without attention to solution, the study of history can produce anger or guilt that are more likely to be impediments than assets in the search for solutions. Far more interesting than revisiting the horrors of slavery, "ethnic cleansing," or other disreputable aspects of life (insatiable greed, crime, exploitation, etc.) that are inimical to democracy, is using history to study efforts to improve society and the short- and long-term effects of such action.

A search for mass participatory democratic movements that have led to desired, albeit transient, consequences is not likely to reveal a rich repository. Historian Goodwyn (1981, 1984) listed but three in the United States: The Shay rebellion against the newly formed United States, the 19th-century self-help cooperative or "populist" movement of southern and western farmers, and the organization of the industrial workers by the CIO in the 1930s. Students should examine those movements to see if these met the movement's criteria for reform, and on the basis of their research add (or subtract) models that can be instructive in producing desired societal change. It would be hard to ignore the remarkable effort that led to the 19th Amendment and the women's vote (i.e., "Catt's Winning Plan"; Evans, 1989; Flexner, 1959) and there is much to be learned from the now nearly forgotten civil rights movement (Branch, 1988; Weisbrot, 1990).

CIVITAS

One effort to make schools more democratic has been launched by R. Freeman Butts and the Center for Civic Education. The goal of the CIVITAS curriculum framework is the development of fully participating, competent, and responsible citizens—citizens with a reasoned commitment to the fundamental values and principles of American constitutional democracy, who find satisfaction in employing those values and principles to serve others, and who fulfill their potential as effective public actors. CIVITAS seeks to foster commitment to constitutional principles and values, while eschewing indoctrination. This goal is to be reached by imparting young people with civic knowledge and skills and providing them relevant experience, all of which is linked to a disposition to look beyond their own particular interests and the social groups of which they are members and seek the common good for the present and for generations to come. Thus, instructional programs based on the CIVITAS curricular framework should convey a profound understanding of the bases of U.S. constitutional democracy that according to this formulation would provide the most promising foundation for a citizen's development of reasoned commitment to sustaining the institutions and furthering the ideals of U.S. constitutional democracy (Center for Civic Education, 1991).

Butts (1988), for the better part of 40 years, has advocated and designed efforts at civic education. He has tried to make us aware that a fundamental goal of education is the preparation of informed and responsible citizenship. CIVITAS is both a monument to him and a culmination of his vision and efforts. In it is to be found the contributions of a wide range of experts who produced an impressive volume. It is an effort to upscale and broaden social studies and in particular the teaching of civics.

CIVITAS is presented in three parts:

Part I: Civic virtue treats the underlying logic of our "system," its dispositions, and commitments.

Part II: Civic participation brings everything related to government and politics into a congruent argument; including a guided tour of participation in decision making with recommendations for a somewhat enhanced student government, community service, research, and debate. It pulls together history, geography, economics, and politics and introduces such issues as diversity and ethnic identity in the treatment of equality in an attempt to create a coherent and integrated social studies. Included are the tensions that have both sustained and divided the United States these past two centuries—power and authority in government and politics, public good versus private interest, the uncoupling of government from its citizenry, pluralism and ethnic identity, the rise (and fall?) of the state, descriptions and explanation of the values and principles that have guided the United States, and how these get translated into political structures (balance of powers, federalism, guarantees of rights and equality, etc.).

Part III: Role of the citizen is a short treatise on the rights and responsibilities of citizenship (including a short detour into the history of civil disobedience), and concludes with a call, perhaps even a plea, for the restoration of civic responsibility and the reestablishment of community

Conscientious social studies teachers will find CIVITAS a useful resource. It can make a contribution to teacher preparation. It is a serious, balanced, and very thorough effort to respond to a clearly defined problem. However, it meets the definition of a camel, an animal created by a committee. It also suffers from too much reverence for the past. It glosses over the hostility of the founding fathers to democracy. Respect and admiration must be shown to those who laid the foundation of the United States and their accomplishments, but not by minimizing the problems they left for us to solve.

From the student perspective, callous and turned off to history and all other social studies, CIVITAS is "same, ole, same ole." It is organized in subjects and although there is recommendation for more spirited approaches to instruction, it, much like the Bradley Commission report on history teaching, is founded on the belief that a better prepared teacher in subject matter, working with better resources, and armed with a range of teaching techniques would be enough to reawaken an interest in civics and thereby prepare students for informed and responsible citizenship. Would that it was so easy. What is lacking is a systematic analysis of the extent to which the daily activities of schooling is antithetical to democracy. Schools are not places where students merely fail to learn the rudiments of citizenship, they are places where students learn to become cynical and virulently antidemocratic. This is particularly true in the treatment of equality, respect for rights, and in the use of knowledge to solve important problems. Equality, diversity, and fairness cannot be treated as sanguinely as they are treated in CIVITAS. These are burning issues that students face every day and a historical perspective in the absence of some efforts at corrective action will simply not suffice. In CIVITAS, students will be provided just enough balanced treatment on all major controversial issues to be unable to participate in the solution to any important problem.

Would we be better off if CIVITAS (or the Bradley Commission recommendations) were to be fully implemented? Of course, but only marginally so. Would students leave high school prepared to be effective, knowledgeable, and informed citizens? A few more than is now the case, but not many more. Would CIVITAS help schools become civic and civil communities? Highly unlikely. Would CIVITAS help produce a society where four times as many African Americans are in higher education than are in prison, instead of the other way around? Absolutely not. CIVITAS is based on expert testimony, not empirical findings. We have no idea what would happen if implemented. We do not know whether it is even possible to implement CIVITAS in high schools as currently constituted.

Making the Classroom Consistent with Democratic Citizenship

It makes little sense to teach a history dedicated to the respect for democratic principles, while in the classroom there is consistent violation of every principle being taught. One other weakness in the Bradley Commission (and other efforts to revive the teaching of history) is that history is presented as an independent discipline. In fact, it is treated as superior to other social science disciplines. If history is to be useful preparation for democratic citizenship, it must be integrated with student government, the study of existing government ("civics"), community service, and cooperative learning.

Nowhere is democratic citizenship less respected than in school. Nowhere is disrespect for democracy more consistently taught by practice and policy than in school. In the great majority of classrooms, students learn that the teacher is boss and whatever she or he says goes, that there is no available mechanism to change a perceived unfair grade, that there is no process by which a student can adequately defend him or herself against a charge of misconduct, and that it is not possible to rectify perceived unfair treatment. It is impossible to effectively teach a history of democracy, if, by teacher behavior and school procedures, democratic ideas and principles are treated with contempt. In the final analysis, one only can learn to be a democratic citizen by practicing democratic citizenship. One learns to be cynical about democracy when there is a huge discrepancy between what is taught in history and the treatment a student receives in the classroom.

Democratic Education: The Development of Citizenship Skills Through Action and Reflection

Democratic citizenship skills are those attributes that facilitate involvement with others in ways designed to generate action for the betterment of the community. Specifically, a skilled democratic citizen can formulate a coherent argument, support that argument with evidence, effectively communicate with a wide range of others, hear what a wide range of others are saying, search for a common ground by negotiating differences, devise with others a plan of action, and engage in a number of specifically designated collective activities consistent with democratic principles to implement the plan.

Democratic skills are developed through school-created opportunities for practice (Gill, Trioli, & Weymouth, 1988; Knight, 1985a). Students are put into situations where they can influence and be influenced by other students, to develop plans of action, and through persuasion and compromise, develop voluntary associations to work for agreed on goals. After a political action is taken, students are helped to analyze the process and progress made by the action.

Unlike current approaches to political participation, in a classroom organized to prepare students for democratic citizenship everyone is encouraged to be a leader and everyone is given ample opportunity to lead. The development of citizenship skills meets the democratic education requirement of universal and equal participation in vital decisions. One vital democratic skill is the art of persuasion, the capacity to reach a general understanding through cooperation, compromise, and the straining for consensus. A necessary secondary democratic skill is learning to accept the legitimacy of disagreement. In any significant issue there will be no consensus.

The right to disagree must be scrupulously respected. The minority must be assured that it will enjoy all the rights and privileges that a citizen has in a democratic community. For this to work, it is necessary that the students learn a particularly important skill: how to disagree without being disagreeable. Students need to be encouraged to recognize the constructive influence a freely dissenting minority has on the ideas of the majority. The minority helps the majority clarify its thinking and forces it to justify its conclusions with logic and evidence. Without such minority, the majority's thinking becomes slack and sloppy.

Students need to be prepared to deal with a politics that has become increasingly nasty. The nastiness has turned many away from politics. And yet, it is only through politics that any of our persisting problems can be solved.

The skills necessary to the resolution of group conflict should be taught in both high school and college. All men and women in positions of leadership, government, or private sector, should be schooled in dispute resolution and all of the antipolarization arts. (Gardner, 1989, p. 78)

Democratic Education: The Building of Community

Experiencing and Inventing Government. Students learn to become responsible democratic citizens by engaging in citizenship activities. Not all citizenship activities involve government, but government establishes the boundaries for citizenship. Even those who are most antigovernment must use the agencies of government to express their opposition. In the teaching of citizenship, it is imperative that classrooms be organized as governments. And indeed, state-supported classrooms are agencies of government (as are, although less controlled, private schools that are subsidized by government). From our perspective, the classroom is more than an agency of government; it is where students learn the rudiments about citizenship. In a democratic classroom, students practice every component of democratic citizenship. They learn to debate issues and support proposals with logic and evidence. They participate in decisions that affect their lives. They learn what rights are and where these rights end through the exercise of rights and by participating in discussions about the definition and boundaries of rights.

Critical for citizenship development is establishing the classroom as an experiment in government. Students in such an experiment should be able to experience various forms of government and be challenged to create new forms. Students should experiment with various early "democracies": representative government where some in class are given the right to vote while others are denied that right. Various justifications can be developed to deny the vote, for example, grades in prior classrooms, failure to conform to dictates of good citizenship (disciplinary actions such as suspensions or detentions), or race or gender, or color of eyes. Each of these restrictions should be discussed and reference to history here is essential. Through the study of a focused history, students will learn that government at every stage of history was an unstable compromise of competing forces and constituencies.

The classroom is the bedrock of citizenship training. It is in the confines of a single classroom that a full range of experiments in government can be tested and analyzed. It is only when students fully appreciate the complexity and difficulty of democratic government that they are able to move to larger units (e.g., school governments; local, regional, and national governments; and international agencies such as the United Nations). As students developmentally expand their grasp and begin to conceptualize where the boundaries that separate the local from more centralized authorities should be, they should never abandon the classroom as the basic unit of preparation for citizenship.

Establishing the classroom as the basic unit of preparation for citizenship could allow for the examination of a variety of arrangements in democratic government. One possibility is to combine direct government with elected representatives. At the classroom level, democracy can be direct, the classroom can select representatives for decision making at larger units (e.g., a school government, a statewide student organization, or a national student assembly). Similarly, at a neighborhood level, decisions could be made by a modified town hall from which delegates could be sent to larger local, regional, and national legislatures and from which executives could be selected (e.g, governors, presidents, prime ministers). Students can experiment with modifications of the existing arrangement in Australia and England where executives are selected from elected legislators. Currently, there is lack of harmony between levels of government. A system in which one set of elected representatives serves at all levels could be examined by students. Students in their government could experiment with a variety of arrangements in which the local control (in this instance the classroom) would be more than an empty slogan.

It is in the classroom that all students can hone "democratic arts" including: active listening, dialogue and debate on public issues, prosocial expressions of anger, creative controversy, political imagination, public judgment, reflection and evaluation, negotiation, and mediation (Institute for the Arts of Democracy, 1992; see Table 3.1).

There is yet another reason to keep the classroom as the basic unit of citizen preparation. In some instances it may be the only feasible place to practice citizenship. In other instances, it becomes the fall back when problems arise at larger and more remote levels of student government.

Table 3.1. Democratic Arts: Capacities for Effective Public Life.

Democratic Art	Characteristics	Benefits
Active Listening	No preset agenda Asking questions Noting what is not said, as well as what is said	Uncovers interests and values Discovers mutual interests Speaker's own understanding evolves
Public Dialogue	Public talk on matters affecting the "commons"	Reveals interests; generates more creative alternatives
Disciplined expression of anger	Not rage: anger that communicates grief over injury rather than hatred Anger that can be "heard	Destructive backlash is less likely Motivates positive change Focuses attention for change
Creative controversy	Critical, constructive open, honest confrontation	Demonstrates all stakeholders are involved Generates more options Builds group confidence
Political Imagination	Re-imaging current reality	Spurs creativity Motivates Enables goal setting
Public Judgment	Derived interactively Discriminating reason	Makes problem solving possible: participants more willing to accept consequences
Reflection and Evaluation	Ongoing assessment of lessons learned	Builds capacities and develops group memory

Table 3.1. Democratic Arts: Capacities for Effective Public Life (con't).

Democratic Art	Characteristics	Benefits
Negotiation	Clear articulation of interests: narrowing of differences; searching for common ground and acceptable compromises	Makes problem solving possible
Mediation	Listening in order to surface differences Helping move from fixed positions in order to probe for interests	Avoids destructive conflict Makes problem solving possible

Note: From Institute for the Arts of Democracy (1992).

Student Government

Student government must be changed from a process that builds contempt for government and political processes to one that teaches democratic citizenship. When the comprehensive high school was developed in the beginning of the 20th century, its core activities were designed to prepare the student—especially the new immigrant student—for citizenship responsibilities. The approach at the time was minimally successful. We simply have refused to learn from history. What was minimally successful in the 1920s is simply absurd in the 1990s. Student government, if anything, has worsened over the years. There is virtually no school matter over which it has control. Furthermore, there are enormous restrictions on participation. Typically, only students acceptable to the school management can be involved in student government. Student government has all of the undesirable features of a "managed" democracy. Administrators and teachers control the process. A few students are permitted to exercise "leadership" in elections that are unrelated to critical school issues. School elections, thus, are reduced to popularity contests. In a sense, school government has been a harbinger of elections for public office, which too, have been reduced to popularity contests. How could it be otherwise? Without developing a sense of citizenship responsibility, which is dependent on informed and considered involvement in the decision making process, the only possibility is for candidates to base their appeal on prejudice, ignorance, or personal attractiveness.

Learning about government begins in the individual classroom, and only after the classroom government is successful and all students understand what government does and what their role is in it, and only after every classroom in the school has a working government does it make sense to talk about school government. And only when students understand student government are they developmentally prepared to understand local, state, and federal governments.

Student government in a democratic classroom is real. It is a far cry from current fantasy student governments. In the democratic classrooms, students make important decisions. One area of important decision making is fiscal. A democratic student government controls a defined budget. This is a necessary condition because the primary responsibility of modern governments is raising and spending money. Student government makes critical budgetary decisions. The student government is permitted to make "mistakes." Reflecting on mistakes teaches accountability. In the process, students learn about zero-sum choices. Spending money for one activity means that something else will not be funded. Student governments should also be involved in the fundraising aspect of government. Student governments in a democratic class-room "tax" their constituents. The government has to deal with tax resistance and legal challenges. Student governments debate and experiment with various approaches to tax collection. The govern-ment can decide to run its operation without a tax and depend on revenues derived solely from voluntary contributions. Such an approach creates dilemmas: Does the government provide services to those who do not, or cannot, make donations? Do persons who make extra large donations receive extra or special benefits? Or, if the government decides to tax, should the levy be a flat tax where everyone pays the same rate, or a progressive tax where the rate is raised according to wealth or income, or a regressive or a fixed fee for all citizens? Taxation is a major issue in equity. Are those who cannot afford the levy denied citizenship (a form of a poll tax)? Are they denied services (e.g., access to dances, athletics, excursions, publications, film nights, club functions)? The government may decide to engage in income-creating activities, pay its employees, and tax them. Here again, there are interesting choices to be con-sidered. At what rate should income be taxed? Are persons not taxed entitled to benefits? Or the student government may decide to charge a value added or sales tax on its income-creating activities (e.g., sales of meals and other school products). Again, there will be problems: What rate of tax? Does a sales tax raise the price of a product or service so as to make it prohibitive to some? Do some students receive entitlements not provided others?

All of the approaches to fundraising are problematic. All can be defended by some form of logic and all have a history that can be studied and brought to discussion and meaningful debate. To add depth to the debate, local "experts" that divide along the political continuum can be asked to provide consultation to the process. And finally, as part of the process of citizen preparation, the discussions that take place in arriving at school government decisions can be generalized to the debates of fiscal policies that are taking place in local, state, and federal governments. Students should be encouraged to make their opinions in these larger debates known through letters, petitions, and delegations to dif-ferent legislative bodies.

Democratic school governments (whether at the class-room, school, or larger span of control) have important executive and legislative and judicial responsibilities. The executive function of a student government is to administer a variety of programs (e.g., student assemblies, excursions, dances, sports days, science and art fairs, safety and security functions, and supervision of community services). The legislative function, in addition to the aforementioned fiscal responsibilities, include establishing the rules by which students must live. The judicial responsibility is to provide due process and to determine consequences for rule infractions.

Student government does not just happen. There must be a clear logic to its development. And it should not move to the next stage without establishing a powerful case that sufficient knowledge and maturity has occurred for the additional responsibility. And at no stage is student government removed from adult supervision and possible remedial intervention. From the very beginning, students are made aware of what is necessary for advancement to the a higher stage of political responsibility, and the specific acts of nonfeasance (not performing an accepted student government responsibility), misfeasance (activity that is improper by a student government representative that would not be improper if done by anyone else), and malfeasance (misconduct or wrongdoing by student government representatives) that would require intervention by adult authority and the nature of the intervention for specific infractions. If something occurs that had not been anticipated, school authorities would negotiate with the student government for an acceptable response. In most instances, this decision would be ratified by a school election. In matters of extreme urgency, school authorities can call a state of emergency and abolish student government for a period of time. However, any intrusion by school officials in student government has a chilling effect on student government and should, if at all possible, be avoided. Any school authority intervention into student government must become part of the learning experience. Both students and school officials need to reflect on both the actions that led up to the intervention and the intervention itself. The restoration of student government should consciously include references to the prior actions and procedures that would lessen the likelihood of a future occurrence. Our experience is that school authorities tend to overreact and if the process of logical development is carried through, the need for teacher and administrator interference in student government would rarely, if ever, be necessary.

We believe the guidelines presented more than two decades ago (Pearl, 1972) for using student government as a means of preparing for democratic citizenship is, if anything, more apt now than it was then.

Democratic Practice in the Primary Grades. In the first few years of school, the student must become acquainted with rational order. During these years, the teacher is totally in charge. There is no organized challenge to that authority. The teacher's primary role in education for citizenship is patently didactic. At this stage the teacher explains the necessity for classroom rules and begins to establish an understanding of individual rights. The teacher (with parental approval) might experiment. One day, the class would be conducted without any rules at all; the next day the students could reflect on what happened. Another day, a class could be modeled after someone who delegated absolute authority and everyone would have to do exactly what the dictator leader demanded. That situation also could be analyzed and reviewed by the children. Instruction in democratic practice should include role-playing of judges, legislators, and executives. Through simulation, the very young can develop a sense of the parameters of democracy.

Preparing for Democracy in the Intermediate Grades. By Grade 4, students should be allowed to experiment with representative government (at both a class and school level). During these years, students should be randomly assigned to governmental functions. The model should be the jury system, in which every citizen is obligated to serve. At this point, the child is beginning to recognize that freedom carries with it responsibility. Every child will get an opportunity to serve as legislator and make the rules. Every child will sit as judge or on the jury, to deliberate what should be done with rule violators. Every child will serve as an executive and have responsibility for a school or class activity.

The initiation of youth into representative government by assignment rather than by election is preferable on a number of grounds. Elections based on ignorance can only debase the democratic process. The only basis for selection can be personal appeal. This is precisely what is corrupting the adult political scene. Premature attempts at elections will limit the experience in leadership to a privileged few. Excluded will be youth who are allegedly limited in ability; the economically deprived and the racial minority will rarely, if ever, get a chance to exercise leadership. The excluded are doubly handicapped because when later in life they, as the underclass, are asked to elect representatives, they will have very limited knowledge of the specifics of the function and thus will hardly be in a position to make intelligent choices, and, their lack of experience will militate against their election into leadership.

The teacher's role changes in this phase of development. The teacher moves from the decision maker to an active participant in deliberation. The teacher refers students to sources; insists on consideration of a range of possible consequences. It is important, even critical, that the teacher allow students to make errors. The teacher must insist that students learn from their errors. If things do not work well—a student activity becomes a shambles or a law meets with wide-scale violation—the teacher can convene the group and say, "Okay, what would we do differently if we had to do it all over? What did we learn from that experience?" and he or she can encourage the students to try again. If students become depressed, the teacher should take measures to restore humor to the process. If students become overly zealous, the teacher should bring the excessiveness to their attention and take corrective measures to mitigate authoritarian tendencies.

Preparing Students for Democratic Citizenship in the Junior High and High School. Students in the junior high (Grades 7-9, or 6-8), the 12- to l5-year-olds, are now prepared to experiment with elections. They can be expected to nominate the candidate, campaign, and vote (first at a classroom level, then if appropriate at larger spans of authority). Students should have developed at this stage of their lives, a sense of the kind of laws that are useful in controlling behavior, the treatment law-violators should receive, and desirable student activities. The responsibilities of student government should include an advisory influence on curriculum and teacher recruitment.

The sequencing of student control is important. It is not wise to establish a student court if the students were not involved in the formation of the rules. It is not wise to involve students solely in the restriction of student behavior; they should also be involved in good things (e.g., planning and executing a dance or an assembly). Student government action that controls student behavior can be appreciated if it is deemed necessary for the valued activity, or as seen as a necessary attribute for the attainment of a desired goal.

The teacher's role at this level changes perceptively from the authority in the classroom to a person who reviews and analyzes authority. At this stage, the teacher clearly enunciates the latitudes of control that are available to the student. The possible restrictions are announced in advance. The major function of the teacher is to return to the student for reconsideration actions which are internally inconsistent, fly in the face of student rights, are illegal, or are opposed by school authorities because it can be convincingly shown that if the action was allowed the results would be, if not disastrous, seriously disruptive to the educational process.

By high school, students should have matured to a point where they can have significant influence in the running of the classroom and the school. Their rights, as well as their responsibilities, have been clearly established. In many areas, the adults function primarily as technical assistants and consultants. If the system breaks down and adult authorities assume responsibility for greater participation in decision making, they must proceed carefully and cautiously because precipitous intervention will seriously retard development of competent citizenship.

Limitations to Student Government. Students cannot be expected to run the school. They should have much more power than they now have, but there are limits to that power. The school is truly a pluralistic institution, with many parties having legitimate stakeholding claims. Accommodation must be made for all. Teachers have rights, and they must be involved in the judicial, legislative, and executive decision making of the school. Just as teacher oppression of students is an intolerable condition, so too would be the reverse. Schools have a social responsibility. Local and more remote communities are entitled to some say in the education of youth. Because this influence has been abused and because these demands have been almost always excessive, inconsistent, and devoid of perceptible logic does not eliminate the legitimacy of community influence on education.

Schools of, for, and by the students are not feasible. Students do not have the political, military, or economic potential to wrest power from adults. Nor is there any persuasive logic to convince adults that they should relinquish all authority over the school. The call for elimination of responsible adult authority from the school is patently anti-intellectual. A sound education requires informed adults to transmit knowledge, focus questions, stimulate debate, supervise controlled experience, offer feedback and evaluation, and in myriad of other ways facilitate student growth. It is inconceivable that such leadership could be accomplished if either teacher or administrator is reduced to flunky roles.

Power in a school consistent with democratic principles is not zero-sum. In fact, the more power the adult shares with students, the more power the teacher or administrator has. Time is the only truly zero-sum game played in school. Time spent on one activity must come at the expense of something else. Time spent by teachers establishing control over unruly youth must eat into time that could be used for productive educational pursuits. If sharing of power can reduce unruliness, the teacher gains time and, ergo, power to go on to other things. That this rarely happens is primarily because there is no consensus about educational goals. If youth and adults have markedly different educational goals, conflict is inevitable and the struggle for control must be zero-sum. There can be similar distortion when the means used to attain goals cannot be defended by logic or evidence.

If, however, there is basic agreement that education should lead to efficacy in the worlds of work, politics, culture, and interpersonal relationships, no battle for control need occur. The goals establish boundaries for debate. Any action proposed from any quarter can be first questioned on its relevance to the goals. If its relevance is established, then negotiation is limited to implementation, and that discussion should not require polarization.

Student Involvement and Conditioning of the Environment. Student involvement in school decision making will not produce disruptive controversy if adults in the community are prepared for it. Before launching into a venture where power is shared with students, those who are to do the sharing must fully understand what is expected of them. Maintaining the classroom as the basic unit of school government reduces the enormity of the task and, as a consequence, control is rarely a difficult problem. Prior to relinquishing any segment of control to students, the teacher, the school board, and other significant adults should convene for a probing discussion of the implications and possible consequences of enhanced student power. If the adult authorities are in disagreement, these differences should be resolved in advance of the undertaking. The various adults involved should be alerted to possible contingencies and to courses of action when emergencies arise. Because of inadequate preparation, an unready community tends to react vigorously against student initiatives, and, in some instances, students are reduced to an even more oppressed condition than they suffered before they were involved in student government.

Inadequate preparation of students can also be disastrous. Educators ask for all hell to break loose if suddenly, without advance notice, an existing authoritarian system is abolished and students are told they are now in charge. If students abuse power, any attempt to clarify the situation after the fact will be interpreted as a betrayal. Power believed to be theirs has been taken away. The friendly "good guy" educator who offered to share power is now the vicious autocrat usurping power. Far less turmoil will occur if the limitation of power is clearly communicated to students at the beginning. "Nice guy" administrators or teachers who are unwilling to recognize that there is power invested in their role that they cannot relinquish will only create problems for themselves.

Distortion and corruption of student involvement in school government will occur. Students will misuse power. In some instances, their power will be illusory. These are conditions to be rectified not causes for abandonment of a necessary project. Nor is it necessary for an entire system to generate student power. Projects can and should start small—the classroom—and only where there is receptivity become larger in the form of grade-level government, school government, and district-wide governance.

Because our society as a whole, and our children in particular, have not been educated to accept democratic responsibility, very few will rush to try. There are too many threats to this initiative and too few rewards. Being passive and dependent does offer an illusion of safety. Many educators (and other adults) will be soured by the student response. They, like those who fear student government as a threat to adult authority, will become distraught when a minority of youth take over student government. Such critics too often will prefer the perfect tyranny of adults to the imperfect involvement of students. It is the adult critics, not the students they condemn, who threaten student involvement in school government and the preparation of democratic citizens. Only as it is demonstrated that students can exercise power will students in large numbers strive for power; and only when the rewards for exercise of power far outweigh the rewards for renunciation of power will the majority become involved. Starting where we are, the development of a truly responsible student body will take some time (Knight, 1996; Pearl, 1972).

Preparing for Democratic Citizenship through Community Service

Competent democratic citizenship requires wide-ranging knowledge. Some of that knowledge is problem-specific, enabling the citizen to bring logic and evidence to a debate on a particular issue. Some of that knowledge is institutional sophistication, creating the government that can best and most fairly serve its people. Some of that knowledge comes through community service. Barber (1992) made a powerful case for community service as a means (he actually came closer to insisting it is the means) for developing necessary citizenship competence. It is his belief that a well-designed community service program is the antidote to the "mistrust, cynicism, disappointment, and bitterness (that) currently weigh(s) down our institutional relations, turning pedagogical allies into enemy camps of faculty, students, and administrators" (p. 230). He argued that "civic education" is an integral part of a liberal arts education and even more importantly liberty depends on the teaching of citizenship. The teaching of citizenship increases in importance and becomes a more difficult challenge at a time when "individuals regard themselves almost exclusively as private persons with responsibilities only to family and job, yet possessing endless rights against a distant and alien state. . . . 'We the People' have severed our connections with 'It' the state or 'They' the 'bureaucrats' and 'politicians' who run It" (p. 231).

Barber's main thesis is that service to the community is a duty and, furthermore, such service is an absolute necessity for the maintenance of freedom. Moreover, this nexus between education and community service was once understood as vital for citizenship preparation. "America's actual history suggests a nation devoted to civic education for citizenship and schools devoted to the nation's civic mission. It assumes that our rights and liberties are not acquired for free; that unless we assume the responsibilities of citizens, we will not be able to preserve the liberties they entail" (p. 246). Barber buttressed his argument by citing the importance that august universities give to community service. The dearth of historical support for community service in kindergarten through Grade 12 does not weaken the gist of Barber's argument. It does mean that its focus needs to be shifted.

Barber presented the Rutgers program with which he has been associated as a model of community service. Community service prepares students for democratic citizenship when it is linked to classroom activity and is guided by the following nine principles. It:

1. makes it an educational experience;
2. helps make "visible" "the crucial democratic relationship between rights and responsibilities (p. 254);

3. provides a "remedy" (for) "antisocial, discriminatory and other forms of selfish and abusive or addictive behavior (that) are often a symptom of the breakdown of civic community" (p. 254);
4. makes possible "respect for the full diversity and plurality of American life is possible and thus has "the greatest likelihood of impacting on student ignorance, intolerance, and prejudice" (p. 255);
5. enables "individuals to feel empowered in the community," if it also entails participation "in the planning process to establish civic education and community service programs" (p. 255);
6. does "not discriminate among economic or other classes of Americans" (p. 255);
7. is "communal as well as community-based . . . (and) built around teams (of say 5 or 10 or 20) rather than around individuals" (p. 255);
8. "teach(es) citizenship, not charity, (because) young people serve themselves as members of the community by serving a public good that is also their own" (p. 256);
9. is "an integral part of liberal education and thus should both be mandatory and should receive academic credit. . . . There are certain things a democracy simply must teach, employing its full authority to do so: citizenship is first among them" (p. 256).

We find Barber's argument for community service persuasive. We differ only in that we believe that community service is but one means by which students are prepared for democratic citizenship. Barber limited his analysis to the university. That too is a worry. Citizenship preparation cannot be restricted to an elite. Every one of the principles that undergird the Rutgers program apply equally, if not more, powerfully to secondary school and even to elementary school students.

There is yet another important difference in our understanding and in Barber's. His proposal for community service is appended to an otherwise unchanged educational system. Community service is an added requirement for graduation. The other requirements remain as courses to be completed. We believe that adding community service to the existing system is probably necessary as a transitional tactic, but we feel its vision (and Barber spoke of vision) is too limiting. For community service to work in our scheme of preparation for democratic citizenship, it would be included as a part of a problem-solving curriculum—perhaps the major knowledge development activity—depending on the problem to be solved. It would be linked to student government (student government could be one of the community services) and would utilize (as Barber suggested) cooperative learning. Unless envisioned as part of an reconstructed educational system—a system that meets democratic requirements—it is unlikely that community service will adequately address the lamentable condition of democracy in the postmodern world. Every level of education is so fundamentally undemocratic (i.e., curriculum, involvement of students in important decisions, guaranteed rights, assignment of responsibilities, and evaluation) that appending community service on to its existing corpus is not likely to lead to a competent democratic citizen. Community service is a necessary but not a sufficient element in the preparation of a democratic citizen.

Effective student government is likely to have serendipitous effects. Students, feeling less alienated and more in control, are likely to make great leaps in traditional academic performance. Hollins (1991), an alienated "at-risk" youth recruited to the University of Oregon Upward Bound Program that we helped design and administer, not only graduated from the university and went on to achieve an advanced degree, insisted that a major factor in his academic success and the academic success of so many of his similarly situated colleagues was the student government that gave to them real power in decisions that affected their lives.

Preparing for Democratic Citizenship through Cooperative Learning

Cooperative learning techniques can be usefully applied to the solving of any problem. It was briefly referred to in the discussion on preparation for work—the ability to work cooperatively is one of the attributes sought in the emerging global economy (see chapter 4). The ability to work cooperatively is a necessary component in culture carrying competence. Without cooperative projects it becomes impossible to establish any negotiated common ground or shared understanding from which benefits can be derived from diversity.

We decided to situate our discussion of cooperative learning in preparation for democratic citizenship to avoid redundancy but also because early in a child's school career there needs to be some balance against the excessive focus on individual achievement. Some cooperative learning schemes do that very well. And further, the very essence of the concept of community requires people working together in various cooperative ventures. There can be no democratic citizenship without cooperative relationships. Therefore, if schools seriously accept the goal of preparation for democratic citizenship, not only must ample opportunities be created for cooperative activities, and the nature of the cooperation must be organized developmentally with the more complex and challenging building on the simple, but there must also be standards developed for students to meet. Cooperativeness is not a simple monodimensional trait. The nature of effective cooperation varies considerably by task, by size of group, and probably most importantly, by the composition of the group. Cooperation is not a universal good. Nor is it synonymous with democracy. Cooperation is entirely compatible with authoritarianism. In the Nurenberg Trials, cooperation with the Nazis constituted crimes against humanity. Most sporting activities are currently organized as very finely tuned cooperative activities governed by authoritarian principles.

Few would dispute the value of cooperation. Supporting cooperative education in schools today is far less controversial than supporting motherhood, God, or heaven forbid, cholesterol-loaded apple pie. Supporters of cooperative education present evidence to show that some approaches appear to produce significantly higher levels of academic performance across a wide range of "subjects" when compared with individual approaches (Davidson, 1985; Newman & Thompson, 1987; Slaven 1989). The gains are sufficiently impressive, although somewhat inconsistent, that we are persuaded that student learning teams in the existing schools would make the classroom less deadly and would produce higher tests scores on the required curriculum. Our concern is not with cooperative learning per se, but with the specific contribution cooperative learning has made to democratic citizen preparation. We are not convinced that cooperative learning as currently practiced will do much to prepare students for democratic citizenship, although we do believe that the techniques designed by leaders in the field (e.g., Kagan, 1989; Johnson & Johnson, 1986; Slavin, 1990) provide excellent tactics to be used to introduce the topic of the demands of citizenship.

Cooperative learning can assist students to master a number of different roles required by a democratic society (e.g., leader, facilitator, and recorder). Working in groups does facilitate the development of a broad range of social skills, and to the extent that the groups are diverse by ethnicity and assumed intellectual capacity these experiences are also generalizable to democratic citizenship.

On the whole, however, we are less impressed with the gains produced by cooperative education then we are depressed with the insistence that schools continue to be lonely places where for so much of the day students are forbidden interaction with each other. We indicated more than 20 years ago that students did not need to be instructed in cooperative learning, they had become quite adept at it without help from teachers—although teachers insisted on calling this cooperation cheating (Pearl, 1972).

In an essential element of democratic citizenship—interracial relationships—cooperative learning has made a contribution to preparation for democratic citizenship and to the achievement of equal encouragement (Hansell & Slavin, 1981; Slavin & Oickle, 1981; Weigel, Wiser, & Cook, 1975). However, although cooperative education is an essential component in the development of a democratic citizen, its importance should not be overstated. In fact, if other changes are not made in the classroom, the gains made by cooperative education will be overwhelmed by the negative aspects of existing school practices. Cooperative education tends to be surrealistic. Because cooperative education is thrown into a mix of contradictory influences, it is very difficult for students to sustain positive influences or to generalize them to out-of-school activities. Without a coherent grounding, the logical consequences of cooperative education is enabling some groups to cooperate with each other at the expense of other groups. Moreover, in the absence of more fundamental changes, the gains in mutual understanding between Whites and Blacks, for example, will not be able to withstand countervailing pressures for racial isolation. The rapidly rising antipathy against immigrants, the surging increase in racism and anti-semitism, the ethnic wars in what was once Yugoslavia, should be powerful enough indicators to convince educators that by itself cooperative learning exercises are insufficient to overcome deep-seated hatreds.

For cooperative education to be a significant factor in democratic education and for it to fully prepare the student for democratic citizenship, greater emphasis must be given to the quality of cooperation and its direct applicability to democratic requirements (knowledge for important problem solving, universal and equal participation in decisions, rights, and equal encouragement). Cooperative education cannot used to a pretext for the negation of individual rights. A student's right not to participate in cooperative education has to be respected. Nor should it be permissible for students to cooperate to gain advantage at the expense of others. It is just as important for students to learn where cooperation is inappropriate as it is for them to learn how to cooperate.

Cooperative learning is no panacea. If the class activity and goals are antidemocratic, incorporating cooperative learning will openly solidify the school's antidemocratic structures and intentions.

Obfuscating the Preparation for Citizenship: Confusing the Public and Private

The close identification of woman with the private sphere of life (Pateman, 1989), helps explain why so many feminists insist on defining the personal as political. And in some instances they are correct. There are political issues in the definition of the private and in the protection of privacy. Certainly, the issues that Pateman illuminated that have served to deny women access to public arenas is clearly a political issue, as are intrusions into private lives (e.g, abortion and the differential treatment prostitutes receive when compared to the considerations given to the men who hire them). But to go further and define feelings about self-political, makes a mockery of education for citizenship competence. The political, by definition, is transcending self to that which is shared with others. Political requires the resolution of a conflict through collective action. Democratic politics requires that the resolution occurs after everyone has had equal opportunity to be informed, has had equal participation in the decision-making process, everyone's rights have been preserved, and the decision does not give unfair advantage to one group at the expense of another. A preoccupation with the personal has led to a significant decline in democratic politics. The knowledge dimension of democratic education should provide students with sufficient information to differentiate between the personal and the political. The establishment of a boundary between the personal and the political brings sense and sensibility to different kinds of conversation and debate. Rather than confusing the political with the private it is necessary at the outset to cultivate an understanding what is subject to a political decision and what rightfully is excluded because of its private nature.

Can Problem Solving be Taught in the Abstract?

Some of the reform directions in recent years have sought to teach abstract problem-solving skills. Students have been directed to learn how to solve contrived problems. There is no investment in the solution, nor is anybody negatively affected by the solution. There is limited utility in such exercises. Nothing is more meaningless, for example, than to ask students 'what would have happened if Columbus had landed on the western shore of the United States rather than on the Atlantic shore. Such a question trivializes history, removes context, minimizes the impact colonialism had on the way the United States and the modern world developed. It is impossible to appreciate the roots of racism from such a question.

Democratic education is used to solve problems that are real, not imaginary, important not trivial, difficult not easy. This is most true in the preparation for democratic citizenship. Democratic citizenship has been taught as a fuzzy abstraction and students by the droves have responded by distancing themselves from it. Efforts to revitalize the study of history do strive to make the subject more concrete, but as we have tried to point out, insufficiently so. Citizenship is not an abstract quality, it is the possession of precise skills and knowledges required for participation in the solution of very real and difficult problems. There is no abstract solution to poverty, justice, violence, crime, the preservation of the environment, and so on. There are specific costs and benefits to all proposed solutions. There are no solutions to serious problems where everyone wins. The world may not be zero-sum, but it is sufficiently finite that in every feasible solution of an important problem, in order for some to gain, others must lose. For students to emerge as democratic citizens they must be able to calculate the positive and negative impact of any solution on the various individuals or groups that are affected, and on something much more difficult to define—the common good. Something as deliciously ambiguous as the common good can only become part of the political process when effort is made to define it in very clear and precise economic, social, political, and environmental terms. Anything short of that will leave us in the paralyzed state we now find ourselves.

What Happens to "Subjects" in the Democratic Classroom?

Subjects have always been arbitrary and in most instances essentially useless. Why useless? Because the knowledge cannot be readily used to solve an important personal or social problem. With "subjects", students are rendered passive. Furthermore when an education is organized by subjects, student feelings of helplessness and hopelessness is fostered. Freire (1968) called the process of the teacher depositing subject knowledge into the head of the student the "bank" approach to education. We must come to recognize that the bank is bankrupt and needs to be foreclosed.

Does that mean that subjects are abandoned and we start over as if they never existed? Of course not. It means adopting a strategy for replacing subjects with a problem solving curriculum, and during the transition phase teachers shape the study of subjects by showing students how the subject that has been learned can be applied to the solving of a specific problems.

It is conceivable that subjects have such a hold on people's understanding of education that there may never be totally replaced with a problem-solving curriculum. A total substitution may not be necessary. What is necessary is for students to gain sufficient understanding that after graduation from high school they can meaningfully participate in the development and analysis of solutions to all of the world's important problems.

What Happens to Reading, Writing and Arithmetic? Science? History and Government? The Arts? Vocational Programs? Health and Physical Education? The command of all of these "subjects" are vital to the development of a democratic citizen. A democratic citizen is literate. It is impossible to be a democratic citizen and not be a proficient reader, writer, and rhetorician. It is impossible to be a competent democratic citizen and not be proficient in mathematics. Every decision that a citizen must make requires complicated calculations. Increasingly political decisions require a working knowledge of science. To make reasoned decisions on such issues as environmental stability, world peace, elimination of poverty, control of crime, requires an understanding of scientific methods, the capacity to make sense of scientific findings and the permissible inferences that derive from them. Rather than reducing the importance of the curriculum now organized as discrete subjects, a problem-solving education elevates their importance by transforming them. A problem-solving education provides a teacher with a sensible answer to the often asked question, "Why do I have to learn that?" Instead of a lame, "You'll need it when you grow up," the teacher can provide a crisp response and show specifically how the learning is related to the problem the student wants to solve. In fact, everything we now call a subject can be incorporated as a resource to be used in the solving of some important problem. But it is the problem that determines how much of which discipline needs to be utilized.

Problem-solving education deprives "subjects" of their exalted status by putting something more important in its place. Subjects no longer are held in high esteem by students. That is the lament of the traditionalists (A. Bloom, 1987; D'Souza, 1991). Their rant does not come together as a coherent analysis, nor will all the classical courses and renaissance men return the world to something wondrous that was lost in the veil of history. Students in the future will challenge the worth of any educational offering as students should. The value of the tomorrow's education will be tested by the teacher's capacity to make a persuasive argument for its usefulness to the solution of some clearly defined, generally recognized, important problem.

SUMMARY

One of the most difficult problems to be solved is the creation of a workable government created by the people and accountable to them. Such a government requires competent citizens. Only a revamped education can prepare such a citizen. An education whose goal is a competent democratic citizen utilizes cooperative learning projects and organically combines the study of the history of democratic thought and projects, with a student government that grapples with real problems, with community service that makes a significant contribution to the building of community while at the same time such community service is so organized as to facilitate the attainment of specifically defined democratic skills and knowledges. Such an education is organized developmentally in ways that are consistent with current knowledge about cognitive growth. Such an education signals the way that fragmented subjects can be reconceptualized into problem-solving curriculum.

Chapter 4

The Problem-Solving Curriculum in a Democratic Classroom: Helping Students Learn How to Solve Important Personal and Social Problems

In this chapter we continue our discussion of a problem-solving curriculum, emphasizing the importance of relevance in curriculum. Relevance is tied to importance, but important knowledge cannot be theoretical abstraction, neither can it be self-proclaimed nor imposed by authoritarian decree. Important knowledge is negotiated. It is linked to goals that students recognize as important. We begin our discussion of problem-solving education with preparation for employment because: students do not have to be persuaded of its importance, and because of the exaggerated importance currently given to work in education.

Preparation for work provides a particularly useful way to introduce an essential feature of a democratic curriculum—

ecology. Every educational activity is ecological and has to be understood as contextual, involving human impact on the social and physical environment and the environment's influence on the human. Every educational activity requires a delicate balance between providing a public or social good and meeting the needs of the individual. Ecology and social-personal balance are of particular importance in preparation for work because the student not only must be prepared to enter the work world as it is, but must also be prepared to participate in the deliberations that change the nature of work that can have far-reaching implications for ecological balance. He or she must be able to find employment in the existing world but also must participate in public policy to ensure that there is work to find.

In this chapter, we discuss in some detail the means by which students learn to solve problems developmentally; we introduce the Vygotsky notion of the importance of play in cognitive development and note how the eradication of play from school has made the classroom unnecessarily grim. We end the chapter with an evaluation of prevailing practice and suggest a transitional process from a subject-based emphasis to a reconstructed school organized around problem solving. We introduce a resonating principle: If the lesson cannot persuasively and pervasively define a specific problem that will be solved by its mastery, it should not be taught.

THE SALIENCY OF CURRICULUM

Curriculum is the reason for schools. Everyone believes schools should be places where what students learn is important. The consensus unravels on the definition of important. Democratic education comes into play both in the definition of important knowledge and in the procedures used to arrive at the definition.

Current definitions of important knowledge and how the definitions were reached cannot be defended either by logic or by evidence. No case is even attempted to establish the importance for what is taught in schools to students. When students ask, "Why do I have to learn this?" the answers provided, if any are at all, border on the nonsensical. Students rather quickly discover that if they persist trying for competent answers they will find themselves in trouble and suffer accordingly. As a consequence, those students who invest in schooling do so because they see school as an obstacle that one must hurdle as part of a course to some desired *future* designation; derive gratifications from feelings of competence, belongingness, usefulness, and understanding from participation in school activities (more on this when we discuss equal encouragement); or find that going along with the school program is less difficult than actively resisting it.

Very few students believe what they are learning in school is important. And these few cannot make a case for the importance of school knowledge for the solution of important personal or social problems.

What is worse for the future of education is the absence of serious debate about important knowledge. It is possible that after a careful and extensive exploration of all possibilities subjects would emerge as the best way to organize the curriculum. But such an examination has not taken place. If nothing else, this book may generate interest and movement toward such a debate. As it is, curriculum is ordained and imposed. Commissions and committees are created (almost at whim) to issue pronouncements of needed change (or to denounce changes that have occurred). Pressure is placed on schools to accept those changes (or to return to normalcy), and after the dust settles things remain pretty much as they have always been. The key actors in the educational process are never included in the discussion. Students are given no voice. Only a ridiculously small number of carefully selected parents are allowed into the decision-making process. The teacher's voice, like the parent's, is barely heard and unrepresentative. The vast majority of teachers find themselves simultaneously attacked for real and imagined problems in the school while they are held responsible for immediate introduction of wide-sweeping curriculum changes that they neither support nor necessarily understand. Except for a brief period in the 1970s when experiments on school-based curriculum were conducted, and teacher knowledge and experience were valued, teachers in general have had limited influence in curriculum design and policy development.

If the logic for existing curriculum is specious, the evidence to support it rests on even shakier ground. The primary criteria used to defend or attack what students learn in school are scores on standardized tests. These measures have never been able to successfully respond to the criticism of race, class, and gender bias (National Center for Fair and Open Testing). But even if standardized tests were fair indications of what students learn in school, it is not shown how that learning is either transferable or generalizable. Moreover, students cannot use school-derived knowledge to solve personal or social problems. It is far worse than that. The criteria used to measure school performance tend to dictate the curriculum. As tests gain increasing power in decisions that involve schools, teachers are covertly influenced or overtly coerced to teach to the test (Bishop, 1995; Cohen, 1988, Darling-Hammond, 1986).

> Education thus becomes an art of depositing, in which the students are the depositories and the teacher the depositor. Instead of communicating, the teacher issues communiques and makes deposits which the students patiently receive, memorize and repeat. This is the "banking" concept of education, in which the scope of action allowed to the student extends only as far as a receiving, filing and storing the deposits. (Freire, 1968, p. 58)

Knowledge in a democratic classroom is useful! Students are given reasons to believe that what they learn in school is needed to solve the problems that they recognize need solving. The problems are both personal and social. In a democratic classroom there is balance between the personal and the social. Teachers take pains to explain why that balance is necessary. Personal problems cannot be solved in an unlivable environment or in a social world destabilized to such an extent that fear of victimization prevents normal social interactions, or if the economy is unable to generate a sufficient number of good jobs for everyone, or if persons are denied access to jobs, housing, or social recognition because of race, religion, ethnicity, class, or gender. Conversely, social problems cannot be solved by persons overwhelmed by personal problems.

> We face many insistently urgent problems. Our prosperity and even our survival depend on the solution of these problems—the threat of nuclear war, the exhaustion of essential resources and of the supplies of energy, the pollution or spoilage of the environment, the spiralling inflation accompanied by the spread of unemployment.
> To solve these problems, we need resourceful and innovative leadership. For that to arise and be effective, an educated populace is needed. Trained intelligence—not only on the part of leaders, but also as followers. (Adler, 1982b, p. 20)

DEMOCRATIC PROBLEM-SOLVING EDUCATION: REINTRODUCING RELEVANCE INTO EDUCATIONAL DISCOURSE

Students have opinions and they have problems. Both provide a basis for relevance in the determination of useful knowledge in a democratic classroom. In a democratic classroom students learn how to back up opinions with logic and evidence. They also learn how to predict the logical consequences inherent in their opinions. Currently, there is not the slightest hint that even our "best" students are able to support their opinions with logic or evidence, nor is there any reason to believe they have tried to calculate the likely consequences if their opinions would become social policy. Democratic education not only brings intellectual defense of ideas into the classroom for the elite, it does the same for everyone else.

But even more than intellectual involvement in important ideas, the democratic classroom aims to be engrossing. It is organized to attract and hold the student's attention. Making education interesting for everyone is one reason it earns the right to be called democratic. Or to put it another way, an uninteresting or uninvolved education cannot be democratic. In a democratic classroom, students are persuaded to be actively interested in becoming knowledgeable about important matters.

Who Determines Important Knowledge?

In the absence of an independent ground, neither God nor science determine important knowledge. In order for everyone to accept the definition of important knowledge, everyone needs to be involved in the debate over that definition. Students must be assisted to learn how to make a persuasive case for importance. Although such a process will not lead to unanimous agreement, it should lead to considerable progress toward a common understanding. The process should continue until the agreement reached is near enough to a consensus to bring a shared sense of legitimacy to a classroom activity. The process should be extensive enough to convince even those who dispute the decision that they were given the opportunity to fully participate in the debate. In the absence of consensus, the debate continues or an understanding among rivaling groups is reached. For example, if the unresolved dispute concerns curriculum, the same general topic can be treated very differently in different classes.

Establishing a procedure whereby the importance of knowledge can be assessed, although complex and confusing, is also immensely rewarding. Education moves from the humdrum to the exciting. Students are elevated from regurgitators to inventors and discoverers. Nothing is taken for granted. Everyday is an adventure. Contexts continually change and that means important knowledge also changes.

Knowledge in a democratic classroom is not stored for future utility. It is utilized daily and the utilization contributes to its constant reformation. Such an approach to knowledge can succeed only when there is thorough understanding and an appreciation of conflict. The accumulation of important knowledge will not occur if the authority overwhelms the student, nor will it occur if debate is truncated prior to a serious and thorough search for a generally acceptable conclusion. Differences should not be allowed to remain unresolved simply because neither time nor effort was expended to reach an agreement. From a democratic perspective, when there is no sustained effort to resolve differences, all diverse opinions are equally valid. Only after all parties have agreed at the outset to strain for shared understanding, to commit themselves to both present carefully reasoned proposals and to listen to carefully reasoned rejoinders, is it possible to come to a temporary understanding of important knowledge.

IN A DEMOCRATIC CLASSROOM PERSONAL AND SOCIAL PROBLEMS ARE SUBJECTED TO AN ECOLOGICAL ANALYSIS

In a democratic classroom preparing students to deal responsibly with important problems takes the form of ecological analysis. The problem is presented as an interaction between the individual and the environment. The solution to the problem requires both individual adaptation to and socially responsible actions on the environment. The four requirements of democratic education—knowledge, participation, rights, and equal encouragement—enter into every solution. A democratic curriculum recognizes that humans are by nature an environmentally altering, interdependent species. The challenge is to find ways to collectively agree on alterations of the environment that both sustain livability while producing and distributing resources in a just manner (i.e., striving to create a world in which every inhabitant can enjoy a useful and gratifying life). That is a daunting challenge. It will not be perfectly met. But, if it is not presented as the background for all educational problem solving, we will continue to have what we have now, a bad situation deteriorating into something worse.

Race is one area that begs for democratic treatment. It is our failure to examine race relations in a broad social context that has left this issue unresolved with periodic outbreaks of violence and a similar lack of analysis results in continued aggression against women. It is our failure to develop an analysis that includes both environmental and economic considerations that has led to a livelihood (employment) versus livability (a healthy environment) mentality to the detriment of both a healthy environment and a healthy economy.

Race issues, gender issues, the environment, and the economy cannot be treated adequately unless these are placed in the context of student preparation for an existing although rapidly changing work world. Discussions about race, gender, the environment, and economics become exercises in sophistry unless the distribution of work and its availability plays a central role in that discussion.

On one hand, education about work must demystify the existing and projected work world so that every student can make an informed choice for a future occupation. On the other hand, the student has to be provided with information and helped to develop an analysis that would inspire every student to participate in the invention of an economy, and more narrowly a work world, that has the potential to provide everyone with useful and fulfilling employment.

Examining Preparation for Work

The simplest but most unsatisfactory part of the problem from an educational viewpoint is preparing students for the existing work world. Even this simple problem has its complications. Preparation for work is perceived as a fundamentally different problem by students and employers. Students, who want their schooling to provide them the skills, the knowledge, the experiences, and the understanding that would qualify them for "good" jobs, perceive the problem as limited access to, and eligibility for, good jobs. Employers perceive the problem as schools failing to provide them with the quality of workers they claim they once had and now need. The National Commission appointed by President Ronald Reagan, in its celebrated 1983 Report, *A Nation at Risk*, condemned state-run schools for failing to prepare the workforce needed by the United States to remain competitive in the emerging transnational economy. Similar charges have been leveled in every other country striving to be competitive in a global economy (e.g., Department of Employment and Training, 1991). Student concerns have not been considered in these analyses; to the contrary, the preponderance of criticism condemns permissiveness (i.e., inviting students into the decision-making process). The prevailing opinion is that education suffers from too much "democracy" (Chubb & Moe, 1990).

A democratic classroom encourages students to carefully assess the validity of the *Nation at Risk* and DEET arguments, while also analyzing the employment opportunities that existing economic policy has created. Students should be encouraged to ponder whether there are sufficient employment opportunities to enable everyone to obtain a fulfilling job. They should question whether the current approach to the production and distribution of goods and services is sufficient to provide everyone with a quality life. It falls to the democratic teacher to cajole and provoke students to invent and defend with logic and evidence systems that could provide better solutions than that which they criticize. The analysis of what is, and the examination of various proposals, provides students with the opportunity to debate a wide range of proposed policies and to identify the positive and negative features of each. Part of that analysis is to help students arrive at some unifying conceptions of quality life, acceptable levels of unemployment, means by which work is created, the differential impact on the environment of different approaches to work, and the means by which work can be accessed.

All Education is "Vocational Education"—Unfortunately. Preparing students for the work world is fast becoming the sole credible justification of secondary and higher education. Learning for the sake of learning may inspire a few academics; it sounds pompous and stupid to most young people. Some stay in school solely to play sports, and even in this instance there is often a vocational component bouncing around as part aspiration and part fantasy. This is especially true for those students who have not been encouraged toward academic success.

How Vocational Education Currently "Works." Vocational education continues to be organized as a static entity. The work world is perceived as an unalterable given, the curriculum is fixed and fed to the student who is then stamped as prepared for some small category of work. Characteristically, the curriculum has little intellectual challenge. The student is more trained than educated. The school system places all the onus for failure on the student (although employers blame the schools for failure to adequately prepare the student). Vocational education is linear and undynamic. The individual student enrolls in a particular vocational program and on satisfactory completion of the program is certified to be a welder, clerk-typist, auto repairer, computer maintainer and repairer, food service worker, and so on, and thus eligible to seek employment in that particular field. That many are unable to find employment in areas where they have been certified as qualified, and conversely, many find themselves successfully employed in these fields without benefit of a vocational education has not altered the approach significantly. The system is not only authoritarian, arbitrary, and inflexible; it is also extremely inefficient. Feedback is inconsistent and frequently nonexistent. Employer contact is hit and miss and often more condemning than useful. Student feedback is all but dismissed. Moreover, in times of rapid change, it becomes virtually impossible for school-based vocational education to keep current and thus students are trained on obsolete equipment.

In reality, schools meet most of the assigned responsibility for work preparation through culling (i.e., separating those who will use higher education to obtain credentials needed for professional careers from those limited to unskilled or semi-skilled occupations).

Although schools long have been given the responsibility for preparing students for the work world, little respect has been given for what was being done. Every decade or so the approach to vocational education is revised. Titles and course descriptions are changed. What never changes is a patently undemocratic social reproduction. Schools continue to prepare different strata of students for very different work futures. The process begins early with ability grouping in the elementary schools, becomes rigidly defined in educational tracks in the secondary school, and is further reinforced with the credentials that can only be obtained by the small minority of students allowed entry first into higher education and then to graduate professional schools (Oakes, 1985). Such an approach serves to restrict the number of applicants for high pay-high status positions to manageable proportions. Deeply ingrained throughout—among teachers, administrators and students—is the belief that ability and motivation vary so greatly that maintaining all students in the same educational stream is absurd. Thus, curriculum is split to accommodate believed differences in capacity and desire. Status goes to the tertiary preparation courses and subjects, to the people who teach them, and to the students who take them. Assignment to track is greatly influenced by race, ethnicity, and social class (Oakes, 1992; Selvin, 1992). And thus, historical arrangements by race, ethnicity, and social class are sustained. Well-situated students continue to get most of the good jobs, the farther down the economic ladder, the less there is available. The maintenance of a prejudicial system can be challenged on fairness, but there may be an even worse consequence from such a system. The lack of democracy may produce an inadequately prepared workforce at every level. The current system locks out the vast majority of the lower income strata from the opportunity to become medical doctors or rocket scientists and, as a consequence, potentially valuable talent is not permitted to develop. The other side of such a divisive system is that many of those bestowed with august credentials may have only illusory competence.

There have been some well-advertised attempts to build partnerships between the business community and schools where businesses generate the worksites and the schools tailor the instructional program to the challenges encountered on the job. These modified apprentices programs have not been very successful. Schools have great difficulty changing curriculum to meld it with job-related experiences. Furthermore, in the most successful programs the entry job, from which there is limited upward mobility without continued education, is often far more gratifying than school experiences (Dayton & Pearl 1987), which means that these programs facilitate premature school withdrawal. It is impossible to have an equitable school to work program as long as the notion of differential ability is so pervasive, or where choice is tied to a needs-based definition of equity (Gewirtz et al., 1995).

In a Democratic Classroom, Students Make the Choices

In a democratic classroom, students are provided with the knowledge they need to make informed choices. This begins with demystification of the work world. Democratic preparation for existing work begins with a serious effort to determine what students need to know to make responsible choices about future work. Necessary knowledge and related experiences are organized developmentally in a coherent scope and sequence. From the individual student's perspective, the problem is knowing what he or she needs to know and do in order to get the best possible job. And from the student as citizen perspective, the problem is knowing which employment policy he or she should support for the public good (i.e., in the best interest of society).

Neither the individual problem of career choice nor the social problem of the optimum employment policy can be solved without access to a relevant body of information. As background, every student should be provided with core knowledge about the terrain of the work world and projections for its future. They should learn to use such resources as as the *Statistical Abstract,* the Internet, OECD projections, and various local resources to examine employment, unemployment, and those not accounted for, by age, education, gender, race, and ethnicity. Students (preferably working in groups, for reasons explained later) would then present various findings to the class or school-parent groups, and, at some stage, to state and local governments. The findings are an invitation to broad-ranging discussions with effort made to identify and assess many possible interpretations. One of the interpretations that will surface will derive from deep-seated distrust of any statistics and that concern will become a part of an ongoing discussion. Students need to be able to establish, to their own satisfaction, the validity of any statement, and struggle to find ways to develop shared understandings of "truth." They will struggle to find satisfactory answers to the following questions: Do the findings of differential employment success by race, ethnicity, gender, and class reflect employer bias? Does the bias of existing workers on jobs tend to drive minorities away? Do the differences reflect a different quality of education received by different categories of students? Is it a matter of logistics—not being where the jobs are? If so, where are the jobs?

By studying work trends, students learn that the demand for educated workers continues to increase, but that the increase is uneven. In the United States, no more than one third of the currently employed work in jobs that require more than a high school diploma or 2 years in a tertiary school. As long as "good" jobs exist in far fewer numbers than there are job seekers, the competition for them will be intense. And given that reality, the pressure on parents to secure for their children a competitive advantage will also be intense. Students should examine the range of possibilities that exist when the demand for good jobs vastly exceeds the supply of those jobs, and they should be made aware of the efforts that have been made to maintain special privilege and competitive advantage.

In developing proposals for employment policies, students should also examine what the future holds, whether current trends will continue, what is likely to happen in good times and during recessions.

> Richard Freeman of Harvard University, found when overall unemployment declines by one percentage point the employment rate increases by 1.9 percentage points for all youth, but by 4.3 points for Black youth. (Breslow, 1995, p. 2)

Unemployment jumps during recessions, but economic downturns are not the only factor affecting employment. Changing outlooks and restructuring have effects as well. In recent years, the highest skilled workers have been victims of layoffs as multinational corporations downsized, reengineered, and outsourced. Students should, through discussion and research, demystify these terms and consider them in their proposed policy initiatives. Articles such as the seven-part series that appeared in *The New York Times* in the midst of a prolonged economic upturn detailing the insecurities that "A Downsizing of America" has wrought (*New York Times,* 1996) can be used to instigate a critique of the distribution of work and stimulate proposed alternatives that can be researched and debated. Part of any education for work must deal with that uncertainty and students need to examine possible avenues for increasing job security. Students should also discuss the role of government as a part of the ongoing employment picture, both as permanent public services (e.g., police, teachers, public works), and as last resort short-term employment during downturns in the economy. In a sense, every high school should in its treatment of work policies organize itself into a think tank merging the attributes of the conservative (Hoover Institution; Heritage Foundation) and the liberal (Institute for Policy Studies) think-tanks as well as think tanks that cannot be neatly categorized.

WHAT DO ALL OF THESE "STATISTICS" AND NEW TERMINOLOGIES HAVE TO DO WITH EDUCATION FOR WORK?

> Therefore, since the world has still
> Much good, but much less good than ill,
> And while the sun and moon endure

Luck's a chance, but trouble's sure,
I'd face it as a wise man would,
And train for ill and not for good.
A. E. Housman, Epilogue

What we know about the work world becomes the primary resource out of which curriculum and instruction that address problems in that area are developed. The first requirement of a democratic education is providing all students with sufficient knowledge to make an informed decision on his or her work future. Students must not only know the statistics, they must know how the statistics were derived. They must also be provided with challenges to these statistics, alternate descriptions and explanations and, if the general conclusion is that prospects are poor, different ideas for improving the situation. Education for and about work is, like all education, an examination of various proposals, assessment of different approaches, and the logic and evidence on which these are based. Such education involves debating different ideas in different contexts and with differing assumptions. Students need to be prepared to deal with good and difficult times.

A DEMOCRATIC APPROACH TO WORK PREPARATION IS DEVELOPMENTAL

Preparation for Work in Elementary School. Very early in their school careers, children should be given a carefully grounded sense of the relationship between education and work. In elementary school, students should become realistically familiar with the organization and distribution of work. They should gain a firm grasp of what people do in various occupations and what it takes to get into those occupations. This can be done in many ways. Medical doctors, computer programmers, lawyers, bus drivers, chefs, accountants, and so forth, can be invited to converse with students in classrooms. Students should prepare for these visits with teacher-led classroom discussions and by conducting rudimentary research. The visits by people in different occupations should be followed by debriefing sessions. Students can also visit worksites and reflect on what was seen afterward. Literature and biography are necessary components in preparation for informed choice of future work. For example, students could do research on scientist

Marie Curie, the only woman to win two Nobel prizes. Students can examine her early life, how she became interested in science, and what she did as a child for fun. Students should be able to present to other students a dramatic sketch on Marie's choice of science as a life career, what particular things she did as a child to move her in the direction of her life's work, what kind of encouragement she received, and so on. In a similar way, other figures such as George Washington Carver, Elizabeth Blackwell, Karl Frederich Gauss, Maria Montessori, Sally Morgan, Joan Kirner, Margaret Thatcher, and so forth, can come to life as persons to be understood and emulated. Biographies should not emphasize uniqueness or "genius" qualities, but rather how and what a particular person did to prepare for a life's work and what can be learned from a particular life that can be useful in planning one's own future. Visits, stories, and biographies must be integrated and organized for active problem solving—the selection and securing of a career or, more realistically, several careers. Unconnected bits and fragments passively learned may actually be worse than no discussion about work.

The understanding of work as preparation for informed choice has to be woven through a variety of classroom experiences. Although it is impossible to expect all work to be equally valued, it is both possible and desirable that all work be treated with respect. In their reading and their discussions with a wide range of occupations, students should be encouraged to discover how humans derive gratifications of competence, usefulness, belonging, security, hope, excitement, meaning, and creativity in almost every work activity. An overemphasis on credentialism and a glorification of wealth can create dissension in families and lessen the respect children have for what their parents do for a living. Shame rather than admiration and pride for what parents do is the logical consequence of most school approaches to work. This is only one of many ways that schools become accessories to youth marginalization, drift, and high-risk activities (Carrington, 1993; Knight, 1985a, 1997; Polk & Schafer, 1972).

No occupation should be viewed as demeaning, but at the same time it is important that the presentations be such that choice is open-ended. Elementary students should be encouraged to dream and the rest of their education should be designed to help them make their dreams a reality. The delineation of a path to fulfillment of a dream with specification of pitfalls and detours brings necessary uncertainty and excitement to the education. The student should be given every opportunity to fully appreciate what must be done to accomplish a designated goal. In many ways, the recreation and refinement of dreams is at the heart of elementary education. The Irish poet W.B. Yeats speaks to the importance of dreams. His poem can initiate a discussion and stimulate an ongoing commitment to the dream process. The more "disadvantaged" the student, the more important are the dreams.

> Had I the heavens' embroidered cloths,
> Enwrought with golden and silver light,
> The blue and the dim and the dark cloths
> Of night and light and half-light,
> I would spread the cloths under your feet:
> But I, being poor, have only my dreams;
> I have spread my dreams under your feet;
> Tread softly because you tread on my dreams.
>   W.B. Yeats ("He Wishes for the Cloths of Heaven," 1899)

In a democratic classroom, students are asked to unleash imaginations. And there is no place where this is more important than in the consideration of "What I am going to be when I grow up." That few of us have realized the dreams of our youth does not lessen their value. Dreams provide focus and exhilaration in tough times. An extraordinary part of the excitement and allure of sport for the young is the dreams that one attached to the activity. Who has not pictured himself winning a World Series by striking out Barry Bonds for the third out, or herself returning one of Steffi Graf's powerful serves for the winning point at Wimbledon, or kicking the winning Grand Final goal. Who, when shooting baskets alone, has not said to him or herself, "It's 2 seconds to go, we're behind 100-98" just before launching a jump shot from beyond the 3-point line?"

A child can survive every disappointment in elementary school except dream-killing. Take away the dreams of children, particularly children mired in poverty and surrounded by crime, violence, and squalor and they are more than abandoned, they are brutalized. When students stop dreaming, ugly things begin to happen. When dreams are killed, nightmares take their place. When children cease to dream, the pessimistic "reality" of drugs and gangs and violence and sexually transmitted diseases and children having babies takes over. The killing of dreams brings out the worst in all of us. And a lot of dream-killing takes place in elementary school. Dream-killing is one of the devastating effects of the sorting process. When students are sorted they are told in no uncertain terms what dreams are permissible. When students are ticketed for low-status work stations, their dreams are trampled. By the fourth grade, students have been given very clear indications what they can dream. In a democratic classroom, students dream and their dreams are represented in writing, pictorially, on film, by music, or as theater. As mentioned, earlier, biography and literature can help add substance to a dream.

The major goals in elementary school in the area of vocational education is to build a foundation of knowledge that can be used for decision making in the existing work world, and to instill a spirit of openness to new ideas. All students should be discouraged from decisions that would preclude a later reconsideration. In the elementary grades, the emphasis is on positive features of all careers. But positive does not mean sugar-coating or distorting.

Currently, children in elementary school learn about work in elementary schools in much the way they learn about history, Africa, or Mars—in the absence of context. Work is presented as a fixed and mysterious system. There is not the slightest suggestion that work is created in response to social and economic policies. That is, tax strategies and other fiscal policies, occupational health, disability, environmental protection and other regulations, wage policies and union negotiations, licensing and credentials, tariffs, and the government as first, last or nonemployer all strongly influence employment opportunity and in many instances determine who works at what. Dorfman argued that children are unable to develop well-organized social philosophies because they are fed a distorted history presented in the tradition of *Babar the Elephant* at best (the glorification of progress, Western culture, and civilization), or in the tradition of Walt Disney at worst (the denial of history). Work in elementary school is presented as either a distortion of reality or is disconnected from reality. The grim and unhealthy aspects of work should not be overdramatized, but it is essential that elementary students be given a realistic foundation for their future work life.

Once a foundation has been established, students should be given a general idea of the skills and knowledge required for different occupations and how work is organized by ladders and lattices. The science base of a medical education should be explained, as should the relationship between medical doctors and others in the health providing occupations, such as nurses, health administrators, laboratory technicians, and so fourth. The skills and knowledges required for occupations should be dissected and arranged developmentally. Efforts should be made to explain to students what they are currently being taught prepares them for future academic work and this in turn prepares them for different careers. In the elementary grades, students should receive road maps to different work futures and be encouraged to travel extensively along a variety of paths before deciding on a life career.

THE GENERAL VALUE OF PLAY IN SCHOOL

Next in importance to dreams in elementary school is play. Play is an important element in all school activity and remains important as the child develops. The characteristics of play, however changes as children develop. In the earliest years play, is an introduction to school and smooths the transition from that which a person does just for fun and that which is tied to a mandatory responsibility. Mark Twain, in *Tom Sawyer*, conveys the way most of us have come to look at work. "Work consists of whatever a body is obliged to do, and play consists of whatever a body is not obliged to do" (*Tom Sawyer*, 1876, Chap. 2). School is perceived to be the equivalent of work by most if not all children. That is in part because of the overly close identification of school to vocational preparation, and partly because of the widespread belief that students must be coerced to learn. The heavy emphasis on coercive education is increasingly burdensome over time, negatively affecting both student and teacher. Later, we discuss the importance of play in teaching and argue that the more teachers consider what they do to be hard work, the less successful they will be. Today, fun and school are seen as mutually incompatible. In fact, there is widespread suspicion of the value of an educational experience if students appear to be enjoying it. A democratic classroom turns that around and makes school less like work and more like play. The transformation is made, not by reducing the intellectual experience of the school, but by raising it. Play is an invitation to students to be creative, to use their imagination. But play is neither undisciplined nor anti-intellectual.

Play is an important element in every phase or aspect of democratic education. Every curricular emphasis can be improved with play. Seemingly insoluble problems take on new dimensions when students are encouraged to play with solutions. One of our criticisms of postmodernism is, that although it claims playfulness, very little play is tolerated. Postmodernism is more snide than playful.

Playfulness as students grow older has to be directed to imaginative solutions and becomes less egocentric and more sociocentric. As children develop, their play becomes more social and less solitary.

We chose the preparation for work to introduce and discuss play because of our observation of how much children like to play at work when they are very young and how this fun aspect of this activity tends to be extinguished as they grow older.

We were drawn to play by our interest in Vygotsky. Vygotsky (1978) attributed a number of important qualities to play and its relation to cognitive development that should be considered by educators. He, emphasized the importance of motivation and the attachment of motivation to needs. Failure to attend to student needs will necessarily lead to the stunting of cognitive growth. As far back as Pestalozzi (1746-1827), the relationship between need gratification and cognitive growth was clearly established; and yet, there is very little application of that principle in schools today. Nowhere is the lack of appreciation of need gratification more apparent than in preparation for work. To complicate matters, educators need not only to know how to gratify needs at any particular moment, but they must further understand how motivation and needs change as students grow cognitively and how these changes are to be incorporated into the planning and evaluation of class-room activities.

Vygotsky argued that young children need activities that bring immediate gratifications—no 3-year-old wants to do something a few days in the future. Here, his views can be contrasted with Sigmund Freud's "pleasure principle." The difference is that Vygotsky believed the child's insistence on immediate gratification is grounded in reality, albeit a primitive reality (Kozulin, 1990), whereas Freud argued that the ego develops through encounters with reality and in that process learns how to delay gratification. In the chapter on equal encouragement we show how the "pleasure" and "reality" principles have undergirded one "deficit" explanation of differences by class in scholastic achievement thereby deflecting attention away from the ways an inequitable system perpetuates itself. Although attracted to Vygotsky, we also differ from him in important respects. We believe the immediate gratification is important at every age and that the differences in school success by class, race, ethnicity, and gender can be explained by the way classroom is organized to provide immediate gratifications of such vital needs as security, relief from unnecessary pain, meaning, belonging, usefulness, competence, excitement, creativity, and hope to some students while denying these gratifications to others (see chapter on equal encouragement for a detailed explanation of how the existing system is organized to ration success and how the inequities of the current system can be changed to an equal encouragement system).

Vygotsky, unsatisfied with previous definitions of play, made imagination the defining characteristic of play. While emphasizing motivation, he also drew attention to the relationship that motivation has to cognitive processes and the importance of context—the particular circumstances of play. But probably even more important to educators, particularly democratic educators, is his understanding of the role of play in cognitive development.

To Vygotsky the imaginary situation in any play is organized by rules. He use as an example a child playing mother with a doll. Vygotsky insisted that this play can only occur if the child obeys the understood rules of maternal behavior. As children develop their use of imagination, play changes. Over time, children's play evolves from games with an overt imaginary situation with covert rules to games with overt rules and covert imaginary situations (Vygotsky, 1978).

According to Vygotsky, young children are unable to differentiate meaning from perception and in preschool ages, a stick can become a horse. Play in this transitional stage separates meaning from a thing or situation. One of the distinctive attributes of human beings is attaching meaning to perceptions. For the young child, the perceived object dominates the relationship. At a certain crucial stage the capacity of the child to successfully create reality is diminished. A child is limited in what can be given meaning. Not everything can be made into a "horse." Play at any age allows imagination to stretch meaning, but as the child grows older the more he or she is bounded by "reality." This does not end the importance of play in education. But for play to be a powerful influence in the education of older children, the rules have to be universally accepted and fairly applied and the emphasis has to be shifted to imagination. There is no better place to put imagination to work than in encouraging students to think about future careers and in imagining how a society should organize work.

There is yet another reason for bringing play into the classroom. Play helps to socialize children—sometimes too much so. Play generates pressure against impulsive action. The reliance on rules conflict with spontaneous action. A child is most under self-control when at play. There is no better way for a teacher to understand the unwillingness of a child to submit to school rules than to realize that the school from the child's perspective is no longer play. But far more important than the control dimensions of play is the aspects that Vygotsky attributed to it. It is through play that a child reaches new achievements and these achievements establish the foundation for more complex cognitive actions and value systems.

Play has the capacity to create what Vygotsky called a zone of proximal development (ZPD). In play, a child can transcend prior levels of performance and can establish new levels of expectation. Because Vygotsky found in play all developmental tendencies, it is a major contributor to development. Thus, play is similar to good instruction it provides a background for changes in needs and consciousness. By acting in imaginary situations, the child begins to develop a sense of where he or she wants to go and initiates the formation of real—life plans. According to Vygotsky, a child attains and displays the highest level of preschool development through play. With the way school is presently organized, play is underutilized in later grades. In the democratic classroom using play to stretch imagination is important in all grades.

Play as Preparation for Work

Children love to play at being grown-up. Playing doctor, lawyer, storekeeper, engineer, scientist, and so fourth is a critically important aspect of a democratic classroom. Such play, if allowed to develop and integrated with reading, field trips, and discussions will establish important foundations. Without teacher intervention it is likely that the boys will play doctors and the girls nurses. Play reveals prejudices and stereotypes. These become invitations to discussion and if kept within the framework of play, much can be accomplished without disrupting the development that comes from spontaneous actions. A teacher might suggest the game be replayed but with girl as the doctor and the boy as the nurse. Such intervention by an adult may disrupt the play and take from it its spontaneity. That is not necessarily bad. The teacher can sustain the play through discussion and variations of a theme. Students may resent teacher intervention and refuse to play, or otherwise respond negatively. But development is a long-slow, and uneven process and momentary setbacks are to be expected and should not be allowed to interfere with long-range educational goals. It is during these periods of strain and setback that a corollary of play-humor—comes to the fore (see the chapter on democratic teaching for necessary attributes of the democratic teacher).

Work Preparation in Middle School. In middle schools, students are given a realistic picture of the opportunity structure. In these years the credential society is demystified. In very clear and precise terms, the relationship between school and work is described and explained. Students are encouraged to connect what they are currently doing to future plans. In a very real sense, dreams are transformed into plans in the middle grades. In these years, students are introduced to the connection between economic policy and job creation. School projects a theatrical production, a television station, a clean-up campaign, a school store, and so on, should be modeled after existing work situations (in middle school, students should play at work). In debriefing discussions students will become more aware of the how work is organized, what specific tasks are to be performed, the skills to be mastered, and gratifications that can be obtained from such work. There is virtually no activity in a middle school that cannot be connected to work, and that includes teaching. Middle school students should be involved in cross-age tutoring, peer instruction, co-operative learning, and peer counseling.

Play as preparation for work in the middle grades changes in character. By middle school, rules in play have long ceased to be covert; moreover, from a play perspective what students know about work (which they associate with school) has led them to believe that rules have become necessarily rigid and thus rules rob play of that which makes it enjoyable. For play to be useful as preparation for future work in the middle school, the emphasis must be on its imaginative aspect and that is the feature that has been most discouraged. The last thing vocational educators believe future employers want are students who are imaginative about work. The emphasis in vocational education has always been on developing a dependable, generally skilled, and adaptable worker, but most importantly, a docile one who obeys the rules. Even if employers were convinced it was in their interest to have an inquiring active intelligence as an employee rather than a passively docile "hinge-head"[1] that would not necessarily result in a more informed questioning and creative workforce. Teachers would have to initiate a fundamental different approach to curriculum. That will not be easy for them to do. They have taken pains (and by the reality of the job) to position themselves as far

---

[1] A term used on the docks by longshoreman in the late 1950s to describe a "company man"- someone who unquestioningly did whatever employers wanted them to do.

from the realities of a work world that is insecure, constantly in flux, and highly competitive. Thus, teachers would continue to emphasize obedience rather than initiative partially because that is what they believe employers want; but far more importantly, that is what they want from their students. Teachers need to be convinced that imaginative play is a critical ingredient in a vocational program for all ages, and most importantly for the middle school years.

The easiest means by which students can play with work is through simulation. Simulation can vary from the highly technical and complex to the simple. Computer simulation is intriguing and offers a wide range of possibilities, particularly if sustained over a long period of time. Not all schools will have such capability. The absence of technology, however, should not inhibit the use of play in the classroom. Simulation through role-play (psycho drama or sociodrama) will do just fine. Beginning efforts can be crude but even these rough efforts should be organized into a coordinated scope and sequence. Every activity in a school should lead to a more challenging activity. Role-play is valuable in its own right. It becomes more valuable depending on the quality of the discussion that it stimulates. But it should not stop at that. Televising the role-play adds to its value, and like video replays for athletes, offers instant opportunities for analysis and reflection.

Televising a class activity is no longer a technically daunting activity. Virtually every classroom has access to some form of video camera and a VCR. Initial efforts can be primitive. With editing they get better. Each step can be an exciting as well as an important lesson. Each step opens up future employment possibilities. Televising student research on work in the community that would involve interviews and depictions of actual work in progress is yet another element in middle school (and high school) preparation for work. Community service can be preparation for work aided and abetted by video-recording. Such activity logically leads to classroom visitations by a range of "experts." These visitors would be invited to view student productions and suggest ways in which these efforts can be improved. In time, the classroom becomes a production studio opening up consideration of fast-growing occupational opportunities. Middle schools are ideal places for play to mature and merge significant cognitive growth with the development of a wide range of skills that have future employment possibilities.

Care should be taken to not overemphasize the future economic value of this kind of activity. Although the skill and cognitive development in work-oriented play is a vital part in preparation for future work, the play can assist students in any important problem solving. Furthermore, the gratifications that come from the play and the cognitive development that play makes possible can and should be transferred to other school projects.

Preparation for Work at the Secondary School. At the high school level students are ready to do serious research. They will have had a range of meaningful work and simulated work experiences. These experiences include shadowing people in work sites and apprenticeships. In discussions about work they are expected to be able to link aspirations with specific characteristics of a desired occupation.

The primary responsibility of work preparation in high school is to discourage premature foreclosure on aspirations. One of the unfortunate consequences of authoritarian schooling is the powerful negative impact it has had on imagination applied to preparation for work. A school influenced narrow vision of future work, nongratifying school experiences, desire for economic independence, the need for immediate income as a response to the powerful force of consumerism and the general availability of "youth" work (fast food establishments, etc.), all have negative impacts on a preparation for lifelong work.

Play at the high school level is continued use of imagination about transforming existing work. More imaginative play is directed at economic planning. Students should be able to make critical appraisals of the credential system, alternatives to it (such as new career ladders; Pearl & Riessman, 1965), and should be prepared to evaluate proposed ways to democratize the work world. High school students use play to, in a sense, return to their early years. The preoccupation is again with rules, but now the interest is in inventing new rules. Throughout the student's school career there has been little opportunity to analyze the rules that govern work nor has the capacity to examine alternative systems and rules been developed. The idea that education is a necessary prerequisite for work is one of the seemingly unchallengeable rules about work. Students can play with the idea that work should be a prerequisite for school. As high school students begin to use their imagination about work other rules come into play, the rules that determine definitions of work, and the rules that determine compensation are all open for consideration.

Some Guiding Considerations About Preparation for Work

In a democratic classroom choices are not made for students, nor are students discouraged from considering any possible future career. If, for example, a student diagnosed with severe intellectual impairment should aspire to be a nuclear physicist, the role of the democratically oriented teacher would be to describe exactly what a nuclear physicist does describe what the student would need to learn at this time and in the future to attain such a goal and encourage that child to the same extent she or he would encourage a student believed to be intellectually gifted.

In a democratic classroom, the alleged intellectually disabled student should have the same access to all of the available resources as the "gifted" student.

We can hear the crescendo of voices screaming at us, "That is cruel! Encouraging people beyond their capabilities only programs them for failure, wounds their egos, damages self esteem and in other ways does irreparable harm." Trying and not achieving could be interpreted as failure. However, by not permitting a student to try, failure, wounded ego and irreparable harm are guaranteed. Encouraging all students to try does not mean that all will succeed. Even when participation is as restricted as it currently is, not every participant succeeds. When only the "gifted" are admitted to some elite institution, some fail. From a democratic perspective the problem is not "the failing" but the interpretation given to effort. With a hierarchical orientation, winning becomes everything. In democracies, effort is appreciated. A democratic education not only levels the playing field, it also redefines failure. In a democratic classroom, trying cannot lead to failure. The gratification derived comes from participation in the process—in the knowledges and skills gained, the comradeship, the security that comes with a sense of understanding of how the world works, excitement in the opportunity to compete, and so on. By emphasizing play and maintaining humor instead of failure, there is exhilaration that comes from participation.

The challenge for a democratic classroom is to find ways to incorporate vocational and academic education. Part of that challenge is to be persuasive in preventing students from prematurely foreclosing on their options and part of the challenge is in keeping everyone eligible for all possibilities.

HOW DOES EXISTING VOCATIONAL EDUCATION FIT INTO A DEMOCRATIC PREPARATION FOR WORK?

Traditional vocational education goes in a direction diametrically opposite from that which is proposed here. Currently, structured vocational education is antidemocratic in both theory and practice and is tied to social reproduction. If a student is assigned to a vocational education track, he or she is not college bound. The distances between the two tracks are too large to bridge both in ways people think and in the ways the programs are organized. Movement toward a democratic education begins by narrowing the gap between the academic and the vocational. The narrowing has to go in both directions. The vocational tracks should be accompanied with a more challenging academic curriculum. Rather than "dumbing down" maths, language, and science the intellectual underpinnings of these "subjects" should be enhanced. The more subjects can be connected to work the more relevant the subjects can be made. Subject knowledge can be used to enter into and solve problems associated with work. But straining at relevance has often contributed to anti-intellectuality. Vocational education can be upgraded by stressing the importance of keeping options open and by generalizing competence where it has been exhibited to where students have not demonstrated either mastery or confidence.

The academic upgrading of vocational education can be accomplished by upgrading the status of the vocational education teacher. That teacher has be included with the currently more highly regarded teacher of the tertiary bound in interdisciplinary teams. The vocational teacher needs to be encouraged to raise expectations and not accept a dumbed down or Vege math, a less than exciting science class or a second-class approach to language. Most importantly, vocational education teachers must insist on first-class citizen preparation for all students. Vocational education will be upgraded paradoxically by lessening its importance and by directing students' attention to other important educational goals—citizenship, culture carrying competence, and personal well-being. The overemphasis on vocation not only has contributed significantly to social reproduction but it has also tended to deaden all of education. An education with a broad base appeal and whose activities are connected will go a long way to reduce student alienation and counter the system's hierarchical tendencies.

There is yet one other way that existing systems can be made more democratic; the tertiary bound should be encouraged to learn about the entire range of the work world because such knowledge is in their long- and short-term interests. The more the tertiary bound understand about what those who never get beyond high school do for a living the better they will be able to make sense of the world they live in. Moreover, the tertiary bound work in "youth industries" to at least the same extent as less upwardly mobile (we do not believe that those who graduate to higher education are more academically able, more intelligent, more disciplined, or in any way superior than those who are are never allowed into institutions of higher learning for reasons we provide later in this book), and those experiences should be brought back into academic discussions.

Upgrading current vocational education can only be partially successful, but partial success can lay the foundation for more powerful changes. Thematic instruction, cooperative learning, and interdisciplinary approaches in vocational education, or in any other curriculum area, are in of themselves insufficient. However, these rather small and tentative changes in educational practice open the door for more fundamental change. Some of the recent efforts to reform education can be significant first steps to important change; they also represent tragic ends if not seen as first steps.

New Business-Driven Initiatives: School to Work

One element of a business orientation to education has been the promotion of privatization; another is business telling schools what they should do. This latter thrust is most apparent in preparation for work. Business leaders have never been satisfied with the worker schools have prepared for them. In recent years, the criticism has become increasingly shrill. Such criticism was at the heart of the President's Commission on Education (National Commission, 1983). Efforts have been made to involve business more in guiding schools to better prepare students for work. These schools-to-work initiatives feature the development of student businesses, job shadowing, mentoring, school business partnerships, youth apprenticeships, and job training. None of this is particularly innovative. All have been tried before in various combinations with limited success. There is the belief that student will be far more ready for work with more serious business investment in schools. Virtually no data support such optimism. Considerable excitement has been generated by one particular business connection with work bound students-mentoring. It is firmly held that when practical minded businessmen serve as mentors youth will get that practical dose of reality that has been missing in their education. At present, such expectation is a declaration of faith. It is possible that some students may benefit from some mentors and it is important that this relationship be carefully evaluated. It is also possible that there will be a serendipitous effect employers will gain a deeper appreciation of the difficulty of teaching in currently constructed underresourced urban high schools and do something substantial to alter those dreadful conditions..

The-school-to-work initiatives tend to ignore the profound effects of "outsourcing" and "re-engineering. In a rapidly changing work world, school-to-work efforts must encourage students to develop broadly applicable skills rather than focusing on skills that can be applied to only one type of job.

The absence of an informing general theory creates strains between the work aspect of schools and the academic requirements. The effort to patch a vigorous school-to-work program on the existing school is not likely to persuade many academic teachers of its importance. In that sense, a school-to-work program attached to the existing curriculum, methods of instruction, and school organization deforms rather than reforms education.

We support all of the proposed activities in a school-to-work program (e.g., partnerships, mentoring, apprenticeships, job shadowing, mentors), but only when they are incorporated into a general education theory. Otherwise, the new school-to-work will resemble the old vocational education and be a vehicle for sophisticated tracking while providing students with a distorted picture of the way work is organized and never initiating discussion on the transformation of work. Without serious efforts to meet all four democratic education requirements—sufficient knowledge to inform work policy and equal encouragement to compete for desirable jobs, meaningful universal student participation in decisions that affect their lives (which would include participating in the formation of the school to work program), and respect for fundamental individuals rights while at the work site as well as in the classroom—it is highly unlikely that school-to-work will overcome the obstacles that are currently encountered (Lynn, 1996).

NEW CAREERS: ONE APPROACH TO DEMOCRATIZATION OF WORK

New careers is the result of positive playfulness. It provides an alternative to the pressures to sort students and orient them to different stations in life with widely disparate rewards.

A democratic effort to prepare for work without a parallel developmental curriculum to alter the work world is no remedy for an already near impossible situation. As mentioned earlier, humans are an environmentally altering species and there is no area of life in which the alteration has been more significant than in the way work has changed in the past century. These changes are the result of social policy. The results rarely met expectations. But contrasting expectations and results should be part of the analysis of social policy undertaken by students nearing high school graduation.

It is difficult to democratically prepare students for work when work itself has been so resistant to democratic practices. Credentialism has been one very powerful way in which existing work has been organized undemocratically. Credentials have been imposed. The establishment of credentials has been an effective means by which access to "good" occupations has been severely restricted. Credentials have also greatly enhanced the role of education in the work world because credentials are issued only to people who have completed rigidly defined courses of study. The justification for credentials is the protection of standards. What has not been established is whether the credentials are in fact standards or obstacles. There are two fundamental issues in the examination of credentials from a democratic perspective: the first concerns whether credentials are necessary to maintain a high level of service or production; the second examines the means by which credentials are obtained for fairness and quality of performance.

New Careers dealt with the latter concern. New Careers also provides an example of the creative use of play. It has an interesting history.

The New Career story begins with the chance meeting of Frank Riessman and Art Pearl in 1962. Pearl at the time was research director for the New York Division for Youth; Riessman, a leader in the highly publicized delinquency prevention program, Mobilization for Youth, that had been initiated by then President John Kennedy's brother, Attorney General Robert Kennedy. Both Riessman and Pearl were psychologists with slightly different perspectives and quite different histories. They questioned the prevailing idea the that existing social hierarchy validly reflected ability and motivation. And both questioned the wisdom and morality of a "poverty" program that had as its mission opening up the opportunity structure to impoverished youth, and yet, expended most of its budget on middle-class credentialed employees. Pearl, at the time, described Mobilization for Youth as a program designed to "open up the opportunity structure for the middle class." Pearl argued that if a program was to be an "antipoverty program then most of the budget should go to poor people." Such an idea was rejected on the grounds that poor people were in no position to teach, counsel, provide health care, or other much needed social services. And the notion that in an antipoverty program the preponderance of the funds should go directly to poor people was dismissed as errant anti-intellectuality.

In 1963, Riessman and Pearl, with funding from the Ford Foundation, brought a wide range of social scientists concerned with causes and effects of poverty to a 2-day conference. They found that the vast majority believed that the poor were poor because of one or more of the following deficits: genetic, accumulated environmental, inadequate socialization, or cultural deprivation. Riessman had just published his book, *The Culturally Deprived Child* (1962), which challenged prevailing opinion. Riessman and Pearl, in very different settings, explored the use of paraprofessionals in a variety of human services. They not only questioned the justifications for excluding "the poor" from consideration as professionals, they also questioned whether existing credentialed professionals could provide adequate services to the poor (Riessman, Cohen, & Pearl, 1964). At this stage of their development, they were "problemizing." What was needed was a creative solution to the problem they had identified; a solution that maintained standards and equity. With the help of Grant and Grant (and several others) they invented *New Careers for the Poor* (Pearl & Riessman, 1965). New Careers illustrates the role of play in the more advanced stages of cognitive development. In New Careers the explicit rules for the attainment of credentials was not changed. The power given to credential-granting institutions was not reduced. The creative effort was restricted to the means by which the credentials were to be obtained. With New Careers, Pearl and Riessman attempted to answer the criticism directed against them for suggesting that the "unqualified" poor should receive the majority of poverty program funds because these were "soft monies," and would no longer be available once the program was discontinued, thus leaving the poor no better off than they were before the program began; whereas when middle-class professionals are paid out of soft monies, the help they provide as teachers, social workers and health practitioners can have a lasting impact and once the funding runs out they have the credentials to access professional positions elsewhere. The challenge was to invent a system that could have both short- long-term positive effects. This they did by turning traditional wisdom on its head. Pearl and Riessman operated with two new principles:

1. Job first then education, in place of education first than job.
2. Tailoring the job to meet the characteristics of the worker rather than fitting people to the job.

For such an approach to be truly open-ended and no one excluded because of background or social condition, the entry position had to be open to all, requiring no prior experience, education, or skills.

What began as play became law. That is an important lesson unto itself. Students can see that the work world is pliable and that calculated change is possible. But that would be an incomplete lesson. Inventing new approaches to careers may constitute no improvement over existing process and no recognized problems may be solved or ameliorated.

New Careers made important progress. In the interest of time and space we restrict our discussion to the largest of the New Career programs—the Career Opportunity Program (COP) for teachers. The problems to be solved by COP were equity and quality. Did COP open up opportunities for people who had been excluded from consideration on the grounds that they lacked the capacity to meet accepted standards of performance? And was the New Careerist at least as competent as the traditionally prepared teacher? The success of COP would have profound implication for one particularly difficult requirement of democratic education—equal encouragement.

COP was a large experiment that had, like all the other New Career programs, a career ladder, a series of negotiable steps culminating in a professional credential. The ladder varied considerably by site but the most were guided by recommendation made by Pearl and Riessman's *New Careers for the Poor* (1965): an entry aide (no prerequisites), teacher assistant (equivalent of 2 years of higher education), teacher associate (equivalent of 4 years in college), and teacher (education and other experiences required for credential). Prospective professionals worked their way up the ladder through a combination of work experience, university courses delivered at the work-site and liberal art courses taken at an institution of higher education (Pearl & Riessman, 1965). In actuality, the education and training received in COP varied greatly by site. The programs were of uneven quality, the one fairly consistent element throughout the almost all sites was the lack of flexibility in tertiary education. The curricular and structural changes recommended in *New Careers for the Poor* were not followed and because this was a critical element of the "dream," evaluation would have to take that into consideration. COP was designed to increase underrepresented minority teachers, demonstrate that inadmissible students can succeed in higher education, lift impoverished people out of poverty, and recruit teachers who could better meet the needs of low-income children, improve staffing in schools, and "respond to the growing belief that the then-present designs of teacher education were inadequate, particularly in preparing teachers for the children of the poor" (Carter, 1977, p. 184). All of these goals have relevance to democratic education.

The evidence supporting the ability of the COP to bring underrepresented minorities into the teaching profession was very powerful (Carter, 1977). The evidence for achievement of the other goals was also strong. However, it is difficult to establish the extent of progress because the program was short-lived, inconsistent within and between sites, and only superficially evaluated. Although participants normally would not have not have been admitted to universities, they did very well in higher education (Amram, Flax, Hamermesh, & Marty, 1988; Carter, 1977) and seemed to better meet the needs of low-income students (Carter, 1977).

The history of New Careers provides yet another good lesson in democratic education because despite its remarkable accomplishments, it was discontinued in the mid-1970s. It rose by a political process and when the political winds shifted, it became a casualty of the political process. In recent years, for somewhat the same reasons for its consideration in the 1960s, the New Career concept is being revived. During the the early 1990s, the new Career concept was passed into law in California as the Paraprofessional Teacher Credential Program and is currently being tested in 15 pilot programs.

Effective New Career programs require the following:

1. There must be a well developed career ladder at agency or other employment setting with clearly defined tasks for each rung of the ladder
2. The gap between each rung must be readily negotiable
3. Colleges and universities to tailor their offerings to meet the characteristics and talents of the participants, and
4. College credits are awarded for skill and knowledge gained on the job (the supervisor on the job serves as adjunct instructor).

Although teaching may be suited for a career-ladder approach, so too is every other profession. And although the original emphasis initially was on public service careers, a "New Career" strategy can just as readily be applied to private sector.

A discussion of New Careers in high school is but one of many ways to stimulate students to dream about restructuring the work world. It provides students with a way to challenge traditional wisdom. It is a clear example of going beyond "problemizing" to "solutionizing" (postmodernists do not have a monopoly on mangling language). It can be a powerful example of democratic education in action.

Students should be encouraged to envision career ladders for every one of their occupational interests. A combination of work and disciplined study can be adapted to any form of work and can be organized developmentally into a career ladder, beginning with entry positions requiring no prerequisites, and terminating with a professional credential. Encouraging such thinking puts new meaning into "youth work," which is not perceived as having potential for career investment.

RIGHTS AND PREPARATION FOR WORK

Every right comes into play in education for career choice. Students should be able to exercise *freedom of expression*—which translates into an opportunity to express interest in different careers, as well as challenge anything said by the teacher about the work world. As amazing as it might seem, students are often strongly discouraged from expressing interest in an occupation that school authorities deem to be inappropriate. And if students persist in expressing unacceptable aspirations the level of disapprobation escalates and a student can find him or herself in increasingly serious trouble.

Students should be guaranteed *privacy* in any decision about future work. One prevalent tactic to discourage students whose aspirations do not correspond to teacher evaluation is public humiliation. And although, *due process* would rarely enter in education about work, students in a democratic classroom cannot be denied an opportunity to explore any work without the same kind of due process they would receive when accused of misbehavior. Career choice includes *rights of movement*. Denial of the right of movement currently governs the assignment to learning tracks. Once assigned to a vocational or any other non-college preparation track students are effectively prohibited from moving to an education that opens the door to the best paying and most influential jobs. Competition for too few good jobs can only be intense. For the competition to be fair, the democratic education requirement of equal encouragement in career choice must be met. In fact, it is in the area of vocational education that the lack of equal encouragement is most prevalent and most damaging. It is in the preparation for different work stations that provides much of the underlying logic for ability-grouping tracking and differential expectations. It is in the consideration of future responsibilities that teachers divide the tertiary bound from those that they deem lack such capability; and once divided, students are treated accordingly.

Many critics of vocational education see as a remedy, integration of high-level academic subjects with vocational training. Without a democratic education, an integrated vocational education is an impossibility. It can produce nothing but anger, often displaced, and will necessarily contribute to increased racial violence and aggression against women. Only when the world of work is demystified is it possible for equal encouragement to good jobs to be more than an empty slogan.

However, it must be noted that if all of the requirements of a democratic education in preparing students for the existing work structure were met, not very much would have been accomplished. At best we would have played musical chairs with jobs. More women and people of color would have good jobs, more White males would find themselves in low-level jobs or be jobless. Preparing for the existing and projected work world is one hand clapping.

LEARNING HOW TO CREATE A GOOD WORK WORLD

There are three considerations in the creation of a good work world. The first One, deals with the creation of sufficient good jobs to go around. The second, deals with the goods and services that are being created. And the third is the impact that job creation has on the environment.

Can everybody who wants to work find a gratifying job? Do the created products and services contribute to a quality life? And do the created jobs come at the expense of the environment? Students need to become familiar with the logic that informs the practices and policies that are used to generate jobs. Jobs do not fall from heaven like manna in the desert. Nor are they fashioned by some invisible hand. Jobs are created by social policies that include both acts of commission and acts of omission—things that are done or things that could be done, but for a variety of political considerations, are not.

There is no consensus on what is the best way to create a high-skill, high-wage, full-employment society. To date, no society has sustained anything close to high-skill, high-wage, full-employment. Those generally described to be conservative believe that an unregulated market is the best way to move toward such a goal. Those on the left (virtually nonexistent at the time of this writing), argue that jobs should be established through an economic plan with government playing a significant role. In between, there are those who are believe that the maximum number of good jobs are produced through a cooperative arrangement of governmental and private enterprise employment.

Prior to high school graduation, students need to understand the logic of each position and the evidence used to support the arguments. Students should be encouraged to become "economists" and engage in forecasting, evaluation of the economy, and assessment of different proposed approaches to remedy problems (e.g., does something like a federal reserve bank whose primary mission is to establish interest rates constitute sufficient management of the economy?).

In one strategic sense, economic policy is constantly altered to run a course between an overheated economy that results in unacceptable levels of inflation, and an underactive economy with unacceptable levels of unemployment. Conservatives believe that the economy will right itself if left alone. Thus, they would favor low taxation, limited regulation, and governmental services limited primarily to the protection of private property. Liberals (or Labor parties in European or Australian political contexts) have, over the years, favored governmental intervention when the economy is in trouble by raising taxes and interest rates and lowering governmental employment during periods of unacceptable high inflation, and, by lowering taxes, interest rates and increasing government employment to offset high unemployment. Liberals also support movement toward a more equitable society through progressive taxation. Students need to be involved in this debate. The debate should not be restricted to existing arguments, but students should view the debate as an opportunity for new thinking.

To fully understand and evaluate economic policy and strategy, students need to be evolved in simulation exercises. They need to design economies and try to determine what would happen with different interventions. The quality of that education is determined by the quality of debate over the knowledge obtained from these exercises. These simulation exercises can be made more sophisticated and more representative as the student advances in grade.

Before students can evaluate an economy, they must have a vision of what the economy should look like. That vision should not be restricted to jobs, but to the capacity of a society to provide everyone with a quality life.

The Elementary Student as Economic Planner. In the early school years, emphasis should be on visions. As students gain mathematical sophistication and more detailed knowledge of the workings of the economy they can become increasingly involved in creating models, assessing the existing economy and proposing interventions to improve its functioning.

The Middle Grade Student as Economic Planner. In the middle grades, students should be encouraged to think about the relationship between economics and the environment and try to design environmentally benign economies. Students should be given an opportunity to fully appreciate the dilemmas in trying to reconcile the economy with the environment. Difficult choices have to be made. At the middle school level students are given the opportunity to understand how much of economic decisions are moral decisions. Students are encouraged to calculate the impact of different economic policies.

The High School Student as Economic Planner. By graduation from secondary school, the ability to engage in economic
planning should be highly developed. The student should have been
given the opportunity to critically evaluate the logical effects of
the range of economic proposals. The student must have been given
every opportunity to analyze the employment implications of
"economic rationalism" (i.e., unrestricted trade in a global economy). Students should be able to calculate the logical consequences
of such policy. They should be able to compare their "theoretical"
calculations with actual experience in different areas of the
world. Nearing graduation, high school students should debate the
long- and short-term impacts on employment of "free trade"
agreements such as North American Free Trade Agreement and
General Agreement on Trade and Tariffs. They should demystify
the dominant slogan that informs much of jargon, if not policy, in
education.

U.S. high school students need to make independent judgments about the nature of the competitiveness of the U.S. economy
and what should be done to improve matters.

Students should be made aware that the global economy is
not an inevitability. They may wish to consider regional self-suf-
ficiency. A democratic education allows students to dig deep and not
be swayed by superficial slogans.

The analysis cannot be limited to just employment.
Students need to consider the effects different economic approaches will have on the environment in their respective countries.

We are entering a new age of global markets and automated
production. The road to a near workerless economy is within
sight. Whether that road leads to a safe haven or a terrible
abyss will depend on how well civilization prepares for the
post-market era that will follow on the heels of the Third
Industrial Revolution. The end of work could spell a death
sentence for civilization as we have come to know it. The
end of work could also signal the beginning of a great social
transformation, a rebirth of the human spirit. The future
lies in our hands. (Rifkin, 1994, pp. 291-292)

One alternative that advanced high school students should
consider is a world with very little work as depicted by Rifkin
(1994) and in Australia, Gregory (1995) predicted on the basis
of longitudinal analysis, no work for youth by the year 2005. How
likely are their forecasts? Rifkin, as all of the economists that
students will examine, should be countered with oppositional

arguments. Glassman 1994, who writes a financial column for *The Washington Post*, in his review of Rifkin came to an almost opposite conclusion, although he does, like Rifkin, support greater involvement of volunteers as the glue that will hold society together.

> The truth is that machines create more jobs and better jobs since they expand the kinds of things people can do. In 1850 most Americans worked on farms, performing drudge labor. Now we produce more food with only 2.7 percent of our work-force, and those erstwhile farmers are software designers, machine-tool operators, TV actors, air traffic controllers and restaurateurs. Of course, the new industrial revolution could turn out to be different from the old one. Rifkin may be right when he writes that in the U.S. "more than 90 million jobs . . . are potentially vulnerable to replacement." The problem is that he presents no solid evidence for this case. (Glassman, 1994 , p. 34)

Wilson (1996) is One of the very few who holds to the liberal ideal with his call for "race- neutral" government, created jobs. Students should look for evidence and try to assemble cases for different positions. That is as essential as any other feature of preparation for work.

In a democratic classroom, students are reminded about the requirements of a democratic society and are asked to consider these in designing their economies. It is perfectly acceptable for students to conclude that some of the requirements of a democratic society cannot be met in their design if they are willing to openly debate their ideas.

How unemployment and undesirable work is assigned is a critical component in an education that prepares students to be economic planners. Historically, and to this day, those at the bottom of the economic ladder did the unpleasant work and were overrepresented among the unemployed. Such assignment has been justified on the grounds that persons doing such work were capable of nothing better. The same kind of thinking is applied to the assignment to different educational tracks, hence arguing different economic futures. Any economy that cannot produce sufficient good jobs for everyone has to defend the procedures used in the relegation to the lower rungs of the occupational ladder and to unemployment. Students in their analyses should indicate what will happen to people who cannot or will not find jobs.

As part of this analysis students should examine taxes. They should devise the ideal marginal tax schedule. They should compare a graduated tax scheme with a flat tax. And they should complete the equation by deciding how tax money should it be spent. They should define a role for government and calculate the importance of government employment.

And perhaps most important of all, students should do environmental impact studies on all inventions of work worlds and strive to create a work world that is compatible with a livable world. This is no easy assignment.

It is only when students are prepared to make an informed career choice in the existing work world and participate in the determination of economic policy can that it can be said that the school has met its knowledge requirement in dealing with work.

THE GOVERNMENT SCHOOL AND PRIVATE ENTERPRISE

No matter what schools do, they are not likely to satisfy corporate leadership. The reverse is also true. No matter what corporations do they will not provide that balance of support to insure that all ideas are given opportunity for full and fair development in schools— corporations are not likely to support high taxes, government employment, favorable treatment of unions, or criticism of corporate despoliation of the environment. Nor are corporations likely to provide sufficient good jobs for all future workers. They will not be able to guarantee permanence or equity in employment or promotion.

To the contrary, major corporations are currently downsizing and terminating workers who have with many years of devoted service. What they will do in the future is totally unpredictable. The failure of business to provide ironclad guarantees is no reason to discourage business-school partnerships, however. There is much to be gained from such cooperation. It is imperative that schools use business facilities for work experience. Schools and business will find it to their mutual advantage to work together to generate resources. The smoother the relationship, the more corporations will like the high school graduate and the easier it will be for the student to transition into an adult work career.

Cooperation, however, is not capitulation! A democratic school must be independent and not controlled by corporations or any other segment of the society. Criticisms of schools by businesses should be encouraged and taken seriously. The reverse is also true. It should be constantly kept in mind that corporate executives have no special expertise in education. They are not particularly knowledgeable about curriculum or pedagogy. Corporate treatment of minorities and women has been far from exemplary. Cooperation coupled with independence permits a more balanced treatment of unions, taxation, environmental impacts, and government employment than many corporations would permit, and allows criticism of corporate policies and political positions that would not be possible if corporations controlled education or any significant piece of it.

SUMMARY: THE DEMOCRATIC SCHOOL AND THE WORK WORLD

For work preparation to break out of the social reproduction trap and meet democratic requirements, it must be interactive and dynamic. Students must be active participants in the development of relevant knowledge and be stimulated to creative play.

By the time a student graduates from secondary school, he or she has a range of work experiences, a sense of what he or she wants to do, a recognition of what it takes to get there, an informed commitment to participate in the creation of the best possible work—the work world that comes closest to achieving full, fair, and gratifying employment and universal quality life without negatively affecting the environment. The class discussions that graduating students have had prepares them to develop an economic plan with sufficient specifics to fix tax rates, establish precisely the division of public and private employment, establish a minimum wage, define licensing and credentialing practices, and Determine environmental impact.

What we propose is a far cry from what happens in any school. What has been defined as *vocational education* has tended to be anti-intellectual. The work world has been viewed superficially and as a fixed entity. There has been a tendency to blame the individual and not critically examine the system. Schooling for work has reinforced inequality (i.e., existing racist and sexist practices).

What we propose is very ambitious. It is also necessary. A democratic approach for work preparation will not happen over night. But it is important to have an ambitious scheme in mind to evaluate progress toward a goal. Such a goal helps redefine teaching. The teacher of the future must be far more involved with the world than teachers have been historically. Education has been conceptualized as an encapsulated process in which teacher and student remove themselves from the real world. That never made much sense. Now it is disastrous. One of the unanticipated negative consequences of a subject-based education is the excuse it has given teachers to narrowly define themselves (e.g., "I teach English," which has come to mean I do not have to be responsible for anything else). To be of the world and guide a democratic problem solving education does not make excessive demands of teachers. They do not have to be experts on everything. They do need to be aware of what is important and help students discover and invent the knowledge that is needed to solve complex problems, among the most complex and difficult of which deals with the future of work and the work of the future.

Teachers, students, and parents will find that even with minimum preparation, efforts to approach work as a complex problem will add excitement and a range of gratifications to classroom activities. They will also find that even small progress in demystifying the work world and in the participation in economic policy decisions will be extremely rewarding, leading both to broadening one's understanding of the world (less feelings of being overwhelmed) and in influencing the direction of the debate.

Chapter 5

Building a Democratic Culture

Education for a democratic culture is as important as preparation for work and preparation for citizenship. In fact, without movement toward a democratic culture, the other educational goals become impossible. Only a democratic culture can produce the shared values that provided the centripetal force that makes possible the restoration of community. Only a democratic culture generates the opportunity To reconceptualize society from me-centered to we-centered; from "problemizing" to solution-oriented. In this chapter, we examine the relationship schooling has with culture. Culture is yet another complex conceptualization that tends to be overly simplified and distorted when applied to schooling. Culture is as protean as democracy. In school, culture is treated as a static entity for pigeonholing or classifying persons or works of art. Schools will not become better places, or even useful places, until "culture" is recognized as dynamic and multifaceted. Complexity of culture, although important, is less crucial to successful schooling than the recognition of its dynamic nature. In a rapidly changing society, schools should not be asked just to transmit culture! Schools should be asked to create culture! It is our position that schools have failed dismally in culture creation, and as a consequence, culture creation takes place elsewhere to the detriment of both the individual and the society. In this chapter, we make the case for a school created-democratic culture as an alternative to both the postmodernist celebration of difference and the modernist (and premodernist) efforts to impose an official canon (assimilationist). We introduce our discussion of culture by revisiting essentialism and perennialism. We examine how these dominant educational philosophies have defined culture and how each treats diversity. We contrast these views with our notion of "democratic culture."

CULTURE AND SCHOOLING

What makes the topic of culture both difficult and intriguing is the required simultaneous analysis of the impact that a wide variety of cultures have on students and the role students play in creating cultures. A general theory of education is needed because culture has been both trivialized and savagely distorted in education. Our task in this chapter is to both bring a focus to culture and to propose the creation of a new culture—"a democratic culture" to replace the inadequate existing "official" school culture and the variety of cultures that impact on a school.

Culture is a much abused term. To many it is a term reserved for a special elite or that which is to be preserved. We believe that everyone is influenced or informed by culture and everyone is involved in its creation. The challenge for schools is learning how to adequately treat the diversity of cultures and in a school and utilize that diversity in the creation of a new democratic culture.

Culture determines what one chooses to learn; culture informs values and taste; culture both limits as well as stimulates. Culture is represented by language, but culture also influences how that language will be used. Culture provides order and meaning to an individual's existence. Culture gives legitimacy to prejudice and to hate. Culture defines love both its expression and the legitimacy of relationships. The schools of today are immersed in a world where advertising has a powerful influence on culture, where traditions that acted as a gyroscope for culture have been weakened, if not destroyed. Perhaps most disturbing is that in the interaction of many cultures, a general acceptance of good and bad, or right and wrong has been obliterated. The erosion of an overarching culture to which there is widespread support and allegiance has created a debilitating vacuum.

we're becoming accustomed to and almost satisfied with people who are either venal or stupid. And with the emphasis on fund-raising for all elections, which is ruining the electoral system, we will be accepting entertainers as our candidates, not those who have learned the processes and practices of government. You can't govern without having the training in it. Even Plato said that a long time ago. You need to be trained in government, to exercise it, to practice it. But the American public is now satisfying itself with entertainers. (Tuchman, 1989, p. 7)

In 1927, Freud (1927/1961) observed that "a culture which leaves unsatisfied and drives to rebelliousness so large a number of its members neither has a prospect of continued existence nor deserves it" (p. 134). He was referring to religion, but his comments apply to schools as currently constituted. Even more important than the continued existence of school culture is survival and development of a civil society. We try to explain how schools managed to contrive such a dysfunctional culture and why heralded "reforms" are insufficient as prelude to a description and defense of democratic culture. A democratic culture begins by creating space, a sanctuary where everyone feels safe enough to engage in open conversation on matters that each believe to be important

A discussion about culture in school begins with the recognition that different cultures go to school and that the school by its response to difference, establishes the latitudes of acceptable school cultures.

We do not go to bed in single pairs; even if we choose not to refer to them, we still drag there with us the cultural impedimenta of our social class, our parents' lives, our bank balances, our sexual and emotional expectations, our whole biographies—all the bits and pieces of our unique existences. (A. Carter, 1979, p. 9)

A satirical writer, Carter's comment about bed is even more applicable to school. And as perceptive as she was, she still only got half of the complexity of culture. It is not only what culture does to us, be it sexual relationships or schooling, it is also what we do to culture. Culture is dynamic. Culture brings stability to a world in flux. And although students "drag their cultural impedimenta" to school, the school responds by dragging in its "cultural impedimenta." The result is an official school culture in various kinds of relationships with a wide range of youth cultures—the "jocks," the "brains," the "fringies," the "grunges," the "gothics," the "homies," the "socs" (acceptably popular), the "druggies," the "skaters," the "gangsters" an so on. Many of these cultures would not have existed without the school, or would have taken different forms if there had been no school, but school officials accept no responsibility for them and often blame youth cultures for the school's failure to educate. These school-inspired or sustained cultures take on their own dynamics and inertia that become part of the individual's impedimenta.

If schools have been perfunctory in preparing students for work and remiss in preparing students for citizenship, they have been more than willing to accept the responsibility for culture carrying. But culture in schools meets the fate of Procruste's victims. Culture is mutilated, everything that does not fit is stretched or lopped. What remains lacks vitality. Culture in schools reduces to transmitting to the student via a specific scope and sequence of study, all of civilization's accumulated contributions to intellectual life that some authority has deemed sufficiently worthy of being transmitted. Almost all of the heated criticism of schools and all the publicized efforts to reform school are directed at this cultural transmission mission.

Culture carrying in existing schools, as we have previously mentioned, has been defined by two somewhat competing philosophies: the essentialists who reduce culture to "the basics" and the perennialists who strive to perpetuate "high culture" through understanding and appreciation of "the great works."

> Education founded upon the Iliad, the Bible, Plato, and Shakespeare remains, in some strained form, our ideal. (H. Bloom, 1994, p. 32)

Culture Carrying the Essentialist Way

The essentialist logic goes like this: Once a student has mastered the basics, he or she has all the necessary intellectual equipment required to build, sustain, or advance a culture. By limiting schooling to the basics, school reduces mission to the readily doable. Investment is limited. Goals are realizable. A "basics" emphasis brings stability to the classroom because the basics tend to remain constant and thus are not subject to transient fads and whims. By limiting school to the tools of culture (i.e., the basics), essentialists claim to remove all distractions from classrooms. One such distraction is controversy. Because the basics are universal and can be applied everywhere, there is no need to bring controversial issues into the classroom. Thus, essentialists perceive important problems to be distractions and exclude them. Essentialists are nothing but effusive in congratulating themselves on their non-doctrinaire approach to education. The neutrality of basics permits an invitation of diversity into the school without having to address any of the issues of diversity. For much of the history of education, the claim to neutrality and the exclusion of controversy was a successful ploy in maintaining wide-ranging political support for public schools. That hardly works nowadays.

As simple as essentialism is, it is not simple enough to avoid controversy. One particularly acrimonious debate concerns the language that should be used in instructing nonnative speakers, Because essentialists tend to use extremely limited definitions of culture, complex issues of language and its relation to social identity (Gumperz, 1982) do not enter into their thinking. Essentialists limit their concerns to simplistic dichotomies. Should the nonnative (i.e., non-English) speakers be first taught in a native tongue and be weaned from it once competence in English is established (which has been the approach most experts in bilingual education support)? Or, should the non-English speaker be immersed into English with no instruction in his or her first language? The opposing sides in the bilingual argument are intransigent. A mutually satisfying compromise is neither immediate nor in the offing.

Yet another dichotomy concerns the appropriate method of instruction in the teaching of language. Should phonics be at the heart of instruction, or should the emphasis be on meaning and be governed by "whole language" principles? As evidence mounts that measured competence in the basics decline, an increasingly shrill attack is mounted against the methods used to teach the basics. And old debates rage anew. Teachers are lambasted for retreating from the use of phonics and deemphasizing spelling and grammar. A similar debate takes place in the instruction of mathematics with drill in multiplication tables a particular focus. We have no doubt that students do not read or do math like they once did, although the comparisons are suspect because conditions and contexts have changed so dramatically in the past few decades.

A general theory of education that is bound by democratic principles is obligated to speak to the issues raised by essentialists. Although a democratic education would find the controversies that are so much a part of essentialist education, overblown, they cannot be ignored. Democratic education by definition is inclusive and requires the development of arguments sufficiently persuasive to convince a majority, while at the same time providing choices to the minority. Inclusivity would mean that students and parents should be able to choose phonics or whole language instruction in a democratic school. In a democratic education, effort is made to keep the debate open while encouraging participants to examine larger issues.

No matter how the debates within essentialist education are resolved, the basics do not lend themselves to resolving larger issues. To a large extent, the retreat to basics is a retreat from reality; something that works very well in authoritarian education. It is an effort to coerce students to a boring and irrelevant education. Essentialists bypass the important issues of culture by ignoring them. Thus, neither bias in culture, that is, patriarchy (Pateman, 1989) and a heavy elite Western emphasis, nor the widespread rejection of a school imposed culture as manifest by youth cultures (Farber, Provenzo, & Holm 1994; Willis, 1990) are examined by essentialists. One possible exception is Hirsch (1988), whose *Cultural Literacy: What Every American Needs to Know* was an effort to extend essentialist principles to consider, in a very superficial way, the issues of diversity. We believe that adding or subtracting items to "culture" borders on the ridiculous and in no way addresses the issue of culture in schools.

Culture Carrying the Perennialist Way

Perennialists make a more interesting if no more defensible case for the content, of education. Their goal is to transmit the great works of culture. Here, the controversy is on what constitutes a classic. H. Bloom (1994) provided a coherent case for perennialism . He critiqued 26 authors from Shakespeare to Neruda. He appended to his work some 200 other authors divided into the Theocratic, Aristocratic, Democratic, and Chaotic ages. More, he allowed, than could be thoroughly digested by any student. His list is, like all such lists, arbitrary. He made no claims for its moral superiority. His criteria for inclusion is immortality, that is, if once read, the reader will not be satisfied until he or she reads it again. H. Bloom found room for women writers, people of color both from within the Western world and from without. He projected his list as an antidote to the six branches of the "School of

Resentment," within which he lumps feminists, Marxists, Lacanians, new historicists, deconstructionists and semioticians He acknowledged his elitism: We need to teach more selectively, searching for the few who have the capacity to become highly selective readers and writers. The others, who are amenable to a politicalized curriculum, can be abandoned to it (H. Bloom, 1994, p. 17). He argues that the Western Canon provides memory and cognition. Without the Canon, we cease to think (H. Bloom, 1994, p 17).

His arrogance in who he deigned to include and exclude does not detract from his appeal. There is much to enjoy in the authors he cited. But reasonability is not necessarily compatible with democracy. His delineated Western Canon, for all its value, like any other ordained common reader, be it his or Virginia Woolf's, cannot form the basis of general education. He, in fact, acknowledges much. The readings must address problems and they must also come to grips with the loss of public and intellectual support for their ideas. What he called the *School of Resentment* was not created out of whole cloth. It came into being as an effort to ordain culture-lost credibility. Perennialists can only hope to attract a small coterie of supporters who, like other splinter groups, try to keep a train of thought alive. The Western Canon fails as sufficient culture because it does not have within it, no matter how defined, the capacity to solve pressing problems. Nor does it adequately address diversity. To the contrary it attempts to pick and choose the worthwhile from the worthless. Although not as empty as essentialism, it treats culture in an inadequate way. Perennialist culture is insufficiently dynamic, even with the elasticity that Bloom brings to it.

Perennialist diversity is achieved by patching a little color and a few women on to a male-saturated Western Canon core. Efforts to tinker with the Western Canon by such patching are not immune from criticism. To the contrary, universities that have amended the classics with such tinkering have been savaged for "political correctness" (D'Souza, 1991).

Coming to Grips with Popular Culture

. . . television is the true "great American educator," and little that the schools attempt to do or undo can compete with it. (Barber, 1992, p. 33)

Presidential and state commissions pontificate about what young people should to be doing with their lives. Then there is reality. Students spend a great deal of their time ignoring commissions and rejecting schooling. It is in this world of the young that our understanding of culture is extended and refined. Popular culture has a huge hold on youth. More accurately, popular cultures have a huge hold on youth. It is through television, motion pictures, records, tapes, and CDs that students not only define themselves, but also their world. The diversity of youth cultures not only splinters youth, it creates problems for them. The cultures can be antagonistic to each other and lead to violent confrontation. Warring gangs are but one example of cultural conflict. Some cultures draw students to drugs and keep them entangled. Some cultures promote interracial conflict, some, violence against women. Some youth cultures seek out and terrorize young gay men. That youth are able to develop and sustain relatively autonomous cultures is not necessarily laudable. But the existence of youth cultures is undeniable and require a powerful and intellectually defensible response from schools. The increase in violence toward the senior end of secondary school can be largely attributed to conflict within and between youth cultures. Neither pretending these cultures do not exist, nor glorifying them are defensible responses.

Many students currently find that school has been defined or constructed for them by "texts" generated in various popular media (Farber et al., 1994). Students tend to find these images of school more powerful than their own experiences. Students have difficulty making sense out of their involvements in school and so the misrepresentations, distortions, and caricatures of schools and teachers in the public media become convincing illusions. A growing number of scholars concentrate their research on the popular media and its impact on the lives and thinking of young people. Such research is consistent with postmodernist thought. It both elevates the importance of the popular culture, and moves intellectual focus to the margins. Scholarly research of popular culture to a very large extent constitutes voyeurism. Little of value can come from such investigation. Popular media reflects the amorphous reality of existing schooling. The media is not the problem, schooling is. It is not the power of the public images and text treatment of schools that needs to be addressed, but the weak reality of schooling and its inability to draw young people to it. Today's students are postmodernist, while their teachers are modernist and even premodernist and their cultures clash. The solution is not to found by transforming teachers to postmodernism, nor is it possible to attract many students back to a modernist world. It is possible that all can meet in a post postmodernist democratic world.

Popular culture needs to be brought into the schools as necessary topics for discussion and as part of the negotiations that are required in democratic schooling.

> . . . popular culture—as represented . . . on television and in comic books and in movies—is based on fantasies created by very ill people, and (the African-American student) must be aware that these are fantasies that have nothing to do with reality. (Baldwin, 1963, p. 11)

Popular culture is undeniably influential. It helps students define themselves given the lack of attraction of more conservative influences. But just as popular culture cannot be ignored, much of it should not be made. There is both activity and passivity in youth cultures (Thompson, 1990). But being active or passive is not the important issue. What matters is the effect the culture has on the individual and the society of which the individual remains a part. There is a powerful conviction that cultural life has been "mediaized" with the implication that only when cultural life is "demediaized" (Farber et al., 1994, p. 10) can schools reoccupy a central place in the lives of students. But is media all powerful, or are schools so peripheral in a student's life that media merely fills a vacuum? We believe that a democratic education will not demediaize the world of youth, it will merely reduce its importance. Media, no matter how technologically advanced, will always be secondary to meaningful personal relationships. In fact, it is the peer relationships, more than the media that sustains current youth cultures. Students find in them a sense of shared belonging that is absent everywhere else. Mostly we learn from popular culture how trivial schools are.

> It is the extraordinary in the ordinary, which is extraordinary, which makes both into culture, common culture. We are thinking of the extraordinary symbolic creativity of the multitude of ways in which young people use, humanize, decorate and invest with meaning their common and immediate life spaces and social practices—personal styles and choices of clothes; selective and active use of music, TV, magazines, decorations of bedrooms; the drama of friendship

groups; music-making and dance. Nor are these pursuits and activities trivial or inconsequential. In conditions of late modernization and the widespread of cultural values they can be crucial to the creation and sustenance of individual and group identities, even crucial to cultural survival of identity itself. There is work, even desperate work, in their play. (Willis, 1990, p. 2)

We are in the process of creating what deserves to be called the idiot culture. Not an idiot sub-culture, which every society has bubbling beneath the surface and which can provide harmless fun; but the culture itself. For the first time, the weird and the stupid and the coarse are becoming our cultural norm, even our cultural ideal. (G. Bernstein, 1992, p. 62)

Our attitude toward our own culture has recently been characterized by two qualities, braggadocio and petulance. Braggadocio—empty boasting of American power, American virtue, American know-how—has dominated our foreign relations now for some decades. . . . Here at home—within the family, so to speak—our attitude to our culture expresses a superficially different spirit, the spirit of petulance. Never before, perhaps, has a culture been so fragmented into groups, each full of its own virtue, each annoyed and irritated at the others. (Boorstin, pp. 13-14, 1960)

Farber et al. (1994) urged us to explore

particular films, television programs, magazine articles, or music videos . . . in detail. . . . This kind of work is conducive to forms of inquiry concerning viewer/listener/reader responses to the content of popular culture texts, and is especially pertinent to the exploration of pedagogical possibilities in this domain. This set of studies (looking at different popular culture "stuff") provides a context of issues and tendencies that will help to frame such on-going critical inquiry. (p.19)

We ask, to what end? What would be accomplished by such exploration? Students are attracted to those cultures precisely because school and all it stands for is ridiculed. The cultures represent the feelings of exclusion. The cultures provide one way, maybe the only way, youth can express their anger for how they have been demeaned and their intelligence insulted. Studying youth culture is yet another way to avoid dealing with real problems. Before popular culture can be a topic for study, the school has to be reinvented and students presented with clear models and visions. For this to occur, teachers need to exert meaningful leadership, otherwise studying popular cultures is an invitation to continuing fragmentation and the ultimate dissolution of society. When a persuasive case has been made that school is a place where students come to solve important problems then it is possible for popular culture to play a meaningful role in the educational process. The case for schooling must be more than a rhetorical exercise. That case has to supported with compelling logic and ever more convincing evidence. It begins with the defining of a particular problem for which students have expressed a desire to solve. And most important of all, it must be shown that through a school-involved process, some generally recognized significant progress was made toward an indicated solution. Teachers may help students define the problem, teachers may help students define the strategy to be used to bring about solution, but only students will be able to provide the evidence powerful enough to convince other students that a school program can help solve an important problem. When students take on that kind of initiative, a new youth culture comes into being with an entirely new meaning attached to the term and that culture becomes centripetal. It draws youth away from marginal cultures where they now find themselves.

Youth cultures not only fail to solve problems; youth cultures represent illusionary power to mask an ever-increased powerlessness. Youth cultures close rather than open doors. They entrap, rather than liberate. They reduce options in a world where far too few options for young people exist. In the postmodern world of youth, the Eriksonian notion of adolescence as the time for experimentation, a psychosocial moratorium, is no longer operative. The risks of experimentation are too great, the rewards nonexistent. Violence; crime; the use of drugs, alcohol, and tobacco; unready pregnancy, AIDS and other sexually transmitted diseases; as well as prison and unemployment are as much a part of youth cultures as the

> extraordinary symbolic creativity of the multitude of ways in which young people use, humanize, decorate and invest with meaning their common and immediate life spaces and social practices-personal styles and choices of clothes; selective and active use of music, TV, magazines, decorations of bedrooms; the drama of friendship groups; music making and dance. Nor are these pursuits and activities trivial or inconsequential. (Willis, 1990, p. 2)

Willis et al. are on safe ground when they stated that youth cultures are not "trivial or inconsequential." To the contrary, they can be deadly.

Before we make the case and present the evidence for a democratic school culture, we briefly examine two other often discussed aspects of culture-feminism and "multicultural" education.

Dealing With Male-Dominated School Culture

> To me the "female principle" is, or at least historically has been, basically anarchic. It values order without constraint, rule by custom not by force. It has been the male who enforces order, who constructs power structures, who makes, enforces, and breaks laws. (Le Guin, 1989, p. 11)

Despite concentrated efforts to create a gender-neutral school (i.e., teaching the same material to all students), the preponderance of evidence supports the contention that school remains a male-dominated enterprise. A powerful culture exists that leads students to recognize, after a 6 years in school, that certain courses of study,(i.e., science and math) are distinctly "masculine," whereas others, (i.e., reading) are less clearly "feminine" (Streitmatter, 1994).

Despite competitive examination results by girls, the longer students remain in school, the more powerful is the socialization to appropriate gender dispositions. The male oriented school culture is sustained by a variety of influences and forces. Curriculum is most resistant to change and therefore traditional bias is most difficult to eliminate. Women continue to be underrepresented in leadership roles in instructional materials and when they are represented they are often made to appear as exceptions. Bias is found in instruction, including the male bias of women in the women-dominated profession of, teaching, who wittingly or unwittingly reinforce the ideas of gender dominance of different intellectual pursuits that lead to different occupational futures. Few teachers or parents encourage girls to be "unfeminine" (Deaux, 1976; Lenney, 1977), and so it is not surprising that so many female students come to believe that doctors and lawyers is men's work and inappropriate for females (Fiorentine, 1987). All of this has a bearing on the overrepresentation of women in "women's work"—teaching, nursing, and social work—and the continued overrepresentation of men in "men's work"—

medical doctors and engineering. Women have made significant intrusions into men's work; there has been no corresponding increase of men in "women's work." The continuation of a male-dominated culture also explains the enormous difference in wage and prestige between "women's work" and "men's work."

With male domination, the adult influence on culture joins with the biases of youth cultures. Students who choose to challenge the male bias in some youth culture pay a particularly heavy psychological price, exacted by their peers. One such price is popularity with both male and female peers. Female peers, who accept traditional socialization, react negatively to those who do not, and young women experience the pain of exclusion and derision. But much more painful and more powerful is the pressure put on young women when they enter into a man's world. There they meet every form of subtle and unsubtle aggression. Even if this pressure suddenly and miraculously disappeared, there would be residual effects because defined roles for men and women are so deeply embedded in both youth cultures and in the school culture Young women would be discouraged from crossing the line because of anticipated conflict (O'Leary, 1974).

The more civilized aspect of male domination is reflected in lack of encouragement. But there is also an ugly side of a male-dominated culture and that is harassment and brutalization.

Which of the Feminisms Informs a Democratic Education?
No particular feminism informs a democratic classroom, although traditional feminism as expressed by Susan B. Anthony and extended through Carrie Chapman Catt comes closest to our democratic ideal of equal encouragement and universal participation. With the enormous activity and arcane analysis associated with much of feminism and the low esteem with which electoral politics is currently held, the marvelous accomplishment of women suffrage tends to be devalued. That women who currently represent the majority of voters in the United States has not resulted in first-class citizenship for women, or that the movements that produced the vote disintegrated in the 1920s can not be blamed on feminists who led the suffrage movements. Schools, however, must accept much of the responsibility for an uninformed and apathetic citizenry.

Feminism has had its impact on modern culture life. The lives of women have changed accordingly, but the changes have not been limited solely to women. Men have been affected, as have social institutions. Feminist thinking has led to improved conditions in the life of well-situated women. It has had little or no impact (perhaps even negative impact) on the life of poor women (Sykes, 1996). In the past two decades, there has been dramatic demarcation between the rich and the poor that has impacted the lives of women and certain minorities. (African Americans and Latinos, particularly those whose origins are in Mexico, have been the most affected in the United States. In Australia, the same case can be made for indigenous Australians). Life has never been so good for affluent women. Life conditions are deteriorating for poor women. The kind of feminist thinking that has produced dramatic changes in life conditions for some women and has markedly altered university curriculum must become a part of the democratic classroom. So, although no particular version of feminism informs the democratic classroom all forms belong there and students, male as well as female, need to be come acquainted with the logic of each and its relevance to solving particular problems. Examining feminism within a democratic classroom brings into focus the antagonistic forces within any social movement. Feminism, like all ethnic, class, or racial movements directed against a felt imbalance of power are torn by three conflicting goals: equality within the system, return to some distant mythic past when power relations were reversed (e.g., matriarchy in place of patriarchy), and a new society established through synthesis.

Multicultural Education

Schools have attempted to address diversity with multicultural education. Although heralded as innovative and significant reform, it has hardly been that. In fact, multicultural education has done little to bring about an understanding of diversity and the dynamics of a deeply divided and hierarchical society; it has managed to fuel a spirited and sometimes ugly opposition. As currently implemented, multicultural education is insufficiently attractive to alter entrenched belief systems. It is superficial, static, cautious, and not organized to solve any problem. It is not oriented to creating a "culture" to which all belong. Multicultural education is a very thin veneer applied to a society that is rapidly unraveling.

In 1920 Yeats wrote:

Things fall apart; the centre cannot hold;
Mere anarchy is loosed upon the world,

The blood-dimmed tide is loosed, and everywhere
The ceremony of innocence is drowned;
The best lack all conviction, while the worst
Are full of passionate intensity.
("The Second Coming")

Yeats could have written that yesterday. But the situation has worsened, the center is smaller, more unstable. And babble about multiculturalism has not helped at all. The problem to be solved is the recreation of a center within which crucial common values are shared and from which, like spokes in a wheel, all of the diverse "cultures" emerge. The center is the core of a *democratic culture*. The core is democratic to the extent that all of the diverse groups have been actively recruited to participate in its development. Each has brought knowledge to it. The rights of each has been respected in its development and those rights are guaranteed as a precondition for further refinement and evolution. And each cultural spoke is equally encouraged to succeed in its development.

Crucial to the survival of the species will be our ability to develop a democratic culture. One need look no further than Somalia, the former Yugoslavia, the former U.S.S.R., the treatment of immigrants in the United Kingdom or Germany, aborigines in Australia and almost any inner-city in the United States to see the future if we fail to construct a centripetal center that has as its intent the drawing, everyone to it. The success in pulling diversity to the center will, of course, be the determining measure.

The ultra-right is dedicated to the establishment of a center. Its center is manifestly undemocratic. The far right has no respect for diversity. It is coercively authoritarian. There is no place in it for pro-choice advocates, gays or lesbians, or even advocates of bilingualism or an amended Western Canon. And yet they are likely to prevail if a democratic alternative is not seriously attempted. Multiculturalism to the intellectual right is assimilationism or, cultural restoration (Ball, 1993) and its symbol is the melting pot (see Fig. 5.1).

Multiculturalism as the "Melting Pot"

The public school, as it was conceived in it development in the United States and Australia and to a somewhat lesser extent in Great Britain, had as its primary mission the socialization of diverse populations—differing in religion, race and ethnicity to the acceptance of the laws, values and mores of the dominant society. The school had a role to play in the melting pot: to facilitate

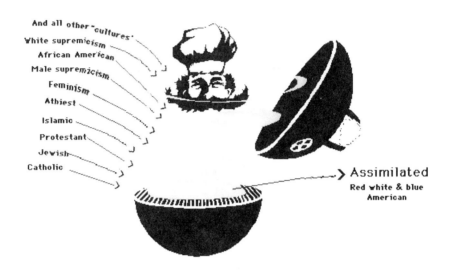

And all other cultures
White supremicism
African American
Male supremicism
Feminism
Athiest
Islamic
Protestant
Jewish
Catholic

Assimilated
Red white & blue
American

Figure 5.1. Multiculturalism as the "melting pot"

assimilation. No matter how different students were in their thinking when they entered school, all would come out the same—knowing their place, being law-abiding citizens, speaking a common language, having loyalty to God, king (or other certified authority), and country, and possessing the skills to be productive workers. That was the system a multicultural education was to replace. However, it was not to be totally replaced. Most of the characteristics of the melting pot were to be retained. There needed to be greater recognition of the contributions of women and minorities, but these recognitions were to be patched on to the existing system. Two models were introduced into schools. There is no evidence that either has had any effect on student attitudes or behavior. One is "pluralism" (see Fig. 5.2); the other the "salad bowl" approach (see Fig. 5.3).

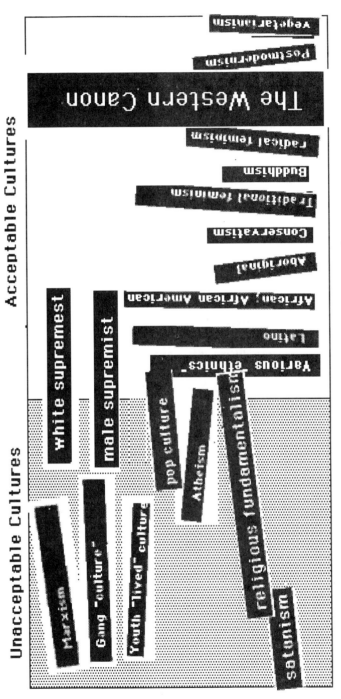

Figure 5.2. Multicultural education as "pluralism"

Multicultural education as "pluralism." Pluralism in general practice calls for all school-recognized cultures to be "celebrated"— one right after another. February, for example, in the United States is Black or African, American History Month. During that month, bulletin boards are graced with pictures of great African Americans whose exploits are lauded. Students get to hear a recording of Martin Luther King Jr.'s "I Have a Dream" speech, and are given the opportunity to become acquainted with W. E. B. Du Bois, Frederick Douglass, Rosa Parks, and Jackie Robinson. Now that they are safely, dead even Paul Robeson and Malcolm X can be celebrated. These celebrations are perfunctory. Names and events are ripped from context. The divisions within a "culture" are not examined, nor are the diverse internal strains that have added both richness and tragedy. It is not explained that all cultures are divided by tensions that are not readily reconcilable. It is impossible to understand the struggle of African Americans for justice without appreciation of at least three conflicting forces that have been so much of the process. One trend is *assimilation*—to do whatever it takes to make it in the "White man's world." And that effort can only be understood with a balanced sense of the costs of such an effort. Understanding the costs of assimilation would be difficult enough for an outsider if there was consistency across time and space. Some who strove to assimilate had to pay a much higher price for attempted assimilation than have others. Some few even got favored treatment. There is nothing in the school-presented Black History parade, which is what it is, that explains how one person whose great accomplishments are never recognized and suffered indignity heaped on indignity trying to be accepted, while another with much lesser accomplishments gets an appointment as a senior fellow to the Hoover Institution.

Another deeply rooted aspiration has been Afrocentric, the maintenance of links to a historical past. (These difference are analogous to the contradictory movements in feminism of "same" and "different"). And yet a third impulse has been efforts to reform (or separate from) the larger society—To create a new society to replace the existing racist society.

The current school approaches to multicultural education do not answer questions, nor do they solve any problems. Actually, the approach creates problems. It leaves a great many White students who have had limited or negative interaction with Black students frustrated, perplexed and angry. The too little knowledge they have been allowed to learn "is a dangerous thing." Not only is insufficient attention given to the complex issue of race relations in the United States (Australia, Great Britain, or everywhere else), but the absence of context allows the celebrations to provide a legitimacy to current injustices by caricaturing bad things no longer in practice.

And once February is over, March comes and its time for Women's History Month, During Women's History Month students get a chance to discover the existence of Lucretia Mott, Elizabeth Cady Stanton, Susan B. Anthony, maybe Virginia Woolf or George Elliot, and a few other remarkable women with the same superficiality that marked Black History. With multicultural education, the principle of equal superficiality is scrupulously observed. And that principle is applied to multiculture when applied to Latinos, Native Americans, and/or Australian aboriginals.

In a world where shared understanding is a prerequisite to the solution of important problems, "pluralism" serves to further fragment. It is impossible to constructively deal with diversity (a) without a clear idea of what constitutes a democratic society, (b) without knowledge of the role of schools in developing and sustaining such a society, and (c) knowledge of how diversity and shared understanding interconnect.

Moreover pluralism as currently defined is as much defined by what is excluded as it is by what is deem acceptable for inclusion. Popular culture does not get its month, nor do "gangs" or politically radical perspectives. A case could be made for their exclusion, but no more reasoned argument is made for exclusion than there is for inclusion. Multicultural education is served up as a package.

Excluding popular culture is missed opportunity. We agree with Farber et al. (1994) that school should "tune in" to popular culture (popular cultures) but for very different reasons. Farber, et al. are intrigued by the different texts and forms of expressions of popular culture and want to invest scholarly attention in them; whereas our primary interest is in examining popular culture for what is not there. We analyze popular culture for its potentiality in preparing youth for leadership in a world that is too much with them. We side with James Baldwin (1963) that the popular cultures that have entrapped youth are "fantasies that have nothing to do with reality" (Baldwin, 1963). We note that Baldwin gave his talk to teachers in 1963. If given in the 1990's he would have commented on how much sicker those who have created popular culture have become and how much more it is removed from reality.

What Willis called *common culture* o r *lived culture* cannot be dismissed or underemphasized. Such culture is critical to young people's lives. It is, however, far from common. Youth cultures are as widely divided from each other as they are from adult-authority driven cultures. And although youth lived cultures are important statements, it also must be recognized *and communicated* that these are inadequate cultures. Teachers need to recognize and interpret to students the notion that these lived cultures of youth reflect the despair, the disarray, and the felt helplessness of passengers on a rudderless ship churning on rolling sea. Willis made a concerted effort to promote positive qualities of youth cultures. We find this analysis unconvincing, but we also recognize that youth cultures are important for youth and therefore, unreal and perhaps even destructive as they may be, these cultures should be an integral part of the curriculum.

It is the claim of cable television representatives that cable is the embodiment of democracy, because every group (and maybe in time every individual) has a channel of its (or his or her) own, which is not exactly what Virginia Woolf meant by A Room of One's Own It is interesting to note that although the programming changes channel to channel, the advertisers remain fairly constant. From our perspective, cable television is the farthest thing from democracy. The dismembering of society, the dispersing of each splinter to its own self-sealed enclave, cannot produce democracy. It can only move in the opposite direction. When splintered, no group is large enough to influence the mass, and choice is limited to consumption. None of the powerless groups can produce much of anything, certainly nothing of substance. Each culture is held captive by ever larger and less accountable corporate enterprises. No longer is there effort to produce for felt need. With the development of a consumer society, production comes first, followed by a campaign to create a want. Which is exactly what happened with "multicultural education" with one important distinction; there has not been much of a campaign to create a need.

Multiculturalism as a "Salad Bowl." A "mixed salad" is a metaphor for something that stands between assimilation and isolated parallel cultures. The mixed salad calls for sharing, equal valuing, elaborating on the extent to which mainstream society is multicultural and identifying the important contributions of different cultures to generally accepted values and understandings. Instead of the assimilated stew, society becomes a "mixed salad,"

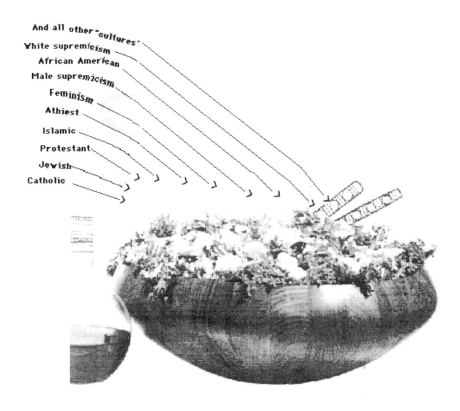

And all other cultures
White supremicism
African American
Male supremicism
Feminism
Athiest
Islamic
Protestant
Jevish
Catholic

Figure 5.3. Multiculturalism as a "salad bowl"

with all cultures equally identified and equally valued. Mixed salad translates into incorporating into teaching ways of thinking that are not mainstream (e.g., the Native American [American Indian] concept of stewardship of resources mixed together with the dominant infatuation with growth). With the salad bowl, there is a conscious effort to develop an understanding of how other people think and arrive at conclusions and the values that inform actions (Kinetz, 1995) Salad bowl or stew as an alternative to multicultural education is a distinction without a difference. The notion that all will be equally valued is the sugar-coating of problems that has continually plagued public education. Equally valuing all cultures does not correspond to reality and there is no compelling force to bring equal valuing about. If there is to be a change in student values, a much more thorough treatment of culture needs to occur in classrooms than is indicated by the mixed salad approach. Students can only be expected to change values if there is something to be gained from such a change. Mixed salad does not offer much for a persuasive argument for value change. It is not sufficient to argue that such a change would be "nice." Nice is not a powerful argument in a situation where school cultures breed like bacteria in warm garbage and when different school cultures are increasingly antagonistic. As communication between different school cultures declines hostility, between them increases. "Jocks" (athletes) don't like the "nerds" (the studious), the "soshes" (popular with the adults) don't like the "druggies," the "Crips" (one street gang) don't like the "Bloods" (another street gang), the reds don't like the blues, the "Grunges" don't like the "Trendies," the "Gothics" don't like the "Head-Bangers," the Christian right doesn't like the secular left, heavy metal doesn't like soft rock, and "nobody likes the Jews" (from a satirical song by Tom Lehrer). "Salad bowl," like "melting plot" and "pluralism," is a fairy tale response to the reality of the school. What's more, students recognize it as such.

Tolerance, Laundry Lists, and Universal Values as a Response to the Dilemma of Diversity

Boyd (1996) looked at efforts to address pluralism in the classroom. He comments on the three perspectives that have informed efforts to address the dilemma of diversity, the heart of which is not the "superficial" characteristic (i.e., food, clothing, art, and music) that he called the "munch, stomp, and dress up" approach, but the more substantial issues of resolving problems of "moral values that form the motivational heart of different ways of life" (Boyd, 1996, p. 612). The dilemma is substantial—how can schools include and provide equal respect to ways of life that not only do not respect each other but are basically incompatible? In an attempt to resolve the dilemma Boyd reviewed the approaches used in schools (The Groundless Tolerance Perspective, The Laundry List of Values Perspective, and the Search for Universals Perspective) and finds all to be inadequate.

The Groundless Tolerance Perspective, or "tolerance as a panacea" or "aren't differences great?" is exemplified by values clarification (Raths, Harmin, & Simon, 1978). This perspective is dismissed by Boyd as superficial, "the appearance of a quick fix to what is a much deeper problem" (p. 618).

The Laundry List of Values Perspective is a "more sophisticated . . . (listing) of 'common values' held by all cultures" (p. 618). Diversity from this perspective is ". . . a smoke screen . . . concealing a 'more solid laundry list' of common values" (p. 618) . . . the shared values act as "'campfire circle crazy glue'" (p. 619) that bind all cultures together. The list is "created by a loose, consultative, trial-and-error process" (p. 619) . . . and "amounts to empirically denying the fact of *reasonable* pluralism" (p. 620) "a facade of commonality to hide multidimensional differences" (p. 620). Boyd believes that listing "the names that different cultures give to 'values' (or concepts) serves only to confuse naming and meaning. (It is the) deeper level of meaning (that) must be shared across cultures for . . . cultural pluralism to gain legitimacy" (p. 620).

The Search for Universals Perspective, is "an attempt is made to look under surface variation (and commonality) to uncover the universally valid values and moral principles . . . that do not vary because they are built into the structure of the universe" (p. 621). Boyd cited Kohlberg's (1984) theory of moral development as an example of such panculturalism (i.e., all cultures go through identical stages in the development of moral reasoning). This perspective, although "more sophisticated" (p. 622) is no improvement over the other two "because 'down deep' those who hold this perspective really believe there is only one moral culture, waiting for someone to find it, the best candidates for the someone probably being them—that is, their own favored cultural group" (p. 622).[1]

---

[1]We come to a similar conclusion about Kohlberg, albeit arriving at it from a very different route. The elitism Boyd found in Kohlberg (and other panculturalists), we find manifest in deficit thinking (attributed to unfavored cultural groups or even individuals and we describe how this leads to unequal encouragement in the chapter in which we treat the democratic requirement of equal encouragement.

Boyd concluded that all efforts at incorporating cultural pluralism fail because none adequately treat the reality of unequal power relationships, the existing hierarchical arrangement of powerful and powerless, the contented and the discontented (Galbraith, 1992) among the various cultures in the schools, and as a consequence all do harm because they disguise reality rather than come to grips with it.

Boyd knitted together a proposal for resolving the diversity dilemma consisting of tolerance (tested by the opportunity for powerless and unpopular values to be expressed); the development of a list of shared "values" (created by ". . . . localized performative efforts at reciprocal intelligibility, with dynamic intelligibility itself understood to carry significant moral weight" p. 628); and, "universals" (". . . . activating and maintaining constructivist institutions of inclusive interchange and shared public identification of value stances that actively support such institutions" p. 628).

Boyd's proposal for resolving the diversity dilemma is a far cry from a school-created democratic culture, but his ideas are consistent with such a goal and the analysis is also consistent, albeit much more limited, with our concerns about the distribution of power in schools and how this affects the educational process. Boyd's argument has limited utility however, it suffers from much the same inadequacies that he found in current perspectives. He, too, is trying to remedy a complex difficult problem with a grossly insufficient proposal that is further handicapped by the absence of a guiding general theory

Muticultural Education as "Stages". Although schools for the most part have given superficial treatment to multicultural education, some scholars have approached the subject with serious intent; among these are Banks and Grant and their colleagues. Both have long histories of dedicated involvement in school equity issues and multicultural education. Both believe that multicultural education constitutes a vital ingredient, if not the most important element, in the achievement of equity. Neither are impressed with what passes for multicultural education and both make similar proposals for change.

Banks (1993) projected a four-level approach to multicultural education. The first level would be called *pluralism.* He described this level as the "contribution approach" marked by celebrations of heroes and holidays and distinguished by the assignment of discrete characteristics to specific "cultures."

Level 2 the *additive approach,* is a little more intrusive and the curriculum is altered by adding to it some content associated with specific "cultures," some concepts that distinguish the culture, and some of its characteristic themes and perspectives. What makes the multicultural approach additive is that no change in curriculum structure is acquired (analogous to what we identified as a"salad bowl"). In Level 3, the "transformational approach" the structure of curriculum is altered to such an extent as to enable students to view ideas, issues, specific events, and particular themes from the perspectives of different cultural groups. The final and highest level, and the one recommended by Banks is the *"social action approach."* The multicultural education provided at this level enables students to reach decisions on problems affecting issues of equity and to engage in social action.

Sleeter and Grant (1994) have a five-level approach and the highest level that they recommend, "multicultural and social reconstructionist, practicing democracy" is similar to 4th level proposed by Banks.

Banks and Grant apparently believe that it is necessary to begin at the lower levels in order to develop the understanding and support for the the higher levels of multicultural education.

There are important similarities between what the higher stages of multicultural education as proposed by Banks and Sleeter and Grant and our ideas of democratic education. There are also important differences. Democratic education is a total concept and transcends multiculturalism. We believe that what Banks and Sleeter and Grant proposed is insufficiently transforming and unless broader issues are considered, (e.g., work, citizenship responsibilities, student rights and participation in governance of the school), the appreciation of diversity will be resisted and efforts at multicultural education will be sabotaged.

We are troubled by the definitions of culture used by Banks and Sleeter and Grant. Culture is not synonymous with ethnicity, race, or gender. Culture is influenced by race, ethnicity, religion, class, age, and gender, and among other things by the availability of work, indulgence in psychoactive chemicals, media, weather, the organization or disorganization of community, the availability of sophisticated weaponry, and architecture. The differences within race, ethnicity, and gender are as interesting in the development of a democratic culture as are the similarities. Dyson (1996)made a powerful argument for the extent to which race intrudes into all U. S. cultures. He was concerned with the deep divisions within African-American life and the dozens of cultures these divisions have spawned (e.g., jazz doesn't talk to hip-hop). He is acutely aware of how much white American cultures continue to be influenced by Black America. He said, Hip-hop's appeal to white youth extends the refashioning of mainstream America by black popular culture. From sports to fashion, from music to film, innovations in American art owe a debt to the creativity of black culture (Dyson, 1996, p. 115).

Some of this influence is positive, most has been negative. Racism is a dominant factor in many cultures. It takes many forms and is often disguised in half-hearted or misguided efforts at multicultural education. Only with the development of truly democratic culture is it possible to transcend "the subtle, subversive ways race continues to poison our lives" (Dyson, 1996, p. 223). If we have made progress in gender equality (and that is not entirely clear), we are regressing in dealing with race. It is a topic that schools treat gingerly, if at all.

DEMOCRATIC CULTURE AS A RESPONSE TO DIVERSITY

In a democratic culture, everyone is invited into the debate over what belongs in the center. The center contains only that which is freely supported by near unanimity. There is no special privilege given to established authority. Nothing is put into the center through an a priori arrangement. For the center to be truly centripetal and to have the capacity to draw everyone to it, students are encouraged to bring to school their lived cultures and all not proscribed by law that is associated with those cultures—dress, hair style, tattoos,and so on Once there is a general consensus on what belongs in the center, each culture that accepts the center is represented as a spoke emerging from the center and students are encouraged to see the classroom from that perspective (See Fig. 5.4.).

Regardless of the sincerity of invitation and the removal of all obstacles for participation, some will find they have nothing to share with others (or what they have is precluded by law) and remain outside. The unwillingness of some to join the center is not a problem if, a very big if, those who choose to remain outside constitute a small and declining minority. As long as the class starts with almost everyone in the center and the trend is for steady movement toward the center, and the center continues to grow (i.e., more and more is shared), a democratic culture is viable. Where there is wide-scale evacuation from the center, democracy is not possible (nor in our opinion is any enduring society).

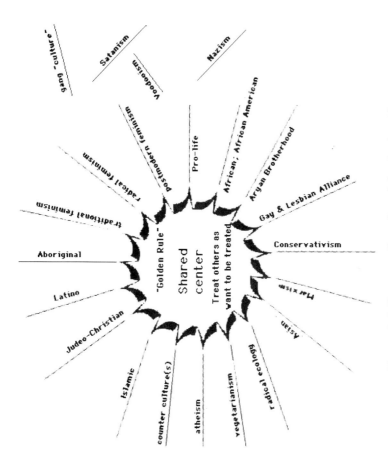

Figure 5.4. Democratic culture's beginning phase

In the development of democratic culture it is not necessary for everyone to like each other. It is necessary that everyone be persuaded to make a serious attempt to understand each other and resist making caricatures of each other. The attempt is to find common ground. Are there values that all share? Are there characteristics that some (or one may have) that all others can live with? Is there a way of settling differences that does not require fight or flight? The striving for a democratic center raises to consciousness two problems a class (a school or a nation) must be able to solve. One problem involves the development of an individual who can lead a gratified existence and be a competent culture carrier in a world of diversity and divisiveness. The other problem involves preparing the individual for the social responsibility to play a significant role in the creation of a center where all can enter and be made to feel welcome. Just as with democratic education for work, individual needs cannot be met without addressing larger issues, so too, individual gratifications cannot be satisfied without a sustaining culture.

What Belongs in the Center?

Without an unchallengeable authority there is no standard to determine what belongs in the commonly accepted center. More clear is what cannot be there. A shared center is not democratic if it encompasses the belief that knowledge must be rationed, permits only some to participate in decision making, does not equally guarantee rights to students, and encourages some while discouraging others. In other words, although not all of the defined requirements for a democratic education have to be part of the initial shared understandings, the active denial of them disqualifies the center from democratic status.

If all are invited to participate and the participation is free and open, it is highly unlikely that the center will be actively antidemocratic. It is also unlikely that it will initially contain any of our designated democratic requirements. The initial center is likely to contain very little.

Bloom insisted that Shakespeare may be the only item in the Western Canon that would make it into the center, where all groups would recognize its immortality. It would be interesting to see if he was right and if Shakespeare would be revived if students were encouraged to evaluate its universal appeal. It may not be possible to find initial agreement on any text—cultures being as antagonistic to each other as they are. The initial agreements may be on rules of procedure or on defining student rights rather than criteria for immortality.

The primary venue for intercultural exchange is in the classroom as part of curriculum and instruction. Youth cultures in the democratic classroom should not be considered as substitutes for the "classics," but as legitimate expressions of culture to be contrasted with teacher introduced topics, and used to enliven discussion and broaden the context for analysis. The argument for timelessness of important cultural creations is convincing only if students are willing to carry the tradition forward. A mutually respectful give and take between generations on culture cannot only be exciting and interesting, it can help generate more of a shared language than is currently possible. It can also deepen appreciation and improve the quality of analysis and criticism. Ignoring television that youth watch does not lessen television's hold on youth. Bringing youth culture into the classroom for thorough analysis in which the teacher, and other invited guests, express their views may do more to extinguish it, (or lessening its impact), than any effort to outlaw its existence or pretend it is not there. There is no better place to begin a coherent discussion about democracy than in the discussion of culture.

We began this chapter with a quote from Barber (1992), "television is the true 'great American educator,' and little that the schools attempt to do or undo can compete with it" (p. 33). We take the opposite position. Schools can compete with television, but more importantly, schools can use television. It just requires an engrossing and challenging school to replace the dull, irrelevant one that many wish to patch up.

Culture is important to students, maybe the most important aspect of their lives. Students spend enormous amounts of their time in cultural activities. It turns them on. They listen to music for hours on end. They do art (we call it graffiti). They watch films and television and bring considerable psychological investment to these activities.

Broadening the discussion about culture is an important ingredient in a democratic classroom, but that in itself is also insufficient. Students need to produce culture. It is not enough to sustain values. Students produce values and intellectual understanding. They embellish language and originate style. The classroom must be a place for symbolic creativity, for the creation of literature and the development of critical capacities. All students should be encouraged to create music, art, drama, dance. School symphony orchestras, marching bands, jazz choirs, and theatrical productions should be continued and even extended, but in addition, students should be encouraged to create new art forms, write, produce, and act in their own plays, compose music, generate dance bands to supplement and supplant disk jockeys at school dances. The same students who perform in *Fiddler on the Roof*, can create their own musicals and generate talent for a school-sponsored teen club. Students, in addition to a school newspaper and a literary journal, can develop television and radio stations. If there are inadequate resources, television and radio studies can be simulated with camcorders, VCRs, and tape cassettes. All cultural art forms should be brought to the center for examination, reflection, and synthesis while at the same time opportunity is created for diverse cultures to become different spokes for different folks. The goal of such a democratic educational endeavor, is encourage each student to broad cultural literacy, while possessing the background and understanding to influence the direction of social policy in local art commissions and the national endowments of the humanities.

Diversifying Staff, a Necessary Component in Democratic Education

In the chapter on work, we presented career ladders as a means by which work can be democratized and to stimulate student imagination. Given the enormous discrepancy between the demography of teachers and demography of students, creating career ladders to a teacher credential is vitally necessary for democratic education (Pearl & Riessman, 1965). Without serious effort to diversify teachers by ethnicity and class, claims for commitment of muticulturalism ring hollow. And there can be no serious commitment to diversifying teaching staffs without establishing career ladders that one can begin to climb with no prior education, skill or experience and with rungs that readily permit the attainment of a professional credential.

Critical Theorists and Democratic Education

A number of scholars over the last few decades have examined education and leveled criticisms similar to ours. They call themselves critical theorists and they too, advocate a democratic education with a strong radical feminist (and postmodernist nuance) bent.[2] We welcome their contributions to the debate. They write with power and passion. They bring a special perspective to areas that have been superficially examined— class bias, sexism, and racism. We would like to see ourselves as their allies, and in many ways we are. But the differences between us are large and need exposition. They speak with the authority of critics but with very little history of sustained involvement in democratic education projects. Thus, the arguments of critical theorists need to be taken on the faith not a record of accomplishments. To recognize and condemn the unjust and the oppressive does not necessarily lead to justice and freedom. One of the expressed goals of the critical theorists is to be anti-hegemonic. As Weiler (1988) said, If feminist teaching is to contribute to what Giroux and others have called the building of counter-hegemony, then we must be conscious of the realities of various forms of oppression and the realities of intersecting and conflicting forms of power (p. 125.)

Anti-hegemonic is not synonymous with democracy, and in fact there is no clear idea of what an anti-hegemonic classroom would look like except that in it teachers recognize and actively oppose all manifestations of hegemony in the classroom. An inadequate definition of democracy leads to inappropriate actions on the part of teachers. The critical educator assumes a moral superiority, the unique ability to recognize right from wrong and thus recreates the vanguard in critical theory that was jettisoned with the decline of Marxism. The anti-hegemonic, feminist teacher is required to support feminist students. Weiler (1988) presented a number of examples of feminist teachers acting as agents against "male chauvinism" by supporting feminist students and identifying with their interests. We oppose such practice not because we believe the critical theorist will indoctrinate students. Our concern is just the opposite. We believe the teacher taking sides will lose contact with students who do not share her or his views. The conceit actually has the effect of justifying the hegemony that is ostensibly opposed. critical theorists claim they are justified by their partisanship because by so doing they empower the powerless. There is no evidence that is what happens, or whether it is even possible to empower someone else. In the democratic class-

---

[2]Prominent among the critical theorists are Jean Anyon, Michael Apple, Madeleine Arnot (also Madeleine MacDonald), Stanley Aronowitz, Henry A. Giroux, Paulo Freire, Patti Lather, Ira Shor, Roger Simon, and Kathleen Weiler. Critical theorists draw heavily on Paulo Freire and Italian Marxist scholar and activist Antonio Gramsci (Gramsci, 1971).

room, students are encouraged to assume power but not at the expense of other students.

Critical theorists cannot seriously consider themselves democratic when they persist in communicating in a language none but them understand. *Hegemony,* for example, is a term "Critical Theorists" appropriated from Marxists—it is a password used to gain admittance into a club; it mystifies rather than clarifies power relationships in schools. In fact, the term tends to distort the nature of those relationships and unnecessarily makes the difficult problem of inequity of power in social relationships more difficult. Basically critical theorists play at politics. Politics is not talking the good talk, or even walking the good walk, it is influencing decisions at the classroom level, and if you are paying attention, you will immediately recognize things are not going the critical theorists way, and they have no clear sense of how things can be turned around with coherent tactics and strategy of change. Publishing the same book every year lamenting hegemonic education is not going to cut it. In a very real sense critical theorists make the mistake for which one of their mentors, Freire, skewered others: creating an exclusive "circle of truth" that enables those included to applaud the work of each other while remaining oblivious to everyone else.

Can Teachers Express Their Political Views in Democratic Classroom?

Of course! But in so doing the teacher relinquishes authority and thereby clearly establishes that not only are students free to disagree with her or him, but further, the teacher must also offer students the opportunity to hear views of adults who oppose what the teacher believes. In the democratic classroom, it is not the power of the speaker, nor the popularity of the opinion, but the power of the argument as established by the logic and the evidence used that prevails.

Having indicated our differences with critical theorists it is also important to indicate where similarities lie. We both share a commitment to problem-solving education and our understanding of what that means comes closest when directed at literacy.

"Hey, What About Me? I Teach Reading to Barely Literate Students." I haven't time for all this high-falutin' knowledge to solve problems. Once I teach my students to read they have all the skills they need to solve problems. Anyway they aren't smart

enough, nor could I possibly teach them enough, in the time I have, to solve the problems you talk about. Furthermore it isn't necessary, we are doing quite well with the education we have. This is how many teachers respond to our call for a problem-solving curriculum

There is probably no more destructive conclusion for a teacher to come to than to accept what currently passes for education. The belief that teaching minimal skills is doing all that can be reasonably done is held by too many people. If we continue to trivialize education we will not only fail to solve important problems but we will also lose a constituency. We will fail to motivate students. Reading is rarely an end unto itself for students who live in comfort and have a future laid out for them. Reading is never an end unto itself for students who struggle for survival in a hostile environment. Reading opens up the world to students, but once it is opened up they need to do something with it. Education to Freire, (1968, 1970, 1985), is acting on the world to change it and then reflecting on those efforts. Reading is too important to waste on trivial assignments.

Science and Math and the Problem-Solving Curriculum. Math and science are as much a part of culture-carrying competence as great works of literature. Just as with reading, students do not learn math and science, they use math and science to learn to solve important problems. Science and math are part of the accumulated inventions of culture and a much larger portion of it belongs in the center of shared understanding than is currently the case.

There is an important difference in examining what exists as shared understanding in science and math than in what has been lumped together in the humanities. With the humanities there is considerable disagreement of who or what belongs—Adrienne Rich or Louise Bogan? Ernest Hemingway or Langston Hughes? That is not the nature of the argument when it comes to science and math. Here, the issue is not what belongs, but who gets how much? As discussed previously, sexual bias in science and math has resulted in female students being unrepresented in advanced classes, and in the math and science class they do attend they are given less attention than male students. This means that women have less access to the center than men. In a democratic classroom, the center is equally accessible to everyone (how that is accomplished is treated in more detail in the chapter on equal encouragement).

In a democratic classroom, students are held to at least as demanding standards as that found in a traditional class. The difference: In the democratic classroom far more students are expected to achieve those standards and that differences in performance by gender, class, race, or ethnicity are NOT expected. For those standards to be met, the approach to math and science must be changed substantially. With the current system of fragmented subjects, instruction should be steered toward the problems that can be solved with what is currently being taught. This will require considerably more biography, anecdotes, and cooperative learning than is currently the case. The emphasis on the instruction must be on current and future usefulness. One way that usefulness can be forcefully demonstrated is the students are encouraged to use what they have learned in meaningful research.

In a democratic classroom drill, is not pitted against explanation, both are necessary. When a student appears to be confused, the instructor is obliged to explain. Drill is important in a democratic classroom, but only after students are persuaded that the activity is worth the effort. Whitehead (1929) in the early part of the 20th century, insisted that there was a natural rhythm to education and that interest has to precede discipline (i.e., drill). The democratic classroom reclaims the common sense of education that seems to have been lost somewhere in the acrimony of meaningless squabbling.

Even in its early stages, a democratic classroom will be recognizably different from the traditional classroom. The democratic classroom will be distinguished by emphasis on the problems that can be solved with mastery of a particular area of concentration. Whitehead insisted there was no reason to teach quadratic equations if it could not be shown that learning how to solve quadratic equations would be useful in addressing current life problems. The rule to follow is that problem-solving education works best when the problem is neither contrived nor trivial. The democratic classroom will also differ from the traditional classroom in that students will be provided much more historical context to the problems they are addressing. History becomes a more fascinating and useful topic when extended into math and science classroom. Understanding the history of the developments in science and mathematics helps demystify these subjects. Mathematics and science grew in response to problems needing solution in agriculture, architecture, navigation and so on and the problems stimulated creativity. Not all mathematical and scientific geniuses showed early promise and seasoning the classroom with anecdote and biography is yet another way to stimulate interest and maintain focus. Math and science are not only employed in the solving of societal problems, but also play a significant role in personal decisions, (e.g., probability largely determines employment choices but also can used to develop contingency plans in all areas of life).

The merging of science and mathematics with history and biography is not done to titillate students, nor is to make life easier for teachers. Stimulating interest must be linked to student mastery of science and math. If students are not demonstrating that mastery then the efforts to stimulate interest may be a distraction and a waste of time. The most powerful motivation for continued investment of time and energy in mathematics and science is competence in the subject matter. Students will continue to grow in any intellectual endeavor in which they believe they are good at it. Although interest can lead to competence, it is much more likely that competence will lead to interest. How competence is determined is a vital matter in educational equity. We make an extensive revisit to competence in the chapter on equal encouragement in the democratic classroom.

Diversity in a Democratic Classroom

The democratic classroom is inclusive. It welcomes diversity, even diversity that has the potential of being anti-social. While all schools must protect students against actions that threaten person and property, the democratic classroom tries to win people to it rather than drive students from it. As discussed in the next chapter most of the problems students have can best be dealt within the school. It is only after the school has tried everything it knows how to do, that students should be referred to some other institution, and then only for the verified protection of the school community.

Diversity in the classroom will be expressed by musical taste, weakly formed political views, diet, sports, "cultures," recreational interests, dress, religious affiliation, and race, gender, or ethnic identity. These are differences that schools should welcome and bring into classroom discussions. As long as the affiliation to the center is strong the differences that students bring to class can only enrich discussion. Figure 5.5 depicts a situation in which there is considerable shared values and understandings. All the students have, after considerable negotiation, agreed to respect individual rights, they have agreed to a core

Rights of expression, privacy
due process, movement

Shakespeare-algebra-biology
shared sense of national history
(agree to disagree on certain points)

shared language
(agree to disagree on certain points)
disagree without being disagreeable
all students welcome at school

community service

Figure 5.5. Diversity in a democratic classroom: more mature phase

curriculum, and acceptable and unacceptable language for the conduct of school activities, to be responsible for building the community. to disagree without being disagreeable, to and make all students feel welcome in the school and to equally encouraged them. With that much in the shared center, student differences energize the classroom. The major problem facing schools is not in the treatment of differences, but in the development of a center of shared interests and understandings. Once it is recognized that such a center cannot be imposed and that the absence of a center is prologue to disaster, the efforts to freely negotiate a center will grow in importance.

Is the Recent Emphasis on Integrative Multidisciplinary Themes and Block Schedules a Significant Step in the Direction of a Democratic Classroom? Yes and no. Such efforts could be a good beginning but unless guided by coherent theory and incorporated into a comprehensive and coherent problem-solving education, such efforts will generate some initial interest that will soon disappear. This sort of tinkering cannot provide the sustained direction a good education needs. Students will not learn enough to solve important problems and the material in and of itself does not stimulate enough interest to break students out of the mental torpor that a life of television watching and other mind-numbing activities produces.

All of the current efforts advertised as "reforms" suffer from a lack of vision. Changes are made without a clear understanding of a desired outcome. What does a high school graduate have to know? What is she or he able to do? How would one determine whether the goal of "educated" has been achieved? How is this to be staged in a coherent scope and sequence? What foundations are developed in elementary grades? Middle school? Secondary school?

In practice, if our goal of a responsible, independent, informed citizen is reasonable, school, go about it backward. Little children are given more latitude than young adults. As they grow older students find themselves more restrained and their ideas less respected. Education for democratic citizenship is a logical development of more freedom coupled with more and more responsibility. A democratic classroom is organized for a logically consistent development of the skills and knowledges required for competent citizenship.

As we write, the pendulum has swung back and the multidisciplinary whole language reforms are being replaced with phonics, spelling, and other drills imposed on disinterested students. The retreat to a more deadly education is the logical consequence of an elite-driven education in which parents and students are left out of the decision making process and where their concerns fall on deaf ears.

WON'T WE SPEND ALL OUR TIME DEBATING WHAT IT IS TO BE LEARNED AND NEVER GET TO THE LEARNING? A SUMMARY OF THE ARGUMENT

Only people who waste enormous amounts of time trying to coerce students to master nonsense and even more time punishing or excluding students who resist school-based learning, question whether debate is necessary in classrooms.

Furthermore, our proposed debate does not come at the expense of knowledge. Students tend to listen to people whose proposals make sense, but even more, they are stimulated by such conversation to do research and acquire new knowledge. Debate facilitates the development of knowledge, it does not impede it. To the contrary, it is the stifling of debate that impedes knowledge.

Democratic education introduces a new form of leadership into education. Leadership in a democracy proposes, defends, and responds to counter proposals. Leadership generates an atmosphere where reason can prevail. Bringing democracy into the educational debate changes the boundaries of discussion. The intellectual context is broadened. Rather than limiting discussions to whether or not "Johnny Can Read" and if not, who's to blame, the relationship of school practice and policy to social and individual problems is examined. The introduction of democracy into the education debate elevates the importance of education.

The bankruptcy of existing educational philosophy is reflected in its inability to incorporate the parts into a whole. Most students resist education because they have no sense of where they, as individuals, and the society of which they are a part, is headed.

Chapter 6

Personal Problems or Difficulties as Problem-Solving Curriculum in the Democratic Classroom

Treating personal problems as problem-solving curriculum rather than attempting to extinguish such behaviors with "aversive reinforcements" or referring students to school personnel specialists is a distinguishing feature of the democratic classroom. Classroom disruption, drug use, reckless teen sex, violence, and vandalism are primarily curricular issues. Punishment or referrals to psychotherapists or counselors reinforce the authoritarian nature of schools, demean students, create division in school populations, establish a pecking order, systematically build inequity, and ultimately breed disrespect for established authority. In this chapter, we indicate how such "problems" can become part of a problem-solving curriculum in a democratic classroom.

Behavioral relationships between teacher and student in the secondary school largely can be summarized in one sentence: What adult authority decrees to be taught, students find irrelevant and what students find relevant is undermined by adult authority's lack of credibility. School fairly reeks with problems that school officials insist are unrelated to their primary mission. Teachers and administrators vehemently deny that drug and other substance abuse, dysfunctional families, violence, gangs, television, graffiti and irresponsible sex are major topics for instruction. Such problems are viewed as interfering with the primary purposes of education and as such are obstacles to effective teaching. Student problems and problems with students are relegated to soft areas of curriculum and are deemed far less important than core subjects such as mathematics or literature. Teachers seem to believe that if student problems and problem students would somehow go away, they could get to the business of educating—unless of course the roof leaked, the copy machine broke down or the computer crashed. Most teachers do not think that the problems they complain about are the logical consequences caused or exacerbated by an undemocratic education. Nor does it occur to them then that what they perceive to be obstacles or interferences are precisely what a problem solving education must address. Currently, public schooling is not made inoperative by disruptive or distracted students, but by the approach taken with students who cannot be coerced to conform to mandated norms or standards of behavior.

Credibility of adult authority is determined by the nature of the relationship. When the teacher attempts to impose authority, taking on the role of guardian, he or she becomes an enemy of democracy (Dahl, 1989), while establishing an adversarial relationship with many students. It cannot be otherwise. If a teacher tries to impose authority he or she will be resisted. The resistance increases when students find the subject irrelevant, are treated as infants, believe the treatment received at school to be unfair, and are convinced that they are doomed to fail in school-mandated projects. In fact, irrelevance, disrespect, feelings of unfair treatment, and assessed incompetence are among the major causes of behavioral problems.

A DEMOCRATIC APPROACH TO SCHOOL DISRUPTIVE BEHAVIOR

School disruptive behavior is currently treated as a classroom management or "discipline" issue, as well as an important school safety issue. Discipline has been a continuing major concern of parents and teachers. According to the annual Gallup Poll, discipline and drugs have been at the top of the list of the public's biggest problems facing public education. In the 1990's the concern over school safety heightened as the incidence of violence in school increased and the weapons, particularly guns, became common on school premises. California serves as an example of a growing epidemic: A survey revealed that "Seven in 10 Californians (69%) worry about the safety of their children" (*Handguns and Violence*, 1994, p. 1). The concern is justified by bloody reality. Violence and fear of violence has triggered a series of get-tough measures. In California, 1995 legislation mandated compulsory school expulsion for a student who brings a gun to school or brandishes any other weapon. The get-tough responses to serious problems have not solved the problem of violence in schools, nor have they appreciably reduced violence in the schools or in the community. Doubling and tripling prison and jail populations have not made streets or schools safe. Such responses may actually have worsened the situation while at the same time seriously threatened democratic practice. Get tough interventions make more difficult solving the problem of school violence or ameliorating less serious classroom disruption.

Get-tough measures are a weak-kneed response to the political pressure generated by the specter of violence. The pressure is motivated by fear, ignorance, prejudice, and the desire for vengeance. No problem has ever been solved when action taken is so motivated. The reasoned alternative is democratic education.

A democratic education approach to discipline not only makes schools and classrooms safer, it also provides important understanding of the workings of a democratic society. Only with a democratic education approach to discipline can students develop a thorough understanding of *justice* both as a concept and as a working system. In a democratic classroom, students can learn to distinguish between justice and vengeance.

Discipline in a democratic classroom meets the four requirements of a democratic education: knowledge (curriculum), participation, rights, and equal encouragement. When discipline fails to meet democratic requirements, school disruption not only continues but becomes increasingly serious. A failed discipline approach triggers increasingly more serious occurrences; minor disruptions escalate into ever more dangerous events. Rather than acknowledging that things are not working, school authorities doggedly continue on a path that should be abandoned. The response to upscaled violence has been more draconian measures. The logical consequence of this is the existing urban high school where control rather than education becomes the major concern.

Knowledge and Discipline

The knowledge component of democratic education in the general area of "behavioral problems," is curriculum designed to provide a solution to an identified problem. The approach taken is similar regardless of the severity of the problem in that all solutions meet democratic education requirements. For the discussion to be comprehensive and not mimic the current approach of meaningless slogans, teachers should introduce students to epidemiology as a method of analysis. Epidemiology brings analytical coherence to any chronic social problem. It also has sufficient breadth to encompass all theories that students will be encouraged to examine. In epidemiology, analysis focuses on the interaction of the triad of host, agent, and environment.

Designing a Safe or Nondisruptive Classroom Environment

The problem to be solved is the design of a "safe classroom" environment. Conducting research on safe environments requires students to examine a number of different possible environmental influences on behavior. One area of investigation would be gratifications or lack there of provided by the environment, the putative negative environmental influences such as those provided by "the entertainment industry" and the alleged positive environmental influences leading to reduction of violence and disruption, such as that allegedly produced by "dress codes."

The studying of behavior brings students to the examination of motivation (i.e., the reasons that underlie individual actions). If the action is deemed rational, the explanation for disruptive behavior must be found in the environment. If it is decided that such behavior is irrational (or arational), explanation must be lodged in either the host (a predisposition to arationality, e.g., limited intelligence, or irrationality, e.g., Tourrette syndrome or attention deficit disorder), or caused by an agent (e.g., a psychoactive ingested substance or a virus). Analyzing school disruption from an epidemiological perspective will require students to examine a wide range of existing hypotheses.

Gratifications Provided by the Environment. A major thesis of ours and perhaps our most powerful argument for democratic education is the positive change democratic education brings to the school environment. We believe that school disruption (and low levels of achievement) are largely the result of consistent selective denial of essential gratifications. One of the hypotheses we would urge students to test is whether the classroom has been organized to ration gratifications, that is, organized to provide some students with important gratifications that are routinely withheld from other students. Students would be asked to ascertain whether students disrupt the classroom or become threats to the safety of others because these students are denied what nondisruptive students receive: the encouragement to risk, relief from boredom or humiliation; meaningful classroom activities, the experience of first class citizenship,[1] useful school-provided learning, opportunities to demonstrate competence; opportunities for excitement in sanctioned classroom activities; hopefulness about the future; and the opportunity to be creative. Not only do we believe that these gratifications are vital determinants of student behavior, but we urge student investigators to take their analysis one step further and seriously consider whether students engage in disruptive behavior precisely because they derive more gratification from disrupting than they are able to derive from conforming behavior. (We would encourage teachers and administrators to also seriously consider such a possibility).

"Culture" As an Influence on Behavior. Culture in school is lively, amorphous and in constant flux. A single student can be "multicultural." One advantage to a democratic education is that it enlists students in the definition of culture and allows the student to define his or her own cultural membership. The school as currently constituted officially recognizes acceptable cultures, and considers only these in its multicultural education. One reason that multicultural efforts have so little influence on students is that students are more influenced by their own "lived cultures" than by the cultures the school defines for them. These youth cultures arrange them-

---

[1] If student research concludes that the problem is made to feel unwanted, then the problem is in the environment and corrections should be made in how students are welcomed into the classroom. If the research concludes that the students, perceives self to be an outsider although every effort has been made to include him or her, then the problem is either in the host or is caused by some form of psychoactive agent and the proposed solution has to be directed to accommodations in those areas, though the possibility of an undiscovered or unconsidered environmental cause should always be kept in mind.

selves in various degrees of compatibility to the official school cultures. School youth cultures take on a more hardened definition to the extent they are identified as threats by adult authority. Most alienated of all are the 'enemy' cultures, the "druggies" and the "gangsters," for whom there is "zero tolerance" and whose members are targeted for search-and-destroy missions by school authorities. We believe that student cultures emerge as the result of dynamic interactions between perceived opportunities for gratifications in the established and formal school cultures, the cultures the student brings from home and local community, the media fabricated cultures; and d) the real or imagined gratifications found in youth-fabricated cultures. The youth-derived cultures increase in importance in reverse relationship to the gratifications found in established school or home cultures.

A Managed Environment As Influence on Behavior. Student attention should be directed to existing efforts at school safety. A wide variety of environmental alterations are possible and many have become popular. Some schools increase police presence on campus. Some campuses are closed and students are forbidden to leave during school hours. Some schools do not allow students on campus without first passing through metal detectors. Some initiate dress codes and forbid the displaying of "gang colors." Each of these managed environments in different ways place student rights in jeopardy and thus are inconsistent with a general democratic educational theory. Most efforts to create a safe environment would fail to meet democratic requirements even if the decision to create them was consensual and was reached after extensive informed discussion and debate by students. The failure to meet democratic requirements is not a sufficient reason to reject any environmental change designed for student safety. Democracy recognizes states of emergency and the need to suspend rights under special circumstances and conditions. The intent of this part of the exercise is to have students generate an exhaustive list of possible safe environmental designs that they would consider, analyze, and ultimately decide to test in specific programs of action.

The Agents of Disruption. If disruption is not a function of the environment, something else must instigate it. What could that be? The identification of possible agents that induce negative behavior can be obtained by consultation with a variety of community and library resources. The intent is not to create junior biochemists or little league medical practitioners but to allow students to gain familiarity with that kind of thinking. The examination of agent influenced behavior leads students to examine "drugs," which is another student problem that needs to be addressed through democratic education.

The Host as the Initiator of Disruption. Almost all approaches to discipline hold the individual accountable for alleged misconduct. Various deficits are attributed to the individuals who are accused of classroom disruption. The deficits can be attributed to genetic, cultural, environmental, or developmental factors. The deficits used to explain disruptive behavior are also used to explain scholastic failure. A careful and thorough examination of deficit versus systemic explanations of student disruptive behavior is crucial to a democratic resolution of a discipline problem. Nothing is more absurd than trying to initiate action without first determining cause. Determining cause is more than revisiting the nature versus nurture controversy. Nor is it merely an academic exercise. The locating of the source of the problem, be it the individual, the stimulating agent, or the situation determines what is to be changed and how the change will take place. Given the lack of resolution of an age old controversy, students should help design a definitive test of the cause of disruptive behavior.

In an introduction to research, students are provided instruction to enable them to distinguish correlation from causation. Students may find that there is a connection between the type of music a student likes, for example, and a propensity for classroom disturbance. That connection however does not necessarily indicate a causal relationship. The music could cause disruption; disruptive students could be attracted to certain music; or, both the music and the disruption may be attributable to some other factor (e.g., culture).

Students should also be introduced to another epidemiological concept—level of intervention. Primary treatment focuses on prevention of a problem—stopping it before it starts. Secondary treatment is concerned with early detection (i.e., intervening in early stages of a problem). Tertiary treatment deals with the full-blown problem. Different strategies are likely to be designed for different levels of problem.

Only after students have considered discipline from an epidemiological perspective (i.e., brainstormed and generated a wide range of possible explanations) are they ready to engage in research. As with all other curricular issues, the class will be organized in student research teams to explore in depth the "best" explanations. Knowledge developed and produced by students as distinct from passively responding to adult initiated instruction is a distinguishing feature of the democratic classroom. The research teams will report back to the class, after which programs for classroom or school discipline will be developed.

Participation in the Development of a Democratic Discipline Program

The first phase of this process is selecting a discipline system. Students will derive their system from the the research they have conducted. They will be asked to select the particular discipline strategies that seem to have the best chance of success and come closest to meeting democratic requirements. The class may decide to test some strategies that do not meet democratic requirements in emergency conditions, but in these instances they must come to this decision consciously and with serious consideration of the harm that such an emergency action has on democratic thinking and practices. This phase of the process meets the democratic requirement to the extent that all members of the class have equal power in what amounts to an informed election process, and each is given equal opportunity to develop and hone citizenship skills (i.e., articulate positions, listen to other students, engage in debate, and negotiate differences).

Participation in a democratic discipline system requires specification of a developed justice system of rules and procedures that would include precise definitions of transgressions, a due process system, and defined consequences for those convicted of violating the rules. Other defining attributes of participation in the discipline system is the means by which the discipline system will be evaluated. If in the process of debating and negotiating, a consensus cannot be reached then the majority plan may be adopted, however, the minority concerns should be an important component in the evaluation of the majority plan. In some instances, two or more systems of justice can be tested and compared. The justice plan (or plans) is an experiment with predictions of specified change over a designated period (e.g., there will be a significant reduction of discipline incidents over a 6-week time span). At the end of that period, the class will reflect on the results and make adaptations. This aspect of the classroom experience follows Friere's (1968) notion of praxis—acting on the world to change it and reflecting on that action.

Democratic Discipline and Fairness (Equal Encouragement)

Nothing angers school administrators more than to be accused of unfairness. Allegations of unfairness are arbitrarily dismissed and those who have made the charges are made to feel uncomfortable (to put it mildly).

A carefully devised system of justice of rights, due process, and clear consequences for proven transgressions will go a long way to produce a fair system. But it would not go far enough. Unfairness is deeply embedded in our institutions and in our ways of thinking. Students need to examine in depth what fairness means in classroom practice. Fairness is not only equal protection under the law, fairness is also equal opportunity to invest in the system. It makes little sense to expect a student to conform to imposed restrictions on behaviors, (a justice system in the final analysis reduces to a bunch of shall nots and or elses), unless that student expects to benefit from the system. That is an element of a justice system less considered in these tough-on-crime days than it was when more liberal practices held sway.

To provide a more level playing field, it is advisable that students have access to an *ombudsman* who can serve as both advocate and counsel. An ombudsman is especially needed in the early grades and during the beginning stages of implementation.

What is important in this process and how it differs from some of the discipline approaches discussed later, is that the rules and due process system are developed only after serious research. Without opportunity to fully examine a problem, student proposals will be as poorly thought through and as ill advised as the discipline programs we later criticize. Student teams should not only evaluate the positive and negative features of each proposal but also detail the paths that must be taken to establish a particular recommendation (e.g., what must be enacted as state or federal law, what requires school board approval, and what is allowed under existing law and policy).

Until a democratic classroom is implemented, it is advisable for teachers in existing classrooms to be as resourceful and thorough in selecting or developing a discipline plan as we believe students should be in the democratic classroom.

Democratic discipline is developmental. It follows the identical logic used for the development of student government. In fact, school discipline is an integral component of student government. It constitutes the justice element of the legislative, executive, and justice triad of checks and balances.

In the early primary years, the teacher is the unchallengeable authority and explains the logic of justice system, the primacy of rights, the workings of a due process system, the limitations on punishments, and the necessity of meeting the criteria of fairness. In the next stage, the teacher serves as the supreme court, ruling on the allowability of student actions, mandating retrials, and overruling excesses of a student court. In the early developmental phases, the teacher is authoritative rather than authoritarian, explaining, not dictating. Even in the earliest stages, the teacher acquaints the student with the importance of logic and evidence by providing students with the basis for a particular decision. As students develop, the teacher relaxes control, increasingly moving to an advisory role. In high school, if the student has had the opportunity to move through every developmental phase of a democratic classroom, the teacher becomes a consultant to the process (Knight, 1991; Pearl, 1972). If the high school attempts to institute a democratic classroom without the benefit of elementary and middle school development, the phases should be telescoped with the teacher beginning as the authority and moving quickly through the advisory to the consultant role. The teacher explains in advance that his or her role will change as soon as students demonstrate the capability of greater responsibility. The students demonstrate responsibility in experiments with ever more developed justice systems.

Examining Existing Discipline Approaches in the Light of Democratic Education

Considerable attention is given to discipline in schools. In a great many programs, students preparing to be teachers insist that discipline is their primary concern when they begin their training. Once on the job, teachers are trained in specific programs that derive from every philosophic orientation. The various discipline programs claim to be informed by theory and point with pride to "proven" effectiveness.

Discipline varies across the entire spectrum of control, from the blatantly authoritarian to those that advertise themselves to be democratic. One text on discipline lists eight different models (Charles, 1989); another has nine (Duke & Meckel, 1984). Literally millions of dollars a year are spent in staff development to train teachers and administrators in one or more discipline techniques.

Behavior Modification. One of the discipline systems draws on the work of B. F. Skinner (1953, 1971) and his principle of behavioral modification. Behavior modification holds the environment responsible for human behavior. According to this approach, a student's behavior is shaped when desired actions are reinforced with rewards and undesirable behavior is extinguished by lack of attention or with aversive reinforcement (i.e., punishment; Axelrod, 1977; Thoresen, 1973). No effort is made to identify underlying reasons for behavior, nor is there any appeal to reason. Students are rewarded when they are "good" and ignored or punished when they are "bad." Behavior modification is overtly authoritarian and is more likely to be employed in classrooms believed to be saturated with students burdened with limited intelligence or characterological problems. There are many variations of behavior modification and the kindest thing that can be said of any behavior modification program is that when it works it represents the benefits of benign dictatorship.

Assertive Discipline. This system is among the most popular approaches to discipline (Canter & Canter, 1976). It has had a powerful impact in the development of school discipline policy in the United States. In Australia, almost every school has been influenced by this approach (Slee, 1995). It, too, fails to meet any of our democratic requirements, although unlike behavior modification it wraps itself in the mantle of democracy. Canter and Canter insisted that their system derives from "basic" student and teacher "rights." "Every student has the right to a learning environment that is free from disruption" (Canter, 1988, p. 59) And teachers have the right to expect support from parents and administrators. Neither of these rights meet the definition of a right. They could be, under appropriate circumstances, educational responsibilities. Providing a teacher the right of support of parents is a conspiracy against the rights of students. Such a right prejudges a situation and assumes the absence of legitimate student grievances against the teacher. In fact, Canters' rights serve to obscure the likely denial of the defensible rights of due process, privacy, right not to be a captive audience, and protection against cruel and unusual punishment. The denial of rights is what makes assertive discipline undemocratic, brutal, and ultimately unworkable. Programs such as assertive discipline are a logical consequence of efforts to solve classroom problems in the absence of a general theory.

Glasser and Dreikers. Discipline in a democratic class-room also differs widely from the Glasser and the Dreikers approaches, both of which claim to be democratic. Prior to 1985, Glasser's (1965, 1977, 1978) approach was clearly authoritarian. His system was designed to coerce students into obeying the rules, although he did suggest that students should contribute to the creation of the rules (without the knowledge developed through research and the citizenship skills required in a democracy). In his 1985 work, *Control Theory in the Classroom,* Glasser acknowledged that students must have good reasons to obey rules. This revelation meant that for successful discipline, secondary school must become "a place where almost all students believe that if they do some work, they will be able to satisfy their needs enough so that it makes sense to keep trying" (p. 15). He listed four essential needs to be satisfied: belonging, power, freedom, and fun. At a superficial glance, Glasser's needs bear close resemblance to the gratifications that we identify as necessary for equal encouragement (see chapter 8). This correspondence in thinking appears even stronger because he defined power as not power over others, but as competence. His need for freedom is vaguely connected to a student's right to movement. However, absent from Glasser's thinking is an adequate grasp of democracy. And he has not thought much about education other than maintenance of control. A general theory of education does not begin with discipline. Discipline is secondary to curriculum. The saliency of curriculum is so obvious it should not have to be stated; and yet, discipline is far more an issue in schools than curriculum and often becomes the major concern of urban high schools.

Dreikers defined his approach as democratic and, more than Glasser, elucidated his understanding of democratic education (Dreikers, 1968; Dreikers, Grunwald, & Pepper, 1982). It is a democracy informed by group dynamist Kurt Lewin (1948).[2] It is a theory that largely limits democracy to teacher leadership. To Dreikurs, the democratic leader is neither permissive or autocratic; that is an insufficient definition of a teacher in a democra-

---

[2]Lewin had a great influence on the formative phases of our thinking. We worked with Ron Lippitt, one of Lewin's distinguished students in cross-age teaching and the Doug Grant New Career project that emerged from Vacaville. At one time our understanding of democracy coincided with the Lewinian conceptualization. However 25 years of experimentation has caused us to move to a "stronger" definition of democracy (Barber, 1984) and far less reliance on "science" and leadership and more on a negotiated development of citizenship.

tic classroom. Dreikurs' democratic teacher is sensitive, caring, and nonintrusive, but that too is not enough for students to develop into enlightened democratic citizens. The democratic elements in Dreikurs' thinking are restricted to classroom process. There is virtually no consideration of outcomes. Education is not perceived as a means to definable ends. That is less a criticism of Dreikurs than it is recognition of the importance of a general theory that informs all of education. A theory that centers on discipline trivializes both education and theory.

Democratic Education and Sex Education

Curriculum is more important in sex education than it is in discipline. However, what passes for sexual education has not only been ineffective but also, because of divisiveness, represents one of the greatest threats to democratic education. Sex education suffers from both an unresolved adversarial confrontation between the "abstinence-only" advocates and the "responsible-choice" advocates; and from a student body not persuaded by either. The battle over sex education is bitter and destructive. School board members find themselves embroiled in the sex education controversy and in many areas find themselves under siege, particularly by the abstinence-only zealots. Sex education is also often a major issue in school board elections and a salient factor in privatization campaigns. Parents worried about a sex education that would permit discussion of abortion, homosexuality, and/or distribution of condoms are attracted to private schools that prohibit such talk.

The Abstinence-Only Orientation. Abstinence-only sex education reduces to adults telling youth how to behave. Proponents establish their case as much by ire directed against an amoral media and a "permissive" amoral education then by substantiating claims with logic and evidence. The media and permissive sex education are blamed for a general moral decline and the undermining of "family values." Abstinence-only sex education sporadically does more than defend itself with appropriation of the moral high ground. There is an effort to provide a statistical case of effectiveness. Such a claim. if true. would add power to the case for authoritarian education and, if it could be demonstrated that democratic education was less effective in preventing teen pregnancy, would be a powerful argument against democratic education. It would not be easy to dismiss Teen-Aid, Inc., an abstinence-only program that claims to have reduced teenage pregnancy by 86% in just 2 years. It would be difficult for a democratic education to come close to that. Unless, of course, the claim was too good to be true.

One aspect of democratic sex education would have students validate various sex education claims. Such investigation could help put sex education on a solid basis and distinguish hyperbole from reality. At the present time such investigation is desperately needed. When *The San Diego Union* sought to verify the Teen-Aid, Inc. claim of an 86% reduction from 147 teenage pregnancies to only 20 in just 2 years they found that "while the 147 figure was well documented, *the number 20 had apparently been made up*" (Elmer-Dewill, 1993, p. 89; italics added).

Reality-Oriented Sex Education. On the opposing side of the sex education debate are advocates of a comprehensive "reality-oriented" program. The underlying argument of this group is that abstinence is not a feasible response to teens, a sizable proportion of whom will be sexually active regardless of what they are told. Such an education would present abstinence as the safest of all courses, monogamous relationship the next most preferable course of action, and, for those who are sexually active, the advisability of safe sex practices (e.g., the prescribed use of condoms and other contraceptive devices). If an unwanted pregnancy does occur, a comprehensive education provides students with an opportunity to consider the pros and cons of abortion. Although diametrically opposed in philosophy and in content, "comprehensive" sex education programs also claim to be effective and moral. Comprehensive reality-oriented educators insist that they do not impose a value system. They try to get students to examine the consequences of different sexual practices and, if students choose to be sexually active, how to engage in safe practices. Religious fundamentalist-oriented abstinence-only advocates, however, view the comprehensive approach as immoral and an invitation to promiscuity. Comprehensive reality-oriented educators perceive their opponents as fanatics trying to impose a narrow worldview on everyone. There is little debate between the two; neither accept the other as legitimate. Sexual education thus disintegrates into an either-or proposition; neither are willing to compromise. Students become the battlefield over which both perspectives fight. And both fail because both are enemies of democracy; the authoritarian, abstinence-only believers are guardians, whereas the permissive, comprehensive educators are anarchistic, emphasizing individual choice while minimizing community responsibility. As such, they too, are enemies of democracy. (Although, unlike the authoritarians who make no claim to democracy, the comprehensive educators perceive themselves to be its defenders). What makes neither group democratic is the limited role provided students.

Sex education will be effective only when students become active developers of knowledge. In the democratic classroom, students are the problem solvers who design programs. Sex education is guided by the same kind of epidemiological analysis required in a democratic approach to discipline. Students examine the environment, the host, and the influence of psychoactive agents; engage in research; and conduct experiments. The approach has to be developmental. In the early grades, sex is not the major emphasis of the curriculum. In these years, students are encouraged to have mutual respect and to develop cooperative relations with each other. In these early developmental years, teachers establish the basis for decisions based on logic and evidence and introduce the intertwined concepts of personal growth and community responsibility that are further developed in sex education organized within a democratic classroom. If in these early grades students develop a sense of the importance of debate and the capacity to disagree without being disagreeable, they build the foundation for inclusive debate when highly charged "hot button" issues are encountered in the upper grades.

The particular problems a sexual education program must address are the elimination of sexual harassment in ways that maintain rights of expression; the establishment of a center that includes religious fundamentalists and "secular humanists"; the defining of the range of acceptable sexual behavior that enables individuals to lead full, rich, and gratifying personal lives while at the same time building a healthy civil community; and, perhaps the most difficult of all, the establishing of a school community in which gay and lesbian students are made to feel welcome.

A Democratic Approach to Drugs and Serious Delinquency

Current Approaches to Drug Education. Schools crusade against the use of all controlled substances. Students are told of the dangers and warned of the consequences. Schools proclaim zero tolerance of use of marijuana, tobacco, alcohol, cocaine, heroin—all of which are lumped together and treated as equal hazards. National campaigns against drug abuse are launched with great fanfare disguising the absence of theory or record of accomplishment. What emerges are advertisements and personal promotions, not serious interventions. Drug Abuse Resistance Education (DARE) is a typical example. DARE was a handsomely endowed and widely publicized effort—a $750 million a year U.S. national program featuring a powerful core curriculum offered by specially trained local police officers in 17 weekly, 45 to 60-minute sessions. After much self-congratulation and 3 years of operation, the official evaluation found no significant decrease in drug use reported by the fifth and sixth grade population that the program targeted.

Blaming the Entertainment Industry. According to Clinton White House anti-drug official, Lee P. Brown, students are "misled and misinformed about the dangers of marijuana" (news release, September, 13, 1995). Blaming the entertainment industry for misinformation has become a popular way to slough off responsibility. This is misplaced attention. Focus should be on what schools are and are not doing to provide relevant information and organizing that information for student use in personal decision making. A school program in which responsibility is diverted from teachers to police officers begins wrong. If it is possible for the police to become effective educators with a few weeks of intensive training than clearly the years teachers spend in preparing for their professional careers are mostly wasted. That teacher preparation is very likely a waste of time does not lead one to the conclusion that minimally qualified people, including police officers, should teach about drugs, but rather that teachers should be better prepared.

An effective drug education program must begin with respect for the intelligence of the students. No slick advertising campaign will do. No set of guardians will coerce students into following the leader. Moreover, teachers as guardians, for all their other deficiencies, lack the power, the disposition, and/or the credibility to coerce. If teachers cannot intimidate students into "being good," what can they do? Conventional wisdom has them removing offenders from school, or failing them in class. But nothing could be more shortsighted, or counterproductive. Students will not be frightened out of destructive behavior. Teachers need to know that when a student is expelled from the school system, whatever positive hold the school has on the student is severed. Once expelled, the student is steered to even more coercive institutions that step up the ante and by so doing increase investment in delinquent ways of life. Being tough ("scared straight" experiments, or military-like "boot camps") actually lead to an increase in recidivism. On the other hand, programs for institutionalized delinquents that emphasize what educators should have been doing—preparing students for the work world and "rewarding prosocial attitudes"—effectively reduce the likelihood of a rearrest (Gibbs, 1995).

One "justification" for taking a tough line with students (i.e., expelling and suspending) is "to send a clear message back to students" (i.e., deter others from following in a similar path). Such justification reveals how little school authorities know about perception. There may be a single message sent but many messages are received. Whatever is sent is filtered by the perceptual bias of the receiver. When principals and teachers take action or make any statement and expect all students to automatically fall into line, all they reveal is arrogance and ignorance. Rather than all of the students getting the message, some few students do interpret the decision as necessary for their protection and for maintaining a school atmosphere conducive for scholarship (these are the conforming students and the message sent to them is that they are "safe"). Some students may interpret the decision as yet another example of class, race, or ethnic bias (although few students are likely to use such terms because an accusation of racial bias is "politically incorrect" in these conservative times). Some may interpret the action as merely another expression of adult authority's obsession with "power tripping." Most students, however, will not be aware that a message has been sent or an action taken. Only with extensive and open interchange is it possible to move from idiosyncratic and phenomenologically unique perceptions and interpretations to shared understanding. But such interchange is impossible in any authoritarian system. It is also impossible with the other enemy of democracy—anarchy. One enemy chills discussion, whereas the other permits students to readily escape from it by choosing to be with like-minded others. Neither provides the leadership for an organized center where sharing can take place. Anarchy serves to centrifugalize and all the talking is within ever smaller groupings that only serves to reinforce differences at the expense of commonality. What is needed is coherence and substance to replace chaos and superficiality. Like all democratic education, the emphasis is on the solution derived from weighing a wide range of approaches.

A Democratic Education Approach to Drugs

A democratic drug education requires an epidemiological analysis in which the host is the afflicted student, the agent is the "drug"—marijuana, alcohol, cocaine, and so on—and the environment is the social setting in which the use and/or abuse of the substance flourishes.

The Drug-Inducing Environment. Asking students to solve any aspect of the drug abuse problem is much more difficult than asking them to address discipline issues. Solutions are restricted by law. Many students believe there is no problem other than that created by adult authorities. Others will be overwhelmed by the magnitude of the problem and by the difficulty of reaching some shared understanding. In this instance (as with many others), the creation of a democratic culture to which all share some allegiance is a time-consuming challenge. To keep this difficult process alive, teachers should facilitate discussions, find ways to keep students from becoming discouraged, serve as mediators, and in some instances serve as arbitrators.

How Much Drugs Can the Environment Tolerate? Teachers must entertain the range of possible proposals from effective zero tolerance to legalization. Another aspect of the environment to be considered would be lived culture (Willis, 1990) and the impact the entertainment industry has on substance use. Also to be considered are the gratifications derived from the environment. Students should analyze whether vulnerability to drugs stem from the lack of necessary gratification in the straight world (i.e., no encouragement to risk, unnecessary pain, lack of meaning, inability to belong, denied usefulness, denied competence, lack of excitement, feeling of hopelessness, and denied creativity), with special attention given to the school environment. The gist of the hypothesis to be tested is when important gratifications are denied, the affected student looks elsewhere for gratification and although the drugs offer some immediate physiological effects (which are discussed under agents), the drug culture or environment may be the primary attraction because it offers important gratifications not provided elsewhere.

The same procedures used for discipline are used for drugs with perhaps slightly more teacher leadership. Once students, with the help of teachers, bring to the table a number of possible drug problem-solving environments that are discussed for an agreed on period of time, students form teams to explore different proposals. The teams not only evaluate the positive and negative features of each position, but they also indicate the paths that must be taken to create the environment (e.g., legalization of marijuana would require either state and/or federal legislation or something like a constitutional amendment established by a statewide initiative). The teams function for an agreed on period before they reconvene to share with the entire class the results of each team's work. The class will strive to reach a consensus, and when that is not possible, issue majority and minority reports. The results of this culminating effort is shared with the broader community.

With drugs, the primary prevention proposals (instituted prior to onset of a problem) will differ greatly from secondary and tertiary prevention proposals in that primary prevention can be introduced at the classroom level, whereas secondary and tertiary will have policy and legal ramifications that extend beyond the school. In helping students with a problem-solving drug education curriculum, teachers make clear where the authority for decisions rest. That which is established by law needs to be clearly communicated and distinguished from actions that are taken by a school board or by the school-site administration.

Drugs as Agent. Drugs carry with them considerable mythology. Students need to sift through fact and fiction of the various substances currently used or contemplated by students. If it is true that "Many youngsters are being misled and misinformed about the dangers of marijuana," then it follows students need to be better educated about marijuana and other control substances (including alcohol and tobacco). If students are not to be misinformed they must discover for themselves the acute and chronic effects of marijuana, cocaine, heroin, methamphetamines, barbituates, LSD, alcohol, tobacco, and the like. That research would involve a search of literature to determine what has been discovered about each of these agents. That research should be conducted by teams, and after the research has been conducted for a designated period, the results presented as works in progress.

Drugs as agents have both physiological and psychological effects. For example, students need to examine the findings that have led to the conclusion that alcohol attacks the liver and the central nervous system. Alcohol is also a depressant and students need to know why people desire the effects of depressants, and why they desire stimulants and hallucinogens. As part of this exercise, students are asked to consider ways in which the desired psychological effects can be attained without recourse to "drugs" (i.e., non-drug-induced "highs").

The Host. Individuals differ widely in their responses to drugs. There are differences in tolerance, allergic responses, the development of dependence, and habituation. There may also be personality and genetic predisposition to drug abuse. Examining host differences completes the epidemiological investigation. And this phase is handled exactly as the other phases—teams study host differences to drugs and report findings.

The intent of this curriculum is to both help students learn how to make decisions based on logic and evidence and to help prepare them for the citizen responsibility for law and social policy in this area. It is not necessary that students agree on the findings; it is necessary that they develop a comprehensive and coherent understanding and debate their ideas in a public forum.

A Democratic Approach to Serious Delinquency

Of all institutions, schools alone can provide effective primary prevention to drug abuse, delinquency, and violence. If students have effectively addressed discipline, sex education, and drugs, they have probably already developed a powerful democratic anti-delinquency program.

Schools not only fail to develop effective primary prevention, they do just the opposite. Polk and Schafer (1972) and Knight (1985a, 1996) indicated how schools create delinquents by denying students opportunity for success in schools while pushing them to the gratifications that delinquency provides. Over the years, tolerance for delinquent behavior has declined and has been replaced by increasingly punitive measures.

Currently, schools make things worse by driving students from school rather than examining means by which alienated students can enjoy gratifying school experiences. As soon as a student begins to fail a class, efforts should be made to establish contact with that student and negotiate with him or her a new education plan.

In the democratic classroom, students will design plans to reincorporate students who have slipped out of the mainstream. Again, there will be an epidemiological analysis of environment, host, and agent with major emphasis on primary and secondary prevention produced by changes in the environment (e.g., cross-age tutoring, cooperative learning team projects, equalization of school-provided gratifications.)

A democratic classroom is heavily invested in secondary prevention. In the democratic classroom, because of its emphasis on inclusiveness, effort is made to facilitate a smooth and inci-dent-free return of students who had been necessarily removed for endangering the education of others.

Tertiary prevention of crime and delinquency in the demo-cratic classroom is reflected in the development of citizen compe-tence for social policy. Such competence would base decisions on careful reading of research and would resist appeals to inflamed emotion.

The Democratic Classroom and Guns

> Fear seems to play an important role in the proliferation of guns among juveniles, particularly urban minorities, according to David Kennedy, a research fellow at Harvard University's Kennedy School of Government. A recent National Institute of Justice study of male juvenile offenders and male students in inner-city high schools found that "self-protection in a hostile and violent world was the chief reason to own and carry a gun." Twenty-two percent of the students reported owning a gun. Thirty-five percent report-ed carrying a gun regularly or occasionally; family, friends, and illegal markets were their primary sources. A majority of students (69 percent) came from families in which men owned guns, and nearly half (45 percent) reported having been "threatened or shot at on the way to or from school." Kennedy remarks that youth culture in the inner cities is akin to prison culture: "captive, lawless, dangerous, self-regulated." Depressing as this is, he adds, it does suggest that the market for guns among juveniles may be malleable: control the fear and you control the guns, which in turn decreases the fear. (Kaminer, 1994, p. 118)

Guns are a major problem for U.S. schools. Guns are the second leading cause of death in the United States, and gun mortal-ity is increasing faster than any other cause of death. In 1996, Australia witnessed a mass killing of 35 men, women, and chil-dren by a lone gunman at the tourist resort of Port Arthur, Tasmania. Australia is presently undergoing a mass debate on the popular culture and its fascination with violence, gun laws and the effect of the media on children's viewing (April, 28, 1996). That discussion should be taking place in schools everywhere, but especially in Australia and the United States, where student research teams should explore and debate different proposals, examining in depth the logic and evidence in support of both the "right-to-bear-arms" advocates and those who favor strict gun control. This study would require a review of the constitutional arguments advanced by "right-to-bear-arms" supporters. Because a democratic education is a problem-solving one, the lesson culminates with plans of action that are realized only after extensive negotiation and compromise.

The democratic classroom is a safe classroom. It deals with violence and fear of violence. In such a classroom, the pros and cons of gun control are debated. But more importantly, the design of a class culture that is perceived to be safe and the marked reduction of fear obviates the desire to bring arms to the classroom (Kaminer 1994).

SUMMARY

A democratic classroom encourages students to produce curriculum and programs to help them solve every level of personal problem. Such an approach is consistent with the goal of an independent democratic citizen and organizes the student to own the problem rather than being dependent on others for solution.

Chapter 7

Rights As an Integral Component of a General Theory of Democratic Education

In our version of a democratic classroom, students have four rights: the right of expression, the right of privacy, the right to due process, and the right of movement, or the right not to be a captive audience. In this chapter each of these are explained and defended in detail. We explain how rights can be defined in the absence of common ground and defend our position that children are born with rights and are taught to be responsible. We contrast our understanding of rights with traditional conservative definitions that are the underpinnings of "thin" democracy." We discuss the proliferation of rights and the confusion of rights and responsibilities and how these serve to muddy the issue. We look at existing classrooms and examine the condition of rights. We give examples of the use of rights in the world that is and how these can provide a foundation for a world that should be.

about one student in five does not agree with the freedoms stated in the Bill of Rights, and on some issues the proportion is even greater . . . these same students who reject the freedoms tend to accept the tenets of fascism. At the same time, these students who manifest the symptoms of authoritarianism are likely to declare themselves to be the "best" Americans and the most loyal supporters of American democracy . . . those who have had a course in Civics tend to be less in agreement with the Bill of Rights. (Horton, 1963, p. 57)

HEART OF THE ARGUMENT

In a democratic classroom, students are born with rights and learn to be responsible. Rights are both an important knowledge issue and something to be honored and exercised in a classroom. In the authoritarian classroom, rights are linked to and are subordinate to responsibility. Only the responsible are allowed rights. This reversal of appropriate order contributes unnecessarily to classroom disruption and unequitable treatment of students. Democratic teachers teach rights by both analyzing and practicing them. Only the four rights just cited have stood the test of time.

Defining Rights

What precisely is a *right*? A right is any unabridged activity that does not restrict the activity of others, or require from others some special effort (e.g., the pay ment of a tax to provide another with subsistence). Freedom of expression is a right because one person's expression does not prevent another from also expressing him- or herself. Respecting one person's privacy does not invade another's. Due process for one does not come at the expense of the due process for another.

Rights, by this definition, must be extremely few in number. Because they are so few and so important, they must be understood and scrupulously protected. In this chapter, rights are considered from two perspectives: first, rights are an important curriculum issue, and second, rights are also vital in defining the nature of the relationship between adult authority and students (as well as between administration and teachers). What troubles us is the extent to which prevailing school practice and curriculum fosters contempt for the underpinning of our cultural and legal definitions of democracy.

Rights, like all of democracy, are not simple. Each right has a fuzzy boundary and can be rescinded in states of emergency. The grey areas and conditions of emergency are important areas of the negotiations that become the practiced curriculum in the classroom. At the present time rights are not highly valued in classrooms and where they exist they are rationed—some students get them, some do not. Those that need them the most get the least.

In the democratic classroom, student rights derive from the U.S. Bill of Rights and other amendments to the Constitution. Similar foundations can be found in British and Australian law (see the review of individual rights and liberties in Australia; Gaze & Jones 1990). The establishment of a bill of rights in the Australian Constitution has been gathering momentum in the 1990s. Freedom of speech, a fundamental value in international law, and present as the initial right in the Bill of Rights of the U.S. Constitution, was not declared a common law principle in Australia until 1988 (Gaze & Jones, 1990).

Our call for student rights is simple and straightforward: In the democratic classroom students should have only the rights that are the entitlements of all citizens.

RIGHTS OF EXPRESSION

Rights of expression are those that have been defined in the First Amendment to the U.S. Constitution:

> Congress shall pass no law respecting the establishment of religion, or prohibiting the free exercise thereof, or abridging the freedom of speech, or of the press; or the right of the people peaceably to assemble, and to petition the Government for a redress of grievances.

Rights of expression did not come easily to the United States. Before rights of expression were accepted, people had to endure centuries of torture and even death for the expression of unacceptable beliefs. In the 15th century, calling the king of England a fool was punishable by death. After the death of Henry VIII, expressing the opinion that his successor Edward VI should not be king was an act of treason. Any expressed negative opinion of Queen Elizabeth was grievous enough transgression to merit a death sentence. Under Queen Elizabeth's reign, screws were tightened on the press, nothing could be printed unless approved by the archbishop. The situation was no better in the colonies. In 1650, Thomas Pynchon's book, *The Meritorious Price of Our Redemption* was publicly burned because sentiments printed in it were not consonant with the colonies' established religion. In 1690, Benjamin Harris, having previously been arrested, imprisoned, and pilloried for publishing a seditious pamphlet in London, found Massachusetts no more hospitable. His newspaper, printed without the required license, was suppressed; the governor did not like what Harris had printed. After that paper was closed down no other was printed in Boston for 10 years. Benjamin Franklin got an early lesson in the consequences of no freedom of expression. His older brother, James Franklin, was jailed in 1721 when his newly begun newspaper, *The New England Courant,* printed criticism of the government. Benjamin took over the publishing responsibility until his brother was released from jail. Imprisonment did not intimidate James and he, by continuing to publish criticism of the government and the church, became an important figure in the effort to establish freedom of expression. Even more significant in that fight was New York's Peter Zenger, who was indicted in 1735 for seditious libel for an unrelenting series of criticisms of the government. The defense at his trial by the venerable Andrew Hamilton established much of the logic that later becomes incorporated in the First Amendment of the Bill of Rights.

> It can hardly be argued that either students or teachers shed their constitutional rights to freedom of expression at the schoolhouse gate. (Justice Abe Fortas, Tinker v. Des Moines Independent School District)

The struggle for acceptance of freedom of expression did not end with the Bill of Rights. Some citizens have had their rights consistently protected, whereas others have been denied rights. Slaves had no rights of expression. For almost 150 years of the Republic, women enjoyed a limited right of expression. Political radicals and trade union organizers found the First Amendment was a now-you-see/now-you-don't proposition. But more than any other group, school children have been denied freedom of expression. It was not until 1965 when 13-year-old Mary Beth Tinker, her 15-year-old brother John, and their friend Christopher Eckhardt went to their Des Moines school with a black band on their arms to protest the Vietnam War that freedom of expression was won for school children. The principals of those schools, being forewarned, decided such protest was unacceptable and suspended the three students. The students took their case to court and after losing in the District Court and surviving a 4-4 indecision at the Federal Court of Appeals, gained vindication with a 7-2 Supreme Court decision (*Tinker v. Des Moines Independent School District*). That decision brought freedom of expression for students and teachers through the "schoolhouse gate." That is, freedom of expression gets through the gate when school officials acknowledge the existence of *Tinker* or decide to abide by it.

Freedom of expression is not a settled matter in public schools, nor in any aspect of public life. Still unresolved are students' rights to express orally unpopular opinions in school, the right to symbolically express an opinion through dress, the right to criticize adult authority in student newspapers, and the right to peacefully assemble to express dissent about school or other government policies and practices.

> The most stringent protection of free speech would not protect a man in falsely shouting fire in a theater and causing a panic. (Oliver Wendell Holmes, Schenk v. U.S.)

As important as it is to define and defend student rights as a necessary ingredient of a democratic school, it is equally as important to be able to define where those rights end. The right of expression has never included libel, slander, or the use of expression to deliberately endanger others. The boundaries of permissible expression are not easily or immutably established. That boundary will be more defensibly established when students debate and reflect on all the arguments. Democracy is not served when adult authority arbitrarily determines permissible student expression. Student awareness of Justice Holmes' famous limitation of First Amendment rights is laudatory, but far more important is discussion and debate of what it means, what the circumstances were that motivated one of the court's strongest supporters of freedom of expression to issue such a ruling, and where it can be appropriately applied. These are not small points. Education about freedom of expression is vital if that freedom is to be secured for anybody.

> If freedom of expression becomes merely a slogan in the minds of enough children, it will be dead by the time they are adults. (Bagdikian, cited in Hentoff, 1980, p. 22)

There is sufficient evidence to support Bagdikian's concern that freedom of expression has been reduced to mere slogan, so much so that unless there is a concentrated and vigorous effort to teach and practice rights of expression, we could lose them. Without those rights, the differences between the Western democracies and the authoritarian regimes we claim to despise would disappear. Avoiding overdramatization or exaggeration, establishing freedom of expression in schools will be as difficult as it is important.

Student Rights of Expression in a Democratic Classroom

Students must be encouraged to express opinions. Criticism of adult authority, teachers, or administration cannot be suppressed. Such criticism can and should be answered by adult authority, not overwhelmed by it. It is imperative that students not be threatened or punished for disagreeing with adult authority. Ridicule or otherwise exploiting the advantage of position has to be viewed as suppression of a right. In a democratic classroom, student newspapers are not censored (although the U.S. Supreme Court recently ruled that school officials can censor). The right of students to petition and assemble are also respected in the democratic classroom. In fact, free speech areas should be created in every school as well as opportunities to debate significant issues.

In a democratic education, libel, slander, and "fighting words" (i.e., the use of racial epithets, sexual harassment, and verbal abuse because of sexual preference) are taken seriously. Action to suppress such expression is given serious consideration and debated thoroughly. The decision to suspend the right of expression must be viewed as extraordinary. Not only should such suppression be rare, it also must be recognized that every suppression threatens freedom of expression.

Is Conversing in a Language other Than English Covered by Rights of Expression? The answer is yes. The language a person uses does more than communicate information to others. Language also expresses identity and loyalty. All oppressed people develop secret codes that they use to communicate with those they trust and to exclude those they do not trust. That is why so many adolescents speak in an argot that their parents and other "old fogies" cannot understand. Any effort to prevent expressing the language of the home in the school is a violation of students' rights. To be democratic, teachers and other officials need to find persuasive reasons for students to become fluent in English without discouraging non-English or limited English-speaking students to remain fluent in their mother tongue. If students resist learning English, school officials should look for oppressive conditions that militate against the mastery of English (see chapter 8).

RIGHTS OF PRIVACY

(George Mason) would have been astounded that the majority of the Supreme Court of the United States should conjure up a constitutional "right of privacy" not mentioned even in statute, and deduce from that conjectural right the further right of mothers to slay their progeny in the womb. (Kirk, 1992, p. 29)

The word "privacy" does not appear in the Constitution. It will be found neither in the original document in 1789, the "Bill of Rights" of 1791, nor in any of the subsequent Amendments that have significantly expanded the rights of Americans.
    The Constitution, however, does protect privacy to a substantial extent. Several kinds of privacy issues are prominent in constitutional law, in legislative discussions, and in political debates. This is more true now, perhaps, than at any other time in United States history. (Bender, 1984, p. 237)

The word *privacy* may not appear in the U.S. Constitution, but it is nonetheless a widely recognized value in society at large and among school children. Somewhat surprisingly, privacy gained the recognized stature as a right under a conservative U.S. Supreme Court, perhaps because it is a "middle-class" right, perhaps because it has been a slowly evolving right, perhaps because intrusion into privacy has become more prevalent and more destructive, and perhaps because of increased recognition of the validity of different lifestyles.
    Justice Louis Brandeis had no difficulty recognizing privacy as a right. He defined it as "the right to be let alone" and asserts that it is "the most comprehensive and the most valued by civilized men" (dissenting opinion *Olmstead v. United States,* 1928). Brandeis had, more than 25 years before *Olmstead,* asserted a right of privacy in the *Harvard Law Review* (1890).
    In *Roe v. Wade,* the critical decision on abortion, the modern definition of *right of privacy* was established, bringing into existence an understanding that there existed an area of private

life into which government cannot pry. It is that definition that obviously disturbs thoughtful conservatives like Kirk, although limiting governmental intrusion would appear to be one of the foundations on which modern conservative thought has been built.

The word *privacy* may not appear in the Bill of Rights, but that does not mean it was not a concern of the founding fathers. The Bill of Rights clearly establishes the foundation on which the right of privacy rests.

> . . . the right of the people to be secure in their persons, houses, papers, and effects, against unreasonable searches and seizures. (Fourth Amendment to the U.S. Constitution)

The Fourth Amendment contains much more than an implication of rights of privacy. In it is a clear recognition of rights of privacy. When coupled with the Third Amendment, which establishes the right of an individual to deny shelter to soldiers in peace time, and the Fifth Amendment's guarantee against self-incrimination, there is even further evidence that from the very beginning, those who created this country understood the importance of privacy. The recognition of its importance grew as the extension of suffrage grew.

It must be remembered that the U.S. Constitution was created by men devoted to liberty but opposed to equality. They believed humans to be selfish and untrustworthy, controlled only by a powerful as well as a good constitution (Hofstadter, 1948). In fact, the idea of democracy is consciously not part of their thinking. It was not until the Civil War ended and the 13th, 14th and 15th amendments were ratified that the nation moved to recognize the importance of equality (Adler, 1987). Democracy requires universal suffrage, which the founding fathers unalterably opposed (otherwise, there likely would have been some founding mothers). As suffrage was extended, so, too, was the concern for privacy. Privacy was an important protection for the emerging labor movement, populists, feminists, the still very vulnerable ex-slaves, the always endangered socialists, anarchists, communists, and other political radicals.

Public school students more so than any other population are vulnerable to the excesses of authority. They are required to attend school and thus are exposed to adult authority not of their choice. The student's concern for privacy includes the right to a personal life, security of one's lockers or desks against unreasonable searches and seizures, and protection of confidentiality (e.g, recognition of the privacy of assessment, personal difficulties, school problems, and school records). As protection of privacy, school authorities must take on the responsibility to discourage malicious gossip.

Students have never had entrenched legal guarantees of privacy. In recent years, the U.S. Supreme Court has ruled that school principals can search students' lockers without the same warrants required of police officers. In democratic education, privacy is an important consideration and there is much more respect for it than is currently the case.

DUE PROCESS

The U.S. Bill of Rights indicated a great concern for due process. The fourth through eighth amendments were designed to reduce the power of established authority in the area of criminal justice. The colonists had been forced to suffer uncontrolled police power and they did not like it. In the Bill of Rights they did something about it. In five amendments they provided protection against search and seizure (fourth Amendment, also important as a right of privacy), prevention of a trial unless there was a reasonable charge, prevention of double jeopardy by denial of retrial after an acquittal, the right not to testify against oneself (fifth Amendment, also important for privacy), a speedy public trial, an impartial jury, access to knowledge about the charges and the right to counsel (sixth Amendment); further protection of the defendant in a trial (seventh Amendment), and no cruel or unusual punishments (eighth Amendment).

All of these amendments are designed to meet one goal: *fairness.* Although the founding fathers were not much for equality in general, there was one area where equality was very important and that was equal treatment before the law. Distrustful as they were of democracy and universal suffrage and as committed as they were to class hierarchy, they were also firm believers in fairness—a fairness limited to a justice system equally applied to all regardless of social standing (slaves excepted and women somewhat so). Even that limited notion of fairness has been difficult to achieve and will not be achieved unless schools attend more to fairness; both in the treatment of students and in the preparation for responsible citizenship.

It is the lack of perceived fairness or guarantees of fairness in schools that produces so much alienation and anger. Only when faced with expulsion, do students have access to a clearly defined due process system. And then it is far too little and too late. Students have long before been dissatisfied with a "justice system" that comes under the general rubric of "discipline." Democratic approaches to discipline were discussed previously (chapter 6), thus here we note that students experience 12 years of schooling without genuine opportunity to appreciate the reasoning for limitation of police powers that are found in the Bill of Rights.

In the absence of a compelling curriculum, which is certainly missing in today's schools, the primary role of teachers is to serve as police trying to coerce students into obedience. In the absence of rights, the student's sole responsibility is to obey. The teacher is an unchallengeable authority. In a system where the authorities make the laws, the very least that must be guaranteed is fairness. Fairness would require presumption of innocence, the right to counsel, a trial before an independent tribunal, and protection against cruel and unusual punishment. Displaying a name on the board (as is the case in one of the more popular discipline systems) for all the class and every visitor to see is the modern equivalent of medieval stocks. And is not public humiliation cruel?

Due process is not limited to disciplinary actions, It also extends to the grades that students receive. Grades are not solely a reflection of what a student has learned in a particular subject. Grades are yet another means used by teachers to control student behavior. A student may meet every requirement for the highest possible grade, an "A," and may actually receive a failing grade if too often late to class or absent. Teachers use the threat of a reduced grade to coerce students from disruptive behavior, however such behavior is defined.

It has been our experience that teachers and administrators contrast significantly on their posture toward student rights; teachers have more of a problem with students exercising their rights of expression, whereas administrators are more troubled by due process.

RIGHT NOT TO BE A CAPTIVE AUDIENCE

Freedom is perhaps the most resonant, deeply held American value. In some ways, it defines the good in both personal and political life. Yet freedom turns out to mean being left alone by others, not having other people's values, ideas, or styles of life forced upon one, being free of arbitrary authority in work, family and political life. (Bellah et al., 1985, p. 23)

School, as currently constituted, is diametrically opposed to "the most resonant deeply held American value." Democratic education has empathy as one of its missions, but it can realize that goal when it works with student's wanting to be left alone. School must come to grips with the unassailable fact that where it tries to go is opposite of where most people want it to go.

The right not to be held captive does not appear in the Bill of Rights. How could it when slavery was permissible in the new nation, as was indentured servitude? And because women had neither voting rights nor access to the workplace, they too often were in effect imprisoned.

The indigenous Australian in some ways parallels the history of the American Black and in some ways that history is similar to the treatment meted out to America's indigenous populations. Aborigines and specified immigrants to Australia found rights to be as illusive and ephemeral as did African Americans, Native Americans, and some immigrants in the United States. Slowly, with many setbacks, rights have been extended to those previously denied; however, there is still much to be achieved.

One place where emancipation has not been extended is the classroom. Long after slaves were freed from captivity, compulsory education laws were passed. Compulsory education laws quickly followed a celebrated 1874 Kalamazoo case that established that states could tax for public education. By 1918 every state had a compulsory education law.

Compulsory education is by its nature coercive. However, there is a solid reason to require students to go to school. Democracy requires an informed citizenry, which means the citizen must be well educated. But to compel a student to become well educated is undemocratic. We have here a large-sized dilemma. How do we resolve it?

With compulsory education, respecting the right not to be a captive will take imagination. If compulsory education is to continue to meet the requirement of informed citizenship, it is absolutely essential that the classroom becomes a place where all students want to be. The right not to be a captive requires an examination of policies that punish for tardiness and absenteeism. In a democratic school, it is far more important to determine why it is that students are unable or unwilling to participate in a class activity and act to change ungratifying conditions, then it is to try to bludgeon students back to the classroom. In fact, lateness and absenteeism only become problems if they impede acquisition of important knowledge. If the school cannot make a persuasive case that what is being taught is worth learning, it is difficult to defend that idea that students must be in a classroom. Asserting that important material is being discussed in class does not make it so.

One reasonable approach to democratizing compulsory education is to increase the number of choices that students have in school. No student should be required to remain in a situation that he or she does not find gratifying. Students should be able to exercise choice over teachers, classes, and schools. Students' claims of unfair treatment have to be taken seriously. Choice can be very difficult for schools. Some classes, schools, and teachers will be much more popular than others. But the difficult is not impossible. If on the basis of increased choice some classes and some schools become undersubscribed (i.e., very few students want to be in them), it is incumbent on the school system to take necessary action to either change the class or find ways to persuade students to want to be there. Classes and schools have to be made more attractive; they have to become places where all students want to be.

The most extreme form of choice would be to define a school as anywhere there is a student. That is not as ridiculous as it may sound. A school is not necessarily a room with teacher in front, X number of chairs, and a chalkboard. In the future, that may be the only place that will not be called a school.

To develop schools that all students want to attend, it will be necessary to talk to students and elicit from them what they do not like about school in very precise terms, and in equally precise terms elicit from them recommendations for improvement. A conversation about schools between adult authority and alienated students would be a giant step toward democratic education. Nothing would do more for teacher credibility than teachers respecting the opinions of their students

The Relationship Between Rights and Responsibilities

There is a necessary relationship between rights and responsibilities. Without responsibilities there can be no rights. The conservative position is that rights are subordinate to responsibility. This is a conclusion drawn from natural law and established tradition. The strong democracy position, as expressed by Barber, is that democratic processes must be developed in the absence of an independent ground (i.e., natural law or tradition). Our position is that tradition works in opposition to democracy. If neither natural law nor tradition can guarantee rights, then rights can only be granted by a responsible community operating with a commonly respected system of laws and procedures. And if rights can only come from a responsible community how can we propose that rights precede responsibilities?

Rights come first because they precede responsibilities developmentally. One needs no talent, no accumulated knowledge, no awareness of the world, no sophisticated philosophy to have a right. It is necessary for a societal body to have accumulated knowledge, philosophical sophistication, and awareness of the world to establish rights, but that is a function of responsibility. Responsible people create rights; that is where rights came from.

Rights precede responsibilities because only with rights can everyone participate in establishing responsibilities. That would not be true if we were indeed, "one nation indivisible, under God, with liberty and justice for all." Neither America, nor Australia, nor Britain, nor anywhere else, have reached such a state. Our pledge must be perceived as a commitment to a goal yet unreached. From the very beginning, both America and Australia have struggled to develop strength from diversity, but diversity has been and continues to be an obstacle to unity. Diversity makes defining responsibility difficult. Conservatives finesse that problem with proclamations of responsibility and condemn as irresponsible all who refuse to accept their pronouncements.

A defensible and credible set of responsibilities under conditions of diversity can only be established by first establishing ground rules for debate. Those ground rules are mutually acceptable "individual rights." It is only after everyone's rights are guaranteed that there can be the necessary debate out of which responsibilities can be democratically defined.

Rights precede responsibilities because democratic education is founded on tradition, not mired in it. Tradition supports a hierarchical society. Rights are necessary to protect powerless minorities and rights are vital because a society is always as vulnerable as its most despised minority (see Table 7.1).

Rights should be a consideration in every school activity. Rights are crucial to the teaching process, both for the teacher and for the student. Rights should constitute a major part of the curriculum in history, government, literature, the arts, and even the sciences. Scientists have paid the price for discoveries that are not politically acceptable. Galileo is a vivid example of a person whose rights were suppressed. Rights are what makes possible administrative accountability to the public. Too often in school, serious abuses of power are covered up simply because

Table 7.1. How Rights Should Be Considered in School.

	Students	Teachers	Curriculum	Evaluation & Assessment	Counseling	Discipline
Rights	Expression	Expression	History of rights	Protection against invasion of privacy	Protection against invasion of privacy	Guarantee of no disciplinary action for exercise of rights
	Privacy	Privacy	Invent rights and determine relationship to responsibilities in government classes and student government	Right to due process in challenge of evaluation of findings	Due process in challenge of counseling decisions and judgments	Clear rules that students participate in creating for use of "fighting words"
	Movement	Surrender some rights to movement when submit to contract to perform duties	Further explore rights in literature	Degree of choice in methods used to evaluate		Clearly define the range freedom of movement
				Voice in interpretation of findings		

there was no freedom to question an impropriety; nor was there a due process system to protect those who chose to expose established authority.

Teaching and Rights. It is nonsensical to consider student rights and not discuss the rights of teachers. Teachers and students have identical rights. To provide rights to teachers and not to students would place students in the vulnerable position presently felt by so many. However, student rights without teacher rights makes instruction impossible. Rights protect both from bullies.

First, providing teachers with rights of expression does not necessarily open the door for indoctrination because indoctrination is virtually impossible. Students do not accept whatever their teacher tells them. Ask any teacher (or parent). Cognition is dialectical. Students initially oppose what they are told and convincing them requires persuasion. Schools today are troubled, not because students mindlessly support their teacher's ideas (or mindlessly oppose them), but because virtually no ideas are being advanced.

Second, in public schools, students are exposed to a variety of ideas. If indoctrination is possible, it can only occur when one idea is allowed to be expressed. That is much more likely to occur in private schools. It is much more a danger in an authoritarian school, which limits the expression of ideas, than in a democratic class where expression of differences of opinion is encouraged.

Indoctrination has always been a fraudulent issue. The actual fear is that students will hear ideas differently from how their parents want them to hear. The real concern of parents, as distinct from the one they raise, is that teachers will unindoctrinate their children. In reality, parents give far too much credit to teachers for what they have come not to like about the ideas and the other general all around weirdness of their children. Television and other media does far more to organize or disorganize thoughts than do schools. That is what should concern us all. The democratic classroom, with its problem-solving approach, has the potential to deal with the problems created by an irresponsible media.

Granting teachers their rights does not ensure a good education. It does not prepare students for citizenship. Schools should do much more. Democracy is advanced when balanced treatment is given to controversial subjects. Balanced treatment is much more likely to occur when teachers are encouraged to express beliefs than when attempts are made to muzzle them. Balanced treatment of controversy is a necessary component of a democratic classroom. The more diverse a staff the more likely there will be balanced treatment of an issue. The diversity should be in economic background, gender, race, and ethnicity but also in worldviews. Assemblies that feature debates between faculty on important issues would enliven any school

The right of teachers to a private life has not yet been completely won. Sexual preference of teachers is not a fully accepted right. In a democratic school, such a right would be guaranteed. In a democratic classroom, discussion about animus against different lifestyles needs to be discussed. The goal of such discussion is not to convert everyone to a standard worldview but to broaden understanding and help students arrive at the consensus that school is a place where all are made to feel welcome, and to help students define the rights of everyone, teachers as well as students.

One right teachers do surrender when they accept employment is freedom of movement. Teachers can only have restricted freedom of movement because they have contracted to be at a certain place to perform specified duties. That contract does not include unwanted advances, defamation, or personal attacks. Having to endure abuse because of captive status works against teachers and students. Schools tend to lend a more sympathetic ear to protests of harassment from teachers than from students. This is unfortunate because students suffer far more from such problems.

Some teacher-student relationship problems cannot be resolved by simple clarification of competing rights. Freedom of movement provides protection from unwanted indignities. There are, because of the unique and sensitive relationships that teachers have with children, occasions when teachers and students consent to relationships that are inappropriate and often illegal. Teachers are made aware of the constraints that goes with the position (i.e., the conditions of professional conduct). When we consider inappropriate teacher-student relationships, the notion that everyone is born with the identical rights and learns to be responsible, no longer seems radical; to the contrary, such order now seems reasonable and the essence of common sense. If, for example, a 13-year-old enters into a willing sexual relationship with a teacher, both are exercising rights, but only the teacher must be held responsible, even if the 13-year-old was the primary instigator of that relationship.

Holding teachers responsible for unprofessional conduct should not require abrogation of their rights. Relationships between teachers and students can be monitored without invasion of privacy.

The Most Important Right for Teachers is Due Process. Due process is the right teachers hold most precious. If teachers are to be held to a high standard, they must be assured that the system that holds them accountable meets the criteria of reasonability and fairness. Teaching is a difficult occupation. It is impossible for a teacher to satisfy every student and every parent. Parents and students who have irreconcilable differences with a teacher in a democratic classroom have the right to choose another teacher (freedom of movement). It is much more difficult for teachers to move away from an unresolved conflict. Only through a carefully devised due process system will it be possible to guarantee teachers and students their rights.

Job security is a valued condition. (The next chapter discusses in detail the importance of security to student success.) The democratic classroom can only operate with a secure teacher. The teacher must be assured that there will be no negative consequences if she or he exercises freedom of expression, and any grievances will be processed through a negotiated due process procedure. The same type of due process system recommended for students in cases of discipline applies to the teacher facing reprimand or dismissal; the teacher is presumed innocent, has access to counsel, is tried by an independent tribunal, and is spared cruel and unusual punishment.

Teacher Rights of Movement. Teacher's rights of movement become a major issue in classrooms in the case of involuntary transfer. Teachers will be up in arms if transferred from one school to another without approval. Such transfers clearly indicate how deeply held the right of movement is (in this instance, the right not to have others impose movement). Unfortunately, teachers who dearly support that right for themselves are often unwilling to recognize its importance to students.

Rights As a Curricular Issue. If there is no independent ground and no natural law, no science, no unchallengeable tradition and no God to define rights, how can there be rights? The most obvious answer comes from the study of history. Students learn about rights by reliving the incidents and debates that brought rights into existence and to general acceptance. The second means by which rights are learned is by negotiating ground rules for the operation of a classroom. In both instances, rights are the focus of a problem-solving curriculum. Learning about rights is essential because it is only when rights are fully understood by the vast majority of students that they will be secure. It is only then that the term inalienable will have meaning. It is only then that rights cannot be taken away at whim. We are a long way from such a time.

Obviously, the study of the history of rights must be compatible with school practice. To teach about rights while simultaneously denying them, only breeds disrespect for those rights and at the same time disrespect for both history and school authority.

A careful review of the the tortuous history of rights should include periods in history when rights were willfully disregarded: pre-revolutionary Salem witch trials, the Eureka Stockade rebellion in Australia, post-World War II McCarthyism, and various intrusions into rights as a result of *political correctness* (political correctness works both ways, those that use the phrase screech about loss of their rights, but they use the term to justify bludgeoning those who speak for the rights of others, particularly feminists, minorities, homosexuals, and lesbians).

Currently, in and out of school, the denial of rights has gained momentum stimulated by a growing fear of crime and violence. The various episodes during which rights were undermined in American, British, and Australian life should be revisited, adequately described, debated in depth, and thoroughly analyzed as part of a deliberate effort to develop a logic for establishing rights.

Experimentation is yet another means by which rights can be established. Classrooms can experiment with situations where rights are honored, where they are outlawed, and where some students get them, while others do not. These experiments have value only if discussion is sufficiently rich and different consequences carefully examined.

It is not expected that all students will perceive rights identically. It is not necessary for a class to reach our understanding of rights. It is necessary that the rights be a living topic in schools. For without broad public understanding, rights will very likely cease to exist.

Rights and Discipline. Simply put, no discipline system should be permitted that violates student or teacher rights. As discussed previously, rights limit what adult authorities can do, and what students can do to staff and to each other. Concern that rights will be an invitation for violence and anarchy becomes a matter for curriculum. Students discuss that possibility, formulate a hypothesis (or hypotheses), and devise experiments. The results of these experiments are presented to the class and reviewed by all class members. It is from such research that a discipline system compatible with democracy will be created (or, if that does not seem possible, a democracy system compatible with some accepted discipline program).

Rights and Administration. Rights both limit and expand the notion of administration. Because of rights and the other requirements of a democratic classroom, administrative power in the classroom is stood on its head. When students have rights, participate in decisions that affect their lives, and are in classes organized for solving pressing social and personal problems, accountability takes on fundamentally different meaning. In an authoritarian system, accountability is upward. Students are accountable to teachers, teachers to site administrators, and site administrators to some central authority. In a democracy, accountability is downward. Administrators are accountable to teachers and teachers to students and parents. In an authoritarian system, the administrator appropriates power. In a democratic system, the administrator tries to create opportunities for others to be empowered. In an authoritarian system, there is considerable entropy. Power is less than zero-sum; in every exchange there are more losers than winners. A democratic system generates a net gain of power; the exchanges are plus-sum, that is, there are more winners than losers.

When students have rights, they have power to act. Without that foundation, everyone has limited power and many are powerless. School administrators play a critical role in the democratic classroom by using their position to clearly define and establish student and teacher rights, to provide leadership in the development of problem-solving curriculum, to encourage teachers to democratic practices in the classroom, to intervene when a school is threatened by its two enemies of anarchy and guardianship, to mobilize a constituency for democratic school practice, and, most importantly, to stand firm when the school is attacked by organized opposition to democratic classroom.

In a well-administered democratic classroom, students gain a measure of power with rights and continue to increase their power by discovering what can be achieved through collective action in ways that could not be done as individuals. When that lesson is learned in a wide range of different problem-solving situations, the student has become informed and competent.

Administrator Rights. Administrators have the same rights held by students and teachers . The way administrators exercise those rights establishes the boundaries of the school's culture. Most studies identify the site manager as the most influential factor in school change. What is true in general applies to an even greater extent to the democratic classroom. The democratic classroom does not require a democratic administrator. It cannot, however, exist with an administrator who is hostile to democratic education.

The rule of thumb to use when initiating a democratic classroom is to begin in a school where the administrator demonstrates support of this practice. That support should extend to all four requirements of a democratic classroom—curriculum, participation, rights, and freedom of movement. It begins with rights.

Rights and Psychological Development. Much of the discussion of rights has been tied to a child's maturational level or stage. An argument has been advanced with considerable support that says that only persons who have attained a level of maturity are sufficiently responsible and have the cognitive capacities to not abuse a right and appreciate its meaning. The conclusion that only the mature should be given rights has been generally accepted, although there is very little evidence to support it.

The position advanced here is that rights should be honored at birth, although there is very little evidence to support such a conclusion (our argument is based on logic). We acknowledge that if students entered school with the same rights as those given to adults, the entering student would rarely understand the meaning of rights and the conditions under which they apply, and because of such ignorance could engage in actions of such severity that the result would be an abrogation of those rights. Understanding of rights will take considerable time to develop (we believe that such understanding is one of the major responsibilities of an educational system). There is no solid evidence to indicate when a student will have developed cognitively to fully appreciate rights. It will be difficult to determine such development in the absence of extensive experimentation. At the present time, very few people (of any age and maturity) understand rights and we believe that is because they have never had the opportunity to develop much of an understanding (nor has the school accepted the responsibility for imparting such understanding). In the absence of more adequate data, it would be reasonable to suppose that appreciation of rights would develop as the student becomes less dependent on adult authority (Piaget, 1993).

We believe that students will learn what rights mean as they experience them, have them explained, and acquire greater ability to apply acceptable rules of logic. If they are encouraged to discuss rights and their limitations, they will develop the ability to independently define and defend the concept of a right.

The surface has just begun to be scratched in the understanding of cognitive development. Not known is the relationship of particular types of stimulation to different dimensions of cognitive growth. Not sufficiently understood is the relationship of democratic processes to cognitive growth. Given the current state of knowledge, a reasonable hypothesis is that maximum cognitive development will occur in a democratic classroom. A corollary of that kind of thinking is that denial of democratic processes and organizing the classroom for differential encouragement will impede cognitive growth for those denied important gratifications. (We explore this line of thinking further in the chapter on equal encouragement.)

Not providing young children with rights in the classroom and developing meaningful conversation about the exercising of those rights creates problems for the classroom. In the earliest grades, students insist on defending what they do on the most garbled understanding of rights. They have heard the term many times, in many places, and on many channels. Those of us who have contended with harassment justified on the basis of "rights" are fully aware of the danger of too little understanding of rights. Teachers will find providing students with rights, defining what those rights are, and dealing with their misuse or abuse as part of the curriculum gives them much more control than they will have when they allow students to define rights willy-nilly.

Rights of Students and the General Public. Ultimately rights are dependent on public understanding and support. Like every other aspect of democratic education, the issue of rights goes hand in hand with increased involvement of the community in education. Part of the problem in education is the warped idea that a small group of people can or should control the process. Without public understanding, there can be no democratic education. That is what lack of independent ground means. Schools, in general, can never be better than the public understanding of them. And that is how it should be.

The Problem With the Proliferation of Rights. We live in a time when claims for rights have reached an all-time high (Will,

1992). Some claim rights for animals, others for trees, still others claim the unlimited use of drugs to be a right. In 1948, as a direct response to the horrors that preceded World War II and that continued throughout it, the United Nations approved an International Declaration of Human Rights. That Declaration states those rights enumerated in the U.S. Bill of Rights plus a clear statement of rights of movement. Those are the rights to which we believe all students and school staff are entitled. However, the Declaration went beyond what is covered in the Bill of Rights. We direct attention to Article 23 and Article 26

Article 23

1. Everyone has the right to work, to free choice of employment, to just and favorable conditions of work and to protection against unemployment.
2. Everyone, without any discrimination, has the right to equal pay for equal work.
3. Everyone who works has the right to just and favorable remuneration ensuring for himself and his family an existence worthy of human dignity, and supplemented, if necessary, by other means of social protection.

Article 26

1. Everyone has the right to education. Education shall be free, at least in the elementary and fundamental stages. Elementary education shall be compulsory. Technical and professional education shall be made generally available and higher education shall be equally accessible to all on the basis of merit.

Neither work nor education qualify as a right because both require actions on the part of others (e.g., a willingness to be taxed to pay for the costs of education or otherwise be involved in the creation of employment opportunities). The Declaration also includes the right to join a labor union and that would qualify as a right because it requires no action on the part of others. It does, however, as all rights should, prohibit others from intruding or limiting rights of movement.

Where in our scheme are property rights, and when property rights conflict with human rights, which prevail? Although property rights is perhaps the most precious right of conservatives, it does not qualify as a right because a right, by definition, requires no actions of others and also must be universally available. However, the protection of private property, the guarantee of work, and the universal access to education are responsibilities of good societies. How these are developed and in what particular form are properly considered as curriculum.

In a democratic classroom not only is there considerable discussion on defining rights, but there is equal concern and discussion on the limitations of rights.

Where Do Rights End? As stated by U.S. Vice-president Spiro Agnew, who had to resign from office after pleading no contest to the charge of criminal behavior, "Your rights end at the tip of my nose." Rights, by definition, are extremely limited and end far before contact with another person's nose. In fact, rights are a major, and often the only legal protection against the intrusion into one's nose because contact with a nose clearly is an invasion of privacy. So where do rights end? They end when another's rights are violated, and when it can be clearly established that the exercise of rights threatens public safety.

SUMMARY: REVIEWING THE RIGHTS-RESPONSIBILITY RELATIONSHIP

Our thesis is that rights precede responsibilities. But a school of rights and no responsibilities is no school at all. The primary responsibility of a school is to develop an informed and responsible citizen. The essence of our argument is although schools have been remiss in respecting students' rights, they have been far more negligent in developing responsible citizens. That is the major reason we have organized this book with the knowledge requirement of democratic education in front. It is through curriculum that students are prepared to meet their personal, economic, civic, and cultural responsibilities. A democratic classroom respects rights and teaches responsibilities and does not confuse the two.

From the equality of rights springs identity of our highest interests; you cannot subvert your neighbor's rights without striking a dangerous blow at your own. (Schurz, 1908, p. 123)

Chapter 8

Equal Encouragement in the Democratic Classroom

THE ESSENCE OF THE ARGUMENT

Every conception of democracy has some commitment to equality. In some ways, equality is an inextricable component of democracy. And yet, of all the democratic attributes, equality is the most problematic, the most difficult to define, and the most divisive. A democratic classroom addresses two different conceptualizations of equality. The first is equality as distributive justice, is the equalization of life condition. The second, equality as fairness, is the extent to which a society acts to ensure that everyone has an equal opportunity to achieve success in all of that society's legally sanctioned activities. Ryan (1982) described the two as "fair shares versus fair play." The distributive justice aspect is a curriculum issue in the democratic classroom and is treated (as we recommend all curriculum issues should be treated) as a problem to be solved through research, discussion, or debate leading to resolution (i.e., a program of action). The latter is an obligation of a democratic classroom and as such is both a curriculum issue and a classroom process. Because we extensively treated curriculum earlier and already established a model of curriculum as a problem-solving process, we only briefly reflect on fair shares in this chapter. The major focus here is on the treatment of students in the democratic classroom. Of particular emphasis is the examination of deficit and system explanations for differential school success.

Although there has been powerful support for the idea of a level playing field where all are equally encouraged, rarely has the classroom met any definition of fair play. Today, although many may give lip service to democracy, fair play may have been discarded in favor of special privilege—the provision of a competitive edge for "us" at the expense of "them." Competitive edge appears to be increasingly favored over fair play in those times when opportunities appear to be shrinking.

Our conception of equality is equal encouragement that we contrast with the conservative definition of equal treatment and the "romantic" definition of equal result. We argue that equal encouragement offers more to an educational system and to a society than an education and a society organized to provide competitive edge.

DEFINING EQUALITY

Conservative Definitions of Equality

The conservative definition of identical treatment has been dominant in educational policy and practice. Equality for conservatives is incorporated into a general worldview that has, according to Kirk (1986), a highly respected conservative scholar, the following "six canons"

(1) Belief in a transcendent order, or body of natural law, which rules society as well as conscience. . . .
(2) Affection for the proliferating variety and mystery of human existence, as opposed to the narrowing uniformity, egalitarianism, and utilitarian aims of most radical systems. . . .
(3) Conviction that civilized society requires orders and classes, as against the notion of a "classless society. " . . . If natural distinctions are effaced among men, oligarchs fill the vacuum. Ultimate equality in the judgment of God, and equality before courts of law, are recognized by conservatives; but equality of condition, they think, means equality in servitude and boredom.

(4) Persuasion that freedom and property are closely linked. . . . Economic levelling, they maintain, is not economic progress.

(5) Faith in prescription and distrust of "sophisters, calculators, and economists" who would reconstruct society upon abstract designs. Custom, convention, and old prescription are checks both upon man's anarchic impulse and upon the innovator's lust for power.

(6) Recognition that change may not be salutary reform: hasty innovation may be a devouring conflagration, rather than a torch of progress. Society must alter, for prudent change is the means of social preservation . . . a statesman's chief virtue, according to Plato and Burke, is prudence. (pp. 8-9)

A conservative conceptualization of equality can only be understood if analyzed as an integral element of a coherent worldview whose primary features are preservation of private property, resistance to change, and aversion to "leveling." Equality in such a philosophy must be restricted. Once the existing hierarchy is viewed as an accurate reflection of the differences in human capability any effort to alter the existing arrangement through "hasty innovation," "abstract designs," and "anarchic impulse" is perceived as destructive tinkering (i.e., messing around with something that is defined to be as good as it can get) can only cause damage to it. Only very recently have conservatives had to consider equality in education. Before equality of education could be generally recognized as an important issue, civil rights had to have legally obtained legitimacy and employment and educational achievement had to be directly connected. The connection between education and employment has become tighter as developed economic countries evolved into credential societies. In a credential society, educational achievement is the prerequisite to a desirable strata of work. Without a credential provided by an accredited institution of higher education, entrance into the professions are prohibited. The evolution into a credential society has not been welcomed by conservatives. They perceive such focus as a vocationalism that adulterates the primary purpose of higher education (A. Bloom, 1987; Kirk, 1979). But because credentialism has become part of the status quo, it must be defended by conservatives as a bulwark against leveling.

Elementary and secondary education are linked to work in a credential society because performance in these lower levels necessarily connect to admission to the institutions of higher education that award credentials. It is education's relationship to work that was the primary focus of the conservative document that stimulated what passed for educational reform in the 1980s and 1990s (National Commission on Excellence in Education, 1983). In a sense, conservatives have been carrying water on both shoulders; on one, lamenting the vocational emphasis in education, and on the other criticizing schools for inadequately preparing students for work. The two diverse strands come together in the insistence that failure in education stems from an erosion of traditional standards.

Because a credential society is dependent on formal education, it became inevitable that education should rise from an insignificant institution to become the primary status flow institution. As the importance of education to economic life rose, so too did those who had been denied credentials to gain access to them. When the denied clamored at the gates, conservatives positioned themselves to be guardians of standards. Standards emerge as a critical concept in the continuing see-sawing debate on equality.

Conservatives have long held that liberty and equality of condition are incompatible; one must come at the expense of the other. Conservatives choose liberty.[1]

Conservative equality necessarily required minimal adjustments in the social structure. Conservative equality respected tradition while discouraging "economic leveling," thus meeting the criteria of "prudent change." Conservative equality strives to provide all with identical treatment. By treating everyone the same, conservatives can support programs that remedy inequity without altering any of their fundamental beliefs. William Bennett, Secretary of Education under President Ronald Reagan, became a spokesperson for that version of equality, which he called *equal intellectual opportunity*. The equal intellectual opportunity approach is conservative because it maintains a traditional curriculum and calls for "clear purpose, high expectations, strong and persistent teaching, and hard work" (Bennett, 1988, p. 34) rather than "imprudent" institutional upheaval or major curricular innovation. Bennett, like most conservatives, blamed liberals for the problems of schooling. He claims that it is the abandonment of the conservative canons that has led to the corruption of education and has produced sloppiness and indolence.

---

[1]Some conservatives such as Milton and Rose Friedman (1979) find equality and liberty to be compatible as " two faces of the same basic value—that every individual should be regarded as an end in himself" (p. 119), but equality is restricted to acceptance of existing treatments.

John Rawls and "Distributive Justice." Conservatives believe equality is achieved when every student receives the identical treatment in the mastery of traditional curriculum. The diametrical alternative to conservative equal treatment is equal result. Rawls (1971) both refined and toned down that concept in his conceptualization of *democratic justice* (we refer to it as *romantic justice* because it meets no requirement of democracy), where differences in wealth and income can only be justified to the extent to which those differences accrue to everyone's advantage.

Ironically, from each according to ability, to each according to need, although not a workable theory of equality, is the sought mission of almost every school and is the avowed mission of conservative elite private schools. The private school's claim to nurture ability and meet individual student needs is what supposedly gives it the competitive advantage over public schools, where individuality is lost in the morass of an insensitive bureaucracy.

THE DEMOCRATIC CLASSROOM AND
EQUAL ENCOURAGEMENT

In the democratic classroom, all students are not treated exactly the same, nor is the aim "equal result." In the democratic classroom, all students are considered equally capable and thus are equally encouraged. What that means in specific action is described and explained later in this chapter. Our conceptualization of equal encouragement is as much a response to liberal programs as it is to conservative efforts, thus it is important that the liberal programs that have been subjected to such an avalanche of both conservative and neoliberal criticism be examined.

The Liberal Definition of Equality as Manifested in the United States in the "Great Society" Programs of the 1960s

Substantial movement toward equality took place during the liberal insurgence that came as a consequence of the great depression of the 1930s. World War II brought about some fundamental changes in race relations in the United States. The need for defense workers opened economic opportunities that made it possible for record numbers of Black Americans to migrate from a closed, authoritarian, legally sanctioned racist south to a more open north. At the same time, breakthroughs in racial equality were being made in the military services. These changes set the stage for momentous events over the next two decades.

In 1954, the U.S. Supreme Court, by a 9-0 vote (*Brown v. Board of Education of Topeka*) invalidated the "separate but equal" dictum that had informed education by race for over more than 50 years. The court called for desegregation of public schools with "all deliberate speed." *Brown v. Board of Education of Topeka* had pivotal significance in the liberal effort to establish equality in education. That decision not only redefined equality, it established a mandate for its achievement.

The Civil Rights Act of 1964, another liberal effort to define equality, prohibited the denial of access on the basis of race or national origin to any program receiving federal funds. Title VI of the Civil Rights Act of 1964 directly affected schools because they increasingly were the beneficiaries of federal resources. The threat of loss of those resources sped the desegregation process. The liberal approach to equality was consolidated by two other federal initiatives—the war on poverty and the provision of the federal government of categorical aid to local school districts to compensate for attributed inequities. The war on poverty had a wide range of different programs, many of which affected education. All were intended to equalize opportunity. The war on poverty program that most directly dealt with education was Operation Head Start, which was designed by social scientists who posited the high rate of school failure in impoverished populations to "accumulated environmental deficits" (Deutsch, 1967; Hunt, 1961). According to this theory, poor children disproportionately failed in school because they entered school with irreversible handicaps developed in the early preschool formative years. The handicaps were caused by home environments unable to provide necessary cognitive stimulation (Deutsch, 1967; Hunt, 1961). To remedy that situation, Operation Head Start provided a preschool experience to a large number of poor children. The education or cognitive stimulation provided at Head Start centers varied considerably. Moreover, in addition to some form of cognitive stimulation, the children were provided nutrition and their parents were offered a variety of services, including, often serendipitously, instruction in community organizing. Operation Head Start, unlike most of the liberal programs initiated during the years when John F. Kennedy and Lyndon B. Johnson were presidents, was embraced by the conservatives that followed them and actually has grown since its initiation in 1965.

Head Start did not violate any conservative canons. It was liberal in the sense that the environment rather than genetics was blamed for educational failure, and it diverted tax dollars from the protection of private property to a social service. The other major federal foray into educational reform, compensatory education, was also begun in 1965 and also has been adopted and only slightly modified by conservative administrations. Because it too violates no conservative canons (neither Head Start nor the Elementary and Secondary Education Act called for any major changes in curriculum, classroom organization, or evaluation), they were liberal only in that they "threw government money after problems" but because there was no insistence on equality of results, nor was there to be favored treatment in the classroom, it was not too difficult for conservatives to accept them. The Elementary and Secondary Education Act provided federal dollars to local districts to compensate for what poor students otherwise lacked. A wide variety of educational interventions met the definition of compensatory education. We were critical of those programs and of analogous programs initiated in Australia (Knight, 1974, 1977a) because they, as we explain later, were based on deficit thinking.

Affirmative Action-Liberal "Social Engineering" Against Which Conservatives Reassert Their Definition of Equality

Affirmative action violates conservative principles and hostility to it has become a major rallying cry of conservatives.

The percentages of African Americans and Hispanics in higher education have increased since the 1960s and White women have increased to such an extent that they now outnumber White men. Asians are in higher education at a much higher rate than would be expected by their proportion of the population. The entering class at University of California in 1994 was illustrative of what is happening in higher education in the United States. If admission criteria had been strictly adhered to, only 1.2% of the class would have been Black and only 5% would have been Hispanic. The majority would have been Asian. To accommodate the special admission of lesser "qualified" students, 9% of Asian and 12% of White "qualified" applicants were denied admission (see Table 8.1). It was this "evidence" that prompted the regents of the University of California to terminate "preferential treatment" on the "basis of race, sex, color, ethnicity, or national origin in the operation of public employment, public education, or

Table 8.1. Freshmen Entering UCLA in 1994.

	Percentage of All Students in the Class	Percentage of Students Admitted on Academic Criteria Alone
Asians	42.2%	51.1%
Whites	30.7%	42.7%
Hispanics	20%	5%
Blacks	7.1%	1.2%
	100%	100%

Source: *Chronicle of Higher Education.* "Other" groups have been omitted. Taken from Hacker (1996)

public contracting." With that action, a conservative group of legislators imposed a conservative definition of equality. However, conservatives are not consistently committed to their definition of equality. They do not challenge affirmative action when it is applied to elite private institutions.

> Princeton accepts only 15 percent of its total applicant pool, it takes upward of 40 percent of those whose parents have been there. These "legacies" have exceeded 10 percent of each Princeton class, compared with a black enrollment of about 6 percent. More often than not, these students, who do not make up a very diverse group, displace candidates with better records. So far as I can see, the universities do not make an explicit or principled defense of this practice. In private, officials may acknowledge that they depend on alumni for financial and other support and the preference for their children is, in effect, a quid pro quo for that kind of loyalty. That such arguments remain unexpressed underlines the hypocrisy of much of the talk about admissions being decided strictly on "merit." (Hacker, 1996, p. 25)

Qualified To Do What? The primary attack on affirmative action is the accusation that lesser qualified people are chosen over the more qualified. What is not asked is whether the criteria used to determine qualifications is valid or even defensible. Is a White male with an SAT score of 1,200 more qualified to teach in a ghetto school than a Black woman with an SAT score of 900? Opponents of affirmative action insist that the White male is more qualified, but to do what, and on what grounds? The only reasonable answer to such questions would require both to teach and to judge competence or qualifications on the basis of performance. The attack on affirmative action precludes such a test. Qualifications to function in a profession reduces to the ability to pass a test that has no established connection to professional performance. In that sense, "standards" could in actuality be obstacles to merit. Obstacles in the sense that persons who could be excellent teachers, physicians, or engineers are denied the opportunity to demonstrate that competence. Our criticism of opponents of affirmative action is in their insistence on support of standards they cannot defend by logic or evidence and may be apocryphal.

Another of our concerns is the extent to which opposition to affirmative action is based on the widespread belief that the conditions that required such action no longer exist (i.e., African Americans have caught up with Whites). We previously mentioned how uninformed a public is. White Americans believe that Black Americans constitute 25% of the population (more than twice the actual situation). Two-thirds of Whites believe that Blacks have caught up with Whites economically and thus need no more special treatment (although the reality is far different; Gladwell, 1995). In recent years, although the education gap between Blacks and Whites has narrowed, the wage and unemployment differential between the two has widened (Breslow, 1995).

It is easy to blame media and particular journalists for disinforming a public. What needs to be stressed here is the extent to which public schools have contributed to misinformation and ignorance. How can a public be expected to know what they have not been taught? Or even have been mistaught? Schools disinform mainly by not challenging the misinformation students bring to class. When an untruth is not challenged, students rightfully interpret the silence as validation.

The Democratic Classroom and Affirmative Action. The democratic classroom operates on an entirely different logic from that which justifies affirmative action. Affirmative action provides special consideration to persons who have suffered exclusion. As practiced, it fails to meet a democratic criterion by how it came into being. For affirmative action to be democratic, it must have been subjected to intense discussion and debate prior to enactment and must have been endorsed by the majority of the citizenry. No such thing happened. Moreover, those who were to be helped should not only have supported the action, they should have made a significant contribution to the proposal. The process that created affirmative action was flawed. Not only was the process top-down, it suffered from a colonial paternalism: providing help to those deemed incapable of helping themselves.

Even more damaging for a democratic resolution of a complex problem was the divisive nature of affirmative action. Affirmative active was divisive in creating conflict between groups, whether so intended as some insist, or unintentional. It was also divisive within groups. Only a small number of targeted populations benefited from affirmative action. The few chosen from targeted populations were not selected as representatives through a democratic process. Affirmative action in that perspective is the opportunity to escape from community, which may partially explain why women, and targeted minorities, have simultaneously gained economically and have become increasingly poor. The simultaneous increase in wealth and poverty is examined as part of a problem-solving curriculum in a democratic classroom

Affirmative Action and "Deficit Thinking". There is yet another reason why affirmative action is incompatible with a democratic classroom. Affirmative action was designed to give preference to certain groups or categories of persons to rectify prior injustices. The democratic classroom is designed to eliminate present injustices that take the form of differential encouragement. Affirmative action accepts deficit thinking. Those attributed deficits are the scars that people supposedly carry from previous mistreatment. Our primary objection to that kind of thinking is that it serves to deflect attention away from an investigation of current inequities.

Deficit thinking was also at the root of the liberal war on poverty programs. Head Start was designed to remedy early prior-to-onset-of-schooling deprivations in the home, and the Elementary and Secondary School Act was to compensate for deficits that students brought to school. Neither set of actions held the school responsible for differential achievement by race, class, ethnicity, or gender. It is our contention that if categories of students are having trouble in school, the school is the place to look first for explanations. In this sense, we find ourselves closer to conservatives than to liberals, although we differ widely in our proposals for remedying inequity.

Liberals and conservatives both support deficit thinking. They differ only in identification of the cause of the deficits. What distinguishes the democratic classroom is the renunciation of all deficit thinking.

Is It a System Problem, or an Individual Deficit Problem?

Deficit Thinking is the Major Impediment to Equal Encouragement. Deficit thinking has a long history. Some form of it has been embraced by the entire spectrum of political and philosophical thought. All types of deficit thinking share one vital common characteristic: "blaming the victim" (Ryan, 1971). In any educational decision, be it differences in academic performance or discipline problems, a choice must be made. Are the differences in behavior due to differences in individuals or are they due to differences in the encouragement individuals receive? In all instances, the preponderance of expert opinion holds the individual responsible. Moreover, school policy and practice justify all school-based decisions on differences between individuals. The alternative: Differential encouragement has been summarily dismissed.

In the long history of deficit thinking, conservative philosophy has dominated. The conservative insistence on a "natural order" that is arranged hierarchically, more than implies the existence of deficits. In a natural order, the persons on top are, by definition, deserving. They have, like cream, risen to the top because of superior intelligence, will, and character, whereas those on the bottom have fallen because they lack those characteristics. Conservatives argue further that in any effort to fundamentally change the order or level the society will not lift the bottom, it will only pull the top down (Kirk, 1986).

THE GENETIC ARGUMENT

No notion of advantage or deficit is more total and more nonredemptive than the idea that intellectual capacity is genetically determined. Once such a notion is accepted, natural order is fixed. Genetic determination of intelligence is the ultimate conservative argument, and probably no argument is more deeply cherished and none more impervious to change. The genetic determination of intellectual capacity has two facets. The first is that humans are arrayed along a continuum from the barely functioning, feebleminded to the awesomely intelligent (genius) with distinguishing steps in between. The second is that it is possible to accurately assess where an individual belongs on this continuum. Moreover, in the determination of intelligence, as would be expected with natural order, "Whites" as a group have been consistently ranked above Blacks and other people of color; the rich over the poor; and for much of history, men over women. It is this consistency over time and space that Jensen (1969) used as one of his major arguments for the inheritance of intelligence. Wide range and accurate assessment is what makes the assignment of deficit to the bottom and gifted to the top so important for educational policy and practice. Because this discussion of genetic determination of intelligence is a much traveled path (Gould, 1981; Houts, 1977; Kamin, 1974; Senna, 1973; Valencia, 1997), only the aspects of the argument that are important to our version of democratic education are highlighted.

The development of tests of intelligence has had profound implications for schooling. The difficulty in reaching agreement on a definition of intelligence did not deter psychologists from measuring it. Nor did it deter school officials from important decisions made on the basis of such measurements. Measured intelligence kept people in their places. And because intelligence was reputed to be inherited, schooling could not be expected to raise it. A persistent feature of measured intelligence was its powerful correlation with existing order.

Whether that intelligence was inherited or came about through interaction with the environment (i.e., nature versus nurture) became an ongoing heated battle throughout the 20th century with one side or the other, depending on the political climate, claiming victory, only to give way to new findings or changed sentiments.

In the early 1910s and 1920s, the most celebrated champions of inherited intelligence in the United States were the highly respected psychologists Robert Yerkes, Lewis M. Terman, and Henry H. Goddard. Goddard, on the basis of intelligence tests given to immigrants at Ellis Island, concluded that the vast majority of Jewish, Italian, Hungarian, and Russian immigrants were feeble-minded (Gould, 1981; Kamin, 1974). Robert Yerkes, president of the American Psychological Association in 1917, led a team that developed the "Army Alpha" test, which was administered to thousands of Army recruits and from which it was determined that the average White male recruit had a mental age of 13 (placing him barely above the "moron" category). On this test, southern and eastern Europeans lagged behind western and northern

Europeans, and African Americans scored lowest of all (barely nudging out the Poles; Gould, 1981).

Terman was a professor at Stanford when he modified the 1911 and last version of Binet's test of intelligence and with his modification, the Stanford-Binet, he gave lasting identity to intelligence testing.

At the same time the intelligence test was being standardized, the comprehensive four-track high school was coming into existence. The intelligence test made possible "scientific" determination of educability, and thus determined the track to which an individual should be assigned. The scientists minced no words about educability. Terman left no doubt that the test indicated who and who could not be educated. He concluded that low intelligence "is very, very common among Spanish-Indian and Mexican families of the Southwest and also among negroes [sic]. Their dullness seems to be racial . . ." (Terman et al., 1917, pp. 91-92 cited in Gould, 1981, pp. 190-191). Although Terman, in his 1937 edition of *Measuring Intelligence* (Terman & Merrill), recanted to some degree (more by what he doesn't say about immutability of inherited intelligence), not only has the damage been done but there are others who pick up the genetic deficit banner he dropped. Increasingly Blacks were specifically identified as being limited in intelligence.

No one went to greater lengths than Sir Cyril Burt (1959) to establish the genetic determination of intelligence and to have that orientation influence school policy. That his effort to prove that intelligence is almost entirely inherited was done with fraudulent twin studies and other data distortions has been well chronicled and needs not be repeated here (Gould, 1981; Hearnshaw, 1979; Kamin, 1974). Burt may be discredited, but his impact lives on. If anything, his influence has increased. It is not that Burt convinced a skeptical audience of the inheritability of intelligence, nor did it fall to those who have carried on after Burt to reflect more deeply on their findings, and to provide a better established and more solidly developed argument. The Arthur Jensens, and the Herrnsteins, and Murrays who picked up the intelligence is inherited thesis (i.e., White is smarter than Black and rich smarter than poor), make no better case than Burt did (Herrnstein, 1973; Herrnstein & Murray, 1994, Jensen, 1969). These social scientists did not discover truth. They merely echoed what people wanted to hear, and reflected existing policy and practice .

Without awareness of Burt or understanding Jensen, teachers in classrooms make "unscientific" judgments of the bright and the dull and act accordingly.[2] How teacher perceptions and actions influence student performance is discussed later in this chapter.

Gardner (1991) gained a considerable following by postulating the existence of seven intelligences: linguistic, logical-mathematical, spatial, musical, bodily kinesthetic, interpersonal, and intrapersonal. He claimed schools would be better places if effort was made to develop all seven intelligences rather than overemphasizing the linguistic and the logical-mathematic. His approach to intelligence is less restrictive than a single-factor theory and it offers latitudes to those not succeeding in existing classrooms. But it is nonetheless a deficit based theory, with not everyone possessing the same deficits. Although such a theory opens some doors, it closes others. A multiple factor or multiple intelligences assumes what has not been demonstrated; that intelligence is an attribute that an individual possesses and that it can be validly measured.

INTELLIGENCE AND THE DEMOCRATIC CLASSROOM

In a democratic classroom intelligence is considered to be unmeasurable and constantly changing. Intelligence is viewed as dynamically interconnected with the student's physical and social environment. To open a fruitful conversation with teachers and students about intelligence, it is necessary to revisit the early efforts at definition. There was a time when a serious discussion about intelligence could take place and not be shortcut by what has become the conversation-ending standard, but nonetheless ludicrous, justification of intelligence testing. Intelligence has come to mean whatever an intelligence test measures. Before intelligence was defined by sophisticated statistical procedures, effort was made to reach a consensus on what was meant conceptually. Although there was wide disagreement, it was generally recognized that a basic element of intelligence was the ability to successfully meet the challenges of the environment. If such a definition is applied to one of the unique characteristics of humans—the

---

[2]When Pearl's youngest son entered the first grade, he was told by the teacher that he should be pleased to know that his son was "college" (higher education) material.

capacity to permanently alter the environment—then intelligence can only be understood as a complex and dynamic compound that integrates individual characteristics with attributes of the physical and social environment. Intelligence from such a perspective can neither be defined away as Skinnerian behaviorists try (they give all credit to the environment); nor can it be a particular attribute of the individual, as individual psychologists have insisted. With such a contextual definition, individuals are intelligent in some situations and unintelligent in others. We are fairly certain that we are not alone in remembering times and places where we not only were unintelligent, but seemingly mindless.

The observation used to justify measured intelligence as a fixed entity, its stability over space and time may in fact be an artifact and the stability actually may be in the environment that one carries about in the form of reputation, confidence (or lack thereof), official records, and so on, and in the enormously restricted environment in which testing takes place (that in effect is what standardization means). Later, we develop this notion as a central feature of an equal encouragement classroom.

Liberal Deficit Theories

Conservatives do not have a monopoly on deficit thinking. Earlier in this chapter we described the importance of accumulated environmental deficits to the liberal initiatives of the 1960s (e.g., Operation Head Start). Accumulated environmental deficits (AED) was the liberal alternative to conservative deterministic genetic explanations of social hierarchy and differential school performance. Both the genetic and the AED explanations accepted the same data, both assumed that students in school were fairly treated and their assessed performance validly reflected what they knew and accurately predicted how they would perform in the future. They differed only in the identification of cause of intellectual deficiency. The AED were liberal because, unlike the conservatives who closed the door on all but a few poor, they offered hope and provided remedy. Programs like Operation Head Start could not guarantee an equal result. What they could do, according to advocates, is level the playing field and thus provide an equal start. It would appear that only the very cantankerous could find fault with such reasonability, openness, and devotion to scientific objectivity. Somehow, we have managed to do it. Despite its wide acceptance in the scientific community and the support it received in the legislature and the executive branches of government, we found AED no more convincing, then or now, than its major rival, the deterministic hereditarians.

We had particular difficulty with the "accumulated" part of AED. Accumulated was a necessary element in this deficit theory because, although it was claimed that the deficits occurred when the child was very young (even prior to birth), the deficits had to accumulate to be detectable in school performance and that did not happen until the fourth grade (Deutsch, 1967). To our way of thinking, if significant differences in school performances were not noticeable until the fourth grade then the most logical explanation for those differences was to be found in the classroom (i.e., in the ways students are treated in the first 3 years of schooling). We readily acknowledge that it is "hell to be poor." Overcrowding, unsanitary living conditions, physical abuse, ever present stressful danger, limited or no access to books and magazines, malnutrition, and homelessness should be unacceptable in societies that claim to be advanced and civilized. Living in poverty is not a consummation to be wished, but it does not necessarily follow that miserable life conditions lead to inadequate school performance.

Too much of AED was supported by analogy. No effort was made to assess the magnitude of deficit and correlate school performance with level of deprivation. There were too many unexplained exceptions to the rule. And then there was race. Race appeared to correlate more with school performance than extent of deficit.

Other Environmental Deficit Theses

Preceding AED and probably the longest running rival of the hereditarians, were the psychoanalysts. At the core of psychoanalytic thinking is the connection between a stable family and psychological health. According to psychoanalytical theory, the failure to provide appropriate support during the formative years leads to flawed characterological development (maldeveloped ego and superego). Children who grew up in chaotic families (a euphemism for poor and particularly poor Black), that is, families in which there was absence of a father figure, inconsistent parenting, the absence of love and support, and so on, are not able to develop healthy egos and therefore exhibit various forms of psychopathology. A flawed ego causes fixation at the pleasure principle stage of development resulting in an inability to delay gratification, and that in turn deprives the individual of the ability to apply self to the cognitive tasks required for successful academic performance. Students governed by the pleasure principle are often truant because the classroom is predicated on delayed gratification.

Inadequate socialization not only explained academic failure, it also was used to explain disruptive behavior. The lack of a strong father figure in the home precluded successful resolution of the oedipal complex. A poorly resolved oedipal crisis creates a maldeveloped superego and an inability to distinguish right from wrong—the resultant psychopathic and sociopathic personality disorders explain a predisposition for classroom disruption, delinquency, and crime (Aichhorn, 1983).

The most powerful influence on national policy of the inadequate socialization thesis was the *Moynihan Report.* This report not only deflected attention away from schools and other agencies, it also cautioned against expecting positive responses to efforts at increasing equity and access. "Unless this damage (to the Negro family) is repaired, all the effort to end discrimination and poverty and injustice will come to little" (Moynihan, 1965, p. 5). How does one repair a family? How does one repair the African-American family when one in three African males between the ages of 15 and 30 is in prison or otherwise caught up in the justice system? It is but a short step from the *Moynihan Report* to the current mantra of "family values" that has become one of the deficit models. Moynihan's arrogance was such as not to condescend to consult with Black scholars, or with anyone else who knew something about the topic. Unfortunately, ignorance has never been a factor when arrogance dictates.

Our quarrel with the *Moynihan Report* is in its uninformed defense of deficit thinking. And that is where its long-term harm to equity has been most seriously felt. Moynihan, in defense of inadequate socialization, plays a role almost identical to that played by Burt in defending genetic inferiority, but with this difference: Burt cooked the data and Moynihan simply did not know what he was talking about.

There are many inadequate socialization theories. Among the most seductive is Maslow's "third force." In his hierarchy of needs, Maslow concluded that one cannot gratify a higher need until the lower need is met. The hierarchy is organized with basic physical needs at the bottom and esthetic appreciation-creativity at the top. In between, in ascending order, are safety-security, belonging-love, self-esteem, self-actualization and enlightenment. The lower four needs are *deficiency needs,* whereas the top three are *growth needs.* Reduced to its impact, inadequate socialization means, if one is poor one cannot grow psychologically (Maslow, 1971).

Kohlberg's (1973) six-stage theory of moral development has a deficit thinking base. Gilligan (1980) exposed Kohlberg's gender bias, insisting that the "feminine voice" is actually morally superior to men and thereby removes the deficit label from women and attaches it to men. She did not carry her argument further to challenge deficit theorizing when applied to class, race, and ethnicity.

Erikson is yet another inadequate socialization theorist. In his eight-stage theory, healthy development only takes place when the individual in earlier stages is provided requisite resources and support. If in infancy a child is deprived of love, nurturing contacts, or is subjected to chaotic care, the child will develop chronic mistrust and not be ready to develop autonomy at the next stage, and so on up the line (Erikson, 1963, 1968). With such a theory, the poor and the otherwise deprived will carry with them the deficits engendered from earlier stage failures.

Inadequate socialization thinking is protean and ubiquitous. One can be found for any occasion. Most people accept one or another variant without reflection and act on them. When those who act on them are teachers, students are denied equal encouragement. When it comes to social policy, it is Moynihan's, "benign neglect" that has carried the day. It is ironic, or maybe characteristic, that when benign neglect became U.S. social policy in 1996 with the enactment of fundamental changes in welfare policy, it was Moynihan who led the fight against such change.

THE "CULTURAL DEPRIVATION" ARGUMENT

Culture is vitally important to democratic education. Earlier, we devoted a chapter to the creation of a democratic culture. Here we examine how culture has been employed to justify inequality. Although cultural deprivation models have a long history, we limit our discussion to the impact that kind of thinking had on the liberal war on poverty and its corruptive influences on the Civil Rights Movement. Oscar Lewis was one of a fairly large number of social scientists and educators who purported to discover cultures that were so organized as to subvert available opportunities. Lewis, in a series of vivid descriptions, depicted a self-perpetuating "culture of poverty" that was incompatible with the culture of the school. The anti-intellectual nature of the poverty culture and its basic lack of future orientation prohibited academic or economic success (Lewis, 1961, 1966). Miller (1958) and Chilman (1966) also made substantial contributions to the cultural deficit thesis. Chilman enumerated 51 cultural characteristics that would prohibit the poor from academic (or any other) success.

The cultural deprivation thesis was similar to the genetic and accumulated environmental deficit thinking in that little could be done to alter the condition through school intervention. It is difficult to invite "cultures" with little or no positive attributes into a school and make them a part of a multicultural approach. There is little incentive for the dominant culture to learn from a deficient culture. Moreover, if one accepts the Chilman argument, it would be a waste of money to try to ameliorate the condition of poverty.

Ignored by cultural deficit theorists are the substantial number of "exceptions": "culturally deprived" successful musicians, artists, scientists, and business executives. Explanation is not necessary when deficits are believed to be self-evident.

Those who claim the existence of race, class, and ethnic bias in schools are required to build a much stronger case.

Culture as a concept grows in importance and changes in emphasis in the years between its re-emergence as a deficit argument to its current use as multicultural education. Our position on multicultural education has been previously stated and need not be repeated here except to note that multicultural education was designed to promote equity and access, and it is our belief that the deficit thinking inherent in it is a major reason it has failed to reach its desired and desirable goal.

Any attempt to camouflage hierarchy of culture with celebration of difference is naive, if not dishonest. Advantage adheres to some cultural activities and disadvantage cannot be eliminated merely by a carefully controlled terminology or with empty, often half-hearted, "celebrations." There can be no circumventing the consequences of cultural membership—who gets what with what, cannot be avoided in any discussion of equity in education. This is particularly true at a time when competition for station in life has intensified and the gap between rich and poor continues to grow. Given the continued, uneven distribution of status by race, ethnicity, and gender, insisting on equal celebration of difference in no way reduces the prevalence of deficit thinking in school policy and practice. Moreover, the serious debate that has occurred in education has been between different deficit theorists. Equal encouragement has not been given much consideration. What has passed for debate has created the illusion that all possible choices have been considered.

EQUAL ENCOURAGEMENT IN THE DEMOCRATIC CLASSROOM

If deficits do not explain differential performance by race, class, gender, and ethnicity (and even differences within a family), what does? We believe unequal encouragement. There is nothing original about our insistence that students are treated very differently in school. And we are not alone in discovering a strong relationship between the treatment students receive in the classroom and social class, race, ethnicity, and gender. Students are abundantly aware of differential treatment (Good & Brophy, 1991).

The justification for differential treatment has always been based on alleged differences in capacity to learn. Students with "deficits" are not given the same education as those without, and students perceived to be gifted are especially encouraged. Teachers need not be condemned for this practice. To the contrary, with very few exceptions, teachers do what they do to be just and to avoid being cruel. Teachers are humane and do not wish to inflict pain by encouraging students beyond their capabilities; nor do they wish to hold a superior intellect back. Teachers want to do what is best for every student and that is the working definition for equality that teachers collectively use. Unfortunately, it is a definition laden with deficit thinking.

Oakes (1985, 1992) has provided ample evidence of the wide difference in the education students receive when assigned to different educational tracks. Oakes, in her research, examines "in the best interests of students" arguments used to defend tracking.

She found no evidence to support this thesis. Moreover, in examining heterogeneous classrooms she found none of the predicted dire consequences. The high-track students were not held back by the low students, nor were the self esteem of low-track students negatively affected by association with the high-track students (Oakes, 1985). Oakes' conclusion was tracking is inequitable. Tracking does not provide students with equal access to a credential society; to the contrary, it prematurely forecloses on student aspirations. Tracking also has a negative impact on citizen preparation. Students do not graduate high school with the same level of understanding of critical social issues.

We have no quarrel with Oakes. We have long opposed tracking. We also know that tracking is difficult to eradicate. Separating students by their alleged ability to learn is held in place not on the basis of theory or evidence, but because it has part of a deeply embedded tradition and it "fits" established belief systems.

We part company when it comes to remedy. Oakes recommended heterogeneous grouping coupled with cooperative learning. Although we support both, neither is sufficient. Oakes remained on the periphery of the problem. Her own evidence suggested that ability grouping would be reinstituted within a heterogeneous class. In fact, as we explain, the search for equity starts in the classroom. We have argued earlier that the democratic classroom begins in a single classroom, so too, does one of its essential requirements: equality.

To promote equity in a classroom it is necessary to identify precisely the nature and practices of unequal treatment *in the classroom* and to undertake specific actions to alter those conditions to determine if significant changes in the direction of equal encouragement can be achieved, and once accomplished determine what if anything that does to student performance.

If there is consistency in school success and failure over space and time and consistency is not to be attributed to "deficits," it must be due to consistency in encouragement and discouragement over space and time. Our task is to identify those differential encouragements, show how they influence school performance, systematically vary them, and accurately assess responses.

What is Equal Encouragement?

In the intense effort to define and celebrate differences, similarity in humans has been largely overlooked. Yet in many ways, all human beings strive for similar gratifications. These gratifications have not been equally available. In the following, we briefly discuss nine universal desires and indicate how they have been unequally made available in classroom

Security. No one disputes the importance of security to the individual and to the society. In school, security, in addition to providing a safe environment, means willingness to risk.

Encouraging risk-taking is not a characteristic of existing class-rooms. For a classroom to encourage risk-taking the teacher must achieve a balance between challenge and support and that balance is only found in democratic classrooms. The two enemies of democracy—guardianship (authoritarian classrooms) and anarchy (open classrooms)—make no effort to achieve such balance. The authoritarian classroom challenges more than it supports because it requires docility (i.e., submission to established authority). And instead of challenging the student, the open classroom relies on "natural curiosity," which means Rogers' (1969) dictum of "unconditional positive regard," applies. Challenge and uncondi-tional positive regard are not compatible. Challenge requires from a teacher far more assertiveness than is allowed in an open class-room. In the democratic classroom, and only in the democratic classroom, there is encouragement to risk and that encouragement is applied equally to all students.

In existing classrooms, inequality is not based on encour-agement to risk but rather on active and persistent differential discouragement to risk. Very early in school life, those who have attributed deficits learn that they should not risk because the costs of risking far outweigh the benefits. Unwillingness to risk distinguishes the achiever from the nonachiever. We believe that unwillingness to risk is less a personality attribute than it is part of the social environment. Teachers communicate clearly who will and will not be punished for risk-taking. Students who have been fearful, insecure, and suffered failures can blossom when encouraged to risk (Hollins, 1991; Meier, 1995).

It is not difficult to determine who in a classroom is and is not afraid to risk. In every class there are some students whose hands are always up (some well before a question is asked), and some students who try to disappear into the woodwork. Where students situate themselves or are situated in relation to the teacher is another indicator of differential nonrisk-taking. Many observers have noted an "action zone"—the front row and seats directly in front of the teacher. It is in this zone that most student talk takes place and some students are allowed (or encouraged) to monopolize discussions (Good & Brophy, 1991; Rist, 1970). Students who monopolize conversation are not necessarily taking risks, they likely are showing off, basking in teacher approval, or merely striving for competitive advantage.

More important than seating arrangement is the nature of the student teacher relationship. Good and Brophy (1991) reviewed the literature and summarized the differences between students who are expected to be capable and those who are not. Depending on how students are perceived, there are wide differences in opportunity to perform, time to think, autonomy, honest feedback, and a key factor in willingness to risk, "respect for the learners with unique interests and needs" (p. 125). Students perceive these differences in treatment. Their perception is not warped (that would be a deficit). It is an accurate reflection of the nature of the student-teacher relationship. Although universal challenge is rarely found in many classrooms, support for students is a classroom characteristic and it is differentially provided.

> Students who need the most help often are the least likely to seek assistance, especially once they have been in school long enough to learn that question-asking sometimes yields teacher criticism (for asking at the wrong time, for not having listened carefully, etc.) or causes the teacher or peers to infer that one is not very bright. (Good & Brophy, 1991, p. 127)

If observation does not identify differences in the discouragement of risk-taking, asking will. Simple surveys will determine who is and is not discouraged from risking in any classroom. It is also helpful to monitor teacher responses to student mistakes. Are all students treated the same when they make an error (as conservatives would desire) or are there detectable differences in how students are treated when mistakes are made? Are some encouraged to try again and others discouraged from future effort? Equal encouragement means creating opportunities for all students to risk and treating error, the inevitable result of risk-taking, with the same degree of support for renewed effort.

Comfort (Relief from Unnecessary Pain). The quest for comfort is universal. Its promise is a major advertising claim. *Comfort* is not a term students use when they talk about school. For most students, school is an uncomfortable place. Students find most "subjects" deadening. According to Goodlad (1984), the only subjects more than 30% of junior and senior high school students found very interesting most of the time were the arts, vocational courses, physical education, and foreign languages. Goodlad was depressed to discover only 25% found "English" interesting, given the importance attached to the subject. Even less interesting than the subjects were to students was the mode of instruction. Most students find school too "boring." As boring as school is in general, it is intensely more so for those assigned to the lower tracks. It is not merely student opinion that low-track classes are more boring than college-bound tracks. Independent observation provides verification of dreary curriculum and instruction (Oakes, 1985, 1992).

The eternally interesting classroom is neither a desirable nor feasible goal. What can and should be eliminated is unnecessary pain. In school, unnecessary pain takes the form of humiliation, shame, boredom, imposed silence, and loneliness. By differentially inflicting these pains, schools unequally encourage. The "good" student rarely suffers unnecessary pain. Students with "deficits" find themselves routinely humiliated and isolated. Attempts to avoid the infliction of unnecessary pain explains tardiness and absenteeism far more parsimoniously than do attributed deficits.

What passes for discipline is often nothing more than public humiliation. The Canters might insist that assertive discipline is intended to be supportive of students when they are good (Canter, 1988), but students are mortified to have names put on the blackboard, or be sent to the office, or worse, have their parents notified that they have been "bad."

Forcing students to work alone on meaningless problems, imposing silence, ridiculing effort (or maybe even more insulting, lavishing praise on inferior work), are other forms of unnecessary pain inflicted disproportionately on poor and minority students.

Different populations have been subjected to public torment. The targets change. With current immigrant bashing, it is Hispanic populations that are shamed in America (in Australia, the original inhabitants, Aboriginals, but also Asian and near-eastern newcomers; in Britain, immigrants from the Caribbean). As discussed previously, neither multicultural education nor bilingual education as currently practiced provides equal encouragement, or equal protection against unnecessary pain. When all the various unnecessary pains are combined they amount to a systematic assault on dignity.

Teachers and administrators are not the only ones who inflict unnecessary pain. Students do it to each other. Bullying, harassment, and name-calling are all part of the existing at-risk school culture. However, students inflicting pain on students does not absolve the teacher from rectifying that situation. Drawing attention to the process, generating projects that address the situation, actively engaging in team-building, counseling individuals, continuously consulting with students, and developing games that strive for new records in avoiding putdowns, all help develop a new culture. If students are to be persuaded to refrain from abusing each other, teacher leadership is required In the democratic classroom, and conscious effort is made to eliminate unnecessary pain. Teachers listen to complaints about humiliation, boredom, blaming, and shaming. There is no imposed silence for silence's sake in a democratic classroom. Every effort is made to eliminate unnecessary pain (and student suggestions are welcome here); every effort is also made to ensure that necessary pain is distributed equally (and again student comments are welcome).

Competence. White (1959) constructed a theory of personality based on the human need to be competent. It is a theory that passes the test of common sense—people do those things that they do well and try to avoid revealing their incompetence. In every arena of life we are quick to attach the label *incompetent* on great numbers of people, and then we are surprised when they lose interest in their assigned responsibilities. Denying people the opportunity to be competent at work, politics, school, health, and so on, does not end the matter. If people are unable to be competent in actions approved by legitimate authority, they will find places and activities where their competence is recognized. Burglars brag of their ability to pick locks, drug dealers of their ability to elude police, school clowns of their talent to irritate teachers, and so on.

Competence in school is measured by evaluated performance (i.e., grades). Students learn very quickly who among their peers are considered competent in school and who are dismissed as incompetents. It is through this system of assessment that a meritocracy is supposedly established. But grades are far less a measure of competence than a means to encourage and discourage. Students know that grades are as much a willingness to be submissive as they are a measure of academic accomplishment.

Competence will be fairly determined when all students are encouraged equally to be competent, when existing competence is equally recognized, and when students who are having difficulty are encouraged to build on the competencies they do have.

In school, competence and relevance are inseparable. It is difficult to encourage students to be competent in matters they find insignificant. Students will strive to be competent when the knowledge and skill they are developing is organized for important problem solving. When encouraged to competence, students with alleged deficits show unexpected and often spectacular growth (Edmonds, 1984; Hollins, 1991; Meier, 1995).

How is equal encouragement to competence attained in a democratic classroom? It begins with shared responsibility. Instructors bear as much responsibility as students when students fail to learn. The sharing of responsibility not only reduces adversarial relationships, it also reduces classroom tension.

> Teaching may be compared to selling commodities. No one can sell unless someone buys. . . . There is the same exact equation between teaching and learning that there is between selling and buying. (Dewey, 1933, pp. 35-36)

In the democratic classroom, all aspects of education, curriculum, instruction, evaluation, discipline, and time schedules are negotiated. Freely communicated is the recognition that competence cannot be judged by an unchallengeable authority.

Belonging. Ours is a society that systematically includes and excludes. In an earlier time, family, neighborhood, union, church, and fraternal order provided psychological centering and opportunity for psychological investment. Such a society was inequitable and blatantly unfair, but it provided gratifications, much of which has been lost. The "existential vacuum" noticed by so many is partially the result of the technological takeover of community. Passive reception has replaced active participation. So much of today's life is centrifugal and impersonal. Belonging is a vital human need. Humans hunger for companionship. They are terrified by isolation. Schools have always included and excluded. Exclusion from welcomed membership in school does not terminate a student's desire for belonging. Students who are demeaned, humiliated, and excluded from first-class membership in school (i.e., those with attributed "deficits") will search for belonging outside of school-sanctioned memberships. They will join cliques, gangs, and so forth, in order to establish identity and they will demonstrate affiliation by dress, music, language, designation of "turf," identifying behaviors, shared values, and other indicators of a "common culture" (Knight, 1997; Willis, 1990). These groups become references for acceptable and unacceptable behavior and in time rob established authority of its legitimacy.

In a democratic classroom, all students are made equally welcome and all students are encouraged to be part of the effort to make the classroom an inclusive community. A democratic classroom by definition is inclusive. Welcoming all students equally not only makes a community out of the classroom, it also prepares the student for community building in the broader community. It is an antidote to racism, ethnocentrism, sexism, and homophobia.

Meaning. Meaning is insufficiently understood in our society. Meaning in school has two fundamentally different *meanings*. In one of its senses, students need to understand what is expected of them in any class activity and in the other, students need to know that what they are learning means something important. They must be persuaded that what is being taught or discovered is something that they want to know. Reading and mathematics have suffered because they have been made unnecessarily mysterious. Educators speak in secret codes. As a result, students are often so confused that they are no longer able to ascertain for themselves what they know. They have lost ownership of their thought processes and thus are unable to determine if they can or cannot read, multiply, or analyze a historical situation.

Meaning in culture is active participation. Culture will not become meaningful until it is recentered and freed from the grip of corporate or governmental-bureaucratic control (e.g., national standards).

In today's classroom, there is wide discrepancy in communicating both senses of meaning. Teachers of students with diagnosed or attributed deficits are not as patient with students, nor are they as clear in providing instructions as are teachers of high-status students. Much more time is spent with low-status students on "discipline" issues than is the case with high-status students. And although there is not much time spent explaining the utility of knowledge to either the upper or the lower tracks, students in the upper tracks know their future plans depend on how well they do in any particular class. Preparing for the future carries with it a kind of meaning not available to vocational or basic track students (Goodlad, 1984; Oakes, 1985, 1992). It is not surprising that "low ability" students find vocational education classes more meaningful than English, Social Studies, or Algebra" (Goodlad, 1984).

In a democratic classroom, all students receive equal justifications for the lesson and are equally demystified on how the lesson is to be learned. In the democratic classroom, students participate in deliberating how equitable and successful communication of both senses of meaning has been. Students assist the instructor in enlightening the class on what is to be done, and students contribute in making the case for utility.

Usefulness. Uselessness is a dreaded condition. In the democratic classroom, Goethe's often quoted "A useless life is early death" is taken seriously. Enforced uselessness is cruel punishment and yet enforced uselessness is the essence of existing classrooms. The *raison d'être* of current education is preparation for future usefulness. And that is one of the reasons students find school so deadly. They are asked to put their lives on hold. Dewey (1897) lamented that focus in his also often quoted ". . . education, therefore, is a process of living and not a preparation for future living" (p. 78). As we have stated earlier, we are not comfortable with that phrase, believing it to be too encapsulating. In our formulation, schools do prepare students for future challenges, but at the same time usefulness is built into day-to-day classroom activity. Usefulness is perceived as a developmental attribute, the skills, insights, and knowledge obtained in the process of being useful provide the basis for continual growth that open doors to a variety of valuable paid and volunteer adult usefulness.

In the democratic classroom, all students are encouraged to be useful and are given a wide range of choices in providing a service and also a wide range of choices in accepting the service of another. Usefulness in school is meaningful problem solving rather than mindless drill and alleged preparation for a dubious and murky future. Currently, those with deficits are offered even less opportunity to be useful than is provided to the favored student. In fact, there is no place in life where disadvantaged or at risk students feel less useful than in school. They rarely are allowed the gratifications of being tutors, or representing the school in student government or in an academic decathlon, and so on. It is the disadvantaged student who is defendant in a student court at which advantaged students serve as prosecutor, judge, and jury. Moreover, the student with deficits is denied the gratification of seeing future utility in school. He or she is not encouraged to perceive the school as a way-station to some future good place.

In a democratic classroom, all activities are organized for usefulness. The problems students solve are problems they perceive to be real and important. All students are recruited to help with the instruction and serve in many different capacities. All engage in cross-age tutoring, all share the results of research with the class, all have valuable roles to play in cooperative education projects, all engage in community service that is integrated with the basic curriculum.

Hope. Russell (1927) said,

It is because modern education is so seldom inspired by a
great hope that it so seldom achieves a great result. The
wish to preserve the past rather than the hope of creating
the future dominates the minds of those who control the
teaching of the young. (p. 110)

A few decades ago, at least in the United States, it would
have been unnecessary to include hope as an unmet human need. It
sprang eternal, it was the essence of our national character and
was manifest everywhere. We largely believed with Franklin
Roosevelt that "the only thing we had to fear was fear itself."
Hopelessness now comes at us from many directions. Pessimism is
reflected in opinion polls and loss of confidence in one's ability to
influence one's future (Morin, 1995). Pessimism is the one
common characteristic in modern American life—middle class and
poor, Black and White alike fear the "American dream" is not for
them. Students with defined deficits have little to be hopeful about.
Their prospects are far more bleak than students without such
impediments. Treating a student as deficient makes the world that
much more hopeless.

In a democratic classroom, serious effort is made to equally encourage all students to be hopeful. But it is more than cheer-
leading. In a democratic classroom, all students are provided reasons to be hopeful. There is a continuous dialogue. Problems are
organized with possible solutions in mind. Students are encouraged to be problem solvers, rather than to be overwhelmed by the
problems they have.

Excitement. Excitement is a legitimate and important
human need. We believe it is a major motivating factor in crime
and other mischief-making. Excitement is not a term students
associate with classrooms, unless there is a fight or someone
lights a fire in the waste basket. But there are rare moments,
treasured and forever relived by a few successful students who
are able to experience the intense feelings of fulfillment that come
with discovery, invention, and creativity. What is rare should be
the norm. All students, rather than a privileged few, should be
encouraged to be excited by what goes on in a classroom.

When the classroom is not an exciting place, some students
will try to make it so. It is not the "good" students who bring
excitement to the class, but the "bad" ones. The troublemakers
create their own excitement and share it with the rest of the class.

They engage in outrageous (i.e., exciting) actions because they believe they have nothing to lose. It is one of the few times students with a stake in the system envy the bad student.

Excitement is another hallmark of the democratic classroom. Excitement is not sufficiently controllable to be a valued or even be a permissible part of the authoritarian classroom. If there is excitement in such a classroom it is bogus, a staged activity in which students are required to perform as if they were excited. Most school-based excitement is relegated to athletics and other co-curricular activities such as opening night of the carefully selected school play, and as such it is restricted to a few carefully screened students.

The open classroom, because it is much less controlled than democracy's other enemy, authoritarianism, is marked by spontaneity and therefore can often be exciting. What is lacking in the open classroom is the opportunity to build on excitement and have excitement be a vital element in the development of important knowledge.

Classrooms can be designed to be exciting if teachers are willing to relinquish control and students are encouraged to participate in activities where they generate important knowledge, make important discoveries, and participate in important decisions. For the classroom to be democratic, the opportunity for such excitement is consciously extended to all students, and when it is apparent that some students find the classroom more exciting than others, the situation is discussed in class and efforts are made to extend excitement to all.

Creativity. Humans are, by nature, a creative species. Each generation creates a new world. School officials, with a similar logic used for assessing intelligence, arbitrarily establish limits on creativity, insisting that only a privileged few are creative. Creativity is in a certain sense undefinable. There are no acceptable criteria for creativity and often it goes unrecognized. Creativity should not be defined solely by school-recognized accomplishment, or by an even more capricious criterion, assessed capacity to be creative. Both "standards" for creativity are powerfully correlated with race, ethnicity, and parental economic condition. The way schools are currently constructed, adult authority decides who can be creative and how that creativity is to be expressed. Those supposedly limited by deficits are not permitted outlets for creativity, or, the perceptions of them are so overpowering, their creativity goes unrecognized.

Unfortunately, when the creativity of those with labeled deficits are not allowed to demonstrate creativity in school-sanctioned activities, the denied often find creative fulfillment in proscribed activities. They are creative in inventing ways to torment teachers with their graffiti and in their complex illegal activities.

In a democratic class, all students are encouraged to be constructively creative and to use creativity for community building, that is, to make the class a far more interesting, exciting, and creative place than is currently the case; and, far more interesting, exciting, and creative than any of the proposed highly advertised "reforms."

What Happens with Equal Encouragement?

Equal encouragement has not had many advocates over the years. Deficit thinking in its many guises has been so pervasive that any effort to truly test deficit thinking through equal encouragement has itself gotten very little encouragement. Pearl and Riessman were astounded to discover at a Ford Foundation sponsored conference in June 1965 how widespread deficit thinking was among scholars. Conservatives at that conference by and large believed that deficits was a primary cause of poverty, whereas liberals tended to the belief that deficits was a consequence of poverty.

Riessman and Hallowitz (1965), Grant (1967), and Pearl (1965), with somewhat different conceptions, devised experiments that questioned deficit thinking. The experiments were successful in the sense that persons with reputed deficits far exceeded expectations. We very briefly summarize these efforts.[3]

The Vacaville New Careers Development Project. Grant was less interested in attacking deficit thinking than he was in demonstrating that persons who had long criminal histories could beat the odds and lead very productive lives. The 18 incarcerated criminals he recruited into his "New Career" experiment had, by the calculus used by the California Department of Corrections, a 95% probability to relapse to crime and be returned to prison within 2 years. Only 1 of the 18 failed to make 2 years of parole, and only 3 of the 18 spent any time in prison over the next 30 years. Three went on to earn doctorate degrees; 3 others, master's degrees. Of those with doctorate degrees, one served as an admin-

---

[3]We discuss in detail these experiments in a companion work on democratic practice in schools.

istrator for an institution of higher education, one became an administrator for New York State's Division for Youth, and one became a high-ranking administrator for the U.S. government's National Institute for Mental Health. In the experiment, the recruited inmates were subjected to a very intensive 4-month training program immediately prior to release from prison.

An important ingredient of the study was the sponsorship the inmates received after release from prison. How much of their spectacular results was due to the training they received and how much was due to sponsorship cannot be ascertained. The researchers did make one concession to deficit thinking in their program. They recruited only those who scored above average on intelligence tests. However, considering all the other baggage the inmates carried with them, this experiment must be viewed as a powerful indictment of deficit thinking. It is a story of particular importance at a time when so much public opinion is disinformed by the malicious myth that rehabilitation is impossible and that the only course open to a public is to "lock them up and throw away the key."

Lincoln Hospital Mental Health Services. The Riessman experiment was not designed to test deficit thinking. The primary motivating factor for this experiment and one of Riessman's key interests was to apply and test the "helper principle" in a variety of human services. Riessman advanced the idea that in the helping of others, people grow and reveal otherwise hidden talents. His work has contributed substantially to our understanding of usefulness as a universal human need. Being reduced to helplessness can lead to the appearance of a deficit and the helping of others may cause the attributed deficits to disappear. In this experiment, Riessman and his associates at Albert Einstein Medical School opened three storefront mental health services, each with 5 to 10 aides who served as bridges between the indigenous population and the professional as expediters, advocates, and counselors. The aides were indigenous poor (mostly of Puerto Rican descent) with limited skill, training, and experiences (and with many attributed deficits; Hallowitz, 1968). The aides increased enormously the services provided to the indigenous poor (Gartner, 1971). The ability of people with supposed intellectual and other deficiencies to perform as well as they did cannot be explained by deficit thinking and constitutes a damaging blow to the notion that poor people lack the capacity to perform at the same level as those not mired in poverty (Hallowitz, 1968).

The Howard University Community Apprentices Program. Pearl undertook a study whose primary purpose was to challenge deficit thinking. In the program designed by Pearl and his colleagues at Howard University, 10 low-income minority (African-American) youth were recruited to serve as aides in child-care, recreation, and research. All those recruited were supposedly riddled with deficits, scored low on IQ tests, came from very deprived backgrounds and thus suffered from accumulated environmental deficits, came from chaotic homes and thus had impaired character development, and were members of deprived cultures. Their deficits were confirmed by poor school performance, high delinquency rates, and an inability to hold a job.

The program called for youth to participate in a 2-week orientation to become familiar with the program and the three options that were available to them—child-care, recreation, or research. At the end of the 2 weeks the 10 youth met as a group to select the 4 students who would work in child-care, 4 in recreation, and 2 in research. For the next 6 weeks, the youth worked half a day and were in school the other half day. From the eighth week on, they worked a 40-hour week and attended twice-a-week evening seminars. They were paid minimum wage only for time worked. All 10 completed the full year of the program, none were incarcerated, their attendance at school and work was exemplary, as were their performances on the job and in school. None gave an indication of deficits, not even the youth who had been diagnosed as a catatonic schizophrenic (MacLennan, 1966; MacLennan & Klein, 1965; Pearl, 1965).

Pearl had taken the most extreme position possible. He categorically rejected all forms of deficit thinking. It is not that he believed that everyone was equally capable, but rather that the differences in intellectual capacity was not measurable and there was no reason to conclude that race, ethnicity, gender, or class contributed to whatever differences that did exist.

Although the findings of this study were not disputed, sufficient criticisms of the project prevented it from being a definitive repudiation of deficit thinking. Its replicability was challenged. Was it not possible, or even likely, that the results reflected unusual leadership and the leadership, not the students was responsible for the results? The second criticism was that the environment in which the experiment took place was so altered that it acted to obscure deficits. It could be validly argued that the success of the participants could not be attributed to equal encouragement, but rather that the participants in the program were beneficiaries of encouragement that ordinary students never receive. Teacher ratios of 10:1 was far more favorable than in existing classrooms. The curriculum, organized for problem solving on the job, is not found in existing classrooms. A special effort was made to provide students with gratifications of competence, usefulness, belonging, relief from unnecessary pain, encouragement to risk, opportunity to be creative, and the knowing what to do and why the learning was important. These gratifications, as we have previously noted, are too rarely found in existing classrooms.

It was easy to test whether the success of the project was due to the participants or the leadership. The program was replicated with a newly released inmate from the California Department of Corrections replacing Pearl as director. The only special qualification the new director had was one he developed while in group counseling in prison. The students in the program he directed enjoyed every bit as much success as the earlier group. So much for charismatic leadership.

The Oregon Upward Bound Program. The more than equal encouragement and the special treatment of the Howard project were criticisms not easy to dismiss. Opportunity to test deficit thinking in a regular school setting came when Pearl, in 1966, was appointed director of the University of Oregon's Upward Bound Program, one of the poverty programs that brought impoverished youth to universities for a summer of educational enrichment. Pearl accepted the position on the condition that every participant who completed the summer phases of Upward Bound would be guaranteed admission to the university. That condition made the University of Oregon program different than all other Upward Bound programs. Another difference was that Pearl was a full professor at the university and continued his normal teaching load. He served as director of Upward Bound as an unpaid extra assignment. The connecting of the Upward Bound to the normal functioning of the university made the test of equal encouragement possible.

As with the Howard University program, Pearl sought out persons who were least likely to succeed in higher education. He brought to the university persons who had shown no promise in high school, were in trouble with the law, and who were in trouble in other poverty programs for disadvantaged at-risk youth. This was not an affirmative action program that brought supposedly unqualified students to the university. It was designed to test the validity of the qualifications. However, merely bringing a group of students with alleged deficits to the university was almost a guarantee for failure no matter how well prepared the students were in summer programs. The students did not meet prejudged notions of what university students should look, sound, and act like. If the problem was, as we hypothesized, unequal encouragement, very little encouragement was what they were likely to be given. Knight headed a tutorial program during this period, drawing volunteers from the mainstream university as tutors to the program. University tutors were able to gain university credit for their work and were expected to attend some of the classes taught by Pearl. University tutors were actively encouraged to adopt an equal encouragement stance within their tutoring.

An effort was made to consciously build a strong team spirit in the Oregon Upward Bound Program, leading to a feeling of belongingness, not only during the summer but also after students enrolled as first-year university students. Part of the program was developing bridge courses in the university where unwelcome students would be made to feel secure and protected from humiliation, given assignments that were carefully explained, given classroom assignments built on demonstrated competence, given opportunities to help other students, and encouraged to aspire to an achievable hopeful future. The program was designed for students to participate in decisions that affected their lives through the establishment of a governance structure with real power. The students' willingness to meet what at first seemed to be an insurmountable challenge was partially a response to the expressed faith that the staff had in them. It was a novel experience to have teachers who expected success rather than failure. Pearl altered the student assessment process in the program. In his classes, his students could only receive an "A" (indication of excellent work), or, not an "A" yet. If Pearl had restricted this approach to competence assessment to just those at-risk students in his programs he would have been subject to the same criticism of his Howard program—this was not equal encouragement, it was special treatment. To meet his developing sense of democratic education he extended that type of assessment to all his classes. That action had many repercussions, not the least of which was a marked increase in popularity. His classes grew in size until enrollment reached 2,500 students, necessitating the conversion into a classroom of the university's basketball court.

There was yet another element to the Oregon Upward Bound program that gave it democratic character. It incorporated the New Career approach (discussed in more depth later in this chapter). Democracy works to the extent to which leadership is shared and becomes interchangeable. Pearl relinquished the directorship first to his graduate students and then to the Upward Bound students who had entered the university as inadmissible students (i.e., with deficits). These students moved up the career ladder as aides to tutors, tutors, counselors, assistants to the director, and to ultimately assume the director position. By the time Pearl left the University of Oregon to join the faculty at the University of California at Santa Cruz, three former students of the Upward Bound program had risen to be its director. Charles Hollins (1991), a former student, a former director of Upward Bound, and later an administrator in an institution of higher learning in California, credited this aspect of the program for much of its success.

Considering the success of so many of its students, University of Oregon's Upward Bound Program is a testament to equal encouragement and a powerful argument against deficit thinking. Students defied conventional judgment to become medical doctors, lawyers, teachers, academics, government administrators, and successes in a variety of other challenging careers (Hollins, 1991).

In the University of Oregon project a systematic effort was made to provide every student with encouragement to risk, to remove all unnecessary pain from the university experience, to demystify the university, to instill a strong feeling of belonging, to create opportunities to be useful, to develop strong feelings of competence in intellectual activities, to inspire hope, to encourage creativity, and to build excitement into educational activities.

New Careers. The New Careers Program (Pearl & Riessman, 1965) provides yet another challenge to deficit thinking and to the potentialities of equal encouragement. New Careers was reviewed earlier and points already made are not repeated here. New Careers was the only war on poverty program that directly brought people out of poverty. New Careers finessed deficit thinking. Rather than excluding the vast majority of the population from consideration of a professional career because of lack of qualifications, New Careers brought everyone to the starting line. Equality in this instance is accomplished through the creation of a career ladder beginning with an entering rung available to all regardless of training, skill, or academic accomplishment. Advancement to a professional status is achieved by negotiating a series of steps terminating with professional status. Promotion is determined by performance on the job as well as by academic performance. Preparing a New Careerist for the next rung involves a combination of on-the-job training, a portion of higher education that focuses on problems encountered on the job and is brought to the work site, and normal higher education liberal art requirements.

There were many New Career programs developed in the late 1960s and 1970s. They encompassed a wide range of fields. Discussion of them have been covered in a wide range of publications (Gartner, 1971; Riessman & Popper, 1968). Because of the multiplicity and fuzziness of the goals of most New Career programs, it is difficult to establish their general effectiveness. Few were carefully evaluated. It is unlikely that any adopted or even understood the opposition to deficit thinking that was a significant part of Pearl and Riessman's motivation in writing *New Careers for the Poor*. New Career programs popped up everywhere with no prior preparation, administered by people who knew nothing about its essential elements. New Careers blew in with the political winds and went out when the political winds changed. What was abundantly clear, however, and acknowledged by many of its most vocal critics, is that large numbers of heretofore considered unemployable poor people, when given the opportunity to work, performed well (Carter, 1977).

New Careers provides yet another demonstration of the fallacy of deficit thinking. Again, substantial persons with alleged deficits were able to achieve far more than they were deemed capable of doing. New Careerists believed that their success was made possible by the networks of support they were able to form among themselves (belongingness), usefulness that came with the career ladder, the feelings of competence that came with recognized high-level jobs and education performance and the hopefulness that the ladder provided (Amram et al., 1988).

Sunshine High School in Melbourne, Australia. In 1976, a group of young teachers organized into a task force by Knight instituted an experiment in democratic education in a working-class suburb in Melbourne, Australia. It was organized as a school within a school. The school used Pearl's (1972) *The Atrocity of Education* as a model. Its focus was to equalize encouragement for all work, citizenship, culture, and personal development. For more than 50 years, few students in that school had been admitted to the university. By the time the experiment ended, the admission rate to the university competed with many of the more exclusive schools (Jones, Metcalf, Williams, & Williamson, 1982). At least one graduate of that program had completed his doctorate by 1995.

Deborah Meier and Central Park East Secondary School. Meier is a passionate advocate of democracy and an equally passionate defender of a vibrant public education. She like we believes that both are inextricably intertwined. She not only "talks the talk," she "walks the walk." Central Park East Secondary School demonstrates the feasibility of democratic education. Rejection of deficit thinking is a key component of the school. And here again students with alleged deficits did very well.

There are fundamental differences between Meier's understanding of democracy and ours. Her understanding is not a general theory. But it goes farther in that direction than the inconsistencies and contradictions that are found in the so-called comprehensive high schools. The five habits of mind that are the intellectual glue for her approach help create an inclusive unifying center. Such a center is essential to any school that wants to be democratic.

> The "five habits of mind" are: the question of evidence, or "How do we know what we know?"; the question of viewpoint in all its multiplicity, or "Who's speaking?"; the search for connections and patterns, or "What causes what?"; supposition, or "How might things have been different?"; and finally, why any of it matters, or "Who cares?" (Meier, 1995, p. 50)

The curriculum in Central Park East Secondary School is much more traditional than what we recommend. But where we come together is in equal encouragement. Her school, like our experiments, emphasized competence. ". . . we . . . build on their natural drive toward competence" (Meier, 1995, p. 21). She stressed belongingness through the building of community. Students are encouraged to risk. Unnecessary pain is avoided. Our two senses of meaning are emphasized. Opportunities for usefulness are created, and students are given reasons to be hopeful.

Equal Encouragement in an Undemocratic Setting: Ronald Edmonds and the Effective School. It is not necessary to establish a democratic school or even move in that direction in order for equal encouragement to be initiated. It is possible to equally encourage all students in existing antidemocratic schools. The late Ronald Edmonds was an acknowledged leader in what has come to be known as the Effective Schools movement. He disputed the notion that students brought deficits to school with them, insisting that it was the *"(s)chool response to family background [that] cause[d] depressed achievement for low-income and minority students"* (Edmonds, 1984, p. 37). Edmonds' synthesis of the research findings led him to define the following as characteristics of an Effective School for disadvantaged minorities:

- strong administrative leadership
- high expectations from students
- a safe and orderly environment
- an emphasis on basic skills
- frequent monitoring of pupil progress using measurable curriculum-based criterion-referenced evaluation (Edmonds, 1979, 1984).

The thrust of the Effective School is to improve the delivery of services to those who have not been encouraged to succeed. It is not directed at changing the nature of schooling.

The Achievement Council, a California-based organization promoting Effective School principles, directs its attention toward another population that has been maligned as "deficient," the Latinos. The council identified the following as "roots" of underachievement of this group: an unchallenging curriculum with tracking for low-ability students, too few able and experienced teachers, ill-prepared and often culturally unaware administrators, inadequate services, and low teacher expectations (Haycock & Navarro, 1988). The Achievement Council's prescription for success follows logically from the diagnosis of the problem—a determined principal, demanding teachers, a rich and rigorous core curriculum, parents as partners of teachers, support services for students and teamwork between administrators, teachers, students, and parents. By implementing these reforms, encouragement of students is made more equal and student performances in what had been a dumping ground high school began to resemble schools where students without deficits matriculated (Haycock & Navarro, 1988).

The Effective School is not a move toward a more democratic school. It does not direct its concern to the development of competent democratic citizens; its focus is on leveling the playing field for those who have been badly served in the past. It is included here only because it provides yet another indication of the fallacy of deficit thinking.

IS EQUAL ENCOURAGEMENT POSSIBLE, GIVEN THE IMPETUS FOR COMPETITIVE ADVANTAGE?

Competitive advantage has become increasingly prevalent as concern about the future grows. Indisputably, the search for competitive advantage is a powerful motivating force. Political parties that cater to it do very well in the United States, England, and Australia. How can equal encouragement survive in such a political climate?

Competitive Advantage and Deficit Thinking

The moral justification of competitive advantage is acceptance of deficit thinking. Very few of those who strive for competitive advantage admit to wanting unfair advantage. They desire only what is reasonable: escape from danger, removal of negative influences on their children, and prevention of disruption of their learning. All of which are attributed to deficits that create chaos and lack of discipline, anti-intellectuality, drugs, and violence in schools. The striving for competitive advantage thus is less wanting special privilege than it is providing an opportunity for a (i.e., my) student to reach her or his potential. Once deficit thinking is removed from the equation, the inclusive (i.e., democratic) classroom in a public school can be seen as precisely that, a secure place where all students are encouraged to reach their potential.

Once the deficit thinking is obliterated, diversity can be seen as an asset, and students in a diverse inclusive school will be expected to grow more and live far more enriched lives than is possible in any homogeneous environment. Deficit thinking has had a curdling effect on social thought

Calculating the Costs of Competitive Advantage

Competitive advantage is expensive. When the cost of competitive advantage obtained through some sort of exclusionary process begins to enter the calculations of a general population there will necessarily be some rethinking. We believe if collective action in the direction of democratic education is not taken these costs, which are currently high and rising, will go from excessive to prohibitive and finally to crisis proportions. The bankruptcy we face is not economic; it is intellectual. In the beginning of this book we enumerated a large number of problems that must be solved if quality of life is to be sustained. We argued then that those problems can only be solved by an enlightened democratic citizenry. We presented as a hypothesis that many of those problems have been exacerbated by self-interest run amok. Once it is understood that crime, violence, drug abuse, environmental devastation, poverty, and the like cannot be explained by individual deficits, then it becomes possible to address them as social conditions that beg for social remedy. Once it is recognized that managed democracy, always a myth, is impossible, it falls to a citizenry enlightened by extensive debate and mutually developed research to explore the range of plausible possibilities to create solutions. Excluding any from the deliberative process limits the range of thought, but also invites trouble. The excluded are going to go away and they will cause trouble.

Ultimately, Equal Encouragement Versus Competitive Advantage is a Curriculum Issue

The arguments presented for equal encouragement and the ones very briefly noted against competitive advantage can only be viewed as an introduction to a serious debate. Equal encouragement versus competitive advantage is a curriculum issue that students need to research. It is one of the problems they need to solve as they invent the future. What we have presented could be the kick-off of such knowledge development.

REASONS TO FEEL HOPEFUL

We are encouraged by the enthusiasm with which students have welcomed equal encouragement in the experiments that we have conducted and their willingness to investigate the issue when it is introduced into the curriculum. But, perhaps most importantly, equal encouragement is in the interest of the majority, competitive advantage benefits a minority. The ultimate justification of a democracy is the resonating belief that when all are enlightened and all are involved in a debate, the decision reached is in the public interest. (See Figure 8.1. on how to establish equal encouragement in the classroom.)

SUMMARY

We have presented a long and complicated argument. Equality is not an easy concept to understand because its nemesis, deficit thinking, is ubiquitous. However, regardless of how prevalent deficit thinking is, it can be countered anywhere, by anyone. Equal encouragement can begin in any classroom. It needs no special mandates or guidelines. It violates no laws or policies. It can be the lived practice of every school.

Why, if it can be introduced in any setting, did we wait so long in this book to introduce it? Equal encouragement can begin in any classroom but equal encouragement cannot be sustained without the other requirements of democratic education being met. The interconnectedness of different democratic requirements is what makes a general theory, a general theory. One sets back the advent of democratic education when aspects of it are begun, but cannot be sustained. For equality to be a workable concept it needs a supportive environment. That is why a democratic education in every instance is a balance between meeting the needs of the individual and the needs of society.

Introduce the topic. Open a discussion on each of the encouragements. Discuss encouragement to risk. Make sure students know what you mean. Describe how you will react when students do risk. Negotiate the limits. Try to anticipate. Describe how you will behave if students go beyond the limits (e.g., a student goes beyond the acceptable). Stop the activity and with humor renegotiate the limits. Emphasize your desire for there to be equalization. Indicate how you will limit some student participation to get others to participate.

Discuss elimination of unnecessary pain. Indicate how you will refrain from humiliating students and what you will do when students put each other down. Explain how you will try to keep students from feeling lonely and what you will do to keep students from being bored. Discuss also what they can do when they feel things are becoming boring.

Discuss the importance of meaning. Indicate what you will do to ensure that students know what is expected of them and what they can do if they do not understand an assignment. Discuss how making sure everybody understands can be accomplished without bogging the class down with incessant questions.

Discuss important knowledge and what you will do to explain the importance of anything you are teaching, while at the same time encouraging students to raise questions that they feel are important that can be treated in the class.

Discuss feelings of belongingness and what you will do to make every student feel welcome, and what you will do when students do not extend a welcome to other students.

Discuss competence and how you intend to build on what students know rather than dwell on mistakes and lack of understanding. Indicate how you will treat students who denigrate the competence of others.

Discuss usefulness as a concept and what you are going to do to create opportunities for all students to be useful in the class (e.g., peer tutoring, peer counseling, different roles in cooperative learning, and teacher helper in a variety of tasks). Elicit suggestions for other ways students can be useful.

Discuss excitement. Elicit suggestions for ways the class can be more exciting. Indicate what you are going to do to make the class a more exciting place. Also, establish the limits to class-induced excitement. Use humor.

Discuss creativity. Indicate how you will create opportunities for students to be creative. Elicit suggestions.

Figure 8.1. Establishing equal encouragement in your classroom.

Discuss hope. Get students to think about the future and elicit suggestions of how the class can help with future aspirations. Encourage dreaming. "Tread softly for these are their dreams."

After reaching some shared understanding, construct an evaluation instrument. The following is a suggestion. It will be changed as the class begins to grapple with equal encouragement.

An equal encouragement survey

In the class, I:	Strong yes	yes	???	no	Strong no
was encouraged to risk					
was not humiliated, bored, or felt lonely					
understood what was expected of me					
believed what I was taught was important					
felt welcomed and at home by the teacher					
felt competent					
felt useful					
engaged in exciting activities					
engaged in creative activities					

Comments:

The teacher will lead a discussion that will go in two directions, both of which should be kept separate. One discussion will involve improving the evaluation instrument, the other generating suggestions for more adequately meeting the goal of equal encouragement. The teacher should alert students that both a good instrument and an adequate plan for equal encouragement will take time and will go through many revisions.

Figure 8.1. Establishing equal encouragement in your classroom (con't).

The evaluation should be done frequently (e.g., once a week) because it will take no more than 5 minutes to administer. Students should keep a record of progress toward equal encouragement.

Aside. In addition to helping develop an important requirement of a democratic classroom, students will use this exercise to gain competence in the use of descriptive statistics.

Figure 8.1. Establishing equal encouragement in your classroom (con't.).

Chapter 9

The Democratic Teacher-Leader, Theoretician, and Researcher: The Heart of the Educational Process in the Classroom

ORGANIZING TEACHING WITHIN A GENERAL THEORY

Although one does not need to be exceptional to teach in a democratic classroom, very few teachers are prepared for such teaching. The path to democratic education is deliberative and arduous. There will be many setbacks. It is imperative that the requirements of democratic teaching be fully understood. Ultimately, it is the classroom teacher who will decide the fate of democratic education. The democratic teacher, first and foremost, is dedicated to the primary purpose of a democratic classroom—the preparation of a democratic citizen. It is against this goal that the teacher in the democratic classroom must be evaluated. In many ways, democratic teaching is easier than traditional teaching. Many restrictions are removed. The class is not organized to be adversarial. The teacher does not have to possess all the knowledge or enforce all the rules. She or he, however, is a democratic leader; having mastered democratic arts and being able to take the initiative when necessary by proposing courses of action and modeling democratic citizenship. The democratic teacher persuades and negotiates, uses logic and evidence rather than the coercive power of authority. The democratic teacher is a gyroscope pulling diverse elements toward the center. She or he understands the requirements of democratic education and shares that understanding with students. The democratic teacher explains how the knowledge developed in the classroom can be used to solve important problems. The democratic teacher organizes the classroom for student participation in decisions that influence classroom activity. The democratic teacher establishes rights as underlying conditions for all classroom activities. The democratic teacher equally encourages all students to competence for present and future success. She or he provides a balance between challenge and support, encouraging all students to grow and extend themselves, while equally supporting students when their efforts are not initially successful. In this sense, the democratic teacher encourages all students to risk, sometimes even to fail, and then to regroup and try again.

A necessary attribute of a democratic teacher is an infectious sense of humor. A person who can not bring humor to the classroom, or takes him or herself too seriously should not teach in democratic classroom. A democratic teacher is able to establish warm supportive relationships with a defined segment of the student population. No teacher can relate effectively with all students, but a school should have on its staff a sufficiently diverse teaching staff so that every student can find a teacher that he or she can trust and can engage in meaningful conversation. An important attribute of the democratic teacher is to be able to define the kinds of students with whom she or he can effectively communicate. A democratic teacher knows what he or she knows and is able to present a persuasive case for how that knowledge can be used for important problem solving.

Perhaps most important of all, the democratic teacher does operate alone; he or she knows who to go to and where to go for help. The democratic teacher works collaboratively and encourages students to do the same. A democratic teacher falls along the entire spectrum of political opinion and is free to express his or her views as long as the class receives balanced treatment on any issue. To meet the goal of democratic teaching, the teacher is necessarily a theoretician and researcher. In this chapter, we discuss the attributes of democratic teaching and the means by which such teachers can be prepared. Merely feeling that one is being "democratic" does not necessarily meet democratic requirements.

Those preparing a teacher to work in a democratic classroom, would critically examine deficit thinking in its many ramifications. Today, those preparing to be teachers and those already in the classroom learn fragments about the evils of racism, sexism, classism, homophobia, and so on, and how important it is to celebrate diversity. They are also told that every student should be provided with a fair chance for educational success. A superficial swipe at equality, or moral posturing is not enough. Prospective teachers rarely if ever learn that the most virulent expressions of racism, sexism, classism are not in acts of commission, but what is not done.

Teacher preparation programs interested in producing teachers who can be effective in democratic classrooms must focus on the development of the above attributes. Far different from what currently happens.

THE STATE OF THE ART

Regardless of what spirit of reform moves education, teaching remains the same. There can be no real reform of education without a markedly different approach to teaching. Despite much discussion, organized by respected commissions and senate committees that bring the best minds to bear on the topic, nothing has changed. Teachers teach as they as they always have. They teach "subjects" with little or no general theory. They are unclear about goals, in fact educational goals are almost never on the reform agenda (Gore, 1995; Postman, 1996). Furthermore, teachers accept little responsibility when students do not learn. We believe it will be impossible to bring about change in teaching in the absence of a general theory of education. Any useful theory of instruction must be subsumed within a general theory of education.

No change in teaching will take place with top-down "steering from afar." Teachers need to play a prominent role in changing teaching. And that change will begin in a few classrooms and grow through a process of planned contagion.

In 1966, Henry Steele Commager, an historian, reviewed the history of teacher education and concluded that great change was needed.

Almost two centuries after Thomas Jefferson and Noah
Webster, a century and a quarter after the pioneering work
of Horace Mann and Henry Barnard, more than half a century
after Jane Addams and Lester Ward and John Dewey we find
ourselves confronted by problems as complex and intransigent as any which these great educators faced. Once again we
see millions of children deprived of equality in education;
millions who do not go on to high school or who drop out once
they are there; millions who are not in fact given an education sufficient to enable them to hold jobs or to perform their
duties as citizens. We see that in a nation dedicated to equali-
tarianism, the standards of schools are shockingly disparate
and that the gap between slums and suburbs is greater now
than it was a century ago. We see that while the South has
quite deliberately condemned the Negro to social, political,
and economic inferiority almost unconsciously the North has
condemned him to educational inferiority—an inferiority
which all but guarantees that it will be a social and economic
and cultural one as well. Nor is this merely a racial matter.
Millions of white children of our urban slums, of the impoverished areas of the country—Appalachia, the Deep South,
mining-country and share-cropper country—are likewise
fobbed off with an education so inadequate that it condemns
its victims to economic and cultural inferiority. (p. 56)

Commager, in reviewing the historical evolution of
teacher education in the United States (a history applicable to
Australia as well, less so for England), saw the decline in standards as an inevitable consequence of trying to please too many
masters.

It is this historical experience which accounts in large part
for the strains and tensions that have clustered about
teacher-training in America in this century. Teacher education here has paralleled all other forms of education in that—
in contrast to the Old World—it is expansionist, ambitious,
equalitarian, functional, and miscellaneous. Just as we asked
our schools generally to take on a vast body of non-academic
duties and responsibilities, so we have expected teacher-
training schools to take on far wider duties than those cus-
tomarily imposed upon them abroad. Teacher-training institutions are expected to prepare for almost every level of
teaching, in almost every kind of institution; they are
expected to teach both technical, or professional, and subject matter courses. Because they were called upon to turn
out teachers in most subjects—even in typewriting and in

football coaching—and at almost every level, they were of necessity forced to settle for pretty low standards. (p. 55)

The 1960s, when Commager (and almost everybody) else was whacking away at teacher education, were optimistic times. It was a time for experimentation and considerable teacher enthusiasm. Teachers, no more than any other profession, enjoy being abused, but there was a fairly general recognition for the need for change and a willingness to give it a go.

The conditions of inequity and the challenges that meant for education (that Commager cited) were generally recognized in the profession. A National Institute for Teaching the Disadvantaged was created (Pearl served as its chair in the final year of its existence). The institute members, who differed considerably in the understanding of the problem they were asked to address, engaged in vigorous debate. That kind of vitally needed debate is missing today. The incomplete resolution of that debate was reflected in a book by Smith, Pearl, and Cohen (1969), the first chapter of which was amplified into *The Atrocity of Education* (Pearl, 1972).

The institute did not reach consensus on deficit thinking. Institute members were divided when they began the debate and remained divided when the institute was dissolved. How could it be otherwise, given the powerful hold that deficit thinking has on both a general public's consciousness and the educated elite. As an example, Commager, a wise and distinguished historian who we highly respect and admire, provided an analysis riddled with deficit thinking.

THAT WAS THE 1960S, IT IS NOW THE 1990S

After 30 years of huffing and puffing and darting off every which way, where are we? Very little has changed (Cuban, 1984). The situation, if anything, is worse. The willingness to grapple with the issues that Commager enumerated has lessened considerably. The mood of the times calls for suppression, not experimentation, growth, or liberation. As a consequence, academic components in teacher education remain weak. There is no more evidence now of effective teacher preparation than there was in the early 1960s. What little evidence does exist is not favorable to teacher education. If anything, administrative inertia has increased, as has centralization. Academic departments in the postmodern age have increased their distance from anything that smacks of teacher education (Bessant, 1996). In fact, they appear hostile to anything associated with an education faculty. State departments of education add requirements to the credentialing process that further bogs down the process and unnecessarily restricts admission to the field. The language used by "educationists" is even more arcane than it was as little as 30 years ago. There is nothing more undemocratic than speaking a language that students and their parents do not understand. Speaking in an unintelligible patois does not enhance the teacher. To the contrary, being inaccessible is viewed with suspicion and serves to undermine the educator's credibility (Goodlad, 1990).

How Does a Teacher Currently Become a Teacher?

One becomes a teacher in precisely the same manner and with the identical logic used by the Wizard of Oz when he appeased the Strawman, "you don't need a brain, all you need is a credential." A person is certified to be a professional teacher when bestowed a credential by the state. Whether the credential granted by the state indicates more competence than the one given the Strawman is open to question.

Professional development has been defined with soft boundaries as all those activities that contribute to the teacher's growth, through various courses in curriculum and instruction, classroom management, competence in a specific subject matter, technological skills, and teaching practice, culminating in a teaching credential. Upon entering the profession, the credentialed teacher experiences random (often one shot and likely to be contradictory) professional development activities: curriculum days, school seminars, visiting speakers and education department development courses, subject conferences, weekend workshops, evening meetings, and short-term and summer school courses. This loose and often disparate collection of activities aims to develop teacher competence in the classroom. The most substantial approach to professional development are tertiary courses leading to higher degrees or additional professional qualifications (accompanied by increased salary or promotion). These professional development tertiary courses, distanced from the classroom, whose content is determined by a remote academic, are not easily applied to classroom practice. In orthodox forms of professional development, teachers are passive recipients of what is purported to be knowledge. Teachers rarely are permitted to reflect on their professional experience or understanding to develop research questions, to contribute to theory, or to construct knowledge about classroom practice.[1] In democratic education, the relationship of teachers, students, knowledge, and research is reconceptualized. Teachers and students become producers of knowledge, not consumers, and thereby redefine their role in the development of professional knowledge.

WHAT A DEMOCRATIC TEACHER EDUCATION PROGRAM WOULD LOOK LIKE

All of the requirements of a democratic classroom are highlighted in preparation for democratic teaching. Because the distinguishing feature of a democratic classroom is persuasion and negotiation, a major aspect of teacher preparation involves honing those skills. It is in developing the ability to persuade and negotiate what would be democratic, that classroom teachers sharpen the requisite keen sense of humor and learn to use logic and evidence to defend proposals.

Democratic Teacher Preparation and Knowledge

A democratic teacher needs to know a lot. Part of what distinguishes the democratic teacher from the traditional teacher is ownership of knowledge. The democratic teacher is knowledgeable about the field in which he or she teaches. We refer not to the dry static knowledge that conservative critics skewer teachers for not having, although they are on safe ground in their claim that teacher education programs do not provide future teachers with sufficient knowledge to be competent in the classroom. Conservative critics are not on safe ground, however, when they define the knowledge a teacher should have. It is not sufficient for teachers to be competent in subjects and technical expertise, especially when teaching and learning are narrowly defined (Goodlad, 1994). Future teachers must be given the opportunity to learn how what they teach can be used to solve important per-

---

[1]The essential school movement developed by Theodore Sizer does create opportunities for teachers to learn from each other. We applaud this aspect of that movement. Our criticism is that it is not theory-based, nor does it recognize the undemocratic nature of current schooling. Teachers helping each other to maintain an undemocratic school system is in our opinion, at best, a giant step sideways.

sonal and social problems, and have a working understanding of the social context of schooling and of youth. Knowledge in a teacher preparation program is not restricted to academic subjects. Prospective teachers should also be provided a wide range of opportunities to demonstrate competence in citizenship arts (e.g., the involvement of students as active participants in problem-solving projects, organizing cooperative learning into a coherent educational plan, rousing students from passive recipients to active learners, and stimulating in all students a thirst for knowledge). In a teacher preparation program the once and future teacher becomes familiar with the students lived culture (Knight, 1997; Willis, 1990) and learns how to introduce this culture into the classroom for penetrating analysis.

A democratic teacher preparation program requires its students to be knowledgeable about the world in general, and the students' worlds in particular, and continually involves prospective teachers in exercises that are designed to show the relevance of school-based instruction to the issues that students confront outside of school. Reflection on the use of knowledge is one important component in the development of citizen responsibility. Being widely read on contemporary issues is essential for all democratic teachers regardless of the ages of their students.

Future and existing teachers need to be taught how to work cooperatively with other teachers and how to enlist an array of community resources. The teacher must, as a result of a teacher preparation program, have in place a working general theory that includes child and adolescent development, to guide not only instruction, but can be used when things are not going according to plan.

Democratic Teacher Preparation and Participation

Teacher education programs must involve the prospective teacher in the decisions of the education program. Future teachers should be involved on course committees in curriculum decisions and in hiring of staff. They should be involved in evaluation of the program and encouraged to make suggestions for improvements. If the future teacher's suggestions are rejected, he or she develops the skill with the support of others to insist that the rejection be supported with logic and evidence. The process in preparing the teacher should, in the most unambiguous way, make clear that the prospective teacher in a democratic teacher education program is considered to be a vital cog in the decision-making process. The process should be organized and formal. It cannot be a now-you-see, now-you-don't proposition, or that student participation is welcomed as long as students agree with the teacher education faculty and administration. In the governance of a teacher education program, substantial disagreements between students and faculty and administration should be expected. A democratic teacher education is distinguished by the procedures used to resolve those differences. In democratic teacher education, the resolution of conflict is perceived as a critical part of the learning process. In the resolution of conflict, the future teacher gains some sense of citizen empowerment, he or she also gains an understanding of how to resolve conflict in elementary and secondary classrooms.

Participation in decision making means that a teacher in a democratic classroom is involved with politics, not necessarily partisan or party politics (although it is difficult to be a citizen and not have some involvement in the "political system"). Politics is arriving at decision under conditions of conflict. By inviting students into decision making, the teacher invites conflict and that conflict requires a resolution that rarely will satisfy all. A person who does not like politics should not be in a democratic classroom, and likely should not be teaching in any classroom, given how deeply embedded education is in politics no matter how defined.

Democratic Teacher Preparation and Rights

The prospective teacher has all the rights a student should have in an elementary or secondary classroom—the right to voice unpopular opinions, the right to privacy, the right to due process, and the right not to be a captive audience. Students in a teacher preparation program must have the right to challenge actions perceived to be unfair, and to remove oneself without penalty from a classroom when the conflict between the teacher and the student cannot be resolved to the mutual satisfaction of both. When these conflicts occur and a negotiated settlement is not reached, either party should have access to binding arbitration with a mutually agreed on arbitrator. For rights to become a reality for students in K-12 classrooms, it is of vital importance that people preparing to be teachers experience rights before they become teachers. Such experiences help define rights, but they also help prepare for states of emergency where rights are temporarily suspended.

Democratic Teacher Preparation and Equal Encouragement

A major portion of a democratic teacher education program is designed to rid the prospective teacher of deficit thinking. Issues of equity are discussed and debated in depth. The future teacher is given the opportunity to understand how important student gratifications are for educational success and how vital it is for all students to be equally encouraged to be secure in the classroom; to be equally spared unnecessary pain and discomfort; to be equally aware of classroom intentions and the importance of what is to be learned; to be made to feel equally welcome in the classroom; to be equally encouraged to competence; to be given equal opportunities to be useful; to be equally encouraged to a hopeful future; to be given equal opportunity to be creative; and to be equally encouraged to engage in exciting activities in the classroom.

It is unreasonable to expect the future teacher to enter the classroom without race, class, gender, or other biases. It is not unreasonable for the future teacher to be aware of those biases. It is also not unreasonable to expect that a teacher be aware that there are students in the classroom he or she cannot equally encourage, and in those instances take the initiative to find classrooms where those students can be with teachers able to provide appropriate encouragements. In a democratic teacher education program, the future teacher learns the importance of generating support for a sufficiently diverse teaching staff so that every student can be equally encouraged.

A democratic teacher does not need to be the class expert. It is far more important that a teacher in a democratic class perceive him or herself as a lifelong learner, discovering and inventing knowledge at the same time her students do. In the democratic classroom, teachers work cooperatively with students, and in that relationship it is as important for teachers to inform the students what they do not know as it is to share with students what they do know.

But first and foremost, a democratic teacher is a theoretician and researcher, developing and testing a general theory. A teacher who claims to be democratic but is not involved with theory development or with significant research that is used to test and develop theory is engaged in self-deception.

No teacher preparation program will produce the perfect democratic teacher. There is no such thing. Nothing could be more useless than a democratic teacher manual. That is the ultimate oxymoron. However, guides and examples can be helpful. It must be constantly kept in mind that no teacher can be democratic all the time and some teachers will never be democratic. Our goals are to help teachers be more democratic than they are and to learn from those who make the most serious attempts at democratic teaching. The most that can be expected from a teacher preparation program organized around the principles of democracy and the requirements of a democratic classroom is a teacher who has the opportunity to grasp and work with the principles of inclusion, persuasion and negotiation and the requirements of important knowledge, participation, rights, and equal encouragement. A teacher preparation program can establish a foundation that the democratic teacher will use to establish networks for support and for the exchange of experiences. A teacher preparation program should be a vital component in the collaborative research that will be part of the continual refinement of democratic education theory. What is presented here is works in progress.

   Reviewing Some Efforts at Preparing Teachers for a Democratic Classroom. In a generally dismal situation, a small groundswell for preparing democratic teachers is developing. Wood (1992) summarized the contributions in his journal, *Democratic Education* and in his book, *Schools that Work: America's Most Innovative Public Education Programs.* Powerful critiques and supportive examples of democratic classrooms can be found in the periodical, *Rethinking Schools.* A group of Australian scholars (Centre for Democratic Education—Melbourne) publish occasional pamphlets on different topics that cast light on different aspects of democratic education (Knight, 1995).
   Novak (1994) compiled a series of reports on programs designed to prepare democratic teachers. These programs share some important characteristics and each would be a distinct improvement of what currently passes for teacher preparation. We restrict our comments to a 3-year program at Ohio University Teacher Education for Civic Responsibility (TECR). TECR has as its goal the "civic mission of teachers in educating their students about the rights and responsibilities of citizenship in a democracy" (Hillkirk, 1994, p. 90). TECR has six key characteristics.

1. Students learn about democracy through a 4-year core liberal arts program designed to build an understanding and an appreciation for citizenship responsibility and

democratic government (as distinguished from students individually selecting from an increasingly wide array of liberal art courses that meet university graduation requirements).

2. Students enter the teacher education program as first-year university students and work together as a team or cohort throughout their 4-year teacher preparation program (contrast this approach with the LaTrobe task force presented later).

3. There is a 4-year teacher education curriculum in democratic education. In the first year, students learn about significant figures in democratic thought (e.g., Jefferson and Dewey) and reflect on their own "schooling experience particularly in relation to the ways that their own understandings and commitments to democratic participation were enabled or hindered" (Hillkirk, 1994, p. 93). In this stage students and instructor examine the premises of current schooling and are asked to consider new ways of organizing a classroom that would better reflect participatory democracy and use the first-year field experience to look at classroom as they really are.

In the second year, students begin to examine "the complex relationship between teaching and learning... studying) child and adolescent development from birth through young adulthood in the year-long course "childhood in America" (Hillkirk, 1994, p. 93). They continue to engage in field study with a focus "on a particular child or adolescent over a three to six-month period" (Hillkirk, 1994, p. 93). In this year students become acquainted with Barak Rosenshine's explicit teaching" (Rosenshine, 1986) and cooperative learning as exemplified Johnson and Johnson (1989). In the second year, "Students prepare and teach two explicit teaching lessons during the course, one in the university classroom and the other in their field experience classroom. Both lessons are videotaped and carefully analyzed in relation to the student's effectiveness in applying the explicit teaching functions" (Hillkirk, 1994, p. 94) and students become involved with cooperative learning in many different situations. Students take a third education course that emphasizes diversity with specific reference to African and Asian cultures. As a means to integrate this course with the introductory methods course, TECR students have organized and implemented a Hunger Day in a middle school the first year, and an elementary school more recently. This experience provides a complex organizational and teaching challenge as the TECR students have prepared and served three different types of meals to public school students: (a) an elite group eats a meal typical for many U.S. families that includes meat, vegetables, and starch; (b) a somewhat larger group receives vegetables and starch; (c) the majority eats a simple meal of rice and water, which is a typical diet for millions of hungry people around the world. TECR students are responsible for organization and food preparation, as well as the overall educational planning for Hunger Day, which ensures that students grasp the symbolic "point" of the experience. Hunger Day thus teaches valuable lessons to all involved (Hillkirk, 1994, p. 95).

In the third year, students continue with "explicit teaching" and cooperative learning, and add inquiry learning, project-centered learning, and group discussion to their repertoire of understandings and skills and observe and apply what they know in an ongoing field experience. They begin to develop curriculum and study a variety of democratic education experience, including Foxfire and whole language.

In their final year, "each student was placed with a cooperating teacher who is familiar with and committed to program goals and philosophy. Prior to, and following, student teaching, each student enrolled in a pre- and post-student-teaching practicum that involves weekly work and time spent in the classroom with the teacher who mentors his or her student teaching experience. Regularly scheduled seminars with a university supervisor are also held throughout the senior year—before during, and after student teaching" (Hillkirk, 1994, p. 95).

4. Field experience is much more intensive and far more varied in TECR than in a traditional teacher preparation program. In TECR, preservice teachers develop strong relationships with experienced teachers.

5. As part of process of learning from model democratic classrooms, TECR students visited whole language programs in Chicago and Milwaukee and Meier's Central Park East Community School in New York

6. TECR is marked by collaboration within the school of education, between the education faculty and other university faculty and between the university and elementary and secondary schools.

It is too early to determine whether this approach to teacher training has had any impact on where it counts—the performance of elementary and secondary school students. But TECR is an exciting venture and we are eager to learn whether through this approach to teacher preparation, classrooms become more democratic and students in them are roused from lethargy to civic responsibility. This 4-year program offers a strong guide to developing clear educational objectives over time, in contrast to the 1-year programs with their busy work agendas.

Only with clearly articulated principles it is possible to determine whether programs are moving in the direction of democracy. Ultimately, it is not what we call ourselves, or even how we are addressed by others that determines whether a classroom is democratic, what matters is the impact on students. It is only possible to call a classroom democratic only when it can be shown that all students in a classroom are able to construct knowledge and apply it to the solution of important social and personal problems, can identify their rights and can perceive that these rights are universally available, are able to participate in decisions that affect their lives, and are equally encouraged to succeed. We have a long way to go before teachers are prepared to exercise leadership in such classroom so our immediate goal must be to develop an increasing number of working models.

There is much to learn from experiments in preparing democratic teachers. We confess some skepticism concerning the effectiveness of the use of off-the-shelf techniques (e.g., whole language, authentic assessment, and particular versions of cooperative learning). It is important that students be exposed to these techniques and discover both the valuable contributions that can be made by them, and also their limitations.

The biggest difference between us and others who are dedicated to the advancement of democratic education, is theory. In the absence of a general theory that addresses all aspects of education, democracy becomes fuzzy and even platitudinous. Without a general theory, goals become imprecise, even contradictory. Our theory brings us to an approach to knowledge far different from almost all others who claim devotion to democracy. We are more specific on rights We are closest to others in calling for student participation in decision making; and although there is a shared belief that equality is an essential element in a democratic classroom, we are farthest apart in suggesting means to achieve equality. Because of the protean nature of deficit thinking and its ubiquitousness, we are concerned that discussion of equality without disciplined effort to eradicate deficit thinking will be counterproductive. Moreover, very few who advocate democratic education reveal a history of reflective effort to institute democratic practice.

ONE APPROACH TO DEMOCRATIC TEACHER PREPARATION: TASK FORCES AT LATROBE UNIVERSITY

The taken-for-granted relationship between the classroom and the voices of authority at the university and state ministry levels was challenged in the early 1970s with work done at LaTrobe University, Centre for Urban Education. In that program the concept of *teachers as researchers* in inner urban schools was developed. Claydon (1975) set out two premises to get the model off the ground: (a) the teacher as the prime originator, working from sound theoretical premises; and (b) the school as the principle arena for theoretical discussion centered on specific situations and problems that are identified by the school itself. The general strategy was to bring policy development and implementation under the one school roof. Teachers were to be responsible for developing both.

Claydon (1973), on arriving at LaTrobe University in 1971, developed an action-research program featuring the use of task forces that brought together teachers and higher education. The program featured 2 years of school-based, action-research, postgraduate teacher education. The purpose of the program was to decentralize research and theory development. In place of university-directed research was a partnership of university faculty and teachers, and administrators in a designated school. Experienced teachers volunteered to participate in the research, were interviewed, and on the basis of expressed interest and commitment to achieve institutional change within 2 years, were selected and formed into task force teams (6-10 on a task force). The research was to lead to changes in two areas that we now define as requirements for a democratic classroom. One of which was participation in decisions that affected one's life and the other was designed to achieve equality (to help students who had histories of limited educational achievement). Both of these understandings were influenced by Knight and his work at the University of Oregon, and the work of Claydon with The Liverpool Educational Priority Area Project that emphasized involving the community in school life (although involving the community was not emphasized by us in the 1970s, we now see such involvement as a necessary element in democratic education).

To determine the nature of the research, a number of schools in Melbourne's inner city and industrialized suburbs (schools with heavy concentrations of "disadvantaged" populations) expressed desire to participate in a cooperative arrangement. Parents, teachers, and administrators came together and identified some specific priority school needs that were to be the focus for the research and program development of the incoming task force. It was an integrated model of staff development where all constituents of the school were encouraged to participate in the formation of school policy. Encouraging the participation of teachers, parents, and administrators in determining school policy can be viewed as a first step in conceptualizing a democratic school. This approach was also a first step in the development of the teacher as researcher.

The role of LaTrobe University staff was to take the brief, assign a task force to the school and design curriculum that would assist the task force research team in fulfilling its brief. The university faculty were to be collaborators and partners in the general development of theory and evaluation. This was a joint learning situation where professional development applied equally to tertiary and school staff. The general premise being applied was the more university scholars work as equal status partners with teachers, parents, and students, and the less they define themselves as outside experts, the more useful they will be in helping to develop and test the early formulations of democratic theory (Claydon, 1975; Pearl, 1972).

Role of Tertiary Staff

The tertiary staff was responsible for instituting dialogue with the school principal and staff over the 2 years of the task force project and for including as many interested staff in the life of the project, especially in the development of school programs. The same group assisted in the dialogue that helped develop general theoretical principles and their translation into strategies for change within the school. There was some subject choice at the university for team members. This choice depended on what areas of knowledge and skill needed to be developed in order to assist in the construction of particular programs, for example, forms of technical knowledge needed for research and evaluation. Tertiary staff also conducted weekly seminars around issues contained in the brief. School-based seminars were integral to the developing relationship between school and tertiary staff. It was impossible to escape the everyday relationships in the school when institution-wide issues became the focus of concern during seminars. A form of collegiality had to be developed to resolve problems. This kind of collegial problem solving contrasts with the individualistic approach associated with most professional development programs for teachers.

There were approximately 20 two-year task force programs in the period from 1971 to 1986. We describe them in detail in an accompanying volume on democratic practice.

What Was Learned From the LaTrobe Task Forces

Bringing together a group of people to work cooperatively as a team is a necessary condition for preparing the democratic teacher. The task force or team is as valuable in a preservice program (Hillkirk, 1994) as it is in an inservice project. Learning to work together as a team is a necessary condition for helping students work as teams. Organizing the task forces to solve a particular problem is also a vital component in preparing a democratic teacher. Task force members saw themselves as leaders and that too is necessary in democratic teachers. The task force although vitally interested in developing cooperative research between the university and the school, was less concerned about the requirements of democracy. As a consequence, serious divisions appeared in several of the task forces. On hindsight, it would have been desirable if prospective members had experimented with some fairly simple problem before being selected to work together. However, the most important lesson from the LaTrobe experience is the difficulty, if not impossibility of incorporate an entire school into a democratic educational experiment. The LaTrobe task forces depended on the leadership of the principal. In Brunswick Girls High School, the principal left, and with that the support for the overall school program slipped back, although many of the projects started during the life of the team were maintained for many years and they in turn influenced other programs. At Sunshine High School, the task force and the principal found themselves in a bitter dispute and that undermined the effort. What the LaTrobe experience brought home is the necessity to develop democratic education in a single classroom and build from there. It also helped make clear the importance of building some mutual understanding of the requirements of a democratic classroom. The principal in a school with one or more democratic classrooms must be sympathetic to the effort, but is not required to be the critical actor. Even if working in different classrooms in different schools, the task force can continue to provide a network of support and consultation. However, if members of a task force decide to move on to something else or to develop antagonistic relationships, the classroom is not negatively affected.

PREPARING THE DEMOCRATIC TEACHER THROUGH A CAREER LADDER

We earlier described New Careers as a way to democratize a profession by creating a negotiable ladder in which the entry rung was open to all requiring no prior skill, training, or experience and the top rung is professional status. A person rises in the profession on the basis of performance on the job and not on marginally relevant tests and remote university courses. Under current practice, one is given a credential before demonstration of competence. Some have the temerity to call this maintaining "standards." In a career ladder, when given the opportunity, persons who otherwise would never have been admitted to a university were able to perform at least as well as admissible students (Amram, Flax, Hamermesh, & Marty, 1988; Carter, 1977). By succeeding far beyond assessed competence, New Careers was able to challenge deficit thinking and indicate means by which success is achieved through equal encouragement. The career ladder increases enormously the pool from which teachers can be selected. By recruiting underrepresented populations into teaching, particularly persons from populations that have lagged behind in educational achievement (African American, Mexican Americans, Native Americans, Australian Aboriginals, etc.) to the teaching profession, it was possible for students from these populations to be encouraged to educational success. The underrepresented teacher becomes a role model and a confidante; new types of relationships can be established facilitating equal encouragement of students. It boggles the mind to observe how much effort is made to celebrate diversity in everything but the composition of the teaching staff. A teaching staff made up of almost all White teachers tells students far more about how much diversity is really celebrated than all of the African-American History months, or Cinco de Mayos put together.

Here, we re-examine New Careers as a better way to prepare all teachers but, in particular, teachers for a democratic classroom. We began this chapter commenting on the haphazard way people are prepared for the teaching profession—a host of courses that have little relationship to each other, a short period of time in practice teaching leading to a credential and the sudden thrust into a classroom with unfamiliar students in unfamiliar settings. Hillkirk (1994) in his effort to develop democratic teachers, devised 4 years of field experience in schools prior to the bestowing of a credential (Hillkirk, 1994). There is no question in our minds that students with 4 years of experience in a classroom will find an easier transition into teaching than those with 6 months (or 45 days as is the Australian experience) of practice teaching. But, contrast that with New Careers. The new Careerist has been working in classroom for a minimum of 4 years and as many as 6 or 8 and is an established effective teacher before obtaining a credential. Moreover, if the New Careerist does not develop the range of skills and experiences that make for good teaching, no credential is awarded and students are spared the experience of an unfit teacher. The career ladder connects professional development with educational practice. It brings flexibility into teacher education.

One of the striking features of New Careers was the powerful effect of mutual support. New Careerists did not have an easy time. They encountered hostility on the job and hostility in institutions of higher education. Most of them were poor and single parents who, in addition to meeting job and higher education responsibilities, also had the additional parental responsibility for as many as three or four young children. They succeeded primarily because of mutual support networks that they developed and sustained. New Careers provides further evidence of the importance of a task force or cohort for successful efforts to break new ground, which the democratic education is certainly trying to do.

New Careers requires the institution of higher education (the credential-bestowing agency) to work collaboratively with the school. This approach is the logical extension of what was established in LaTrobe in the 1970-1980s and is what Ohio University is presently striving to accomplish (Hillkirk, 1994).

It is lamentable that the only reason that New Careers has been reestablished is to recruit underrepresented populations into teaching. The need to alter teacher education is not sufficiently recognized and it is likely that New Careerist will be hampered by being required to take the hodge-podge of courses that currently inadequately prepare persons for the teaching profession.

New Careers and the Democratic Classroom

It is extremely difficult to adequately prepare someone for a democratic classroom with abstract discussions of principles and requirements. It is fairly easy to persuade prospective teachers that (a) education should be used to develop knowledge that enables students to solve important problems; (b) students should be permitted to participate in decisions that affect their lives; and (c) students should have rights, and be equally encouraged. But democratic education is more than abstract description. It is a living entity: exciting, invigorating, constantly changing, and constantly challenging. It requires continual support and access to consultation. That kind of support is required in a career ladder and is virtually impossible to achieve in current teacher preparation arrangements.

Democratic education sounds wonderful and easy from some remote place like a university, but once in the classroom the teacher meets unexpected resistance, not the least of which is a lack of credibility. Many students are not interested in developing knowledge. Some play games with participation; rights are abused; movement is restricted by school policy and state law; and efforts at equal encouragement are sabotaged by students, parents, and other teachers. Eagerness is replaced by disillusionment and dedication with cynicism. Almost every new teacher will try to rush the process. Democracy is developmental, it takes time and one must proceed with caution. There is need for contingency planning.

With New Careers, the development of democratic teaching can coincide with movement up the career ladder. Movement toward democratic education can take place after the New Careerist has gained credibility as a teacher and has established a healthy relationship with students. The collaborative relationship with higher education permits the university instructor to develop a sense of the obstacles encountered in the development of democratic teaching. It is difficult to envision democratic education without career ladders playing an important role in teacher preparation.

SUMMARY

Not everyone should teach in a democratic classroom. Only those dedicated to democratic principles and provided with appropriate preparation for multiple challenges are likely to succeed. The attributes of a democratic teacher are not overly demanding, but current teacher preparation not only fails to address those attributes but often militates against them. The LaTrobe experience is one promising model. The democratic teacher can be prepared through New Careers. It is not important how a teacher is prepared for the democratic classroom as long as the preparation instills in the teacher a dedication to theory development and research and a rich understanding of the requirements of democratic education.

Chapter 10

Democratic Evaluation and Research

The goal of democratic research and evaluation is not the mere acquisition of knowledge, but rather the development and evaluation of knowledge that can be applied to the solution of a generally acknowledged problem. The difference between research and evaluation reduces to the question being asked, the identical procedures are used and the same limitations are placed on interpretation. Democratic research and evaluation meets the four requirements of democratic education: the knowledge obtained is used to solve important social and personal problems, students' rights are protected, students participate in every phase of the activity; and the research and evaluation is bound by a dictum of equal encouragement. These requirements are met in all four elements of research and evaluation: the formulation of the question, the data-gathering, the interpretation of the findings, and the implementation of the results. In democratic research data do not speak, data are always interpreted and the quality of the interpretation depends on the extensiveness and the inclusiveness of the debate. Democratic research and evaluation thus becomes a valuable component of the elementary and high school curriculum.

WHAT IS RESEARCH?

Research is a systematic and disciplined means to provide a firm answer to a specific type of question organized as a testable hypothesis. The search is for truth. But truth is illusive and constantly changing. Truth is always a work in progress. It is the constantly changing aspect of truth that conservatives find so worrisome. They want truth to stay put and become upset when someone moves it around on them. Evaluation is a subset of research. Evaluation is a systematic and disciplined means to provide a firm answer to a different type of question. In evaluation judgment decisions are made. Although the type of question is different in research than it is in evaluation (often, it is difficult to distinguish the difference, and it usually is not necessary), the means by which the answer is found is identical. The systematic and disciplined means of approaching a problem in both research and evaluation requires a question organized as a testable hypothesis, a specified and precisely defined set of procedures for collecting data, a complete and precisely explicated procedure for the manipulation and presentation of the data, and a defensible logic for interpreting the findings. Research or evaluation is asking a question in such a way that a specific answer can be obtained, stating how the information required for the answer is going to be obtained, revealing in a precise and detailed way how the information was gathered, justifying the statistical manipulation, making all that information obtained available to everyone and concluding by explaining how the question was answered.

Democratic research is fundamentally different from traditional research. The question asked is often different. As we have learned from the study of perception, the view of a problem is very different when the vantage point is a distant laboratory or academic tower than when one is immersed in it. The vaunted virtues of traditional research are detachment and objectivity. That tradition should be maintained and serves a necessary purpose, but only if there is another way of approaching truth to bounce off against it.

Democratic research meets all four requirements of democratic education. The knowledge obtained in the research is directed toward solving a problem that has been identified as important through a democratic process. Rarely is that the process in traditional research. Democratic education is inclusive; everyone participates in every phase of the research (that would be intolerable in traditional research). Care is taken that research does not violate anyone's rights (a concern of the traditional researcher, certainly, but difficult to ensure from a distance). And the research is governed by a commitment to a special understanding of equality—equal encouragement (not only not understood by the traditional researcher, but so much of traditional research has been dedicated to proving the existence of fundamental inequality, which is the cornerstone of conservative thinking). A democratic approach is an essential element of a general theory. It makes little sense to submit a democratic education to antidemocratic evaluation and research and expect to get a fair hearing. The satisfactory part of democratic research and evaluation is that anyone can do it.

What has been called the *scientific method* is a set of ritualized procedures for each phase of the research process—hypothesis, data collection, statistical manipulation, reporting findings, and interpreting results. The slavish devotion to procedure is intended to release the researcher (evaluator) from personal responsibility for the findings and thus through objective detachment give to the results the added authority of independent ground (i. e., "science"). This approach to research and evaluation has had a stultifying and distorting impact on education. The effort to apply Science to education has led to a warped phrasing of questions and too often, produced useless answers.

Democratic research is not an isolated or isolating process designed by remote "objective" researchers. It is directed toward a problem that has emerged out of the challenges individuals and groups of individuals face daily in life, especially in confronting institutions. In democratic research, students are active participants in framing the questions and in interpreting the answers. This is an untidy process, punctuated by debate and heated emotion. The participants have a lot at stake in the answers. Democratic research violates the "research method" canons of objectivity and detachment. The lack of objectivity and detachment is what makes democratic research so vital and useful.

The established scientific method rests heavily on the data. The data, objectively obtained, are expected to speak for themselves. When Galileo dropped a 16-pound ball and a 1-pound ball from the Leaning Tower of Pisa and both hit the ground at the same time, he rested his case. There was no need for him to interpret the findings and defend his conclusions against Aristotelian adversaries. It was not quite as easy for him when he tried to present data showing that the earth revolved around the sun and not, as it was officially believed, the other way around. In this instance, his data did not speak, nor was he able to debate his opposition. Galileo learned a lesson that scientists throughout history have learned, data speak only under certain political conditions, otherwise data needs to be interpreted and for an answer to be fairly found, the conditions for interpretation must be conducive to democracy (i.e., inclusive and open), otherwise established authority will ordain the answer.

In a democratic approach to research, it is assumed that data never speak and the critical dimension is interpretation. That interpretation can only be persuasive when the debate is thorough and open to everyone.

PARTICIPANTS NOT UMPIRES

rookie umpire: I call them as I see them.
seasoned umpire: I call them as they are.
grizzled veteran umpire: they ain't nothin' until I call them.

At heart, the defense of democratic research and evaluation rests on the absence of an independent ground. Traditional research and evaluation derives from independent ground (i. e., science). Objectivity and detachment protect the independent ground. If independent ground is not a defensible concept, objectivity becomes illusory and detachment a handicap.

In the absence of independent ground, knowledge or truth emerges as a debate between different formulations. Only when the resolution of debate involves the widest diversity of opinion can there be valid claim to firm knowledge, or truth. In the physical sciences, the debate may not be extensive. Although, even here the debate has been far too restricted. In the biological and social sciences, where there is far greater controversy and where results can benefit some at the expense of others, the little debate that has been tolerated has been warped and one-sided—those who are hurt by the findings are not allowed to participate.[1]

---

[1] Foucault made a similar point when he discussed the "archeology of silence" in the lack of discourse between reason and madness as a direct result of the advance of the science of psychiatry:

The language of psychiatry, which is a monologue of reason about madness, has been established only on the basis of such a silence. I have not tried to write the history of that language, but rather the archaeology of that silence. (Foucault, 1965, cited in Eribon, 1989, p. 93)

One important area of biological research that impinges directly on education has been the effort to determine the inheritance of intelligence and the differences in inherited intelligence by race, ethnicity and social class. Educational policy and practices are directly influenced by determinations of educability. A very powerful and extensive defense of the measurements of intelligence (IQ) has been on the basis of detached science.

It is on the basis of such research that that African Americans and children in poverty have been categorized as constitutionally inferior to white and economically advantaged populations. The people who have made these claims all come from advantaged situations (that could include a few non-representative persons from populations vilified by the research findings). When a spokesperson from a population deemed to be disproportionately unintelligent, challenges those conclusions, the challenge is summarily dismissed as non scientific. There is no debate. Our argument with those who have studied IQ is not that they are bad scientists (although in some celebrated instances they clearly were) but that such an issue cannot be adequately studied by any undemocratic method no matter how sophisticated and disciplined. Every aspect of the problem of intelligence-its expression, its effects, its generalizability, etc., need to be debated with differences in understanding negotiated. Which means, that until the debate is settled, truth has not been established.

In place of a fictitious scientific dictum upheld by an unchallengeable independent ground, is the understanding that everything about intelligence (and all other educational research) is overtly political. Currently, the politics is camouflaged by hiding behind "science." Given its history, it is impossible to deny that decisions made about intelligence have been political from Burt (1909) through Herrnstein & Murray (1994). While the politics is incontestable, it is also true that there has been no attempt to make the political decisions democratic.

The issue of educability is of vital importance in education. Challenging the basis for its assessment does not reduce its

---

We draw a similar conclusion with Foucault on the misuse of science as it applies to human deficits (including madness) we go off in opposite directions when it comes to remedy. Foucault extended the silence with an impenetrable language and with an approach to research that excludes even more than the "science' that he excoriated. He opened up no avenues for the "mad" to participate in social policy. Social policy and Foucault are incompatible. Foucault pushed everything to the margins. We try to draw all to the center.

importance. Educational decisions on imputed intelligence are made every day and the consequences have momentous impact on both the individual and the society. The traditional approach has emphasized scientific appraisals of the individual to the exclusion of a careful analysis of differential encouragement to intellectual competence. The relied on defense is that the research on intelligence has meticulously met the standards of "science." It is precisely that reasoning that brings us to democratic research.

CONTRASING TRADITIONAL AND DEMOCRATIC RESEARCH

Hypothesis

Framing the question makes or breaks the research. Ask a pointless question, you get a pointless answer. In traditional research, much is made over the hypothesis—the framing of the question. The emphasis is on technical importance not on theoretical importance. If the hypothesis is so framed as to permit a significant test—a simple yes or no answer—it meets the traditional science test. Whether the question is worth asking gets into values and outside of the purview of detachment and objectivity . But traditional approach to testing a hypothesis limits further what can be learned from the test. It is drummed into the researcher's head that there can be no ultimate test of a hypothesis. Every research must end with the statement that more work needs to be done on this important subject. It is one of the rituals of the scientific method. No research can end the matter because all hypotheses are null hypotheses. The only thing that can be tested is the denial of truth. Truth cannot be proved by science, but science can ascertain untruth. Science grows through exposing untruths. This is an important concept that established traditional researchers tend to keep to themselves. That is not how the findings are reported in the nontechnical media. Nor is that how research is used to influence social policy. Scientific breakthroughs are made more exciting than merely reporting that another untruth has been shot down today. Understanding the scientific method reveals that there has never been a scientific determination of the inheritance of intelligence. What science has supposedly found through testing null hypotheses is the untruth of an environmental etiology of intelligence. By a process of elimination, a conclusion is reached. If it is untrue that intelligence is shaped by the environment what else but inheritance can determine it.

Democratic research is comfortable with the underlying logic of the null hypothesis. Democracy has been badly damaged by untruths. And the more of them demolished the better. However, democratic research is more common sense than slavish ritual. Democratic research is interested in useable knowledge, not ultimate truth.

Validity

Validity is crucial for traditional research. It is equally crucial for democratic research. In both, a powerful case must be made that measurements actually are what they purport to be. Otherwise the data cannot be taken seriously. With traditional research, validity is determined by technically driven criteria. In the physical sciences, a standard is created against which all other measures are judged. Thus, it is technically possible to measure distance in ways that very few contest. In education, validity is determined by less direct methods. And therein lies a substantial problem. Validity is often arbitrarily or operationally defined. The arbitrarily determined operational definition of intelligence used by Jensen (and others) is "whatever an intelligence test measures."

> Abraham Lincoln apparently was not a great believer in operational definitions. It has been reported that he once approached a farmer and asked, "How many legs has a cow?" "Why, four, Abe." "But," asked Lincoln, "If you call a tail a leg how many legs does he have then?" "In that case he has five." "Wrong," says Lincoln, "Calling a tail a leg doesn't make it one."

And calling an IQ test a test of intelligence doesn't make it one, either.

An operational or indirect definition of intelligence is necessary because there is no generally accepted, valid, directly observable standard of intelligence. We earlier briefly reviewed the processes used and the assumptions made in the measurement of intelligence (e.g., whether intelligence is a single general factor or a clusters of factors or traits, or whether there was one, two, three, or seven of it). We do not retrace those arguments pertaining to a measurement no matter how defined that causes far more harm than good. We raise it only to make the case that when an attribute cannot be measured directly, traditional validity requires a sophisticated statistical verification. The case for IQ validity rests on positive correlation with other tests, future school success, or "known groups." Thus, two often used tests, the Stanford-Binet and the Wechsler, each use the other for "validation." An IQ test is "valid" if it accurately predicts future school performance. An IQ test is also "valid" if the people who are supposed to score high, score high and those who are supposed to score low, score low. If, for example, someone designed an IQ test on which African Americans, Australian Aboriginals, and West Indian English immigrants topped the scale, while upper class Whites concentrated at the bottom, the test would immediately be scrapped and denounced as invalid. The technical case for IQ validity is made more secure when supported by all three correlations (e.g., other tests, future school performance, and known groups), which of course happens, and that is one of the reasons IQ becomes a statistical vampire. Every time you think it is killed, the stake is pulled out of its heart and it gets up and bites someone (e.g., Herrnstein & Murray, 1994).

How in democratic research would the validity of intelligence be determined? The most likely answer to such a question is that after wide-ranging discussion it would be decided that intelligence is an unmeasurable concept and thus no attempt would be made to measure it. Assume, however, that after extensive discussion among the widest range of students, parents, teachers, and so on, it was decided that the capacity to learn was an important issue and effort should be made to validly assess such capacity, the first step would involve negotiating a definition of intelligence. Assuming a consensus on such definition, the next step would be negotiating an acceptable measurement of intelligence. Assume the accepted measurement was rating the performance on multichallenge exercises ranging from consumer math problems (e.g, tomatoes cost 75 cents a pound in the neighborhood and 50 cents 5 miles across town at a supermarket, where would you shop today, and why?), to the ability to analyze an oral treatise ("we will play tapes of two presidential candidates, tell me in your own words what they said and on the basis of what you heard explain how you would vote"), to extricating oneself when alone and confronted by menacing gang members on a dark urban street. A range of observers from widely differing perspectives would rate the performance on negotiated criteria. Validity, in this instance, would be the degree of confidence the rater had in his or her score and is comparable to the rating of gymnastic or diving competitors. There are obvious legitimate questions about this type of procedure. Would the students know in advance what the questions would be (as some high-status subjects do in currently administered IQ tests)? Of course not. The agreement would be on the nature of the material to be used and a representative committee would construct the items. Would a new test of intelligence have to be created for every situation? Perhaps. That would depend on the discussion and the expressed satisfaction with existing tests. Would an established IQ test ever be used in democratic research (or evaluation)? Very likely. An IQ test would be appropriate in evaluating democratic education. If poor and minority IQ scores jumped an average of 40 points after experiencing democratic education that would be a far more persuasive measure than could be obtained with the use of nonnormative measures. (If the scores did not rise, that would be cause for concern in the democratic classroom). Democratic research will be viewed with considerable skepticism. The research should be persuasive enough to withstand scrutiny and criticism and traditional measures are often necessary to make a persuasive case.

There are potential political problems in the determination of any measure. In democratic research, decisions made on validity and the reasons for those decisions are out in the open. And if serious enough questions about the validity of a measure arise, it can be thrown out and new efforts at validity attempted. Such rethinking is a characteristic of democratic research; stopping midstream and rethinking the problem is more difficult in traditional research, primarily because the range of debate is so limited. Most everyone on a traditional research team thinks alike.

Intelligence tests rose to prominence not because of scientific curiosity or research design sophistication. The tests were acceptable solely because the scores conformed to dominant societal belief and therein lies its claim to validity. The tests were fiddled with until the groups who were supposed to score high, scored high and those who were supposed to score low, score low. That much of the measurement is bogus is immaterial (see Hearnshaw 1979; Gould, 1981). IQ remains scientifically defensible because it has been politically acceptable, and that has been its sole justification. The problem with traditional measures of educability is not its defense, as shaky as these have been at times, but rather its unwillingness to open debate to the "less scientific" and consider other opinions. We are no closer to understanding educability now than we were before the subject became a matter of scientific scrutiny. The debates that needed to occur still need to occur. The people who have been excluded because of lack of a credentials, remain excluded. The issue of validity needs to be debated and the idea of intelligence as an inherited attribute, versus those who credit the environment for it, versus those who hypothesize intelligence as ecological—an organic interaction of the individual and the social and physical environment—needs to be widely debated. Moreover, if the environment is a factor in educability, the conditions of the environment that facilitate intellectual growth need to be identified and tested. Efforts to conduct research on optimal learning conditions suffer from the same stifling conditions and limited inquiry that is found in research on educability.

If the question of "who can learn what" was raised in a democratic classroom, the most likely research question would be to determine the optimum conditions for learning, and whether these differed by individual, class, culture, gender, ethnicity, race, and so on. Such research would require students, parents, and teachers and partners in higher education to scour the literature, digest the findings, come together to decide whether enough was known to reach a conclusion on definition of conditions for optimum learning and once that was done attempt, to arrive at a measurement. Validity in this instance would be a combination of consensus on concept and construct validity. The measurement would be considered valid if it accurately reflected the definition and the logic used by the group. If the measurement sought is of classroom climate—the balance of challenge and support and the extent to which that balance was equally provided all students—only after this was done could the question of individual or group differences in learnability be legitimately raised.

The validity of democratic-research depends on the quality of the evidence. Evidence in democratic oriented research is not suffocated by research orthodoxy. Evidence can be any observation as long as the conditions of observation are fully explicated and serious effort is made to justify the measurement. Validity has to meet the organizing sense of democracy persuasiveness. If debate is encouraged and everyone is equally involved in determining the validity of a concept, consensus will or will not emerge, its persuasiveness will be determined and none of the scandals associated with IQ will occur. [The effort to maintain a detached objective science available only to the privileged was largely responsible for the IQ scandal]. Determining validity through the resolution of open debate will lead to a higher quality of evidence, (i.e., more valid than mindless adherence to a ritual can produce). The danger is not that democracy will do violence to validity, the danger is that democracy will be lost in the strain to determine validity, which is what happens when a few voices dominate the conversation.

Reliability

Reliability is stability or dependability of measurement. As with validity, traditional research has developed many sophisticated determinants of reliability. Test and rapid retest of alternative forms is commonly used to guard against change that has occurred through growth or familiarization with particular items With multiple item tests, half of the test is correlated with the other half. When raters are used, the degree of agreement between raters determines reliability. Many of these techniques would be employed in democratic research without making a fetish of them. It makes good sense to demonstrate that a measure is reliable. Rubber yardsticks are inadequate measures of height. But without validity, reliability is an illusion of scientific precision.

In education, when validity is hard to come by, traditional researchers retreat to reliability. Reliability in this instance, is worse than illusion. it is cruel deception. Reliability is useless as a measure of intelligence. Among the most stable measures of intelligence is height. Height is a very reliable measure. It holds up over space and time. The same person measures very nearly the same when in New York on Tuesday and Singapore on Saturday. Height in late childhood is predictive of adult height and the nearer to adult status the more predictive height is. No IQ test has been as reliable as height as a measure of intelligence. With all of its scientific virtues, we don't believe we can sell it as a test of intelligence. It would not be politically correct. Too many short people of considerable influence would not permit it. And yet, the primary "scientific" defense of IQ is its stability over space and time. The same kind of people get the same type of IQ scores in 1996 as they did in 1920 and people who score low on IQ tests when they are young (not too young) score low as they get older. We discussed why we are not impressed with this argument in the chapter on equal encouragement.

Reliability is important in democratic research, but not as a substitute for validity. If the case for validity cannot be made in democratic research that is the end of it.

Raters are used in democratic research. In traditional research, raters are usually trained to enhance reliability. In democratic research it is frequently advisable to not train the raters and thus sacrifice some reliability for validity. In rating classroom climate from a variety of perspectives, for example, the training of the raters could produce a forced consensus that would result in less independent judgment and the loss of valuable insights. What is determined by rigid observance to rules in traditional research is resolved through discussion in democratic research.

Standardization

Standardization is yet another requirement of traditional research. Because the intent of traditional research is to remove from consideration all extraneous factors to ensure a definitive test of the hypothesis, it is imperative that standardized conditions be met. But because the administering of an IQ test, for example, is standardized, the test is less a measure of intelligence than it is a measure of the ability (or willingness) to complete a certain number of tasks in a specified time. Standardization fits neatly with conservative identical treatment definition of equality.

In some instances of democratic research standardization is required in other instances it is an impediment. Although the absurdity of meeting the condition of standardization by testing someone in English who does not speak English is generally recognized in traditional research, other more subtle factors that involve race, class, ethnicity, and youth lived culture are superficially considered. In democratic research standardization is carefully scrutinized by all concerned before decisions about appropriateness are made.

Representativeness

Representativeness is as important to democratic research as it is to traditional research. It is imperative that the research accurately describes the population to which the research applies. Too much research has been conducted with special populations and therefore cannot be replicated or generalized. As indicated earlier, Dewey's laboratory school was much too unique to be given credence as a democratic school. In our experiments, we went to extremes to ensure that the least unlikely candidates would be included in our research to construct the most severe test of deficit thinking possible. We are not certain that some of the experiments that claim to be democratic have met the require-ment of inclusiveness. In any research purporting to be democra-tic, if a restricted population is involved in the experiment, or if the conditions of the experiment are special, those limitations must be reported. It is in the interest of representativeness that we argue that experiments to test and develop democratic theory in democratic education be conducted and replicated in the most ordinary classrooms.

Control and Contrast Groups

In democratic research, as in traditional research, it is obligato-ry to state what would have happened if a particular treatment had not occurred. In traditional research great effort is made to ensure the control group (the group that did not receive the treatment) be identical with the experimental group (the one that did). Techniques are devised for random assignment to the two groups. Random assignment is certainly desirable, but there is no assurance that a carefully crafted random assignment precludes contamination. For example, if students are randomly assigned to experimental and control group classrooms in the same school with the experimental class being provided equal encouragement and the control receiving ordinary treatment, it is virtually impossible to prevent contagion because students and teachers will discuss what is happening. Traditional research often becomes consumed with complicated acceptable alternatives to random assignment (e.g., precision matching), which is the ensuring that the contrast group is identical with the experimen-tals when random assignment is not possible. There are also efforts to convince self and others that contamination has not occurred with "double-blind" restrictions (i.e., neither students nor teachers are supposed to know what is happening to whom). The reality is that some sort of contamination usually takes place, and because of the restrictions on discussion, the extent of conta-mination cannot be determined. In democratic research, the prob-lems of the research are openly discussed and effort is made through such discussion to determine whether it is possible to assess what would have happened to a comparable group of stu-dents who were denied treatment. When it is possible to meet rigid experimental conditions or acceptable alternatives, this is done. When such conditions cannot be met, full explication for excep-tions is given and a case is made using the available data. Again, the difference between the traditional and the democratic is the difference between submission to rigidly defined rules and making sense out of data through extensive discussion and negotiation.

Statistical Significance of the Findings

Traditional research is heavily dependent on statistical manipulation of the findings. The use and interpretation of complex statistics is yet another way to limit accessibility of research. The meticulous use of statistics is a hallmark of traditional research. Much is made of the statistical significance of a difference between experimental and control groups. When the difference between an experimental group and a control group is so great that it could not occur more than once in 100 (or more likely, once in 20 times) it is assumed that the difference is real and represent a successful test of a hypothesis. From purely statistical significance, small differences can be made to seem important (especially if the numbers in the experiment are large), whereas large differences in small samples can be statistically insignificant and dismissed as unimportant. In traditional research, statistics "speak," which limits the conversation considerably.

In democratic research, statistics are demystified and the interpretation is not bound by statistical significance. In democratic research, there is no shopping around for a statistical treatment that produces a significant difference. In democratic research all factors are considered and all interested parties are brought into the discussion in interpreting the significance of the findings.

EVALUATION

Evaluation is systematic judgment about performance. The methodology adapts and develops the canons, techniques, and principles of research, although there is much debate about evaluation methodologies due to their specificity (Wolf, 1990).

Evaluation covers a wide territory. Student performance is evaluated, but so too are programs. There is a growing consensus that current approaches to evaluation are not adequate and often lead to biased if not meaningless results (Bishop, 1995).

Whereas educational research is increasingly irrelevant to practice, evaluation often controls practice. Currently, evaluation is used to drive a conservative agenda. At other times, evaluation is used, although not as blatantly, to support left-leaning causes. Regardless of the virtue of the cause, evaluation lends itself to abuse of power. Those who control the evaluation exercise enormous power over both individuals and programs. Evaluation is the prime mechanism used to steer from afar. Evaluation justifies de facto central control while the illusion of local control is fostered. The student is rendered powerless and held hostage by centralized authority imposing a "standard" against which all students are evaluated.

Evaluation is not to be avoided. To the contrary, evaluation is an imperative for sound educational practice. What is needed is balance, a democratic evaluation that is open to negotiation, accountable, responsive, and responsible.

Ensuring Quality Evaluation

Validity and reliability of evaluation is a negotiated process that requires significant input from the parent and the student, particularly if the evaluation is of student academic progress. The school authority presents an assessment of student performance from the school or system perspective and parent and students present their concerns and assessments. The evaluation is negotiated with the understanding that if neither party is satisfied, additional information will be provided or there is recourse to binding arbitration. Validity and reliability must meet two often incompatible standards—one relates to the system of which the student is a part and the other pertains to the individual student. The former tends to be standardized, whereas the latter is tailored for each individual. In the evaluation of student performance, appropriate is a better evaluation measure than standardization (appropriate would likely include authentic assessment but would not be limited to what is currently meant by authentic assessment).

Representativeness has a unique meaning when applied to democratic evaluation of student performance. Because of the requirement of equal encouragement, care is taken to assure that evaluation of students is doubly representative. The items on the test (or whatever is used to assess performance) must be representative of the domain (subject, topic, project, problem) on which the student is being evaluated (i.e., a history test must reflect the important events and ideas of the period being studied). The testing must also be a representative sample of the student's performance. The evaluation is also nonrepresentative if one student took the test while confident, rested, and secure and another is exhausted and distraught by anxiety. Or, more typically, if one student was encouraged to succeed and another not so encouraged. In this instance, the lack of representation is not with the test, but with the student readiness or willingness to perform representatively. It is impossible to accurately determine whether a low test score reflects lack of knowledge or unreadiness for the test. We believe that with intelligence and performance testing, the bias is more in the testing than in the test, which might explain why results are constant over space and time although tests may have been changed.

Authentic assessment (Wiggins 1989, 1991) is widely regarded as a major breakthrough in evaluation methodology. Authentic assessment replaces piecemeal and often meaningless tests and unaccountable teacher judgments of student performance (e.g., grades) with extensive samples of student accomplishment. Authentic assessment enables students to speak for themselves rather than be interpreted by the teacher or judged by tests of dubious validity. A student, for example, can have a video made of a dance performance and have an enduring record maintained in a portfolio that can be judged at any time by a variety of others. With that video, the student is not at the mercy of a particular teacher or some possible biased judge. It is possible for students to maintain portfolios in any subject. The portfolios can contain performance over an extended period of time and thus eliminate the possibility of judgment based on a nonrepresentative day, or of an accomplishment soon forgotten. Authentic assessment is preferable to what currently exists, and what is called authentic assessment would be a part of the democratic classroom evaluation—but only a small part. Much more important in democratic evaluation is the negotiated process by which performance goals are selected and the negotiated means by which these goals will be assessed. It makes little sense to authentically assess what should not be assessed at all.

Authentic assessment addresses some of the most obvious deficiencies of norm-referent and criteria-referent testing, but it is a far cry from democratic evaluation. The student is still the specimen and not necessarily an active participant in the evaluation process. Despite movement in the direction of democracy, authentic assessment falls far short of equal powered negotiation and binding arbitration of irreconcilable differences.

In democratic evaluation, students do not evaluate themselves, but students are not arbitrarily evaluated by someone else either. The evaluation is shared. It is a negotiated synthesis of different assessments each of which are defended by logic and evidence. Those of us who have relied on students to be a part of the evaluation of performance find that students have little difficulty proposing a grade for themselves (not always inflated by the way). They find it much more difficult to defend an assessment with logic and evidence. The negotiation that occurs with students focuses less on the grade (the outcome) and more on the process used in arriving at a judgment (evidence and logic). In this sense, evaluation is as much a part of the curriculum as any other problem to be solved.

We have been involved with democratic research and evaluation for more than 30 years. Too little of that has become part of the shared body of recognized scientific knowledge. We accept a major responsibility for its absence. We have not made a sufficiently vigorous attempt at inclusion. In a companion volume on democratic practice, we will provide more detailed description and discussion of specific projects in which democratic research and evaluation was used. Here we merely provide references for the interested reader: Brunswick Girls High School, Melbourne, Australia (Claydon, 1975; Engish, 1975; Gill, 1975); Sunshine High School, Melbourne, Australia (Jones, Metcalf, Williams, & Williamson, 1982). Community Apprentices, Washington, DC (Fishman, Mac Clennon, & Pearl, 1964); the Vacaville New Career Program for Prisoners, Vacaville, California (Grant, 1967; James, Lester, & Royer, 1965); and Northland Secondary College, Melbourne, Australia (Galati-Brown, 1995).

There will be those who will claim that we have been carried away by our enthusiasm and have greatly distorted traditional research and evaluation, insisting that there is far more flexibility in these methods than we are willing to admit. Those who defend existing practice can point to adaptability in every phase of the process.

We have been engaged in an ongoing 30-year debate with colleagues, who agree with our conclusions about research and evaluation in general and testing in specific but who insist the problem lies not in the methodology but only in its misapplication. We are constantly reminded of the range of research possibilities: quantitative or qualitative approaches to measurement, experimental, quasi-experimental or ethnographic study designs, of the varieties of parametric and nonparametric statistics, and the range in types of scaling. All of which supposedly gives to established research and evaluation enough flexibility to be readily utilized to advance democratic education or any other theoretical formulation. This is an important argument that deserves thorough analysis. We believe research and evaluation should not be evaluated solely on how it has been used (or misused). Others have examined the connection between politics, ethics, and ideology and research and called for examining the latent as well as manifest bias in research activity (e.g., Sjoberg, 1975). However, we believe that purging research of bias is necessary but not sufficient. Only when research and evaluation are integrated into a coherent theory that not only helps frame the questions but also defines the procedures that are to be used in attaining the answers can the artificiality and often irrelevance of research and evaluation be eliminated.

Criticism of traditional research has become increasingly popular. Many have accepted our position and have included students and teachers in collaborative work in research and evaluation. Such utilization broadens the understanding, eliminates the likelihood of silly error, builds growth and understanding in students, and most importantly, helps in the development of theory. All of which is important, but a far cry from integrating the research into a general theory.

Postmodernist undermining of science extends into educational research and has opened the door to a variety of approaches and interpretations.[2] Ethnography has made for more imaginative research, as has postpositivist interpretative inquiry (Caulley, 1992). Postpositivist inquiry is holistic and "ecologically valid" (conducted in natural settings), goes beyond the data, the sampling is informed by the purposes of the study rather than by mechanistic formula, and features "negotiated outcomes." However, the differences between postmodernist research and democratic research far exceed the similarities. Postmodernist research is not solution-oriented, it is part of the process of "problemizing." Nor is there commitment to general or global theory, that is too grand a notion for those satisfied with local theories (not designed to explain much). Conversely, our research is conducted to further understanding of democracy and its applicability to the educational process. Every local finding contributes to the refinement of a general education theory. Thus,

---

[2]An interesting example to the extent to which postmodernism has influenced social science, one of the acknowledged leaders in psychology Bruner (1966), decided that it is through "narrative" that psychology is demystified.

the research is governed by the same general principles that governs every other aspect of democratic education—the solving of a defined problem. And in all things democratic, our concern for equal encouragement of everyone to make a contribution to research cannot be over-emphasized as an attribute that distinguishes us. It is our firm belief that only with such a commitment will it be possible to determine the ultimate limits to democracy.

IN SUMMARY

Traditional research, like all of science, is being challenged. In one sense, traditional research is an intellectually lazy way to attack a problem. For research to be democratic, active intelligence is required. That intelligence needs to be used to construct valid and useful measures and for persuasive argument. In the final analysis, it is persuasiveness rather than dazzling manipulation of numbers that will make the case for democratic research.

In none of its ventures has science been objective. All research is designed to value or judge. Scientists are advocates and their advocacy provides the basis for the questions they ask and for the measurement they use. The advocacy influences the interpretation. Elimination of subjectivity is an impossible task. Subjectivity can, however, be identified and mitigated. What should be eliminated is the illusion of objectivity.

Every mathematical and statistical approach used in traditional research is used in democratic research, but none have elevated status and none have priority in the collection, analysis, or interpretation of data. Every aspect of democratic research is negotiated. This means that different methodological approaches must be understood. The instructor or research director is required to expose less sophisticated students and co-workers to differing methodologies and encourage them to explore them before making a decision.

In this sense, research is no different than any other aspect of the curriculum. Every part of the curriculum is research and concerns the systematic development of knowledge. Students use research to solve personal and social problems and they learn research methods by solving those problems.

Chapter 11

Last Thoughts

It was the best of times, it was the worst of times.
—Charles Dickens (1859, Book 1, Chapter 1)

We began this volume with the assertion that the world is faced with a series of extremely daunting challenges. We indicated throughout that the problems are getting worse, the fabric of society is unravelling, and there is seemingly neither the will nor a sufficiently endorsed program to reverse an ever accelerating tide. Our conclusion is that the future very much depends on the education received by the present generation. We believe nothing less than a democratic education is equal to the challenge. That education must be directed to development of social capital of a particular kind and would include: (a) knowledge organized for the solution of important problems and presented in a manner that makes such knowledge equally available to all students; (b) the equal development in all students of of citizenship skills linked to democratic values to be used to participate in the democratic process; (c) the unconditional guarantee to all students of four "inalienable" rights—expression, privacy, due process, and movement; and (d) equal encouragement of all students in all school-sanctioned activities. These four requirements are inextricable and without all four organized as a coherent general theory, the future looks bleak indeed.

331

We put forth a companion argument. The enormous problems we face can neither be avoided nor can they solved by a small educated elite. The days of overrated managed democracies are behind us. What we need is a generally enlightened citizenry. And only a democratic education is capable of producing such general enlightenment.

The matter is further complicated. Everyone favors a democratic education, at least very few openly oppose it, but few agree on what it means.

We offer a particular prospectus on democracy. It has no special virtue, except that if it errs at all, it errs on inclusiveness. But hopefully, in the inevitable discussion of how to make the classroom more democratic, our thinking will be included. It is not a theory that was created out of whole cloth, nor was it the concoction of armchair philosophers. It derived from involvement in a long and continuous programs of action and reflection.

Inclusiveness is an important aspect of democracy and the primary virtue of a public (i.e., government) school is inclusiveness. The private school is distinguished by exclusiveness. In many ways, the current and past public school practices and policies have undermined the public school's most valuable attribute. A necessary part of inclusiveness in the democratic classroom is an array of visions of democracy to debate. We are gratified to find that democratic education is becoming an increasingly salient topic in education as indicated by the American Education Research Association 1996 presidential address by Linda Darling-Hammond (1996). Darling-Hammond's major focus is on teacher involvement in research. We too believe that teachers need to be involved in research, but whether the preparation should be in learning observational methods or by helping to define the research as directed by theory needs further exploration. Darling-Hammond cited research that is organized to help teachers work effectively with diverse learners. Developing a body of knowledge that helps teachers reach a broader spectrum of students is to be encouraged, but so too is carefully reviewing such research so that it does not become a mask for deficit thinking. In broaching the importance of meeting diverse student needs, an absolute necessity in democratic education, Darling-Hammond ignored the obvious, the vital importance of bringing diversity into the teaching ranks. Somehow, the indispensable role that a career ladder (New Careers) approach plays in making schools more democratic and how that should be addressed to make teaching more democratic is not included by those who now call for democratic education.

Ultimately, education can never be better or more democratic than its teachers. There is currently no evidence to indicate that teachers are committed to democracy, no matter how defined. Concern should be directed at the prevailing antidemocratic tendencies of teachers. We have cited research that reveals the opposition of teachers to student participation in decision making. Few teachers have identified themselves as advocates for student rights. In fact, as violence in schools has escalated, teachers tend to support the curtailing of student rights to allegedly increase safety and security in the school. The American Federation of Teachers has identified itself as a supporter of democratic education and has published a position on rights and responsibilities (see Figure 11.1). What is promoted as a Bill of Rights contains no rights. Nowhere is there recognition of students' rights of expression (which may at times be considered discourteous or disrespectful, that is always a matter of interpretation). There is no recognition of rights of privacy (and how such rights may be respected while trying to fulfill the responsibility of keeping the school safe, orderly, and drug free). There is no mention of due process (an absolute necessity if there are to be discipline codes). And perhaps most grievous of all there is no indication of how this promulgation will facilitate the right of equal encouragement. Nowhere in what should more accurately be described as desired conditions of employment is there willingness to consider that many of the problems caused by students in the classroom are themselves a response to unequal encouragement generated by the deficit thinking of teachers.

The one exception to community responsibilities to teachers in the teacher union document is a responsibility of teachers to the community (i.e., teachers know their subject and how to teach it). But how will that be determined? This responsibility of teachers to the community can only be assured if students and parents have unalienable rights of expression, otherwise a charge of teacher incompetence can be interpreted as disrespect. The position of the teacher union is more far restrictive on rights than that taken by Kirk, in that there no rights extended to students, only responsibilities, and what is worse these responsibilities are masqueraded as rights.

By summarily abrogating students rights, teachers endanger theirs. The teacher union would find unacceptable a contract that contained the provision: "all teachers have a right to work in school districts and schools that have clear non-negotiated discipline codes for teachers with fair and consistently enforced con-

A Bill of Rights And Responsibilities for Learning:
Standards of Conduct
Standards for Achievement

The traditional mission of our public schools has been to prepare our nation's young people for equal and responsible citizenship and productive adulthood. Today, we reaffirm that mission by remembering that democratic citizenship and productive adulthood begin with standards of conduct and standards for achievement in our schools. Other education reforms may work; high standards of conduct and achievement do work—and nothing else can work without them.

Recognizing that rights carry responsibilities, we declare that:

- All students and school staff have a right to schools that are safe, orderly, and drug free.
- All students and school staff have a right to learn and work in school districts and schools that have clear discipline codes with fair and consistently enforced consequences for misbehavior.
- All students and school staff have a right to learn and work in school districts that have alternative educational placements for violent or chronically disruptive students.
- All students and school staff have a right to be treated with courtesy and respect.
- All students and school staff have a right to learn and work in school districts, schools, and classrooms that have clearly stated and rigorous academic standards.
- All students and school staff have a right to learn and work in well-equipped schools that have the instructional materials needed to carry out a rigorous academic program.
- All students and school staff have a right to learn and work in schools where teachers know their subject matter and how to teach it.
- All students and school staff have a right to learn and work in school districts, schools, and classrooms where high grades stand for high achievement and promotion is earned.
- All students and school staff have a right to learn and work in school districts and schools where getting a high school diploma means having the knowledge and skills essential for college or a good job.
- All students and school staff have a right to be supported by parents, the community, public officials, and business in their efforts to uphold high standards of conduct and achievement.

A campaign of the American Federation of Teachers

Figure 11.1. The American Federation of Teachers'"Bill of Rights"

sequences for misbehavior and in the interests of safety these consequences will be imposed and all grievances against the school or due process for the teacher will be waived."

Life in classrooms can be excruciating without the guarantee of basic rights. And it is precisely because so many students are denied these rights by both enemies of democracy—guardianship and anarchy—that school for them is excruciating. There is a necessary connection between rights and responsibilities. A good society and a working classroom must have both. But in our understanding of democracy, students enter school with rights and are taught to be responsible. If students do not learn to be responsible while at school, they are not likely to learn much of anything. Current definitions of school discipline policy are virulently antidemocratic.

When control and suppression become the dominant thrust of a school, when inadequate analysis sacrifices rights in a convulsive response to violence, crime, disruption and the fear thereof, the capacity of the school to educate is first reduced then eliminated. Forcing students to submit to established authority teaches a terrible lesson (even worse when that coercion is advertised as a commitment to rights). Submission through the use of force and fear is not conducive to either individual growth or societal health. When students are compelled to mindlessly obey rules that have been devised by "their betters," they are denied the opportunity for reflection. Reflection is necessary if there is to be inculcation of important social and "family" values. *Values* is a term conservatives throw around with abandon, compile moralistic books about them (e.g., Bennett, 1993) but do little to advance them. With no understanding of the critical relationship between civil rights and associated responsibilities it is difficult to either maintain control over a classroom or prepare students to develop the values that are necessary for leadership in a just and civil society.

For all the other controversies in education and differences in interpretations of democratic education, the one area that cannot be ignored is equality. It is not enough for teachers to insist that they treat everyone the same (disregarding evidence to the contrary). It is not enough to take umbrage at charges of discriminatory treatment of students and refute the charge with nothing more than angry denial or avowed commitment to civil rights principles. The most devastating manifestations of racism, sexism, ethnocentrism, homophobia, and discrimination by social class is not found in what a teacher does, but in what he or she does not do. Teachers do not need to overtly demean a student, the same negative result is achieved by not encouraging that student to the same extent that another student is encouraged.

Equal encouragement is not a luxury to be doled out as a charitable exercise. It is essential for survival of the species. The handwriting is on the wall, and in the headlines. The choice is to find common ground on the basis of a working system of equality or disintegrate in ever more devastating ethnic cleansing, tribal warfare, gang insurrection, and militia uprisings. The terminology used to profess allegiance to equality is self-serving and tends to deflect attention away from a serious analysis of an increasing intensity of violence.

Racism is a ugly force in Australia, the United States, and Great Britain. Racism, violence against women and gays, and other intergroup (and intragroup) violence and brutality will not be addressed with festive interludes (e.g., extracurricular celebrations of diversity). A pleasant dance around the maypole will not extinguish a raging fire. A developing situation of this magnitude must be recognized for what it is—a frightening, if not yet critical problem, that unless solved will grow and grow. A solution will require students working in diverse teams (by race, gender, ethnicity, sexual preference, economic situation, etc.), doing the necessary research, and debating the findings to produce a well defended solution. Some of the debate will not be pleasant, but honest confrontation moderated by resolute teacher leadership is far better than the violence unleashed when we fail to educate.

We attached four requirements to our proposed democratic classroom because we believe all knit together into a coherent general theory applicable to everything that takes place in a classroom. It is not necessary that others who believe in democratic education see democratic education as we do. We believe our most important contribution is to bring definition to democratic education and thus widen the debate. The four requirements do not finesse any of the disagreements about democracy. They provide a bridge for all to be included in the debate. One of the areas that we hope gains recognition is the importance of curriculum change. Curriculum is an area where Darling-Hammond, for example, advocates adjustments but still maintained a subject-based curriculum. We question whether a subject-based curriculum, no matter how adjusted or tweaked, can serve the interests of a democracy. That is a question that needs ongoing extensive debate.

DEMOCRATIC EDUCATION WILL NOT JUST HAPPEN, IT NEEDS AN ORGANIZED ADVOCACY

We are pleased by awakened interest in democratic education, but alarmed by the slovenly way the term democracy is bruited about. Being nice is not democracy. Liking children is not democracy. Cooperative learning is not democracy. Purging school of its troublemakers is not democracy. Making school more enjoyable places for students is not democracy. Democracy is theoretically driven and although there are alternative understandings of democracy, there is no mindless democracy.

Even with all of the recent jumping on the democratic bandwagon and the emphasis on making schools better places for young people, the constituency for democratic schooling remains small and if anything, it is losing ground to blatantly authoritarian schooling. The antidemocrats are in the ascendancy. Democracy is sea change and building both an understanding and a commitment for widesweeping change will require careful development and equally careful organizing. Arousing a population from somnolence to involved intellectual interaction will not be easy. Galbraith (1992) labeled the support for status quo as "the constituency of contentment." Although the contented do not constitute a majority, they are very comfortably in control. Hutton (1995) calculated that "constituency of contentment" as being no more than 40% in Britain, which he called a 40-30-30 society. A similar distribution would apply to the United States and to Australia. However, the situation is changing. As the rich get richer and everyone else gets poorer, the percentage falling into the contented class declines (Pearlstein, 1995), and the potential for change grows. One substantial group of malcontents are high school students. Engaging that population in meaningful debate and discussion is a logical beginning of the process.

Although discontentment is growing and reflected in a wide array of social statistics, The discontented are not organized for impacting social policy. In fact, the discontented tear each other apart. Hutton, comments to that effect in his chapter, Divide and Rule (1995, pp. 193-225). The discontented beating up on each other is what fills the prisons and disrupts the urban classroom.

A democratic classroom has as one of its missions the establishment of a constituency of discontentment organized for social good. The discontented are mobilized in debates over the applicability of knowledge to perceived problems—the solution of which leads to the amelioration of discontent. As students begin to appreciate democracy, they will realize that no solution is real until full understanding of it is shared by a resoundingly large majority. We spent a very large part of this book elaborating useful knowledge and identifying possible problems that could be solved with it. Democracy has as one of its manifestations the making of knowledge public. Alternatives to existing unsatisfactory practices and policy can only come about when a public generally knows enough to replace that which is inadequate or unfair with something better. Keeping people in the dark, teasing them with too little information, or deliberately misinforming them is recipe for disaster. It is not enough to want to do better or to ask for more responsibility. The necessary steps for effective social change include a democratic education in which all students learn how to use knowledge to solve important problems.

One of our democratic education requirements is universal and equal participation in decisions that affect one's life. Students are provided with what is necessary to develop the skills and knowledge necessary to take responsibility for solving their own problems, and the problems that bedevil the wider society. Government by the people, or participation in governance is the most commonly understood definition of democracy, but such participation does not happen automatically and unless there is sustained effort to educate students as to its importance and to provide students with necessary citizenship skills, the current trend away from active participation will continue. We hope we have proposed some useful remedies to apathy. It is those who are now apathetic, the discontented, that become the constituency for sustained change. There is a symbiotic relationship between the constituency for democratic education and an education for enlightened and active citizenship. One builds on the other.

We end this book with references to Will Hutton, a highly regarded perceptive journalist. In his *The State We're In* (1995) Hutton presented a compelling argument of a society in dire straits. The situation in Britain as he described is far worse than we have reported and may be more severe than in mainland Europe, the United States, or Australia, but only marginally so (Head, 1996; Pearlstein, 1995) and the differences are meaningless because all societies seemingly are heading in the same direction.

It is fitting we end with Hutton, because he too sees a world in deep trouble. He concluded with the fervent hope that the British (Americans, Australians, Israeli, Germans, Russians, etc.) will come to their senses, see the error of their ways, and rectify the ugly situation in which they find themselves. He believes "Keynesian economics is (the) best" way to go (pp. 226-256). It will not be that easy. It will take more than high hopes, good intentions, or a suggestion or two. Getting out of this mess will require understanding, skill and knowledge (i.e., democratic citizens). And democratic citizens requires democratic education. "Loyalty to Conservatism is not political, it is the instinct of the upper middle class" (Hutton, 1995, p. 41).

This is not a book of wishful thinking. Nor are we so excited by our accomplishments that we could not wait to share them with you. This is the culmination of more than three decades of investment in the evolution of theory. It is replete with hard won successes and heart-wrenching setbacks. No one has welcomed democratic education with open arms. We coaxed and pushed and tried to persuade. We made many mistakes. In retrospect we ask ourselves how we could be so stupid. Our understanding of education and democracy has grown considerably over time. A theory that was fragmented and disjointed has come together as a general theory. As a general theory it has a long way to go. It has become apparent to us that one of the reasons that education is in difficulty is that so little of it is clearly theory-driven, and where there is theory, there are often contradictions between the theory that governs the curriculum and that which informs the discipline, school management, and instruction.

What we find so exciting is that the seeding ideas of the 1960s and 1970s are still alive and vibrant in the 1990s. New Careers (Pearl & Riessman, 1965), which was nipped in the bud, has come back in recent state legislation. Given that every postindustrial society has forgotten how to employ its youth in the new world economy, the New Careers concept is worthy of a more thorough examination by academics, social policy experts, and legislators.

Our analysis of democratic education is that it must begin small and develop from a solid foundation. There are many lessons to be learned from the 1960s. Democracy did not fare well in the 1960s mainly because too many of the programs were patently undemocratic. The early Civil Rights Movement was powerfully democratic as were the anti-Vietnam War teach-ins in which a handful of people participated when only a tiny minority opposed the war in the United States and Australia. Democracy became an early casualty of the 1960s when preoccupation with violence and destruction and conversation-closing rhetoric drove efforts at persuasion from the scene. It was also a time when postmodernist preoccupation with problems and the disrespect for solutions grew and monopolized the arts and the academy. The frustrations and impatience with the war and the slowness with which a society addressed its problems were certainly understandable, but the consequences of giving vent to undemocratic impulses were tragic.

We know that there is much work to be done. With all the spirited loyalty to sporting teams, the titillating extracurricular activities in extraneous bedrooms by royalty and presidents, a scintillating murder trial or two, state-initiated major events, and casino-led recoveries, getting someone's attention on such a mundane matter as democratic education may be difficult. A society unravels while its people are deflected to more entertaining pursuits. Yes Virginia, there is a Nero, alive and doing very well.

We are in *The State We're In* because we have fairly consciously produced a state of mind that has led to a mindless state. It is not that people cannot think, it is that they are not going to waste their time thinking about something as useless and boring as politics. In that sense, politics and school are identical. What seems difficult for many people to recognize is that politics and education in any society with democratic pretensions have always been inextricably connected. The education a society gets is what the politics of that society delivers and what the politics delivers is a direct result of the education the society gets.

Both politics and education suffer from the lack of quality debate, acquired knowledge to support a thesis, understanding, command of logic, and encouragement to own a vision. The vision killers are presently having a field day that will continue until schools become places where dreams are nurtured and ideas debated.

Of course some of you say. But how can things get better with the "state we're in." The issues are overwhelming and isn't this a terrible time to try to make things better? It seems as though everyone is cynical about government schooling. Where can I start? How can I make the first step? I am only a first-year teacher. Won't tomorrow be a better time to start? Next week? Next year? Next century? It seems so hopeless. If I can get my students just to read, I'll be doing well. Schools can only do so much. I'm just a teacher.

In reality, no time is the right time to make a classroom more democratic. We can only start where we are and with the students we have. We start with those who are ready to go, one classroom at a time. Because we do not have the security of numbers (at least when we begin) we need the security of sound theory. Theory gives direction for those important first steps toward reconstruction. Theory is the compass that keeps the educational mission on track.

Isn't this really foolish? Who is going to let us initiate a democratic experiment, particularly at time like this?

No one will let you and they won't make it easy. But democracy understood is difficult to stop. Most will stand aside and watch, their faces showing disdain or disbelief. Some will openly oppose democracy as we learned to our discomfort (but also to a great deal of satisfaction). Some will malign you, attach invidious labels to your efforts. But as the democratic classroom takes shape, extends beyond an empty slogan to be understood in terms of operating principles, its significance will change. Who seriously would oppose persons applying knowledge to solving important problems and participating in decisions that affect their life? Who will oppose the rousing from political apathy? Who is opposed to rights? And who opposes fairness and equity? The clearer these principles are enunciated, the more likely they will be translated into programs of perceived action, and although it is true that opposition to democracy will grow, but far more importantly, the more democratic education is seen in practice, the more support it will get. It will take some teachers providing leadership as intellectual presence, modeling democratic values, to make it happen.

What Hutton (1995) described and what Kaplan (1994) predicted is a society coming unglued, evacuating the center, moving to the margins, and fragmenting. A democratic classroom begins a recentering process by demonstrating that effective collective action by diverse inclusive communities is possible. The lessons learned are energizing. The actions taken bring external validity to breakthrough ideas.

But, one classroom at a time, won't it take forever?

We won't get there any faster by not starting, nor by trying to go faster than existing understanding and support. We have encountered the tired old "now is not the time to start" argument throughout our careers. The right-wing variant is that change is not needed, if anything, we need to go back to the "good old days." The left variant, very popular in the 1960s, proceeded along the line that fundamental changes could not be achieved under capitalism, and only "after the revolution" would education change be possible. One of the good things about the current situation is that you don't hear that wheeze anymore.

In truth, there is no way of determining how fast schools could turn around and become "democratic." We do know that social change is not linear. The start may be one classroom at a time, but if the idea catches on, democracy will accelerate rapidly. If parents, students, teachers, and others paying attention are impressed by how spectacularly better a democratic classroom is than a classroom informed by democracy's enemies, guardianship, and anarchy, the momentum will pick up. To keep democracy growing, a sense of theory is an imperative. It is out of theory that tactics and strategies are developed. It is on the basis of theory that progress is evaluated. Theory is what connects action to research. It moves the academic researcher to the classroom. In the case of the practicing teacher it strengthens professional competence.

The progress of democratic classrooms can be sped by cooperation, collaboration, and effective networking.

Functioning networks are necessary, and are especially important for beginning teachers. Networks bring together the beginner with an established teacher with institutional credibility who can help the new teacher get started with democratic innovation. Networks help develop the critical mass necessary for implementing any curriculum change. A network is a clearinghouse for ideas as well as for evaluation. It is through networks that teachers moving toward a democratic classroom can discover what works and what is to be avoided. There are many places to start to develop connections and to establish networks. Wood and the journal, *Democratic Education*, which emphasizes teachers in classrooms, has both useful suggestions and potential contacts. The same holds for the periodical, *Rethinking Schools*. In Australia, The Centre for Democratic Education is developing precisely such contacts and Holdsworth and his Youth Participation journal, *Connect,* is another excellent resource By all means, check in with Goodlad and his group at the University of Washington. And surf the Internet. It is also possible to create your own network of friends and colleagues..

Where does one begin to implement change?

Wherever it is easiest; easiest for the teacher (i.e., doing what is most comfortable); and easiest because resistance is least. Make a deliberate choice. Have a very clear time line and subgoals. Examine progress at a predetermined time. Although the tactic is to begin anywhere with any democratic requirement, always keep in mind a long-term strategy organized by the big picture. Trying to do everything at once will surely be overwhelming.

Curricular change begins with existing curriculum. It is rare that one can do anything else, although a more seismic change in the form of a democratic alternative school is always a possibility. If the situation is one in which the curriculum cannot be modified in the slightest, determine how to use what is being taught to solve an important problem. Share that thinking with your students. Ask them to consider how they can put to use what they are learning. If being able to win at Trivial Pursuit or Jeopardy or use a superior grade for entrance into a prestigious institution is the best they can do, keep working at it. In most instances, some modification in the curriculum is possible. The subject matter can be extended or pointed in a direction that lends itself to problem solving. The next move is to interdisciplinary studies that can be organized around solving a particular problem. It is but a short step from interdisciplinary studies to a particular problem-solving topic.

In any phase of curriculum change from the standard curriculum to important problem solving, the nature of the instruction can be tilted toward the democratic. With any curriculum, students should be oriented to produce rather than consume knowledge. They should be encouraged to work in teams. They should do research. They should debate findings. They should devise applications. They should evaluate their efforts. A democratic curriculum is as much a means to establishing a way of thinking as it is a way to amass a body of knowledge. A democratic teacher moving students from passive to active learning can enliven even the dullest and most irrelevant curriculum.

Well before there is substantial curriculum change and as a part of developing a democratic frame of mind, schools can rearrange the school day. The rescheduling of bells (retimetabling the curriculum), particularly in high schools, is part of what is currently called *restructuring* in the United States. Fewer classes per day in larger blocks of time do not necessarily make for a more democratic classroom. The primary purposes of such restructuring is to reduce the number of students a teacher interacts with in a day, the number of class preparations that has to be made, and the number of trips through the hallways students make (thus reducing the likelihood of truancy, tardiness, and altercations). There is also the anticipation that longer blocks of time will result in much more active learning on the part of the students. Although restructuring was not intended for the democratic classroom, such moves can help the democratic classroom. Longer blocks of time is ideally suited for research, debate, and genuine problem-solving activities.

Any classroom can establish rights. Teachers can make abundantly clear the rights a student has in her or his classroom. Precise limits can be established for rights of expression, privacy, due process and movement, and the logic for the rights provided as well as the relationship between rights and responsibilities.

Any classroom can bring students into the decision-making process. A teacher can decide or negotiate what domain of decisions can be given to students. The students can make the class rules, establish a system of justice, and plan class activities. Each of these can be evaluated and used as a reference for examining governments and developing citizen responsibility. All of the paradoxes of participation that Phillips (1991) discussed in her book can be a topic for discussion as a class develops its approach to classroom decision making.

Any classroom can provide equal encouragement. Equal encouragement does not require change in policy or law. No teacher is prohibited from equally encouraging. Any teacher in any classroom can equalize gratifications. Effort can be made to encourage all equally to risk and learn, to equally remove all unnecessary discomfort (consciously curtailing humiliation, boredom and isolation), to make the class equally meaningful, to encourage all equally to competence, to create equal opportunities for usefulness, to equally welcome all, to create equal opportunities for the expression of creativity, to equally inspire all to hopefulness, and to make the classroom an equally exciting place for all.

In the beginning, in order to fashion a democratic classroom, do not think narrowly about democracy and its myriad restrictions and contradictions. Think of it as a way of including everybody in the formation of the future

. . . one classroom at a time.

References

Adler, M. (1982a). *The Paideia proposal.* New York: Macmillan.

Adler, M. (1982b). The Paideia proposal: Rediscovering the essence of education. *The American School Board Journal,* 17-20.

Adler, M. (1987). *We hold these truths: Understanding the ideas and the ideals of the Constitution.* New York: Macmillan.

Aichhorn, A. (1983). *Wayward youth.* Evanston, IL: Northwestern University Press. (Originally published in 1925 as *Verwahrlostejugend.* Vienna: Psychoanalytischer Verlag.)

Amram, F., Flax, S., Hamermesh M., & Marty, G. (1988). *New careers: The dream that worked.* Minneapolis: University of Minnesota.

Apple, M. W. (1979). *Ideology and curriculum.* London: Routledge & Kegan Paul.

Aronowitz, S., & Giroux, H.A. (1985). *Education under siege: The conservative, liberal and radical debate over schooling.* South Hadley, MA: Bergin & Garvey.

Australian Electoral Office, Research Report. (1983). *A qualitative analysis of attitudes toward enrollment and voting,* Australian Electoral Office, Canberra, Australia.

Axelrod, S. (1977). *Behavior modification for the classroom teacher.* New York: McGraw-Hill.

Bagley, W. C. (1938). An essentialist platform for the advancement of American education. *Educational Administration and Supervision, 24*, 241-256.

Baldwin, J. (1963). A talk to teachers. In R. Simonson & S. Walker (Eds.), *Multi-cultural literacy* (pp. 3-12). Saint Paul, MN: Graywolf Press.

Ball, S. J. (1993). Education, majorism and "the curriculum of the dead." *Curriculum Studies, 1*(2), 195-214.

Ball, S. J. (1994). *Educational reform: A critical and post-structural approach.* Buckingham & Philadelphia: Open University Press

Banks, J. A. (1993). Multicultural education: Characteristics and goals. In J. A. Banks & C. A. McG. Banks (Eds.), *Multicultural education: Issues and perspectives* (2nd ed., pp. 3-27). Boston: Allyn & Bacon.

Bantock, G.H. (1970). *T.S. Eliot and education.* London: Faber & Faber.

Barber, B. (1983). *Strong democracy: Participatory politics for a new age.* Berkeley: University of California Press.

Barber, B. (1984). *Strong democracy: Participatory politics for a new age.* Berkeley: University of California Press.

Barber, B. (1992). *An aristocracy of everyone.* New York: Oxford University Press.

Barker, R. (1964). *Ecological psychology: Concepts and methods for studying the environment of human behavior.* Stanford, CA: Stanford University Press.

Beer, S. (1956). Pressure groups and parties in Great Britain. *American Political Science Review, L,* 1-23

Beer, S. (1958). Group representation in Britain and the United States. *Annals, CCCXIX,* 130-140.

Beer, S. (1969). *British politics in the collectivist age.* New York: Vintage Books, Random House.

Bell, D. (1973). *The coming of the post industrial society: A venture in social forecasting.* New York: Basic Books.

Bellah, R. H., Madsen, R., Sullivan, W. M., Swidler, A., & Tipton, S. M. (1985). *Habits of the heart: Individualism and commitment in American life.* New York: Harper & Row.

Bender, P. (1984). Privacy. In N. Dorsen (Ed.), *Our endangered rights: The ACLU Report on civil liberties today* (pp. 237-258). New York: Pantheon.

Bennett, W. J. (1988). American education: Making it work. Washington, DC: Government Printing Office.

Bennett, W. J. (Ed.). (1993). The book of virtues: A treasury of great moral stories. New York: Simon and Schuster.

Bentley, A. (1908). *The process of government.* Chicago: University of Chicago Press.

Berelson, B., Lazarsfeld, P., & McPhee, W. (1954). *Voting.* Chicago, IL: University of Chicago Press.

Bernstein, G. (1992, June 3). *Guardian,* p. 62.

Bernstein, R. (1985). *Habermas and modernity.* Oxford, UK: Basil Blackwell.

Bessant, B. (1996). Lessons from the past: Lessons for the future. *Australian Educational Researcher, 23*(1), 17-30.

Bestor, A. E. (1953). *Educational wastelands.* Urbana: University of Illinois Press.

Bestor, A. E. (1955). *The restoration of learning.* New York: Knopf.

Bimber, B. (1995). *The decentralization mirage: Comparing decision making arrangements in four high schools.* Santa Monica, CA: Rand.

Bishop, A. (1995). *Just testing? Uses and abuses of student assessment* (Pamphlet No 4). Melbourne, Centre for Democratic Education.

Bloom, A. (1987). *The closing of the American mind.* New York: Simon & Schuster.

Bloom, H. (1994). *The Western Canon: The books and the school of the ages.* New York: Harcourt Brace.

Boorstin, D. (1960). *America and the image of Europe.* New York: Meridian Press.

Boyd, D. (1996). Dominance concealed through diversity: Implications of inadequate perspectives on cultural pluralism. *Harvard Educational Review, 36*(3), 609-630.

Bradley Commission on History in the Schools. (1989). Building a history curriculum: Guidelines for teaching history in schools. In P. Gagnon and the Bradley Commission on History in the Schools (Eds.), *Historical literacy: The case for history in American education* (pp. 16-47). Boston: Houghton-Mifflin.

Branch, T. (1988). *Parting the waters: America in the King years 1954-63.* New York: Simon & Schuster.

Breslow, M. (1995, January/February). Racial divide widens, Why African-American workers have lost ground. *Dollars and Sense,* pp. 1-4.

Bruner, J. (1996). *The culture of education.* Cambridge, MA: Harvard University Press.

Brunswik, E. (1956). *Perception and the representative design of psychological experiments.* Berkeley: University of California Press.

Buckley, W. (1968). *Up from liberalism.* New York: Arlington Press.

Burt, C. (1909). Experimental tests of general intelligence. *British Journal of Psychology, 3,* 94-177.

Burt, C. (1959). Class differences in general intelligence. *British Journal of Statistical Psychology, 15,* 1-49.

Butts, R. F. (1988). *The morality of democratic citizenship: Goals for civic education in the Republic's third century.* Calabasas, CA: Center for Civic Education.

California State Department of Education. (1987a). *Caught in the middle.* Sacramento, CA: Author

California State Department of Education. (1987b). *Second to none.* Sacramento, CA: Author.

California State Department of Education. (1992). *It's elementary.* Sacramento, CA: Author.

Canter, L. (1988, September). Assertive discipline: More than names on the board and marbles in a jar. *Phi Delta Kappan,* pp. 57-61.

Canter, L., & Canter, M. (1976). *Assertive discipline: A take charge approach for today's education.* Santa Monica, CA: Canter and Associates.

Carnegie Foundation for the Advancement of Teaching. (1990). *Campus life: In search of community.* Princeton, NJ: Princeton University Press.

Carnegie Foundation for the Advancement of Teaching. (1995). *The elementary school.* Princeton, NJ: Princeton University Press.

Carrington, K. (1993). *Offending girls.* Australia: Allen & Unwin.

Carter, A. (1979). *The Sadeian woman.* London: Virago Press.

Carter, W. T. (1977). The career opportunities program: A summing up. In A. Gartner, F. Riessman, & V. Carter-Jackson (Eds.), *Paraprofessionals today* (pp. 183-221). New York: Human Services Press.

Cassirer, E. (1932). *The philosophy of the Enlightenment* (F. Koelin & J. Pettegrove, trans.). Princeton, NJ: Princeton University Press.

Caulley, D.N. (1992). *Notes on the basic characteristics of postpositivist interpretive inquiry.* Melbourne: La Trobe University.

Center for Civic Education. (1991). CIVITAS: *A framework for civic education* (C. A. Quigley, editorial director). Calabasas, CA: Author.

Chancellor, J. (1990) *Peril and promise: A commentary upon America.* New York: Harper & Row.

Charles, C. M. (1989). *Building classroom discipline* (3rd ed.). New York & London: Longman.

Chilman, C. (1966). *Growing up poor.* Washington, DC: Government Printing Office.

Chubb, J., & Moe, T. E. (1990). *Politics, markets, and America's schools.* Washington, DC: Brookings Institute.

Claydon, L. (Ed.). (1973). *Renewing urban teaching.* Cambridge: Cambridge University Press.

Claydon, L. (Ed.). (1975). *The urban school.* Carlton, Melbourne: Pitman Pacific Books.

Cohen, S . A. (1988). *Tests: Marked for life?* Ontario, Canada: Scholastic.

Cohn, J. S. (1992, Spring). A lost political generation? *The American Prospect, 20,* 29-40.

Commager, H.S. (1966). Challenges for teacher education. In *Frontiers in education, 19th yearbook* (pp. 54-62). Washington, DC: American Association of Colleges of Teacher Education.

Commager, H.S. (1980). Comments. In M. Kaplan (Ed.), *What is an educated person.* New York: Praeger.

Counts, G. S. (1932). *Dare the school build a new social order.* New York: Day.

Cuban, L. (1984). *How teachers taught: Constancy and change in American classrooms, 1890-1980.* New York: Longman.

D'Souza, D. (1991). *Illiberal education.* New York: The Free Press.

Dahl, R. A. (1956). *A preface to democratic theory.* Chicago: University of Chicago Press.

Dahl, R. A. (1958). A critique of the ruling elite model. *American Political Science Review, LII,* 463-469.

Dahl, R. A. (1959). *Who governs? Democracy and power in an American city.* New Haven, CT: Yale University Press.

Dahl, R. A. (1989). *Democracy and its critics.* New Haven, CT: Yale University Press.

Dalin, P., & Rust, V. (1996). *Towards schooling in the 21st century.* Cassell: London.

Darling-Hammond, L. (1986). A proposal for evaluation in the teaching profession. *Elementary School Journal, 86,* 531-551.

Davidson, N. (1985). Small group learning and and teaching in mathematics. A selective review of the research. In R.E. Slavin, S. Sharan, S. Kagan, R. Hertz-Lazarowitz, C. Webb, & R. Schmuck (Eds.), *Learning to cooperate, cooperating to learn* (pp. 211-230). New York: Plenum.

Dayton, C., & Pearl, A. (1987). *The work ability compact as dropout prevention in five California demonstration schools—Los Angeles, San Diego, Fresno, Richmond & Santa Maria, 1986-87, final evaluations.* Sacramento: McConnell Clark Foundation, Industrial Educational of California and California State Department of Education.

Deaux, K. (1976). Sex: A perspective on the attribution process. In J. Harvey, W. Ickes, & R. Kidd (Eds.), *New directions in attribution research* (pp. 335-352). Hillsdale, NJ: Erlbaum.

Department of Employment and Training (DEET). (1991). *Australia workforce in the year 2000.* Canberra: Australia Government Printing Service.

Deutsch, M. (1967). *The disadvantaged child.* New York: Basic Books.

Dewey, J. (1987). My pedagogy. *School Journal, 8*(1), 77-80.

Dewey, J. (1916). *Democracy and education.* New York: Macmillan.

Dewey, J. (1933). *How we think.* Lexington, MA: D.S. Heath & Co.

Dewey, J. (1938). *Experience and education.* New York: Macmillan.

Dewey, J. (1956). The school and society. In *The child and the curriculum and The school and society.* Chicago: University of Chicago Press. (Original works published 1900)

Dionne, E. J., Jr. (1991). *Why Americans hate politics.* New York: Touchstone Books, Simon & Schuster.

Directorate of School Education (DES). (1993). *Schools of the future.* Melbourne , Victoria.

Dorfman, A. (1983). *The empire's old clothes: What the Lone Ranger, Babar and other innocent heroes do to our minds.* New York: Pantheon Books.

Down, A. G. (1977, October). Why basic education? *The National Elementary Principal,* pp. 28-32.

Dreikurs, R. (1968). *Psychology in the classroom* (2nd ed.). New York: Harper & Row.

Dreikurs, R., Grunwald, B., & Pepper, F. (1982). *Maintaining sanity in the classroom.* New York: Harper & Row.

Duke, D. L., & Meckel, A. M. (1984). *Teacher's guide to classroom management.* New York: Random House.

Dunne, F.P. (1954). *Mr. Dooley, now & forever.* Stanford, CA: Academic Reprints.

Dyson, M. E. (1996). *Race rules: Navigating the color line.* Reading, MA: Addison-Wesley

Eagleton, T. (1987, February 10). Awakening from modernity. *Times Literary Supplement,* p. 192.

Edmonds, R. B. (1979). Effective schools for the urban poor. *Educational Leadership, 27*(1), 15-27.

Edmonds, R. (1984). School effects and teacher effects. *Social Policy, 15*(2), 37-40.

Elmer-Dewill, P. (1993). Making the case for abstinence. *Time,* p. 89.

Engish, J. (1975). BGHS: A personal view. In L.F. Claydon (Ed.), *The urban school* (pp. 119-141). Melbourne: Pitman Pacific Books.

Eribon, D. (1991). *Michel Foucault.* Cambridge: Harvard University Press.

Erikson, E. H. (1963). *Childhood and society* (2nd ed.). New York: Norton.

Erikson, E. H. (1968). *Identity: Youth and crisis.* New York: Norton.

Evans, S. (1989). *Born for liberty.* New York: The Free Press.

Farber, P., Provenzo, E. F., Jr., & Holm, G. (1994). *Schooling in the light of popular culture.* Albany: State University of New York Press.

Fiorentine, R. (1987). Men, women and the premed persistence gap: A normative alternatives approach. *American Journal of Sociology, 92,* 1118-1139.

Fishman, J., MacClennon, B., & Pearl, A. (1964). *Community apprentices.* Washington, DC: Center for Youth & Community Services, Howard University.

Flexner, E. (1959). *Century of struggle.* Cambridge, MA: Harvard University Press.

Foucault, M. (1965). *Madness and civilization: A history of insanity in the age of reason* (R. Howard, trans.). New York: Pantheon.

Foucault, M. (1984). *The Foucault reader* (P. Rabinow, ed.). New York: Random House.

Freire, P. (1970). Cultural action for freedom. *Harvard Educational Review* (Monograph Series No. 1).

Freire, P. (1968). *Pedagogy of the oppressed.* New York: Seabury Press.

Freire, P. (1985). *The politics of education: Culture, power and liberation.* South Hadley, MA: Bergin & Garvey.

Freud, S. (1927). The future of an illusion. In J. Strachey (Ed.), *Standard Edition of the Complete Psychological Works of Sigmund Freud* (Vol. 21, 5-56). London: Hogarth Press. (Original work published 1961)

Friedman, M., & Friedman, R. (1979). *Free to choose.* New York: Harcourt, Brace Jovanovich.

Galbraith, J. K. (1992). *The culture of contentment.* New York: Houghton Mifflin.

Galati-Brown, R. (1995). An education for all: The Northland Secondary College story. *The Beacon.*

Gardner, H. (1991). *The unschooled mind: How children think and how schools should teach.* New York: Basic Books.

Gardner, J. (1989, Fall). Building community. *Kettering Review,* pp. 73-81.

Gartner, A. (1971). *Paraprofessionals and their performances: A survey of education, health and social service programs.* New York: Praeger.

Gaze, B., & Jones, M. (1990). *Law, liberty and Australian democracy.* Melbourne: The Law Book Company.

Gewirtz, S., Ball, S. J., & Bowe, R. (1995). *Markets, choice and equity in education.* Buckingham, UK: Open University Press.

Gibbs, W. W. (1995). Trends in behavioral science: Seeking the criminal element. *Scientific American, 272*(3), 100-107.

Gill, P. (1975). Involving parents: Practical steps toward articulating schooling and the culture of students. In L. F. Claydon (Ed.), *The urban school* (pp. 163-173). Melbourne: Pitman Pacific Books.

Gill, P., Trioli, R., & Weymouth, R. (1998) A disciplined partnership: Code of behaviour at Princes Hill Primary School. In R. Slee (Ed.), *Discipline and schools.* Melbourne: Macmillan Company of Australia.

Gilligan, C. (1980). *In a different voice.* Cambridge, MA: Harvard University Press.

Gladwill, M. (1995, October 16-22). Fundamental ignorance about the numbers. *Washington Post National Weekly Edition,* p. 7.

Glasser, W. (1965). *Reality therapy.* New York: Harper & Row.

Glasser, W. (1977). 10 steps to good discipline. *Today's Education, 66,* 60-63.

Glasser, W. (1978). Disorders in our schools: Causes and remedies. *Phi Delta Kappan, 59,* 331-333.

Glasser, W. (1985). *Control theory in the classroom.* New York: Perennial Library.

Glassman, J. K. (1994, February 13-19). Book review *The End of Work* by Jeremy Rifkin. *Washington Post National Weekly,* p. 34.

Good, T. L., & Brophy, J. E. (1991). *Looking in classrooms.* New York: Harper & Row.

Goodlad, J. L. (1984). *A place called school.* New York: McGraw-Hill.

Goodlad, J. L. (1990). *Teachers for our nation's schools.* San Francisco: Jossey-Bass.

Goodson, I. (1992). Studying school subjects. *Curriculum Perspectives, 12*(1).

Goodwyn, L. (1981). Organizing democracy: The limits of theory and practice. *Democracy, 1*(1), 41-60

Goodwyn, L. (1984, June). The new populism: A hell raising tradition waits to be reborn. *The Progressive, 48*(6), 18-20.

Gore, J. M. (1995). *Emerging issues in teacher education.* Commonwealth Information Services. Canberra: Australian Government Publishing Service.

Gould, S. (1981). *The mismeasurement of man.* New York: Norton.

Gramsci, A. (1971). *Selections from prison notebooks.* New York: International Publishers.

Grant, J. D. (1967). *New careers development project* (Final report). National Institute of Mental Health Project OM-01616.

Gregory, R. (1995). *Higher education expansion and economic change. Efficiency and Equity in Education Policy* [Government report, p. 7]. National Board of Employment, Education and Training. Centre for Economic Policy Research, ANU, Canberra.

Greider, W. (1992). *Who will tell the people: The betrayal of American democracy.* New York: Simon & Schuster.

Gross, B. (1953). *The legislative struggle.* New York: McGraw-Hill.

Gumperz, J. J. (1982). *Language and social identity.* Cambridge, UK: Cambridge University Press.

Gunn, M. (1996, March 23-24). Political knowledge a big turn off say teenagers. *The Australian,* p. 6.

Hacker, A. (1996, July 11). Goodbye to affirmative action. *New York Review of Books,* pp. 24-28.

Hallowitz, E. (1968). The expanding role of the neighborhood service center. In F. Riessman & H. I. Popper (Eds.), *Up from poverty: New career ladders for nonprofessionals* (pp. 94-101). New York: Harper & Row.

Handguns and Violence. (1994). *A survey of California and national polling* [pamphlet]. San Rafael, CA: Wellness Institute.

Hansell, S., & Slavin, R. E. (1981). Cooperative learning and the structure of interracial friendships. *Sociology of Education, 54*, 98-106

Hargreaves, A. (1989). *Curriculum and assessment reform.* Buckingham, UK: Open University Press.

Hargreaves, A. (1994). *Changing teachers, changing times: Teachers' work and culture in the postmodern age.* London: Cassell.

Hargreaves, A (1996). Transforming knowledge: Blurring the boundaries between research, policy, and practice. *Educational Evaluation and Policy Analysis, 18*(2), 105-122.

Harvey, D. (1989). *The condition of postmodernity: An enquiry into the origins of cultural change.* Oxford, UK: Basil Blackwell.

Harwood, R. C. (1992, Spring). Citizens and politics: A view from Main Street. *Media & Values.*

Haycock, K., & Navarro, S. M. (1988). *Unfinished business: Fulfilling our child's promises.* Oakland, CA: The Achievement Council.

Head, S. (1996, February 29). The new, ruthless economy. *New York Review of Books*, pp. 47-52.

Hearnshaw, L. S. (1979). *Cyril Burt psychologist.* London: Hodder & Stoughton.

Hentoff, N. (1980). *The first freedom: The tumultuous history of free speech in America.* New York: Delacorte Press.

Herrnstein, R. J. (1973). IQ. *Atlantic Monthly, 213*(3), 43-64.

Herrnstein, R. J., & Murray, C. (1994). *The bell curve: Intelligence and class structure in American life.* New York: The Free Press.

Hillkirk, K., (1994). Teaching for democracy: Preparing teachers to teach democratically. In J.M. Novak (Ed.), *Democratic teacher education: Programs, processes, problems, and prospects* (pp. 89-101). Albany: State University of New York Press.

Hirsch, E. D., Jr. (1988). *Cultural literacy: What every American needs to know.* New York: Vintage Books.

Hofstadter, R. (1948). *The American political tradition.* New York: Knopf.

Hollins, C. E. (1991). *It was fun from the beginning.* New York: Carlton Press.

Horton, R.E., Jr. (1963a). American students and the Bill of Rights. In H.H. Remmers (Ed.), *Anti-American attitudes in American schools* (pp. 18-60). Evanston, IL: Northwestern University Press.

Houts, P. L. (1977). *The myth of measurability.* New York: Hart Publishing.

Hunt, J. McV. (1961). *Intelligence and experience.* New York: Ronald Press.

Hutchins, R. M. (1936). *The higher learning in America.* New Haven, CT: Yale University Press.

Hutton, W. (1995) *The state we're in.* London: Jonathan Cape .

Jackson, K. T., & Jackson, B. B. (1989). Why the time is right to reform the history curriculum. In P. Gagnon & The Bradley Commission on History in Schools (Eds.), *Historical literacy: The case for history in American education* (pp. 3-15). Boston: Houghton Mifflin.

James, M. R., Lester, E. A., & Royer C. L., (1965). *New careers development project: Retrospective analysis of the pilot study.* Sacramento , CA: Institute for the Study of Crime and Delinquency.

Jameson, F. (1984). Postmodernism, or the cultural logic of late capitalism. *New Left Review 146,* 53-92.

Jamieson, K. H. (1992). *Dirty politics: Deception, distraction and democracy.* New York: Oxford University Press.

Jencks, C. (1977). *The language of post-modern architecture.* London: Academy Press.

Jensen, A. R. (1969). How much can we boost IQ and scholastic achievement? *Harvard Educational Review,* 33, 1-123.

Johnson, D.W., & Johnson, R. T. (1986). *Learning together and alone: Cooperation, competition, and individualization* (2nd ed.). Englewood Cliffs, NJ: Prentice-Hall.

Johnson, D.W., & Johnson, R. T. (1989). *Cooperation and competition: Theory and research.* Edina, MN: Interaction.

Jones, D., Metcalf, M., Williams, D., & Williamson, J. (1982). Sunshine High School: A school curriculum and self-evaluation project. In T. Knight (Ed.), *Task force team report no. 7.* Bundoora, Australia: School of Education, La Trobe University.

Kagan, S. (1989). *Cooperative learning resources for teachers.* San Juan Capistrano, CA: Resources for Teachers.

Kamin, L. J. (1974). *The science and politics of IQ.* Potomac, MD: Erlbaum.

Kaminer, W. (1994, May). Crime and community. *The Atlantic,* 231(2), 111-120.

Kaplan, R. (1994). The coming anarchy. *The Atlantic, 233*(2), 44-76.

Kariel, H.J. (1989). *The desperate politics of postmodernism.* Amherst: University of Massachusetts Press.

Kaye, H. J. (1994, Winter). E. P. Thompson, Marxist historian and radical democrat. *New Politics,* pp. 224-230.

Kelly, P. (1992). *The end of uncertainty.* Melbourne: Allen and Unwin.

Kennedy, P. (1993). *Preparing for the twenty-first century.* New York: Random House.

Kenway, J. (1995). *The responsibility of marketing your school* (Pamphlet No. 7). Melbourne: The Centre for Democratic Education.

Key, V. O. (1961). *Public opinion and American democracy.* New York: A. A. Knopf.

Kilpatrick, W. H. (1983). The case for progressivism in education. In G. Hass (Ed.), *Curriculum development: A new approach* (pp. 24-27). Boston: Allyn & Bacon.

Kilpatrick, W. H. (1936). *Remaking the curriculum.* New York: Newson.

Kinetz, M. (1995). Multicultural education: It's in the eye of the beholder. *California Schools, 53*(4), 14-20.

Kirk, R. (1979). Simplicity and audacity in reform: A call for reactionary radicalism. *Modern Age, 23*(3), 226-232.

Kirk, R. (1986). *The conservative mind* (7th ed.). Washington, DC: Regnery Books.

Kirk, R. (1992). The marriage of rights and duties. *The Intercollegiate Review, 27*(2), 27-32.

Kneller, G. (1961). Education, knowledge, and the problem of existence. *Harvard Education Review, 31*(3), 422-441.

Knight, T. (1985a). An apprenticeship in democracy. *The Australian Teacher, 11,* 5-7.

Knight, T. (1985b). Schools and delinquency. In A. Borowski & J. Murray (Eds.), *Juvenile delinquency in Australia* (pp. 257-282). Sydney: Methuen.

Knight, T. (1991). Democratic schooling: Basis for a school code of behaviour. In M. Lovegrove & R. Lewis (Eds.), *Classroom discipline* (pp. 117-144). Melbourne: Longman.

Knight, T. (1993, September 5-9). *A human service society: Renewing the relationship between education, work and schooling.* Paper presented at The European Educational House, School year 2020. I.M.T.E.C. Bogensie, Germany.

Knight, T, (1995). Parents, the community and school governance. In C. Evers & J. Chapman (Eds.), *Educational administration: An Australian perspective* (pp. 254-273). Australia: Allen and Unwin.

Knight, T. (1996, April). *Rights and responsibilities: Basics for a democratic school.* Paper presented at the 4th International Conference of Democratic Schools, Hadera, Israel.

Knight, T. (1997). Schools, delinquency and youth culture. In I. O' Connor & A. Borowski (Eds.), *Juvenile crime, juvenile justice and juvenile corrections* (pp. 79-97). Melbourne: Longman.

Kohlberg, L. (1973). The contribution of developmental psychology to education: Examples from moral education. *Educational Psychologist, 10,* 2-14.

Kohlberg, L. (1984). *Essays on moral development. Vol. 2: The psychology of moral development.* San Francisco: Harper & Row.

Kornhauser, W. (1959). *The politics of mass society.* Glencoe, IL: Free Press.

Kozol, J. (1991). *Savage inequalities: Children in America's schools.* New York: Crown.

Kozulin, A. (1990). *Vygotsky's psychology.* Cambridge, MA: Harvard University Press.

Le Guin, U. K. (1989). Is gender necessary? *Dancing at the Edge of the World* (pp. 4-17). New York: Grove.

Lenney, E. (1977). Women's self confidence in achievement settings. *Psychological Bulletin 84,* 1-13.

Lewin, K. (1948). *Resolving social conflicts.* New York: Harper.

Lewis, O. (1961). *The children of Sanchez.* New York: Random House.

Lewis, O. (1966). *La Vida: A Puerto Rican family in the culture of poverty—San Juan and New York.* New York: Random House.

Lippman, W. (1922). *Public opinion.* New York: Harcourt.

Lipset, S. M. (1960). *Political man.* Garden City, NY: Doubleday.

Lynn, L. (1996, Spring). School to work: Problems and potentials. *Rethinking Schools,* pp. 1, 22-23

Lyotard, J. F. (1986). *La condition postmoderne: Rapport sur le savoir* [The postmodern condition: A report on knowledge]. J. F. Lyotard (trans.). Manchester: Manchester University Press.

Macaulay, T.B. (1924). Milton, *Macaulay's literary essays.* London: Thomas Nelson and Sons.

MacLennan, B. W. (1966). New careers as human service aides. *Children, XIII*(5), 190-194.

MacLennan, B. W., & Klein, W. J. (1965). Utilization of groups in job training for the socially deprived. International *Journal of Group Psychology, XV*(4), 424-433.

Margolis, M. (1979) *Viable democracy.* London: Macmillan

Marx, K. (1875). Critique of the Gotha program. In L.S. Feuer (Ed.), *Marx and Engels: Basic writing on politics and philosophy* (pp. 112-132). Garden City, NY: Anchor Books, Doubleday.

Maslow, A. (1958). *Toward a psychology of being* (2nd ed.). New York: Van Nostrand Reinhold.

Maslow, A. (1971). *The farther reaches of human nature.* New York: Viking.

McClosky, H. (1964). Consensus and ideology in American politics. *American Political Science Review, LVIII,* 361-382.

Meier, D. (1995). *The power of their ideas.* Boston: Beacon Press.

Meisel, J. H. (1962) *The myth of the ruling class: Gaetano Mosca and the "elite."* Ann Arbor: University of Michigan Press.

Michels, R. (1959). *Political parties: A sociological study of the oligarchical tendencies of modern democracy* (E. Paul & C. Paul, trans.). New York: Dover. (Original work published 1911)

Miller, W. B. (1958). Lower class culture as a generating milieu of gang delinquency. *Journal of Social Issues, 14,* 5-19.

Miner, B. (1996). Milwaukee voucher schools close. *Rethinking Schools, 10*(3), 19.

Morin, R. (1995, October 16-22). Across the racial divide: A new survey reveals the depths of our differences. *Washington Post Weekly Edition,* pp. 6-10.

Moynihan, D. P. (1965). *The Negro family: The case for national action.* Washington, DC: U.S. Government Printing Office.

Nash, G. B. (1989). History for a democratic society: The work of all people. In P. Gagnon and The Bradley Commission on History in the Schools (Eds.), *Historical literacy: The case for history in American education* (pp. 234-248). Boston: Houghton Mifflin.

National Commission on Excellence in Education. (1983). *A nation at risk: The imperative for educational reform.* Washington, DC: U.S. Government Printing Office.

Neill, A. S. (1963). *Summerhill: A radical approach to childrearing.* New York: Hart.

Newman, F. M., & Thompson, J. (1987). *Effects of cooperative education learning on achievement in secondary schools: A summary of research.* Madison: University of Wisconsin, National Center on Effective Secondary Schools.

Novak, J. (Ed.). (1994). *Democratic teacher education: Programs, processes, problems, and prospects.* Albany: State University of New York Press.

Oakes, J. (1985). *Keeping track: How schools structure inequality.* New Haven, CT: Yale University Press.

Oakes, J. (1992). *Educational match-making: Academic and vocational tracking in comprehensive high schools.* Santa Monica, CA: Rand Corporation (R-4189 NCRVE-/UCB).

Ohlin, L., & Cloward, R. (1960). *Delinquency and opportunity.* Glencoe, IL: The Free Press.

O'Leary, V. (1974). Some attitudinal barriers to occupational aspirations in women. *Psychological Bulletin 81,* 809-826.

Passmore, J. (1970). *The perfectibility of man.* New York: Charles Scribner.

Pateman, C. (1970). *Participation and democratic theory.* Cambridge, UK: Cambridge University Press.

Pateman, C. (1985). Feminism and democracy. In G. Duncan (Ed.), *Democratic theory and practice* (pp. 204-271). Cambridge: Cambridge University Press.

Pateman, C. (1989). *The disorder of women: Democracy, feminism, and political theory.* Cambridge: Polity Press in association with Basil Blackwell.

Pearl, A. (1965). Youth in low income settings. In M. Sherif & C. Sherif (Eds.), *Problems of youth* (pp. 89-109). Chicago: Aldine Publishing.

Pearl, A. (1971, November/December). Further thoughts on an ecological theory of value. *Social Policy,* pp. 27-30.

Pearl, A. (1972). *The atrocity of education.* New York: Dutton.

Pearl, A., & Riessman, F. (1965). *New careers for the poor.* New York: Macmillan.

Pearlstein, S. (1995, December 11-17). The winners are taking all: In the new economy more and more of us qualify as "losers." *Washington Post Weekly,* pp. 6-8.

Phillips, A. (1991). *Engendering democracy.* Cambridge, UK: Polity Press.

Polk, K., & Schafer, W. E. (Eds.). (1972). *Schools and delinquency.* Englewood Cliffs, NJ: Prentice-Hall.

Polsby, N. A. (1963). *Community power and political theory.* New Haven, CT: Yale University Press.

Postman, N. (1996). *The end of education: Redefining the value of schooling.* New York: Vintage Books.

Raths, L., Harmin, M., & Simon, S. (1978). *Values and teaching: Working with values in the classroom* (2nd ed.). Columbus, OH: Charles E. Merrill.

Ravitch, D. (1989). The plight of history in American schools. In P. Gagnon and The Bradley Commission on History in the

Schools (Eds.), *Historical literacy: The case for history in American education* (pp. 51-68). Boston: Houghton Mifflin.

Rawls, J. (1971). *A theory of justice.* Cambridge, MA: Harvard University Press.

Riessman, F. (1962). *The culturally deprived child.* New York: Harper & Row.

Riessman, F., Cohen, J., & Pearl, A. (1964). *Mental health of the poor.* New York: The Free Press.

Riessman, F., & Hallowitz, E. (1965). *Neighborhood service centers program: A report to the U.S. Office of Economic Opportunity on the South Bronx neighborhood service center.* New York: Lincoln Hospital Mental Health Services.

Riessman, F., & Popper, H. I. (Eds.). *Up from poverty: New career ladders for nonprofessionals.* New York: Harper & Row.

Rifkin, J. (1994). *The end of work: The decline of the global labor force and the dawn of the post-market era.* New York: Putnam.

Rist, R. (1970). Student social class and teacher expectations: The self-fulfilling prophecy in ghetto education. *Harvard Educational Review, 40,* 411-451.

Rogers, C. (1969). *Freedom to learn.* Columbus, OH: Merrill.

Rosenshine, B.V. (1986). Synthesis of research on explicit teaching. *Educational Leadership, 43*(7), 60-69.

Russell, B. (1927). *Selected papers.* New York: Random House.

Ryan, W. (1971). *Blaming the victim.* New York: Random House.

Ryan, W. (1982). *Equality.* New York: Random House.

Sampson, A. (1992). *The essential anatomy of Britain: Democracy in crisis.* London: Hodder & Stoughton.

Saul, R. J. (1997). *The unconscious civilization.* Melbourne: Penguin Books.

Schattschneider, E. E. (1942). *Party politics.* New York: Farrar & Rinehart.

Schattschneider, E. E. (1960). *The semi-sovereign people.* Hinsdale, IL: Dryden Press.

Schumpter, J. A. (1942). *Capitalism, socialism and democracy.* New York: Harper Torchbooks.

Schurz, C. (1908). *The reminiscences of Carl Schurz, Vol II.* New York: Doubleday, Page & Co.

Selvin, M. et al. (1992). *Who gets what and why: Curriculum decision making at three comprehensive high schools.* Santa Monica, CA: Rand.

Senna, C. (1973). *The fallacy of I.Q.* New York: The Third Press, Joseph Okpaku Publishing.

Sjoberg, G. (1975). Politics, ethics and evaluation research. In M. Guttentag & E.L. Struening (Eds.), *Handbook of evaluation research* (Vol. 2, pp. 29-51). Beverly Hills, CA: Sage.

Skinner, B F. (1953). *Science and human behavior.* New York: Macmillan.

Skinner, B. F. (1971). *Beyond freedom and dignity.* New York: Alfred A. Knopf.

Slavin, R. E. (1990). *Cooperative theory: Theory, research and practice.* Englewood Cliffs, NJ: Prentice-Hall.

Slavin, R.E., & Oickle, E. (1981). Effects of cooperative learning teams on student achievement and race relations: Treatment by race interactions. *Sociology of Education, 54,* 174-180.

Slee, R. (Ed.). (1995). *Changing theories and practices of discipline.* London: Falmer Press.

Sleeter, C. E., & Grant, C. A. (1994). *Making choices for multicultural education: Five approaches to race, class and gender* (2nd ed.). New York: Merrill.

Smith, B.O., Pearl, A., & Cohen, S. (1969). *Teachers for the real world.* Washington, DC: American Association Colleges of Teacher Education.

Soros, G. (1997). The capitalist threat. *The Atlantic Monthly, 336*(1), 45-58.

Spanos, W.V. (1993). *The end of education: Toward posthumanism.* Minneapolis: University of Minnesota Press.

Streitmatter, J. (1994). *Toward gender equity in the classroom: Everyday teachers' beliefs and practices.* Albany: State University of New York Press.

Sutherland, M.,(1988). *Theory of education.* London: Longman Group.

Sykes, R. (1996, June 7). Women stint on aid. *The Age,* p. 17.

Terman, L. M. et al. (1917). *The Stanford revision extension of the Binet-Simon scale for measuring intelligence.* Baltimore, MD: Warwick & York.

Terman, L. M., & Merrill, M. A. (1937). *Measuring intelligence: A guide to the administration of the new revised Stanford-Binet tests of intelligence.* Boston: Houghton Mifflin.

Thompson, J. (1990). *Ideology and modern culture.* Stanford, CA: Stanford University Press.

Thoreau, H.D. (1981). Slavery in Massachusetts. In *Walden and other writings* (pp. 661-679). New York: Random House. (Original work published 1984)

Thoresen, C. (Ed.). (1973). *Behavior modification in education* (The Seventy-second Yearbook of the National Society for the Study of Education). Chicago, IL: The University of Chicago Press.

Truman, D. (1951). *The governmental process.* New York: A. A. Knopf.

Tuchman, B. (1989). *A world of ideas: Conversations with thoughtful men and women about American life today and the ideas shaping our future* (B. Moyers, ed.). New York: Doubleday.

Valencia, R. R. (1992). *The evolution of deficit thinking in educational thought and practice.* New York: Falmer Press.

Veblen, T. (1918). *The higher learning in America: A memorandum on the conduct of universities by business men.* New York: Viking.

Vygotsky, L. S. (1937). *Thought and language.* Cambridge, MA: Harvard University Press.

Vygotsky, L. S. (1978). *Mind in society: The development of higher psychological processes* (M. Cole, V. John-Steiner, S. Scribner, & E. Souberman, eds.). Cambridge, MA: Harvard University Press.

Wallas, G. (1962). *Human nature in politics.* Lincoln: University of Nebraska Press.

Weigel, R. H., Wiser, P. L., & Cook, S. W. (1975). The impact of cooperative learning experiences on cross-ethnic relations and attitudes. *Journal of Social Issues, 31,* 219-245.

Weiler, K. (1988). *Women teaching for a change: Gender, class and power.* New York: Bergin & Garvey.

Weisbrot, R. (1990). *Freedom bound: A history of America's civil rights movement.* New York & London: W.W. Norton.

White, R. (1959). Motivation reconsidered: The concept of competence. *Psychological Review, LXVI,* 279-333.

Whitehead, A. N. (1929). *Aims of education.* New York: Macmillan.

Wiggins, G. (1989). A true test: Toward more authentic and equitable assessment. *Phi Delta Kappan, 70*(9), 703-713.

Wiggins, G. (1991). Standards, not standardization: Evoking quality student work. *Educational Leadership,* 18-25.

Will, G., (1992, December 14). Our expanding menu of rights. *Newsweek,* p. 90.

Willis, P. (with Jones, S., Canaan, J., & Hurd, G.) (1990). *Common culture: Symbolic work at play in the everyday cultures of the young.* Buckingham, London: Open University Press.

Wilson, W. J. (1996). *When work disappears: The world of the new urban poor.* Chicago: University of Chicago Press.

Wolf, R. M. (1990). *Evaluation in education.* New York: Praeger.

Wood, G. (1992). *Schools that work: America's most innovative public education programs.* New York: Dutton.

Yates, L. (1993). *Education of girls; policy research and questions of gender.* Hawthorne: ACER.

Author Index

Subject Index